Annual Editions:
Archaeology, 11/e

Edited by
Mari Pritchard Parker and Elvio Angeloni

http://create.mcgraw-hill.com

Copyright 2014 by McGraw-Hill Education. All rights reserved. Printed in the United States of America. Except as permitted under the United States Copyright Act of 1976, no part of this publication may be reproduced or distributed in any form or by any means, or stored in a database or retrieval system, without prior written permission of the publisher.

This McGraw-Hill Create text may include materials submitted to McGraw-Hill for publication by the instructor of this course. The instructor is solely responsible for the editorial content of such materials. Instructors retain copyright of these additional materials.

ISBN-10: 1259161145   ISBN-13: 9781259161148

Contents

i. Preface 1
ii. Correlation Guide 3
iii. Topic Guide 5

Unit 1 7

1. About Archaeologists and Archaeology 8
    1.1. The Awful Truth about Archaeology by Lynne Sebastian 10
    1.2. Zahi Hawass, Egypt's 'Indiana Jones,' Thinks Giza Pyramid Holds Hidden Treasure by Owen Jarus 12
    1.3. Distinguished Lecture in Archeology: Communication and the Future of American Archaeology by Jeremy A. Sabloff 14
    1.4. CSI: Italian Renaissance by Tom Mueller 21

Unit 2 27

2. Problem Oriented Archaeology 28
    2.1. The First Americans by Heather Pringle 30
    2.2. Ancient Migration: Coming to America by Andrew Curry 35
    2.3. Beyond the Blue Horizon: How Ancient Voyagers Settled the Far-Flung Islands of the Pacific by Roff Smith 38
    2.4. Prehistory of Warfare by Steven A. LeBlanc 42
    2.5. Uncovering America's Pyramid Builders by Karen Wright 47
    2.6. A Coprological View of Ancestral Pueblo Cannibalism by Karl J. Reinhard 51
    2.7. Beer and Bling in Iron Age Europe 58
    2.8. Woman the Toolmaker by Steven A. Brandt and Kathryn Weedman 60
    2.9. Bushmen by John Yellen 62

Unit 3 69

3. Techniques in Archaeology 70
    3.1. Lasers in the Jungle by Arlen Chase, Diane Z. Chase, and John F. Weishampel 71
    3.2. Archaeology of Titanic by James P. Delgado 74
    3.3. Mayas Mastered Rubber Long before Goodyear by Thomas H. Maugh II 79
    3.4. Profile of an Anthropologist: No Bone Unturned by Patrick Huyghe 81
    3.5. Interbreeding with Neanderthals by Carl Zimmer 86

Unit 4 91

4. Prehistoric Archaeology 92
    4.1. Human Evolution: The Long, Winding Road to Modern Man by Chris Stringer 93
    4.2. When the Sea Saved Humanity by Curtis W. Marean 96
    4.3. A New View of the Birth of Homo sapiens by Ann Gibbons 100

iii

  4.4. Refuting a Myth about Human Origins by John J. Shea   103
  4.5. Rethinking the Hobbits of Indonesia by Kate Wong   109
  4.6. Putting Stonehenge in Its Place by William Underhill   114
  4.7. The First Vikings by Andrew Curry   117

Unit 5   121

5. Historical Archaeology   122
  5.1. Uncovering Secrets of the Sphinx by Evan Hadingham   124
  5.2. Home away from Rome by Paul Bennett   128
  5.3. Carthage: The Lost Mediterranean Civilisation by Richard Miles   131
  5.4. The Weapon That Changed History by Andrew Curry   136
  5.5. Lofty Ambitions of the Inca by Heather Pringle   139
  5.6. Return to the Trail of Tears by Marion Blackburn   143
  5.7. Living through the Donner Party by Jared Diamond   147
  5.8. The Great New England Vampire Panic by Abigail Tucker   153

Unit 6   159

6. Contemporary Archaeology   160
  6.1. Maya Archaeologists Turn to the Living to Help Save the Dead by Michael Bawaya   161
  6.2. Archaeologists Race Against Sea Change in Orkney by Sara Reardon   164
  6.3. Ruined by Michael Marshall   167
  6.4. Archaeology of the Homeless by Nicole Albertson   171

Preface

Annual Editions: Archaeology has been compiled by its two editors with the intent of presenting a vivid overview of the field of archaeology as practiced today. It is our hope that these readings, in keeping with its previous editions will make the old bones, shards of pottery, and stone tools of the past pop into the present. The book's purpose is to present an approach in which archaeologists speak for themselves of their own special experiences. The student is shown that archaeology is a historical as well as a living, public science. The idea is to give the student the necessary basics in order to transform passive learning into active learning. This way, information is both perceived and conceptualized. Hopefully, the light bulb will go on when students read these articles.

This book is organized into six units, each of which contains several articles of various themes on "doing" archaeology. Each unit is introduced by an overview that provides a commentary on the unit topic. It is highly recommended that the student read the unit overviews, as they are presented with humor and also contain challenges and puzzles to solve.

A number of additional features are designed to make this volume useful for students, researchers, and professionals in the field of archaeology. While the articles are arranged along the lines of broadly unifying themes, the *Topic Guide* can be used to establish specific reading assignments tailored to the needs of a particular course of study. In addition, each unit is preceded by an overview, which provides a background for informed reading of the articles and emphasizes critical issues. *Learning Outcomes* accompany each article and outline the key concepts that students should focus on as they are reading the material. *Critical Thinking* questions found at the end of each article allow students to test their understanding of the key points of the article. The *Internet References* section can be used to further explore the topics online.

Instructors will appreciate a password-protected online *Instructor's Resource Guide* and students will find online quizzing to further test their understanding of the material. These tools are available at www.mhhe.com/createcentral.

The organization of this book is both suggestive and subjective. The articles may be assigned or read in any fashion that is deemed desirable. Each article stands on its own and may be assigned in conjunction with, or in contrast to, any other article.

Annual Editions: Archaeology may serve as a supplement to a standard textbook for both introductory and graduate archaeology courses. It may also be used in general, undergraduate, or graduate courses in anthropology. The lay reader in anthropology may also find the collection of readings insightful.

It is the desire of those involved in the production of this book that each edition be a valuable and provocative teaching and learning tool. We welcome your criticisms, advice, and suggestions in order to carefully hone new editions into finer artifacts of education. We would be most grateful for the time you take to give us your feedback.

Editors

Mari Pritchard Parker is an adjunct professor at Pasadena City College and a Registered Professional Archaeologist with more than 25 years of cultural resources management experience in coastal California, the Great Basin, and the Desert Southwest. Ms Pritchard Parker earned a Bachelor's degree in Anthropology from California State University, Fullerton, in 1986 and a Master's degree in Archaeology from the University of California at Riverside in 1995. Her interest is primarily in ground stone analysis and replication, textile conservation, and ceramic studies. She has served as guest editor for the *Pacific Coast Archaeological Society Quarterly* on two special issues on ground stone analysis. She is also the founder of the Milford Archaeological Research Institute, a non-profit organization dedicated to educating the public and future archaeologists in the study of archaeology and past lifeways of the Desert Southwest, with particular emphasis in the Fremont culture.

Elvio Angeloni received his BA from UCLA in 1963, his MA in anthropology from UCLA in 1965, and his MA in communication arts from Loyola Marymount University in 1976. He has produced several films, including *Little Warrior*, winner of the Cinemedia VI Best Bicentennial Theme, and *Broken Bottles*, shown on PBS. He served as an academic adviser on the instructional television series *Faces of Culture*. He received the Pasadena City College Outstanding Teacher Award in 2006, and has since retired from teaching. He is also the academic editor of *Annual Editions: Physical Anthropology, Classic Edition Sources: Anthropology*, co-editor of *Roundtable Viewpoints Physical Anthropology*, and co-editor of *Annual Editions: Archaeology*. His primary area of interest has been indigenous peoples of the American Southwest. evangeloni@gmail.com

Academic Advisory Board

Members of the Academic Advisory Board are instrumental in the final selection of articles for the *Annual Editions* series. Their review of the articles for content, level, and appropriateness provides critical direction to the editor(s) and staff. We think that you will find their careful consideration reflected in this book.

Lauren Arenson
Pasadena City College

Robert J. Jeske
University of Wisconsin, Milwaukee

Melinda Leach
University of North Dakota

Bethany A. Morrison
Western Connecticut State University

Susan C. Mulholland
University of Minnesota—Duluth

Amanda Paskey
Cosumnes River College

Fred Valdez, Jr.
University of Texas, Austin

Larry J. Zimmerman
Indiana University Purdue University Indianapolis

Correlation Guide

The *Annual Editions* series provides students with convenient, inexpensive access to current, carefully selected articles from the public press. **Annual Editions: Archaeology, 11/e** is an easy-to-use reader that presents articles on important topics such as *cultural diversity, gender, social change,* and many more. For more information on other McGraw-Hill Create™ titles and collections, visit www.mcgrawhillcreate.com.

This convenient guide matches the articles in **Annual Editions: Archaeology, 11/e** with **Images of the Past, 7/e** by Price/Feinman.

Images of the Past, 7/e by Price/Feinman	Annual Editions: Archaeology, 11/e
Chapter 1: Principles of Archaeology	CSI: Italian Renaissance
	Distinguished Lecture in Archaeology: Communication and the Future of American Archaeology
	The Awful Truth about Archaeology
Chapter 2: The First Humans	A New View of the Birth of *Homo sapiens*
	Human Evolution: The Long, Winding Road to Modern Man
	Refuting a Myth about Human Origins
Chapter 3: The Hunters	Ancient Migration: Coming to America
	A New View of the Birth of *Homo sapiens*
	Bushmen
	The First Americans
Chapter 4: The Origins of Agriculture	
Chapter 5: Native North Americans	A Coprological View of Ancestral Pueblo Cannibalism
	Return to the Trail of Tears
	Uncovering America's Pyramid Builders
Chapter 6: Ancient Mesoamerica	Lasers in the Jungle
	Maya Archaeologists Turn to the Living to Help Save the Dead
	Mayas Mastered Rubber Long before Goodyear
Chapter 7: South America: The Inca and Their Predecessors	Lofty Ambitions of the Inca
Chapter 8: States and Empires in Asia and Africa	Ruined
	Uncovering Secrets of the Sphinx
	Zahi Hawass, Egypt's 'Indiana Jones,' Thinks Giza Pyramid Holds Hidden Treasure
Chapter 9: Prehistoric Europe	Archaeologists Race Against Sea Change in Orkney
	Beer and Bling in Iron Age Europe
	Putting Stonehenge in Its Place
	The First Vikings
Chapter 10: The Past as Present and Future	Archaeology of the Homeless
	Distinguished Lecture in Archaeology: Communication and the Future of American Archaeology
	Maya Archaeologists Turn to the Living to Help Save the Dead
	Ruined

This convenient guide matches the articles in **Annual Editions: Archaeology, 11/e** with the corresponding chapters in **Discovering Our Past: A Brief Introduction to Archaeology, 6/e** by Ashmore/Sharer.

Discovering Our Past: A Brief Introduction to Archaeology, 6/e by Ashmore/Sharer	Annual Editions: Archaeology, 11/e
Chapter 1: Introduction	Bushmen
	CSI: Italian Renaissance
	Distinguished Lecture in Archaeology: Communication and the Future of American Archaeology
	The Awful Truth about Archaeology
Chapter 2: Archaeology's Past	Distinguished Lecture in Archaeology: Communication and the Future of American Archaeology
	Putting Stonehenge in Its Place
	Uncovering America's Pyramid Builders
Chapter 3: Contemporary Approaches to Archaeology	Distinguished Lecture in Archaeology: Communication and the Future of American Archaeology
	The Awful Truth about Archaeology
Chapter 4: How Archaeology Works	Archaeology of Titanic
	Bushmen
	Lasers in the Jungle
	The Awful Truth about Archaeology
Chapter 5: Fieldwork	Archaeology of Titanic
	Bushmen
	The Awful Truth about Archaeology
	The Weapon That Changed History
Chapter 6: Analyzing the Past	A Coprological View of Ancestral Pueblo Cannibalism Bushmen
	CSI: Italian Renaissance
	Mayas Mastered Rubber Long before Goodyear
	Profile of an Anthropologist: No Bone Unturned
Chapter 7: Dating the Past	Ancient Migration: Coming to America
	A New View of the Birth of *Homo sapiens*
	Human Evolution: The Long, Winding Road to Modern Man
	The First Americans
Chapter 8: Reconstructing the Past	Beyond the Blue Horizon: How Ancient Voyagers Settled the Far-Flung Islands of the Pacific
	Home away from Rome
	Putting Stonehenge in Its Place
	The Great New England Vampire Panic
	Uncovering America's Pyramid Builders
Chapter 9: Understanding the Past	Prehistory *of* Warfare
	Ruined
Chapter 10: Archaeology Today	Archaeology of the Homeless
	Maya Archaeologists Turn to the Living to Help Save the Dead
	Profile of an Anthropologist: No Bone Unturned
	Zahi Hawass, Egypt's 'Indiana Jones,' Thinks Giza Pyramid Holds Hidden Treasure

Topic Guide

This topic guide suggests how the selections in this book relate to the subjects covered in your course.

All the articles that relate to each topic are listed below the bold-faced term.

About archaeologists
A Coprological View of Ancestral Pueblo Cannibalism
A New View of the Birth of *Homo sapiens*
Distinguished Lecture in Archaeology: Communication and the Future of American Archaeology
Human Evolution: The Long, Winding Road to Modern Man
Lasers in the Jungle
Maya Archaeologists Turn to the Living to Help Save the Dead
Prehistory *of* Warfare
The Awful Truth about Archaeology
Uncovering Secrets of the Sphinx
Zahi Hawass, Egypt's 'Indiana Jones,' Thinks Giza Pyramid Holds Hidden Treasure

Burials, reburials, and human remains
Beer and Bling in Iron Age Europe
CSI: Italian Renaissance
Living through the Donner Party
Lofty Ambitions of the Inca
Profile of an Anthropologist: No Bone Unturned
Putting Stonehenge in Its Place
The First Vikings
The Great New England Vampire Panic
Uncovering America's Pyramid Builders
Zahi Hawass, Egypt's 'Indiana Jones,' Thinks Giza Pyramid Holds Hidden Treasure

Classical and biblical archaeology
Carthage: The Lost Mediterranean Civilisation
Home away from Rome
Lofty Ambitions of the Inca
Uncovering Secrets of the Sphinx
The Weapon That Changed History
Zahi Hawass, Egypt's 'Indiana Jones,' Thinks Giza Pyramid Holds Hidden Treasure

Cognitive and ideological archaeology
Distinguished Lecture in Archaeology: Communication and the Future of American Archaeology

Cultural Resource Management (CRM)
Archaeologists Race Against Sea Change in Orkney
Maya Archaeologists Turn to the Living to Help Save the Dead
Uncovering America's Pyramid Builders

Epistemology (method and theory)
A New View of the Birth of *Homo sapiens*
Distinguished Lecture in Archaeology: Communication and the Future of American Archaeology
Human Evolution: The Long, Winding Road to Modern Man
Refuting a Myth about Human Origins
The Awful Truth about Archaeology
Woman the Toolmaker

Ethics and laws
Archaeology of the Homeless
Maya Archaeologists Turn to the Living to Help Save the Dead

Ethnoarchaeology
A Coprological View of Ancestral Pueblo Cannibalism
Ancient Migration: Coming to America
Beer and Bling in Iron Age Europe
Beyond the Blue Horizon: How Ancient Voyagers Settled the Far-Flung Islands of the Pacific
Bushmen
Living through the Donner Party
Lofty Ambitions of the Inca
Refuting a Myth about Human Origins
Rethinking the Hobbits of Indonesia
Return to the Trail of Tears
The First Americans

Ethnographic analogy
A Coprological View of Ancestral Pueblo Cannibalism
Bushmen
Living through the Donner Party

Experimental archaeology
Bushmen
Mayas Mastered Rubber Long before Goodyear

Forensic archaeology
CSI: Italian Renaissance
Rethinking the Hobbits of Indonesia
The First Vikings
The Great New England Vampire Panic

Garbology
Archaeology of the Homeless

Gender and sex roles
Living through the Donner Party
Woman the Toolmaker

History and historical archaeology
A Coprological View of Ancestral Pueblo Cannibalism
Archaeology of Titanic
Bushmen
Carthage: The Lost Mediterranean Civilisation
CSI: Italian Renaissance
Home away from Rome
Living through the Donner Party
Lofty Ambitions of the Inca
Mayas Mastered Rubber Long before Goodyear
Return to the Trail of Tears
Ruined
The First Vikings
The Great New England Vampire Panic
The Weapon That Changed History
Uncovering Secrets of the Sphinx
Zahi Hawass, Egypt's 'Indiana Jones,' Thinks Giza Pyramid Holds Hidden Treasure

Looters, grave robbers, and pothunters archaeology
Maya Archaeologists Turn to the Living to Help Save the Dead
Zahi Hawass, Egypt's 'Indiana Jones,' Thinks Giza Pyramid Holds Hidden Treasure

Neolithic
Beer and Bling in Iron Age Europe
Bushmen
Putting Stonehenge in Its Place
Uncovering America's Pyramid Builders

Paleolithic archaeology
Ancient Migration: Coming to America
A New View of the Birth of *Homo sapiens*
Bushmen
Human Evolution: The Long, Winding Road to Modern Man
Interbreeding with Neanderthals
Refuting a Myth about Human Origins
Rethinking the Hobbits of Indonesia
The First Americans
When the Sea Saved Humanity

Politics in archaeology
Maya Archaeologists Turn to the Living to Help Save the Dead
Return to the Trail of Tears
Zahi Hawass, Egypt's 'Indiana Jones,' Thinks Giza Pyramid Holds Hidden Treasure

Problems in archaeology
A Coprological View of Ancestral Pueblo Cannibalism
A New View of the Birth of *Homo sapiens*
Archaeologists Race Against Sea Change in Orkney
Bushmen
Human Evolution: The Long, Winding Road to Modern Man
Mayas Mastered Rubber Long before Goodyear
Prehistory *of* Warfare
Refuting a Myth about Human Origins
Rethinking the Hobbits of Indonesia
The Great New England Vampire Panic
Uncovering America's Pyramid Builders
Uncovering Secrets of the Sphinx
Woman the Toolmaker

Public archaeology
Archaeology of the Homeless
Maya Archaeologists Turn to the Living to Help Save the Dead
Zahi Hawass, Egypt's 'Indiana Jones,' Thinks Giza Pyramid Holds Hidden Treasure

Salvage and conservation
Archaeologists Race Against Sea Change in Orkney
Archaeology of Titanic
Return to the Trail of Tears
The Weapon That Changed History

Techniques in archaeology and forensics
A Coprological View of Ancestral Pueblo Cannibalism
Archaeology of Titanic
Beer and Bling in Iron Age Europe
Interbreeding with Neanderthals
Lasers in the Jungle
Mayas Mastered Rubber Long before Goodyear
Rethinking the Hobbits of Indonesia
The First Vikings
The Great New England Vampire Panic
When the Sea Saved Humanity

Tombs and pyramids (also see burials)
Lasers in the Jungle
Uncovering America's Pyramid Builders
Uncovering Secrets of the Sphinx
Zahi Hawass, Egypt's 'Indiana Jones,' Thinks Giza Pyramid Holds Hidden Treasure

Unit 1

UNIT

Prepared by: Mari Pritchard Parker, *Pasadena City College* and Elvio Angeloni, *Pasadena City College*

About Archaeologists and Archaeology

Ozymandias [1817]
I met a traveller from an antique land Who said: Two vast and trunkless legs of stone Stand in the desert. Near them, on the sand, Half sunk, a shattered visage lies, whose frown And wrinkled lip, and sneer of cold command Tell that its sculptor well those passions read Which yet survive, stamped on these lifeless things, The hand that mocked them and the heart that fed. And on the pedestal these words appear: "My name is Ozymandias, king of kings: Look on my works, ye Mighty, and despair!" Nothing beside remains. Round the decay Of that colossal wreck, boundless and bare The lone and level sands stretch far away.

—Percy Bysshe Shelley

So just who is an archaeologist? The job description presented by the mass media is very different from the reality of today's anthropological archaeologists. Archaeologists in the Americas, after all, are trained as anthropologists. Our goal is to reconstruct cultures of the past based on the material remains that managed to survive the "ravages of time." So today's archaeologists are concerned with the reconstruction of human behavior, not just with the collection of treasure objects.

If human behavior were a baseball game, the anthropologist would be in the broadcaster's booth. But long before the game was over, in a seeming paradox, the anthropologist would run into the stands to be a spectator, chow down on a good, fresh, steamy, mustard-covered hot dog, and then rush onto the field to be a player and catch a high fly to left field. This is the eccentric nature of anthropology. This is why anthropology is so interesting.

If one compares anthropology, psychology, sociology, and history as four disciplines that study human nature, anthropology is the one that takes the giant step back and uses a 360-degree panoramic camera. The psychologist stands nose to nose with the individual person, the sociologist moves back for the group shot, and the historian goes back in time as well as space. However, the anthropologist does all these things, standing well behind the others, watching and measuring, using the data of all these disciplines, but recombining them into the uniqueness of the anthropological perspective: much the way meiosis generates novel genetic combinations.

Anthropology is the science of human behavior that studies all humankind, starting with our biological and evolutionary origins as cultural beings, and continues with the diversification of our cultural selves. Humankind is the only species that has evolved culture as a way of adapting to the world. Academically, anthropology is divided into four major fields: cultural anthropology, physical anthropology, linguistics, and archaeology. Anthropologists hold in common a shared concept of culture. The ultimate goal shared by all anthropologists is to generate a behavioral science that can explain the differences and similarities between cultures. In order to achieve this, anthropologists view people from a cross-cultural perspective. This involves comparing the parts and parcels of all cultures, past and present, with each other. This is the holistic approach of anthropology: considering all things in their broader social and historical contexts. A grand task, indeed. One that requires, above all, learning to ask the "right" questions. If there is one thing that anthropologists have learned, it is that the kinds of answers you get depend upon the kinds of questions you ask.

What is culture? Culture is the unique way in which the human species adapts to its total environment. Total environment includes everything that affects human beings—the physical environment that includes plants, animals, the weather; beliefs; values; a passing insult; or an opportunistic virus. Everything that human beings learn is cultural.

Culture is the human adaptive system shaped by its particular time and space. It consists of learned ways to manipulate the environment by making and using tools and it involves shared values and beliefs which are passed down from one generation to the next by means of language. Cultures change and evolve over time. But whether they are high civilizations or small tribes, they do eventually cease to exist.

Archaeology is the subfield of anthropology that studies these extinct cultures. Archaeologists dig up the physical remains, the tools, the houses, the garbage, and the utensils of past cultures. And from this spare database, archaeologists attempt to reconstruct these past cultures in their material, social, and ideological aspects. Is this important to anthropology? Yes, this is anthropology. Because these once-living cultures represent approximately ninety-eight percent of all cultures that have ever existed. They tell us what we have been, what we are today, and what we might become in the future.

How do archaeologists do this? Today, the mass media, including the Internet, is the major source of our understanding of the modern world, and it underscores the cultural values and cultural myths that all humans use to rationalize the way they live. The media is as much a response to our demands as we are to its manipulations. Its themes play a medley in our minds over and over again, until they fade into our unconscious only to be recycled again, pulled up, and laid before us like the ice cream man's musical chimes of our childhood. But the commercial media will also respond to a rational, skeptical, and articulate public, a public that has been educated to think scientifically with a very strict set of rules and regulations that test the veracity of conclusions. This is where anthropology in general and archaeology in particular have a role to play: spreading the word about the scientific method and the wonderful results that can be derived from its use in understanding our species.

Postmodernists may argue that knowledge is only knowable in a relative sense. But we know what we know in a very real pragmatic sense because we are, after all, humans—the cultural animal. It is our way of knowing and surviving. Let us proceed now to see how archaeologists ply their magical trade.

The Awful Truth about Archaeology

Dr. Lynne Sebastian

Learning Outcomes

After reading this article, you will be able to:

- Discuss the importance of archaeology as a discipline.
- Discuss the differences between the way archaeology is really practiced and the way it is usually portrayed in the media.
- Describe the ways in which archaeology can be truly exciting.

"Ohhhh! You're an Archaeologist! That sounds soooo exciting!" Whenever I tell someone on a plane or at a dinner party what I do for a living, this is almost always the response that I get. Either that, or they want to talk to me about dinosaurs, and I have to explain gently that it is paleontologists who do dinosaurs; archaeologists study people who lived long ago.

The reason people think archaeology must be exciting is that they have spent WAY too much time watching *The Curse of the Mummy*, *Indiana Jones and the Temple of Doom*, and *Lara Croft, Tomb Raider* (do you suppose that she actually has that printed on her business cards?). Perhaps it is a flaw in my character or a lapse in my professional education, but I have never once recovered a golden idol or been chased through the jungle by thugs, and I appear to have been absent from graduate school on the day that they covered bullwhips, firearms, and the martial arts. I have not even, so far as I can tell, suffered from a curse, although I have had few nasty encounters with serpents, scorpions, and lightning.

I'm sure that members of every profession are exasperated by the way that they are portrayed in movies and on television, and archaeologists are no exception. Every time we see Sydney Fox (*Relic Hunter*, another great job title) fly off to an exotic country, follow the clues on the ancient map, and rip-off some fabulous object to bring home to the museum, we want to root for the bad guys who are trying to bring her career to an abrupt and permanent halt.

What would really happen if a mysterious man wearing an eye patch showed up at Sydney's university office and gave her the map, just before expiring as a result of slow-acting poison? Well, of course, first there would be a lot of unpleasantness with the campus police . . . but leaving that aside, she would spend months writing grant proposals to get funding for a research expedition and more months getting the needed permits and authorizations from the government of the exotic country. Then she would have to persuade the Dean and her department Chair to give her release time from teaching. And when she and her research team finally arrived in the exotic country, they would spend months meticulously mapping the site, painstakingly removing thin layers of soil from perfectly square holes, and recording every stone, every bit of stained earth, every piece of debris that they encountered, using photos, maps, sketches, and detailed written notes. Finally, at the end of the field season, the team would return to the university with 70 boxes of broken pottery, bits of stone, and all manner of scientific samples to be washed and cataloged and analyzed. And in the end, all that material would be returned to a museum in the exotic country.

Now, of course, nobody would want to watch a TV show where even the beauteous Sydney did all that, but this kind of tedious, detailed work is one important aspect of "real" archaeology. Just about every archaeologist that I know has a copy of an old Calvin and Hobbs cartoon somewhere in his or her office. In it, Calvin, who has spent an exhausting day doing a make-believe archaeological excavation in his backyard, turns to Hobbs in disgust and says, "Archaeology has to be the most mind-numbing job in the world!!" And some days it is. Worse yet, it is detailed work that involves a lot of paperwork and delicate instruments but has to be done outdoors in every sort of adverse weather. When it is 20 degrees and you are hunched down in a square hole in the ground trying to write a description of layers of dirt with a pen that keeps freezing solid or when the wind is blowing sheets of sand straight sideways into your face while you are lying on your stomach using a dental pick to expose a broken shell bracelet so you can photograph it before you remove it—these are experiences that can cause a person to question her career choice.

But you know what? Archaeology really IS exciting, and not for any of the reasons that Indy or Lara would suggest. Archaeology is exciting because it connects with the past in a way that nothing else can, and sometimes that connection can be stunningly immediate and personal. I worked one year on the Hopi Reservation in Arizona, excavating a site that was going to be destroyed by road construction. We found that one of the three "pithouses" or semi-subterranean structures on the site appeared to have been cleaned out and closed up, presumably in the expectation that someone would return to live in it again.

A flat slab had been placed over the ventilator opening, perhaps to keep out dirt and debris and critters, and the slab was sealed in place with wet mud. But no one came back, and eventually the small pithouse burned.

When we excavated the pithouse, we found the imprint of human hands, perfectly preserved in the mud, which had been hardened by the fire. That little house was built in AD 805, but I could reach out and place my hands in those handprints left there by someone a thousand years before. And more important, the Hopi school children who visited the site could place their small hands in those prints made by one of their ancestors, 50 generations removed. We lifted each one of the children into the pithouse, and let them do just that—like children everywhere, they were astonished that they were being encouraged to touch rather than being forbidden to do so.

Afterward we sat together on the site and talked about what life was like for that Hisatsinom (the Hopi term for the people we call Anasazi) person. We talked about food and looked at the burned corn kernels and the squash seeds that we had found. We talked about shelter and tools and looked at the three houses and the broken bits of stone and bone and pottery that we were recovering from the trash areas at the site. One of the houses had burned while it was occupied, and we looked at the fragments of the rolled up sleeping mats and baskets of corn and other possessions that the people had lost. We talked about the family that had lived there, how much the parents loved their children and how they must have worried about providing for them after such a terrible loss. And we talked about the migration stories that are a central part of Hopi oral history, and about what the Hopi elders had told us about the place of this particular site in those stories. I like to think that those children, who reached back across the centuries and touched the hand of their fifty-times-great grandmother, came away with a stronger sense of who they were and where they came from and a richer understanding of the oral traditions of their people.

But what if I had been not me, Dr. Science, purveyor of meticulous and mind-numbing archaeological techniques, but rather Lara Croft, Tomb Raider? If Lara had been rooting about in this site, searching for "treasures," she would have quickly dismissed that small pithouse, although she might have smashed that burned mud with the handprints in order to rip away the slab and check for hidden goodies behind it.

No, she would have focused on the other house, the one that burned while it was being used. She would have pulled out all those burned roof beams whose pattern of rings enabled us to learn that the houses were built in AD 805, probably using them for her campfire. She would have crushed the remnants of the burned sleeping mats and baskets of corn. She would never have noticed the stone griddle still in place on the hearth or the grease stains left by the last two corn cakes cooking on it when the fire started. She would have kicked aside the broken pieces of the pottery vessels that were crushed when the burning roof fell, the same pots that we put back together in the lab in order to estimate the size of the family and to recover traces of the items stored and cooked in them.

No, Lara would have missed all that we learned about that site and the people who made their homes there. Instead, she would have seized the single piece of pottery that didn't break in the fire and clutching it to her computer enhanced bosom, she would have stolen away into the night, narrowly escaping death and destruction at the hands of the rival gang of looters.

Is archaeology the most mind-numbing pursuit in the world, as Calvin claims? Or is it "sooo exciting" as my airline seatmates always exclaim? Both. And much more. What Lara and Indy and the others don't know is that archaeology is not about things, it is about people. It is about understanding life in the past, about understanding who we are and where we came from—not just where we came from as a particular cultural group, but what we share with all people in this time and in all the time that came before.

Critical Thinking

1. Why do people think archaeology must be exciting?
2. Why wouldn't people watch a show about "real" archaeology?
3. Why does the author claim that archaeology "really is exciting"?
4. What made the author's work on the Hopi reservation meaningful?
5. What would the author have done if she were Lara Croft, Tomb Raider rather than "Dr. Science"?
6. What does the author think archaeology really is and why?

Create Central

www.mhhe.com/createcentral

Internet References

Anthropology Resources on the Internet
www.socsciresearch.com/r7.html

Archaeological Institute of America
www.archaeological.org

Society for American Archaeology
www.saa.org

LYNNE SEBASTIAN is Director of Historic Preservation with the SRI Foundation, a private nonprofit dedicated to historic preservation, and an adjunct assistant professor of Anthropology at UNM. She is a former New Mexico State Archaeologist and State Historic Preservation Office, and she is currently the President of the Society for American Archaeology.

Sebastian, Lynne. From *Albuquerque Tribune*, April 16, 2002. Copyright © 2002 by Lynne Sebastian. Reprinted by permission of the author.

Article

Prepared by: Mari Pritchard Parker, *Pasadena City College* and
Elvio Angeloni, *Pasadena City College*

Zahi Hawass, Egypt's 'Indiana Jones,' Thinks Giza Pyramid Holds Hidden Treasure

OWEN JARUS

Learning Outcomes

After reading this article, you will be able to:

- Discuss the importance of tourism to Egyptian archaeology.
- Explain why there may be important discoveries waiting to be made in the Valley of the Kings.
- Discuss the importance of Zahi Hawass to Egyptian archaeology.

Zahi Hawass is back.

The famous, and at times controversial, Egyptologist is free of legal charges, free to travel and is launching a worldwide lecture tour with the aim of getting tourists back to Egypt, he told *LiveScience* in an interview.

Hawass also said that he believes there are some fantastic discoveries waiting to be made, including more tombs in the Valley of the Kings and a secret burial chamber, containing treasure, which he believes to be inside the Great Pyramid built by the pharaoh Khufu (also known as Cheops).

It's a turnaround for the archaeologist, who, just a few months ago, was under investigation and banned from traveling outside Egypt. At the time, there were a number of allegations related to his tenure as Egypt's antiquities chief in Hosni Mubarak's former government. These allegations reportedly included allowing antiquities to travel out of the country illegally, wasting public funds and using his position inappropriately to aid a charity run by Suzanne Mubarak (wife of the deposed Hosni Mubarak). He was banned from travelling outside Egypt while under investigation.

Hawass was head of the Supreme Council of Antiquities for nearly 10 years and became Egypt's first-ever antiquities minister near the end of Mubarak's regime. A revolution succeeded in tossing out Mubarak in February 2011 and Hawass was dismissed from his post a few months later. "All the accusations against me were dropped, were completely false, and this is why everything's finished, I can travel, I can do anything," he told *LiveScience* in an interview after a lecture held here on Monday at the Royal Ontario Museum.

The massive gallery where the lecture was held was filled to capacity, with a waiting list just as robust. The museum's director Janet Carding said that Egypt's ambassador to Canada, Wael Aboul-Magd, helped bring Hawass to Toronto and was in attendance.

Hawass said that Toronto is only the beginning. He'll be in Montreal on June 6 and will be launching a worldwide tour.

"I'm traveling the whole world. I'm going to Brazil, going to Argentina at the end of the month, going to Australia, New Zealand, everywhere to promote tourism to Egypt and to bring the tourists back because, I think, I'm the only one who can really bring the tourists back to Egypt," he told *LiveScience*.

Tourism plummeted after Egypt's revolution, resulting in lower ticket sales at ancient sites, a situation that has the antiquities ministry strapped for cash.

"We don't have any money at all for excavation or preservation," he told the audience.

A Hidden Chamber inside the Great Pyramid

In the interview, and in his lecture, Hawass said that he is excited at the robot work that has been going on over the past two decades at the Great Pyramid. One chamber in the pyramid called the "Queen's Chamber" (although there is no evidence it was ever used for a queen's burial) contains two shafts that go up into the pyramid but do not exit outside.

Robots have been up these shafts and found that both contain doorways with copper handles. When a robot drilled through one of the doors, they found a small chamber with what might be a sealed door behind it.

Ultimately, these shafts may point the way to a secret burial chamber where Khufu (Cheops) was buried, Hawass said. While the pyramid already has three known chambers (one of which contains a sarcophagus), he said the true burial place of the pharaoh has yet to be found.

"I really believe that Cheops' chamber is not discovered yet and all the three chambers were just to deceive the thieves, and the treasures of Khufu [are] still hidden inside the Great Pyramid, and these three doors could be the key to open this burial chamber," he said in the interview.

"There is no pyramid of the 123 pyramids in Egypt that have these type of doors with copper handles," he added. "Really, I believe they're hiding something."

Another Era for Archaeology

Hawass is also very enthusiastic about finding new tombs in the Valley of the Kings. Within the past decade, two new tombs, KV 63 and 64, have been excavated and Hawass told *LiveScience*, and the Toronto audience, that he believes there are many more to be found.

"The tomb of Thutmose II, not found yet, the tomb of Ramesses VIII is not found yet, all the queens of dynasty 18 [1550–1292 B.C.] were buried in the valley and their tombs not found yet," he said in his lecture. "This could be another era for archaeology," he added in the interview.

Finding these tombs will pose a challenge. Ground-penetrating radar tests conducted while Hawass was antiquities chief had difficulty locating tombs and he said he believes that radar will not be effective in finding them.

Pharaohs Were Buried with their Brains

If they find these pharaohs, they may also find their brains. Hawass and Dr. Sahar Saleem of Cairo University looked at CT scans of 12 royal mummies that date to between 1493–1156 B.C.

Based on their findings, detailed in the *American Journal of Roentgenology*, Hawass doesn't believe the Egyptians removed the brains of their dead pharaohs. "All these ideas about removing brains came from Herodotus," he said, referring to a Greek historian who lived more than 2,400 years ago. "It was wrong."

Hawass pointed out that "the brain of Tutankhamun was desiccated (dried) out but still it's there."

A Return as Antiquities Minister?

After a recent article in *Smithsonian* magazine, there was speculation that Hawass could be plotting his return as antiquities minister.

In the *LiveScience* interview, Hawass poured cold water over this idea, saying that it does not appeal to him at all.

"To become a minister, I don't like," he said.

"I only wear a suit and a tie when I come to give a lecture, but all my life, I'm in my jeans," Hawass said, adding he disagreed with the decision to make antiquities a cabinet-level position and hates the meetings required for a cabinet minister. "I can't stand being in the cabinet listening for nine hours of nonsense."

In terms of a future role in Egypt's antiquities ministry, Hawass said he plans to wait a year or two until the situation in Egypt improves. "In a year or two, after everything is relaxed, I would like to continue [building] the 24 museums" that are underway, he said. He also would like to help train young archaeologists and aid in repatriating Egyptian artifacts that are now abroad.

"All of this I need to continue," he said. "I hope one day I'll be able to do that."

Critical Thinking

1. In what ways has Zahi Hawass been important to Egyptian archaeology?
2. How important is tourism to Egyptian archaeology?
3. What evidence is there that important archaeological discoveries are yet to be made in Egypt?

Create Central

www.mhhe.com/createcentral

Internet References

NOVA Online/Pyramids—The Inside Story
www.pbs.org/wgbh/nova/pyramid

The Ancient Egyptian Pharaohs
www.ancient-egypt-online.com/ancient-egyptian-pharaohs.html

Jarus, Owen. From *Live Science*, June 9, 2013. Copyright © 2013 by Tech Media. Reprinted by permission.

Article

Prepared by: Mari Pritchard Parker, *Pasadena City College* and
Elvio Angeloni, *Pasadena City College*

Distinguished Lecture in Archaeology
Communication and the Future of American Archaeology

What follows is the revised text of the Distinguished Lecture in Archaeology, presented at the 95th Annual Meeting of the American Anthropological Association, held in San Francisco, California, November, 1996.

JEREMY A. SABLOFF

Learning Outcomes

After reading this article, you will be able to:

- Discuss the pros and cons of the professionalization of archaeology.
- Explain the ethical obligation that archaeologists have toward "action archaeology."
- Discuss ways to improve the academic system so as to make archaeology more "relevant" to the public.

I offer these remarks with somewhat ambivalent feelings. While it is an honor indeed to be asked to give the Archaeology Division's Distinguished Lecture, I nevertheless must admit that it is a daunting challenge. I have looked at many of the superb Distinguished Lectures that have been presented to you in recent years and subsequently published in the *American Anthropologist* and am very impressed with what our colleagues have had to say. Most of the recent talks have focused on aspects of the ongoing debates on modern archaeological theory and methods. I certainly could have continued this tradition, because, as many of you know, I have strong feelings about this topic. However, I decided to pursue a different, more general tack, which I hope you will agree is of equal importance.

In a few short years, we will be entering a new millennium. Will American archaeology survive in the twenty-first century? Of course it will. But will it continue to thrive in the new millennium? The answer to this question is a more guarded "yes." There are various causes for concern about the future health of archaeology. I would like to examine one of these concerns and offer some suggestions as to how this concern might be eased.

My theme will be archaeologists' communication with the public—or lack thereof—and, more specifically, the relevance of archaeology to non-professionals. In thinking about this theme, which has been a particular interest and concern of mine, it struck me how one of my favorite cartoons provided an important insight into the whole question of archaeological communication. I know that many of you have your office doors or bulletin boards festooned with a host of "Calvin and Hobbes," "Shoe," "Bloom County," "Doonesbury," or "Far Side" drawings that unerringly seem to pinpoint many of life's enduring paradoxes and problems. In particular, the "Far Side" cartoons by Gary Larson, who is now lamentably in early retirement like several of our master cartoonists, often resonate well with archaeologists' sensibilities. This cartoon, while not specifically targeting archaeologists or cultural anthropologists, as Larson often did pinpoint a central concern of my discussion.

While archaeologists may think they are talking clearly to the public, what the latter often hears, I believe, is "blah, blah, blah, *tomb,* blah, blah, blah *sacrifice,* blah, blah, blah, *arrowhead.*"

I will argue that the field of American archaeology, despite some significant progress in the past decade, is still failing to effectively tell the public about how modern anthropological archaeology functions and about the huge gains archaeologists have made in understanding the development of ancient cultures through time and space.

More than 25 years ago, John Fritz and Fred Plog ended their article on "The Nature of Archaeological Explanation" (1970:412) with the famous assertion that "We suggest that unless archaeologists find ways to make their research increasingly relevant to the modern world, the modern world will find itself increasingly capable of getting along without archaeologists." Although Fritz and Plog had a very particular definition of relevance in mind relating to the development of laws of culture change, as did Fritz in his important article on "Relevance, Archaeology, and Subsistence Theory" (1973), if one adopts a broader view of the term *relevance,* then the thrust of their statement is just as important today—if not more so—than it was in 1970.

How can this be true? Archaeology appears to be thriving, if one counts number of jobs, money spent on archaeological field research, course enrollments, publications, and public fascination with the subject as measured in media coverage. But is the public interest, or, better yet, the public's interest, being served properly and satisfied in a productive and responsible fashion? With some important exceptions, I unfortunately would answer "no." Why do I think this to be the case?

In the nineteenth century, archaeology played an important public and intellectual role in the fledgling United States. Books concerned wholly or in part with archaeology were widely read and, as Richard Ford has indicated clearly in his article on "Archaeology Serving Humanity" (1973), archaeology played an important part in overthrowing the then-dominant Biblical view of human development in favor of Darwinian evolutionary theory. Empirical archaeological research, which excited public interest and was closely followed by the public, was able to provide data that indicated that human activities had considerable antiquity and that archaeological studies of the past could throw considerable light on the development of the modern world.

As is the case in most disciplines, as archaeology became increasingly professionalized throughout the nineteenth century and as academic archaeology emerged in the late-nineteenth and early-twentieth centuries, the communications gap between professionals and the public grew apace. This gap was accentuated because amateurs had always played an important part in the archaeological enterprise. As late as the 1930s, before academic archaeology really burgeoned, the gap between most amateurs and professionals was still readily bridgeable, I believe. The first article in *American Antiquity,* for example, was written by an amateur, and, as I have discussed in detail elsewhere, the founders of the journal hoped that it "would provide a forum for communication between these two groups" (Sabloff 1985:228). However, even a quick look today at *American Antiquity* will indicate that those earlier hopes have been dashed. It may be a terrific journal for professionals, but much of it would be nearly incomprehensible to non-professionals, except perhaps to the most devoted amateurs.

In 1924, Alfred Vincent Kidder published his landmark book *An Introduction to the Study of Southwestern Archaeology.* This highly readable volume both made key advances in scholarly understanding of the ancient Southwest and was completely accessible to the general public. As Gordon Willey (1967:299) has stated: "It is a rarity in that it introduces systematics to a field previously unsystematized, and, at the same time, it is vitally alive and unpedantic.... He wrote a book that was romantic but not ridiculous, scrupulously close to the facts but not a boring recital of them." How many regional archaeological syntheses could have that said of them today? Happily, the answer is not "none," and there is some evidence of a positive trend in the publication of more popularly oriented regional and site syntheses (see, for instance, Kolata 1993; Plog 1997; or Schele and Freidel 1990, among others). Marcus and Flannery's (1996) recent book on Zapotec civilization is a superb example of how such accessible writing can be combined with a clear, theoretically sophisticated approach, as well.

Kidder also was deeply concerned about the relevance of archaeology to the contemporary world and was not shy about expressing his belief that archaeology could and should play an important social role in the modern world (a view which is paralleled today by some post-processual [e.g., Hodder et al. 1995] and feminist [e.g., Spector 1993] concerns with humanizing archaeological narratives). Kidder's views were most clearly expressed by him at a 1940 symposium at the American Philosophical Society on "Characteristics of American Culture and Its Place in General Culture." As Richard Woodbury (1973:171) notes: "Kidder presented one of his most eloquent pleas for the importance of the anthropological understanding of the past through the techniques of archaeology." Kidder (1940:528), for example, states: "it is good for an archaeologist to be forced to take stock, to survey his field, to attempt to show what bearing his delvings into the past may have upon our judgement of present day life; and what service, if any, he renders the community beyond filling the cases of museums and supplying material for the rotogravure sections of the Sunday papers." Lamentably, his prescription for the practitioners of archaeology has not been well filled in the past half century.

The professionalization of archaeology over the course of this century obviously has had innumerable benefits. In the most positive sense, the discipline has little resemblance to the archaeology of 100 years ago. With all the advances in method, theory, and culture historical knowledge, archaeologists are now in a position to make important and useful statements about cultural adaptation and development that should have broad intellectual appeal. Ironically, though, one aspect of the professionalization of the discipline, what can be termed the academization of archaeology, is working against such broad dissemination of current advances in archaeological understanding of cultures of the past. The key factor, I am convinced, is that since World War II, and especially in the past few decades as archaeology rapidly expanded as an academic subject in universities and colleges throughout this country, the competition for university jobs and the institutional pressures to publish in quantity, in general, and in peer review journals, in particular, has led in part to the academic devaluation of popular writing and communication with the general public. Such activities just don't count or, even worse, count against you.

In addition, I believe that it is possible that some archaeologists, in their desire to prove the rigor and scientific standing of the discipline within the academy and among their non-anthropological colleagues and university administrators, have rejected or denigrated popular writing because it might somehow taint archaeology with a nonscientific "softness" from which they would like to distance the field.

If popular writing is frowned upon by some academics, then popularization in other media, such as television, can be treated even more derisively by these scholars, and consequently too few archaeologists venture into these waters. Why should the best known "archaeologist" to the public be an unrepentant looter like Indiana Jones? Is he the role model we want for our profession? When I turn on the television to watch a show with archaeological content, why should I be more than likely to see Leonard Nimoy and the repeated use of the term *mysterious*? It should be professional archaeologists routinely helping to write and perhaps even hosting many of the archaeology shows on television, not just—at best—popular science writers and Hollywood actors. In sum, I strongly feel that we need more accessible writing, television shows, videos, CD-ROMs, and the like with archaeologists heavily involved in all these enterprises.

Forty years ago, Geoffrey Bibby, in his best-selling book *The Testimony of the Spade,* wrote in his foreword (1956:vii):

> It has long been customary to start any book that can be included under the comprehensive heading of "popular science" with an apology from the author to his fellow scientists for his desertion of the icy uplands of the research literature for the supposedly lower and supposedly lush fields of popular representation. This is not an apology, and it is not directed to archaeologists. In our day, when the research literature of one branch of knowledge has become all but incomprehensible to a researcher in another branch, and when the latest advances within any science can revolutionize—or end—our lives within a decade, the task of interpreting every science in language that can be understood by workers in other fields is no longer—if it ever was—a slightly disreputable sideline, but a first-priority duty.

Bibby was making a point that is similar to one made years ago by C. P. Snow (1959) that scholars in different disciplines do not read or are unable to read each others' works, but should! However, I believe that Bibby's argument can easily be expanded to include the lay public, which should be able to readily find out what archaeologists are doing. If they are interested in the subject, and they have no accessible professionally written sources to turn to—like *The Testimony of the Spade*—is it any surprise that they turn to highly speculative, non-professional sources? Unfortunately, Bibby's wise call has gone relatively unheeded. Where are all the *Testimony of the Spades* of this generation, or even the *Gods, Graves, and Scholars* (Ceram 1951)?

But even encouraging communication between archaeologists and the general public is not sufficient, I believe, to dispel the lack of popular understanding about the modern archaeological enterprise and the potential importance of archaeological knowledge. With all the problems that the world faces today, the conflicts and ethnic strife, the innumerable threats to the environment, and the inadequacy of food supplies in the face of rising populations, there never has been a more propitious time for archaeology's new insights into the nature of human development and diversity in time and space to be appreciated by people in all walks of life. In order for better communication to have a useful impact, I believe that the profession has to heed Fritz and Plog's call and strive to be relevant. Moreover, we should pursue relevance in both the general and specific senses of the term. In its broadest sense, *relevance* is "to the purpose; pertinent," according to *The American College Dictionary,* while in its more narrow definition, *relevance* according to *The Oxford English Dictionary,* means "pertinency to important current issues."

All things being equal, archaeology could be justified on the basis of its inherent interest. But all things are rarely equal, and therefore archaeological activities and their relevance to today's world do need justification. To what is archaeology pertinent? In the general sense, archaeology's main claim to relevance is its revelation of the richness of human experience through the study and understanding of the development of past cultures over the globe. Among the goals of such study is to foster awareness and respect of other cultures and their achievements. Archaeology can make itself relevant—pertinent—by helping its audiences appreciate past cultures and their accomplishments.

Why should we actively seek to fulfill such a goal? I firmly believe in the lessons of history. By appreciating the nature of cultures both past and present, their uniqueness and their similarities, their development, and their adaptive successes and failures, we have a priceless opportunity to better grapple with the future than is possible without such knowledge. For example, as many of you are aware, I have long argued that new understandings of the decline of Classic Maya civilization in the southern Maya lowlands in the eighth century A.D. can shed important light on the ability of the ancient Maya to sustain a complex civilization in a tropical rain-forest environment for over a millennium and the reasons why this highly successful adaptation ultimately failed (see Sabloff 1990). The potential implications for today's world are profound.

This form of striving for relevance is powerful and should have great appeal to the public, but it is not necessarily sufficient in terms of outreach goals for general audiences. Archaeology also needs to attempt to be relevant, where possible, in the narrower sense, too. As some of our colleagues in the Maya area, for instance, begin to take the new archaeological insights about sustainable agriculture and the potential for demographic growth and begin to directly apply them to modern situations, then archaeology clearly is becoming pertinent "to important current issues" (see, for example, Rice and Rice 1984).

In relation to this latter goal, I would argue that we need more "action archaeology," a term first coined by Maxine Klehidienst and Patty Jo Watson (1956) more than four decades ago (in the same year that *Testimony of the Spade* first appeared), but which I use in a more general way to convey the meaning of archaeology working *for* living communities, not just *in* them. One compelling example of such action archaeology is the field research of my colleague Clark Erickson, who has identified the remains of raised field agriculture in the Bolivian Amazon and has been studying the raised fields and other earthworks on the ground. He has been able to show that there was a complex culture in this area in Precolumbian times. Erickson also is working with local peasants in his field study area to show them how Precolumbian farmers successfully intensified their agricultural production and to indicate how the ancient raised field and irrigation techniques might be adapted to the modern situation so as to improve the current economic picture (see Erickson 1998). This is just one example of many that could be cited, including the close collaboration between archaeologists and Native American groups in, for example, the innovative research of my colleague Robert Preucel (1998) at Cochiti Pueblo, or in organizations like the Zuni Archaeological Project (see Anyon and Ferguson 1995), in the many pathbreaking modern garbage projects initiated by William L. Rathje and his colleagues (Rathje and Murphy 1992), in the thoughtful archaeological/environmental development project initiated by Anabel Ford and her collaborators at El Pilar in Belize and Guatemala (Ford 1998), or in cooperative projects between archaeologists and members of the local communities in locations such as Labrador or Belize that have been reported on by Stephen Loring and Marilyn Masson in recent Archaeology Division sections of the *AAA Newsletter* (October and November 1996). However, we need many more examples of such work. They should be the rule, not the exception.

This kind of work in archaeology parallels the continued growth of action anthropology among our cultural colleagues. The potential for collaboration among archaeologists and cultural anthropologists in this regard, as advocated, for example, by Anne Pybum and Richard Wilk (1995), is quite strong. Explorations of the possibilities of such cooperation should be particularly appropriate and of great importance to the Archaeology Division of the American Anthropological Association, which I know is interested in integrating archaeology within a general anthropological focus, and I urge the Division to pursue such an endeavor. Applied anthropology in its action form need not—and should not—be restricted to cultural anthropology.

It is depressing to note that the academic trend away from public communication appears to be increasing just as public interest in archaeology seems to be reaching new heights. Whatever the reasons for this growing interest, and clearly there are many potential reasons that could be and have been cited, including a turn to the past in times of current uncertainties, New Age ideological trends, or the growing accessibility of archaeological remains through travel, television, and video, there is no doubt that there is an audience out there that is thirsting for information about the past. But it does not appear that this interest is being well served, given the ratio of off-the-wall publications to responsible ones that one can find in any bookstore. I have written elsewhere (Sabloff 1982:7) that "Unfortunately, one of the prices we must pay for the privilege of sharing a free marketplace of ideas is the possibility that some writers will write unfounded speculation, some publishers will publish them, some bookstores will sell them, and some media will sensationalize them. In this way, unfounded speculations become widely spread among the general population of interested readers." I went on to suggest that "Perhaps the best solution to this problem is to help readers to become aware of the standards of scientific research so that scientific approaches can be better appreciated and pseudoscientific approaches can be read critically" (p. 7).

In order for this solution to work, however, archaeologists need to compete effectively in this free market. Why must we always run into the most outrageous pseudo-archaeology books (what Stephen Williams [1991] has termed "fantastic archaeology") in such visible places as airport news shops? I simply refuse to believe that among the large pool of professional archaeological writing talent that there aren't some of our colleagues who can write books that can replace *Chariots of the Gods?* (Von Däniken 1970). If we abandon much of the field of popular writing to the fringe, we should not be surprised at all that the public often fails to appreciate the significance of what we do. So what? Why does it matter if many archaeologists don't value public communication and much of the public lacks an understanding of archaeology and what archaeologists do and accomplish? There are two principal answers to this question, I believe. First, I strongly feel that we have a moral responsibility to educate the public about what we do. Good science and public education not only are compatible but should go hand in hand. The overwhelming majority of us, whether in the academic, government, or business world, receive at least some public support in our work. I believe that we have a responsibility to give back to the public that provides us with grants, or contracts, or jobs. We need to share with them our excitement in our work and our insights into how peoples of the past lived and how our understandings of the past can inform us about the present and future; and we need to share all this in ways that everyone from young schoolchildren to committed amateur archaeologists can understand and appreciate.

Moreover, the better the public understands and appreciates what we do, what we know, and how we come to know it, the better it can assess the uses and—unfortunately—the abuses of archaeology, especially in political contexts. In this age of exploding ethnic conflicts, a public that has been educated to understand the nature of archaeological research and is thus able to cast a critical eye on how archaeological findings are used in modern political arenas clearly is preferable to people who lack such understanding. On a global scale, the use of archaeological myths in some of the former Soviet republics by various ethnic groups to justify repression of others is just one example—unfortunately!—of many kinds of abuses of archaeological data that could be cited (see Kohl and Fawcett 1995).

Second, there are eminently practical reasons for emphasizing and valuing public communication. Namely—and obviously—it is in our enlightened self-interest! As governmental, academic, and corporate budgets grow tighter and tighter, we are increasingly vying with innumerable groups and people, many with very compelling causes and needs, for extremely competitive dollars. If we don't make our case to the public about the significance of our work, then, in Fritz and Plog's (1970) words, we will surely find our public increasingly capable of getting along without us. How many of our representatives in Congress or in state legislatures really understand what archaeologists do and what they can contribute to the modern world? How many of them get letters from constituents extolling the virtues of the archaeological enterprise and urging them to support archaeological research both financially and through legislation? Unless we educate and work with our many publics, we are certain to find our sources of support, many of which have been taken for granted in recent years, rapidly drying up.

Let's turn our attention from the general problem to potential solutions. How can American archaeologists rectify the situation just described and particularly promote more popular writing by professional scholars? One answer is deceptively simple: we need to change our value system and our reward system within the academy. Just as Margaret Mead and other great anthropological popularizers have been sneered at by some cultural anthropologists, so colleagues like Brian Fagan, who has done so much to reach out to general readers (see, for example, Fagan 1977, 1984, 1987, 1991, and 1995, among many others), are often subject to similar snide comments. We need to celebrate those who successfully communicate with the public, not revile them. Ideally, we should have our leading scholars writing for the public, not only for their colleagues. Some might argue that popular writing would be a waste of their time. To the contrary, I would maintain that such writing is part of our collective academic responsibility. Who better to explain what is on the cutting edge of archaeological research than the field's leading practitioners? Moreover, we need to develop a significant number of our own Stephen Jay Goulds or Stephen Hawkings, not just a few.

Why do some scholars look down at archaeologists who are perceived as popularizers? There are probably a host of reasons, but one of them definitely is pure jealousy. Some archaeologists are jealous of their colleagues who successfully write popular books and articles because of the latter's writing skills. They also are jealous, I believe, of the visibility that popular communication brings those who enter this arena, and they are jealous of the monetary rewards that sometimes accompany popular success. But since such jealousy is not socially acceptable, it tends to be displaced into negative comments on the scholarly abilities of the popularizers.

Not only do we need to change our value system so that public communication is perceived in a positive light, more particularly, we need to change the academic evaluation and reward system for archaeologists (and others!), so that it gives suitable recognition to popular writing and public outreach. Clearly, these activities also can be counted as public service. But they further merit scholarly recognition. I also would include the curation of museum exhibits in this regard, especially ones that include catalogs or CD-ROMs that are accessible to broad audiences. Effective writing for general audiences requires excellent control of the appropriate theoretical, methodological, and substantive literature and the ability to comprehend and articulate clearly the core issues of the archaeology of an area, time period, or problem, and therefore should be subject to the same kind of qualitative academic assessment that ideally goes on today in any academic tenure, promotion, or hiring procedure. However, such a development would go against the current pernicious trend that features such aspects as counting peer-review articles and use of citation indices. I strongly believe that the growing reliance on numbers of peer-review articles and the denigration of both popular and non-peer-review writing needs to be reversed. As in so many areas of life, quantity is being substituted for quality, while the measurement of quality becomes increasingly problematic. As the former editor of a major peer-review journal, as well as the editor of many multi-author volumes, I can assure you that the quality of chapters in edited books—often discounted as non-peer-reviewed writings—can be and frequently are of as high or higher quality than peer-reviewed articles. However, many faculty and administrators appear to be looking for formulae that shortchange the qualitative evaluation of research and writing, no matter what form of publication. The whole academic system of evaluation for hiring, tenure, promotion, and salary raises needs to be rethought. In my opinion it is headed in the wrong direction, and the growing trend away from qualitative evaluation is especially worrisome.

As a call to action, in order to encourage popular writing among academics, particularly those with tenure, all of us need to lobby university administrators, department chairs, and colleagues about the value and importance of written communication with audiences beyond the academy. Academics should be evaluated on their popular as well as their purely academic writings. Clearly, what is needed is a balance between original research and popular communication. In sum, evaluations should be qualitative, not quantitative.

Concerning non-academic archaeologists, we need to raise the perceived value of general publications and public outreach in the cultural resource management arm of the profession and work toward having public reporting be routinely included in scopes of work of as many cultural resource management contracts as is feasible. In some areas, fortunately, such as in the National Parks Service or in some Colonial archaeological settings, such outreach already is valued. Positive examples like this need to be professionally publicized and supported.

I would be remiss if I didn't point out that there clearly is a huge irony here. The academic world obviously is becoming increasingly market-oriented with various institutions vying for perceived "stars" in their fields with escalating offers of high salaries, less teaching, better labs, more research funds, and so on, and most academics not only are caught up in this system but have bought into it. At the same time, those scholars who are most successful in the larger marketplace of popular ideas and the popular media and who make dollars by selling to popular audiences are frequently discounted and denigrated by the self-perceived "true scholars," who often have totally bought into the broad academic market economy and are busy playing this narrower market game!

To conclude, I hope that I have been able to stimulate some thought about what might appear to be a very simple problem but which in reality is quite complicated. In order to fulfill what I believe is one of archaeology's major missions, that of public education, we need to make some significant changes in our professional modes of operation. The Archaeology Division can form a common cause with many other units of the American Anthropological Association to realize this goal. This is a four-field problem with four-field solutions! The Society for American Archaeology has just endorsed public education and outreach as one of the eight principles of archaeological ethics. This Division can also play a key role in such endeavors by working within the American Anthropological Association and using its influence to help change the emphases of our professional lives and the reward systems within which we work. To reiterate, I strongly believe that we must change our professional value system so that public outreach in all forms, but especially popular writing, is viewed and supported in highly positive terms. We need to make this change. There are signs that the pendulum of general communication in the field of American archaeology is starting to swing in a positive direction. Let us all work to push it much further!

I am sure that we all have heard the clarion call to the American public—"will you help me to build a bridge to the twenty-first century"—many, many times. It is my belief that, unfortunately, the bridge to the twenty-first century will be a shaky one indeed for archaeology and anthropology—perhaps even the proverbial bridge to nowhere!—unless we tackle the communication problem with the same energy and vigor with which we routinely debate the contentious issues of contemporary archaeological theory that past lecturers to this group have delineated for you. The fruits of our research and analyses have great potential relevance for the public at large. The huge, exciting strides in understanding the past that anthropological archaeology has made in recent years need to be brought to the public's attention both for our sakes and theirs.

References

Anyon, Roger, and T. J. Ferguson 1995 Cultural Resources Management at the Pueblo of Zuni, N.M., U.S.A. Antiquity 69 (266):913–930.

Bibby, Geoffrey 1956 The Testimony of the Spade. New York: Alfred A. Knopf.

Ceram, C. W. 1951 Gods, Graves, and Scholars: The Story of Archaeology. New York: Alfred A. Knopf.

Erickson, Clark L. 1998 Applied Archaeology and Rural Development: Archaeology's Potential Contribution to the Future. In Crossing Currents: Continuity and Change in Latin America. M. Whiteford and S. Whiteford, eds. pp. 34–45. Upper Saddle, NJ: Prentice-Hall.

Fagan, Brian M. 1977 Elusive Treasure: The Story of Early Archaeologists in the Americas. New York: Scribners. 1984 The Aztecs. New York: W. H. Freeman. 1987 The Great Journey: The Peopling of Ancient America. London: Thames and Hudson. 1991 Kingdoms of Gold, Kingdoms of Jade: The Americas before Columbus. London: Thames and Hudson. 1995 Time Detectives: How Archaeologists Use Technology to Recapture the Past. New York: Simon and Schuster.

Ford, Anabel, ed. 1998 The Future of El Pilar: The Integrated Research and Development Plan for the El Pilar Archaeological Reserve for Flora and Fauna, Belize-Guatemala. Department of State Publication 10507, Bureau of Oceans. and International Environmental and Scientific Affairs, Washington, DC.

Ford, Richard I. 1973 Archaeology Serving Humanity. In Research and Theory in Current Archaeology. Charles L. Redman, ed. pp. 83–94. New York: John Wiley.

Fritz, John M. 1973 Relevance, Archaeology, and Subsistence Theory. In Research and Theory in Current Archaeology. Charles L. Redman, ed. pp. 59–82. New York: John Wiley.

Fritz, John M., and Fred Plog 1970 The Nature of Archaeological Explanation. American Antiquity 35:405–12.

Hodder, Ian, Michael Shanks, Alexandra Alexandri, Victor Buchli, John Carman, Jonathan Last, and Gavin Lucas, eds. 1995 Interpreting Archaeology: Finding Meaning in the Past. New York: Routledge.

Kidder, Alfred V. 1924 An Introduction to the Study of Southwestern Archaeology, with a Preliminary Account of the Excavations at Pecos. Papers of the Southwestern Expedition, No. 1. Published for the Department of Archaeology, Phillips Academy, Andover. New Haven, CT: Yale University Press. 1940 Looking Backward. Proceedings of the American Philosophical Society 83:527–537.

Kleindienst, Maxine R., and Patty Jo Watson 1956 'Action Archaeology': The Archaeological Inventory of a Living Community. Anthropology Tomorrow 5:75–78.

Kohl, Philip L., and Clare Fawcett, eds. 1995 Nationalism, Politics, and the Practice of Archaeology. Cambridge: Cambridge University Press.

Kolata, Alan L. 1993 The Tiwanaku: Portrait of an Andean Civilization. Cambridge: Blackwell.

Marcus, Joyce, and Kent V. Flannery 1996 Zapotec Civilization: How Urban Society Evolved in Mexico's Oaxaca Valley. New York: Thames and Hudson.

Plog, Stephen 1997 Ancient Peoples of the American Southwest. London: Thames and Hudson.

Preucel, Robert W. 1998 The Kotyiti Research Project: Report of the 1996 Field Season. Report submitted to the Pueblo of Cochiti and the USDA Forest Service, Santa Fe National Forest, Santa Fe, NM.

Pyburn, Anne, and Richard Wilk 1995 Responsible Archaeology Is Applied Anthropology. In Ethics in American Archaeology: Challenges for the 1990s. Mark J. Lynott and Alison Wylie, eds. pp. 71–76. Washington, DC: Society for American Archaeology.

Rathje, William L., and Cullen Murphy 1992 Rubbish!: The Archaeology of Garbage. New York: HarperCollins.

Rice, Don S., and Prudence M. Rice 1984 Lessons from the Maya. Latin American Research Review 19(3):7–34.

Sabloff, Jeremy A. 1982 Introduction. In Archaeology: Myth and Reality. Jeremy A. Sabloff, ed. pp. 1–26. Readings from Scientific American. San Francisco: W. H. Freeman. 1985 American Antiquity's First Fifty Years: An Introductory Comment. American Antiquity 50:228–236. 1990: The New Archaeology and the Ancient Maya. A Scientific American Library Book. New York: W. H. Freeman.

Schele, Linda, and David A. Freidel 1990 A Forest of Kings: The Untold Story of the Ancient Maya. New York: Morrow.

Snow, C. P. 1959 The Two Cultures and the Scientific Revolution. Cambridge: Cambridge University Press.

Spector, Janet 1993 What This Awl Means: Feminist Archaeology at a Wahpeton Dakota Village. St. Paul: Minnesota Historical Society Press.

Von Däniken, Erich 1970 Chariots of the Gods? New York: G. P. Putnam's Sons.

Willey, Gordon R. 1967 Alfred Vincent Kidder, 1885–1963. In Biographical Memoirs, vol. 39. Published for the National Academy of Sciences. New York: Columbia University Press.

Williams, Stephen 1991 Fantastic Archaeology: The Wild Side of North American Prehistory. Philadelphia: University of Pennsylvania Press.

Woodbury, Richard B. 1973 Alfred V. Kidder. New York Columbia University Press.

Critical Thinking

1. What is the theme of these remarks?
2. Describe the important and public role of archaeology in the nineteenth century.

3. How and when did the gap between amateurs and professionals become unbridgeable?
4. What have been some of the benefits of the professionalization of archaeology? How and why has this worked against the dissemination of current advances in archaeological understanding of cultures of the past?
5. Why have some archaeologists rejected or denigrated popular writing in archaeology?
6. Why is it not a surprise that people turn to speculative, non-professional sources for their interest in archaeology?
7. To what is archaeology pertinent and why, according to the author?
8. Why do we need more "action archaeology"? What is one "compelling example"?
9. What is the evidence for increasing public interest in archaeology? Why should archaeologists take responsibility for educating the public?
10. How can American archaeologists rectify the situation, according to the author?
11. Why do some scholars look down at archaeologists who are perceived as popularizers, according to the author?
12. What changes does the author recommend with respect to the academic evaluation and reward system?
13. What does the author recommend with respect to the non-academic archaeologists?
14. What is the "huge irony," according to the author?

Create Central

www.mhhe.com/createcentral

Internet References

American Anthropologist
www.aaanet.org

Archaeology Magazine
www.archaeology.org

Smithsonian Institution Website
www.si.edu

The New York Times
www.nytimes.com

JEREMY A. SABLOFF is from the University of Pennsylvania Museum of Archaeology and Anthropology Philadelphia, PA 19104.

Acknowledgments—I am honored that I was asked to deliver the Archaeology Division's 1996 Distinguished Lecture and grateful to the Archaeology Division for its kind invitation to deliver this important talk. I wish to acknowledge the growing list of colleagues, only a few of which have been cited above, who have accepted the crucial challenge of writing for general public. May your numbers multiply! I also wish thank Paula L. W. Sabloff, Joyce Marcus, and the reviewer for this journal for their many insightful and helpful comments and suggestions, only some of which I have been able to take advantage of, that have certainly improved the quality of paper.

Sabloff, Jeremy A. From *American Anthropologist*, vol. 100, no. 4, December 1998, pp. 869–875. Copyright © 1998 by American Anthropological Association. Reprinted by permission of the American Anthropological Association and the author.

Article

Prepared by: Mari Pritchard Parker, *Pasadena City College* and
Elvio Angeloni, *Pasadena City College*

CSI: Italian Renaissance

TOM MUELLER

Learning Outcomes

After reading this article, you will be able to:

- Discuss the methods used by paleopathologists to determine how people in the distant past lived and died.
- Evaluate the ethical and practical value of exhuming the dead.
- Discuss the importance of synthesizing knowledge gained from archaeology, physical anthropology, history, and medicine in order to understand the human past.

Inside a lab in Pisa, forensics pathologist Gino Fornaciari and his team investigate 500-year-old cold cases.

High on the facade of Santa Maria Antica, among soaring Gothic spires and forbidding statues of knights in armor, pathologist Gino Fornaciari prepared to examine a corpse. Accompanied by workmen, he had climbed a 30-foot scaffold erected against this medieval church in Verona, Italy, and watched as they used hydraulic jacks to raise the massive lid of a marble sarcophagus set in a niche. Peering inside, Fornaciari found the body of a male in his 30s, wearing a long silk mantle, arms crossed on his chest. The abdomen was distended from postmortem putrefaction, although Fornaciari caught no scent of decomposition, only a faint waft of incense. He and the laborers eased the body onto a stretcher and lowered it to the ground; after dark, they loaded it into a van and drove to a nearby hospital, where Fornaciari began a series of tests to determine why the nobleman died—and how he had lived.

The victim, it appeared, had suffered from several chronic and puzzling conditions. A CT scan and digital X-ray revealed a calcification of the knees, as well as a level of arthritis in elbows, hips and lumbar vertebrae surprisingly advanced for anyone this young. Abronchoscopy showed severe anthracosis, similar to black lung, although he hadn't been a miner, or even a smoker. Histological analysis of liver cells detected advanced fibrosis, although he had never touched hard liquor. Yet Fornaciari, a professor in the medical school at the University of Pisa, saw that none of these conditions likely had killed him.

Of course, Fornaciari had heard rumors that the man had been poisoned, but he discounted them as probable fabrications. "I've worked on several cases where there were rumors of poisonings and dark plots," Fornaciari told me later. "They usually turn out to be just that, mere legends, which fall apart under scientific scrutiny." He recited the victim's symptoms in Latin, just as he had read them in a medieval chronicle: corporei fluxus stomachique doloris acuti et febre ob laborem exercitus: "diarrhea and acute stomach pains, belly disturbances, and fever from his labors with the army."

Gino Fornaciari is no ordinary medical examiner; his bodies represent cold cases that are centuries, sometimes millennia, old. As head of a team of archaeologists, physical anthropologists, historians of medicine and additional specialists at the University of Pisa, he is a pioneer in the burgeoning field of paleopathology, the use of state-of-the-art medical technology and forensic techniques to investigate the lives and deaths of illustrious figures of the past.

Its practitioners worldwide are making startling discoveries. In December 2012, a team of scientists published results from an examination of the mummy of Pharaoh Ramses III, showing that he had died from having his throat slit, likely murdered in the so-called "harem conspiracy" of 1155 B.C. This May, *Smithsonian* anthropologist Douglas Owsley said he'd found evidence of cannibalism at Virginia's Jamestown Colony, probably in the winter of 1609; cut marks on the skull and tibia of a newly exhumed 14-year-old girl's remains indicated that her brain, tongue, cheeks and leg muscles were removed after her death. Scholars have reconstructed the faces of Renaissance figures including Dante and St. Anthony of Padua based on remains of their crania (Petrarch's head, it emerged, had been swapped out at some point with that of a young woman). They are currently sifting the subsoil of a Florentine monastery for remains of Lisa Gherardini, a noblewoman believed by some art historians to be the model Leonardo da Vinci used when he painted the Mona Lisa.

But no one has made more important and striking finds than Gino Fornaciari. Over the past half-century, using tools of forensics and medical science as well as clues from anthropology, history and art, he and his colleagues have become detectives of the distant past, exhuming remains throughout Italy to scrutinize the lives and deaths of kings, paupers, saints, warriors and castrati opera stars. Fornaciari himself has examined entire noble populations, including the Medici of Florence and the royal Aragonese dynasty of Naples, whose corpses have been, in effect, archives containing unique clues to the fabric of everyday life in the Renaissance.

Such work is not without its critics, who brand scholars such as Fornaciari as little more than grave-robbers, rejecting their efforts as a pointless, even prurient, disturbance of the dead's eternal rest. Yet paleo-sleuthing has demonstrated its value for the study of the past and future. As Fornaciari has solved some of history's oldest riddles and murder mysteries, his work also holds life-and-death relevance. By studying modern killers such as malaria, tuberculosis, arteriosclerosis and cancer, whose telltale signs Fornaciari has found in ancient cadavers, he is helping to understand the origins of diseases and to predict the evolution of pathologies. "Gino Fornaciari and his team are prime movers in the field," says bioarchaeologist Jane Buikstra of Arizona State University, author of *The Global History of Paleopathology*. "They're shaping paleopathology in the 21st century and enriching discussion in a range of other fields, too."

Fornaciari's current "patient," the nobleman interred at Santa Maria Antica, was Cangrande della Scala, warlord of Verona, whose family ruled the city and a swath of northeastern Italy with an iron hand seven centuries ago. They reigned at the beginning of the Italian Renaissance, that blaze of artistic creativity and new self-awareness that illuminated the end of the Middle Ages and permanently altered human consciousness. Cangrande was a paradigmatic Renaissance man: Giotto painted his portrait, the poet Boccaccio celebrated his chivalry and Dante lauded him lavishly in the Paradiso as a paragon of the wise leader.

In July 1329, he had just conquered the rival town of Treviso and entered the city walls in triumph when he fell violently ill. Within hours he was dead. Several medieval chroniclers wrote that, shortly before his conquest, Cangrande had drunk at a poisoned spring, but Fornaciari doubted this hypothesis. "I'm always skeptical about claims of poisoning," Fornaciari says. "Since Cangrande died in the summer, with symptoms including vomiting and diarrhea, I originally suspected that he'd contracted some sort of gastrointestinal disease."

The answer to the puzzle was contained in Cangrande's body, naturally mummified in the dry, warm air of his marble tomb, making it a treasure trove of information on Renaissance existence. His pathologies, unfamiliar today, made perfect sense for a 14th-century lord and warrior on horseback. The curious arthritis visible in Cangrande's hips, knees, elbows and sacro-lumbar region indicates what Fornaciari terms "knightly markers," disorders developed by cavalrymen during a lifetime in the saddle, wielding weighty weapons such as lances and broadswords. His liver disease may well have been caused by a virus, not alcohol, because hard liquor was unknown in Cangrande's day. The knight's respiratory ailments were likewise linked to life in a world lighted and warmed by fire, not electricity. Torch-lit banquet halls and bedchambers, where chimneys became widespread only a century later, and the smoky braziers used in army tents while on campaign, caused the kind of lung damage that today could be found in coal miners.

Strangest of all, however, were the results of pollen analysis and immunochemical tests conducted on Cangrande's intestines and liver. Fornaciari isolated pollen from two plants: Matricaria chamomilla and Digitalis purpurea. "Chamomile," he told me, "was used as a sedative; Cangrande could have drunk it as a tea. But foxglove? That shouldn't have been there." The plant contains digoxin and digitoxine, two potent heart stimulants, which in doses like those detected in Cangrande's body can cause cardiac arrest. During the Middle Ages and the Renaissance, foxglove was used as a poison.

In fact, the symptoms mentioned by contemporary chroniclers—diarrhea, stomach pains and fever—matched those of digoxin and digitoxine poisoning. Hence, Fornaciari concluded, Cangrande had been murdered. As it happens, a contemporary chronicler reported that a month after Cangrande's death, one of the nobleman's doctors had been executed by Mastino II, Cangrande's successor, suggesting the doctor's possible involvement in a plot to kill his master. Who ultimately was responsible for the murder remains a mystery—an assertive fellow like Cangrande had plenty of enemies—although the ambitious Mastino II himself now emerges as a prime suspect. "I thought the poisoning story was just a legend, but sometimes the legends are true," Fornaciari says. "Paleopathology is rewriting history!"

Fornaciari trained as a medical doctor, and when I met him in his office at the department of oncology at the University of Pisa, he was applying his expertise to the present, peering through a microscope at samples from biopsies performed at the nearby university hospital. "I have to distinguish benign from malignant tissues," he said, nodding to trays of samples stacked beside the microscope. "I have to be right, or there could be serious consequences for the patient—a surgeon could remove a healthy lung or breast, or leave a deadly malignancy in place."

Now age 70, Fornaciari is an exemplar of that by now endangered species, the Italian university professor of the old school, who combines an almost fin de siècle formality with personal warmth and a disarming passion for his work. The son of factory workers in Viareggio, a coastal town near Pisa, Fornaciari earned his M.D. at the University of Pisa in 1971. He's always been fascinated with the past, and from the outset of his medical training made forays into the health, quality of life and lifestyles of distant eras. During medical training he also took courses in archaeology and participated in excavations of prehistoric and Etruscan sites throughout Tuscany. In the early 1980s, the center of gravity of Fornaciari's work began to shift from present to past, as he joined Vatican researchers charged with examining the remains of several prominent saints, including Pope Gregory VII and St. Anthony of Padua.

In 1984, Fornaciari agreed to lead an investigation of the most significant noble remains then to have been exhumed in Italy, the 38 naturally and artificially mummified bodies of the Aragonese royal family of Naples—major figures in the Italian Renaissance, buried in the Neapolitan basilica of San Domenico Maggiore. Fornaciari began to collaborate with scholars in Pisa and across Italy, who coalesced into an interdisciplinary team centered in Pisa. His investigators, here and in other parts of Italy, range from archaeologists to parasitologists and molecular biologists.

"Gino recognizes the fundamental importance of historical documentation and context in ways that I haven't seen anyone else do," says Clark Spencer Larsen of Ohio State University, a physical anthropologist who, with Fornaciari, co-directs a field project in Badia Pozzeveri, a medieval monastery and cemetery near Lucca. "He's knowledgeable in many other areas as well. He's pragmatic and interested in whatever answers the question, 'How are we going to figure this out?'"

By now, Fornaciari had become the go-to guy for old bones in Italy, and was tackling an ever-growing range of centuries-old corpses, including an entire community overwhelmed by the Black Plague in Sardinia, and a cache of 18th- and 19th-century mummies in an underground crypt in northeastern Sicily. Then, in 2002, he and his team struck the mother lode of paleopathology when they were invited by the Italian minister of culture to investigate the 49 graves in the Medici Chapels in Florence, one of the most significant exhumation projects ever undertaken. Fornaciari still leads the ongoing investigation.

Recently, I drove out to visit his main paleopathology laboratory, established by the University of Pisa with a grant from the Italian Ministry of Research Institute. The structure is housed in a former medieval monastery, set on a hillside ringed by olive trees east of Pisa. When we arrive, a half-dozen researchers in lab coats are measuring human bones on marble tabletops, victims of a virulent cholera epidemic that ravaged Tuscany in 1854 and 1855, and entering anatomical data into a computer database. At another counter, two undergraduates apply glue to piece together the bones of medieval peasants from a cemetery near Lucca.

Fornaciari explains the procedures used to solve historical puzzles. Researchers begin with a basic physical exam of bones and tissues, using calipers and other instruments. At the same time, he says, they create a context, exploring the historical landscape their subjects inhabited, consulting scholars and digging into archival records. For the past 15 years, they've used conventional X-ray and CT imaging at a nearby hospital to examine tissues and bones; conducted histological exams similar to those Fornaciari applies to living patients for a better understanding of tumors and other abnormalities; and relied on an electron microscope to examine tissues. More recently, they've employed immunological, isotopic and DNA analysis to coax additional information from their samples.

Work is done at many locations—here and at Fornaciari's other Pisa laboratory, and in university labs throughout Italy, particularly Turin and Naples, as well as in Germany and the United States. On occasion, when examining illustrious, difficult-to-move corpses such as Cangrande della Scala or the Medici, Fornaciari cordons off an area of a church or chapel as an impromptu laboratory, creating kind of a field hospital for the dead, where he and his fellow researchers work under the gaze of curious tourists.

The laboratory, stacked with human bones, could easily seem grim—a murderer's cave, a chamber of horrors. Instead, with its immaculate order and faint dry cedar-like scent, its soft bustle of conversation, this is a celebration of living. In the final analysis, it's a laboratory of human experience, where anatomical investigation mingles with evidence from medicine, biography and portrait paintings to resurrect fully fledged life stories.

Some of the most compelling tales surround the dynasties of the Aragonese and Medici. Among Fornaciari's most memorable "patients" is Isabella of Aragon, born in 1470, a shining star at the greatest courts of Italy, renowned for her intellect, beauty, courage in battle and remarkable fortitude. She knew Leonardo da Vinci; some art historians also believe she could have been the model for the Mona Lisa. She conducted famous love affairs with courtier Giosuè di Ruggero and condottiero Prospero Colonna, as well as, one scholar maintains, with Leonardo himself. Even an objective scientist such as Fornaciari isn't immune to her charms. "Knowing that I had Isabella of Aragon in my laboratory, one of the most celebrated ladies of the Renaissance, who'd known Leonardo da Vinci—he'd made the magnificent theater backdrops for her wedding feast—all this raised certain emotions."

All the more so when Fornaciari took a close look at Isabella's teeth. The outer surfaces of those in the front of her mouth had been carefully filed—in some cases the enamel had been completely removed—to erase a black patina that still covered the teeth farther back. Electron microscopy revealed parallel striations on the front teeth, indicating abrasions made by a file. The black stain, it turned out, resulted from ingestion of mercury, in her day believed to combat syphilis. Proud Isabella, jealous of her celebrated beauty, had been attempting to hide the growing discoloration associated with her disease. "I imagine poor Isabella trying to preserve her privacy, not wanting to appear with black teeth because people would know she had venereal disease," says Fornaciari.

His examination of Isabella's grandfather, Ferrante I, King of Naples, born in 1431, also produced significant results. This great lord presided over a literary salon where leading humanist scholars converged, but he was also a gifted warrior, who with astuteness, courage and calculated—or, as his critics said, sadistic—savagery, maintained the independence of his kingdom against powerful enemies, both foreign and internal. No less a figure than Lorenzo the Magnificent de' Medici traveled to Naples to kneel in submission before him. Ferrante died in 1494 at the age of 63, celebrated by contemporaries for maintaining his intellectual and physical vigor to the end of his life, although portraits completed during his later years showed that he had put on weight and occasionally appeared to be in pain.

Fornaciari debunked the myth of Ferrante's enduring good health. Although the king's mummified body had been lying in its cedar coffin for five centuries, and in 1509 had been badly damaged by a fire in the basilica, Fornaciari managed to recover a segment of Ferrante's intestine, which when rehydrated showed a pattern of yellowish spots that looked sinisterly familiar to him from analyses of modern biopsies. Extracting DNA from mummified tissue, Fornaciari found mutation in the K-ras gene—clear proof that Ferrante had suffered from advanced colon cancer, most probably a colorectal adenocarcinoma. Fornaciari had made medical history, by identifying an oncogene mutation in an ancient tumor; his results offer potentially important data for studying the evolution of the disease.

Fornaciari subsequently analyzed bone collagen of King Ferrante and other Aragonese nobles, revealing a diet extremely reliant on red meat; this finding may correlate with Ferrante's cancer. Red meat is widely recognized as an agent that increases risk for mutation of the K-ras gene and subsequent colorectal cancer. (As an example of Ferrante's carnivorous preferences, a wedding banquet held at his court in 1487 featured, among 15 courses, beef and veal heads covered in their skins, roast ram in a sour cherry broth, roast piglet in vinegar broth and a range of salami, hams, livers, giblets and offal.)

Maria of Aragon, another famous beauty of the Renaissance, noted for her proud, fiery temperament, whose intellectual circle included Michelangelo, was found to have syphilitic lesions and human papillomavirus (HPV). Fornaciari's identification of the latter in an ancient cadaver also offered new clues to the evolution of the virus.

King Ferrante II, who died young and surpassingly handsome at 28, shortly after the great Carpaccio painted his portrait, was found to have head lice, as well as poisoning from the mercury he used in an attempt to vanquish the infestation. An anonymous, richly dressed member of the Aragon family, about 27 years of age, had a fatal dagger wound in his left side, between the eighth and ninth ribs, with signs of massive bleeding.

Fornaciari also studied electron micrographs of tissue samples from an anonymous 2-year-old Aragonese child who died around 1570. He observed the lethal smallpox virus—which reacted to smallpox antibodies after centuries in the grave. Concerned that the virus could still be infectious, the Italian Ministry of Health threatened to close Fornaciari's lab and impound the tiny cadaver, until Fornaciari reported that he had already sent samples for testing to the United States and Russia, where specialists pronounced the smallpox DNA biologically inert and therefore harmless.

Fornaciari uncovered some of his most moving and detailed personal stories during exhumations of the Medici, begun in 2003. A driving force in the artistic, intellectual and economic life of the Italian Renaissance, the noble house helped to establish Florence as the cultural center of the Western world. The Medici were the patrons of Brunelleschi, Leonardo da Vinci, Michelangelo, Botticelli and Galileo Galilei. "You can't really remain indifferent to someone like Cosimo I de' Medici, one of the architects of the Renaissance," Fornaciari says. An inexperienced teenager who suddenly came to power in Florence in 1537, Cosimo rescued the city-state of Florence, turning a foundering republic at the mercy of foreign powers into an independent duchy that was once more a major player on the European stage. He founded the Uffizi Gallery, freed Florentine territories from foreign armies and built a navy, which was instrumental in preventing the Ottoman takeover of the Mediterranean Sea during the Battle of Lepanto in 1571.

The wealth of biographical information available on Cosimo I allowed Fornaciari to synthesize contemporary testimony and forensic investigation. Documentation concerning Cosimo and his descendants is some of the most extensive in early modern history—the online database of the Medici Archive Project contains descriptions of some 10,000 letters and biographical records on more than 11,000 individuals. Portraits of Cosimo I in museums around the world depict his evolution from a shy, seemingly wary youth in 1538 to a bearded warrior in a polished suit of armor in 1565, and an elderly, corpulent and world-weary figure, gazing absently into space, toward the end of his life in 1574. Reports by court physicians and foreign ambassadors to the Florentine duchy recount Cosimo's medical history in excruciating detail: He survived smallpox and "catarrhal fever" (likely pneumonia) in youth; suffered in later life from paralysis of his left arm, mental instability and incontinence; and had a painful condition of the joints described by contemporaries as gout.

Fornaciari found that Cosimo's remains indicated he had been an extremely robust and active man, in whom Fornaciari also noted all of the "knightly markers"—sacro-lumbar arthritis, hypertrophy and erosion of certain parts of the femur, rotation and compression of the upper femur, and other deformations—typical of warriors who rode into battle on horseback. He noted nodes between Cosimo's vertebrae, signs that as an adolescent, the young duke had worn heavy weights over his thorax, most probably suits of armor. Fornaciari also noticed pervasive arthritis and ossification between the sixth, seventh and eighth thoracic vertebrae, possible signs of diffuse idiopathic skeletal hyperostosis (DISH), a disease of the elderly linked to diabetes. "We see Cosimo getting fatter in his portraits, and the presence of DISH suggests he may have had diabetes, too," says Fornaciari. "The diet of the Medici and other upper-class families often contained many sweets, which were a sort of status symbol, but often caused health problems."

Another vivid marker was Cosimo's poor dental health. The right side of his mandible is marred by an enormous gap, the result of a serious periodontal disease; an abscess had eaten away his first molar and a considerable chunk of bone, leaving a massive crater in his jaw. Fornaciari's examination of the Medici, the Aragonese and other high-born individuals has revealed appalling abscesses, decay and tooth loss, bringing home just how painful daily life in that period could be, even for the rich and famous.

Cosimo's wife, Eleanora of Toledo, was the daughter of the Spanish viceroy of Naples and related to the Hapsburg and the Castilian royal families. Her face was immortalized by the Renaissance master Bronzino, who in a series of portraits captures her transformation from a radiant, aloof young bride to a sickly, prematurely aged woman in her late 30s, shortly before her death at age 40. Fornaciari uncovered the maladies that beset her. Dental problems plagued her. Slightly curved legs indicated a case of rickets she had suffered as a child. Childbirth had taken a major toll. "Pelvic skeletal markers show that she had numerous births—in fact, she and Cosimo had 11 children," Fornaciari says. "She was almost constantly pregnant, which would have leached calcium out of her body." Further analysis indicated that Eleanora had suffered from leishmaniasis, a parasitic disease spread by biting sand flies that can cause skin lesions, fever and damage to the liver and spleen. DNA testing also revealed the presence of tuberculosis. "She was wealthy, and powerful, but her life was brutally hard," Fornaciari says.

Ultimately, Fornaciari also dispelled murder allegations directed against one of Cosimo and Eleanora's sons. On September 25, 1587, Cardinal Ferdinando de' Medici, second surviving son of Cosimo I and Eleanora of Toledo, visited his elder brother Francesco I in the opulent Medici villa in Poggio a Caiano, in the countryside near Florence. The brothers had been on bad terms for years, their relations poisoned by ambition and envy: Cardinal Ferdinando resented the fact that the coveted ancestral title, Grand Duke of Tuscany, had gone to Francesco after Cosimo's death, and violently disliked his new sister-in-law, Bianca Cappello. Her young son Antonio, fathered by Francesco and legitimized when the couple had married, seemed likely to inherit the throne eventually. This gathering seemed a chance to mend bridges between the brothers and restore family peace.

Shortly after the cardinal's arrival, Francesco and Bianca fell ill with ominous symptoms: convulsions, fever, nausea, severe thirst, gastric burning. Within days they were dead. Cardinal Ferdinando buried his brother with great pomp (Bianca was interred separately) and banished his nephew Antonio to a golden exile—whereupon Ferdinando crowned himself the new Grand Duke of Tuscany.

Rumors spread swiftly that the couple had been murdered. Cardinal Ferdinando, some whispered, had cleared his path to the ducal throne by killing the couple with arsenic, often preferred by Renaissance poisoners because it left no obvious traces on its victims. Others said that Bianca herself had baked an arsenic-laced cake for her detested brother-in-law, which her husband had tasted first by mistake; overcome with horror, Bianca supposedly ate a slice of the deadly confection as well, in order to join her beloved Francesco in the grave. A cloud of foul play enshrouded the unfortunate pair for centuries.

In 2006, four medical and forensic researchers from the University of Florence and the University of Pavia, led by toxicologist Francesco Mari, published an article in which they argued that Francesco and Bianca had died of arsenic poisoning. In the *British Medical Journal,* they described collecting tissue samples from urns buried beneath the floor of a church in Tuscany. At that church, according to an account from 1587 recently uncovered in an Italian archive, the internal organs of Francesco and Bianca, removed from their bodies, had been placed in terra-cotta receptacles and interred. The practice was not uncommon. (Francesco is buried in the Medici Chapels in Florence; Bianca's grave has never been found.) Mari contended that the tissue samples—in which concentrations of arsenic he deemed lethal were detected—belonged to the grand duke and duchess. The rumors, argued the researchers, had been correct: Cardinal Ferdinando had done away with Francesco and his bride.

Fornaciari dismantled this thesis in two articles, one in the *American Journal of Medicine,* both of which showcased his wide-ranging skills as a Renaissance detective. Tissue samples recovered from the urns were likely not from the doomed Medici couple at all, he wrote. Those samples, he added, could have belonged to any of hundreds of people interred in the church over the centuries; in fact, the style of two crucifixes found with the urns attributed to Francesco and Bianca dates from more than a century after their deaths.

Even had the tissues come from the couple—which Fornaciari strongly doubts—he argued that the levels of arsenic detected by Mari were no proof of murder. Because arsenic preserves human tissue, it was routinely used in the Renaissance to embalm corpses. Since the couple's bodies had certainly been embalmed, it would have been surprising not to have discovered arsenic in their remains. Fornaciari added that since Francesco was a passionate alchemist, arsenic in his tissues could well have come from the tireless experiments he performed in the laboratory of his palace in Florence, the Palazzo Pitti.

As a coup de grace, Fornaciari analyzed bone samples from Francesco, showing that at the time of death he had been acutely infested with plasmodium falciparium, the parasitic protozoan that causes pernicious malaria. Fornaciari observed that malaria had been widespread in the coastal lowlands of Tuscany until the 20th century. In the three days before they fell ill, Francesco and Bianca had been hunting near Poggio a Caiano, then filled with marshes and rice paddies: a classic environment for malarial mosquitoes. He pointed out that the symptoms of Francesco and Bianca, particularly their bouts of high fever, matched those of falciparium malaria, but not arsenic poisoning, which does not produce fever.

Virtually anyone working in the public eye in Italy for long may run into la polemica—violent controversy—all the more so if one's research involves titanic figures from Italy's storied past. The recent row over a proposed exhumation of Galileo Galilei offers a prime example of the emotions and animus that Fornaciari's investigations can stir up. In 2009, on the 400th anniversary of the great astronomer's first observations of heavenly bodies with a telescope, Paolo Galluzzi, director of Florence's Museo Galileo, along with Fornaciari and a group of researchers, announced a plan to examine Galileo's remains, buried in the basilica of Santa Croce in Florence. They aimed, among other things, to apply DNA analysis to Galileo's bone samples, hoping to obtain clues to the eye disease that afflicted Galileo in later life. He sometimes reported seeing a halo around light sources, perhaps the result of his condition.

Understanding the source of his compromised vision could also elucidate errors he recorded. For instance, Galileo reported that Saturn featured a pronounced bulge, perhaps because his eye condition caused him to perceive the planet's rings as a distortion. They also planned to examine Galileo's skull and bones, and to study the two bodies buried alongside the great astronomer. One is known to be his devoted disciple Vincenzo Viviani and the other is believed, but not confirmed, to be his daughter Maria Celeste, immortalized in Dava Sobel's *Galileo's Daughter.*

Reaction to the plan was swift and thunderous. Scholars, clerics and the media accused the researchers of sensationalism and profanation. "This business of exhuming bodies, touching relics, is something to be left to believers because they belong to another mentality, which is not scientific," editorialized Piergiorgio Odifreddi, a mathematician and historian of science, in *La Repubblica,* a national newspaper. "Let [Galileo] rest in peace." The rector of Santa Croce called the plan a carnivalata, meaning a kind of carnival stunt.

The plan to exhume Galileo is on hold, although Fornaciari remains optimistic that critics eventually will understand the validity of the investigation. "I honestly don't know why people were so violently, so viscerally against the idea," he says. He seems stunned and disheartened by the ruckus he's kicked up.

"Even some atheists had reactions that seemed to reveal decidedly theistic beliefs, akin to taboos and atavistic fears of contact with the dead. Surely they must see this isn't a desecration. And we wouldn't be disturbing his last rest—we could even help restore his remains, after the damage they undoubtedly suffered in the great flood of 1966 that hit Florence."

It's as if he is summing up his entire life's work when he adds quietly: "Investigating that great book of nature that was Galileo would hardly harm his fame. On the contrary, it would enrich our knowledge of Galileo and the environment in which he lived and worked."

Critical Thinking

1. What have been some of the startling discoveries about how famous historical figures lived and died?
2. What are the pros and cons having to do with exhuming the corpses of people of the past?
3. What are some of the forensic techniques used to determine cause of death of people from the distant past?
4. How important is it to synthesize biographical information with forensic investigation in order to solve historical puzzles?

Create Central

www.mhhe.com/createcentral

Internet References

Society for Historical Archaeology
www.sha.org

Zeno's Forensic Page
http://forensic.to/forensic.html

Mueller, Tom. From *Smithsonian*, July/August 2013. Copyright © 2013 by Tom Mueller. Reprinted by permission of the author.

Unit 2

UNIT

Prepared by: Mari Pritchard Parker, *Pasadena City College* and
Elvio Angeloni, *Pasadena City College*

Problem Oriented Archaeology

What are the goals of archaeology? What kinds of things motivate well-educated people to go out and dig square holes in the ground and sift through their diggings like sifting flour for a cake? How do they know where to dig? What are they looking for? What do they do with the things they find? Let us drop in on an archaeology class at Metropolis University.

"Good afternoon, class. I'm Dr. Penny Pittmeyer. Welcome to Introductory Archaeology. Excuse me, young lady. Yes, you in the back, wearing the pith helmet. I don't think you'll need to bring that shovel to class this semester. We aren't going to be doing any digging."

A moan like that of an audience who had just heard a bad pun sounded throughout the classroom. Eyes bugged out, foreheads receded, sweat formed on brow ridges, and mouths formed into alphabet-soup at this pronouncement.

"That's right, no digging. You are here to learn about archaeology."

"But archaeology is digging. So what are we going to do all semester? Sheesh!" protested a thin young man with stern, steel granny glasses and a straight, scraggly beard, wearing a stained old blue work shirt and low slung 501's with an old, solid, and finely tooled leather belt and scuffed cowboy boots. A scratched trowel jutted from his right back pocket where the seam was half torn away.

Dr. Pittmeyer calmly surveyed the class and quietly repeated, "You are here to learn about archaeology." In a husky, compelling voice, she went on. "Archaeology is not *just* digging, nor is it just about Egyptian ruins or lost civilizations. It's a science. First you have to learn the basics of that science. Digging is just a technique. Digging comes later. Digging comes after you know why you are going to dig."

"No Egyptian ruins . . . ," a plaintive echo resonated through the still classroom.

"You can have your ruins later. Take a class in Egyptian archaeology—fine, fine! But this class is the prerequisite to all those other classes. I hate to be the one to tell you this, people, but there ain't no Indiana Jones! I would have found him by now if there were." Dr. Pittmeyer said this with a slightly lopsided smile. But a veiled look in her light eyes sent an "uh-oh" that the students felt somewhere deep in their guts. They knew that the woman had something to teach them. And teach them she would! Dr. Pittmeyer half sat on the old desk at the front of the classroom. Leaning one elbow on the podium to her right, she picked up a tall, red, opaque glass, and took a long and satisfying drink from it. Behind her large-framed black glasses, her eyes brightened noticeably. She wiped away an invisible mustache from her upper lip and settled onto the desk, holding the red glass in her left hand and letting it sway slightly as she unhurriedly looked over the students. Her left eyebrow rose unconsciously.

The quiet lengthened so that the students filling out the Day-Glo-orange drop cards stopped writing, conscious of the now loud silence in the room.

"OK! Let's go!" Dr. Pittmeyer said with a snap like a whip swinging over their heads. The startled students went straight backed in unison.

"Archaeology is a science, ladies and gentlemen. It's part of the larger science of anthropology. The goals of both are to understand and predict human behavior. Let's start by looking at an area, or subfield, of archaeology that we may designate as problem-oriented archaeology. Humans evolved in Africa, Asia, and Europe, or what we refer to as the Old World."

Dr. Pittmeyer simultaneously turned out the lights and clicked on the PowerPoint projector. On the whiteboard, she wrote rapidly with a harshly bright, purple pen in a hieroglyphic-like scrawl. Dangling from her neck was a microphone that was plugged into a speaker that was then plugged back into an old, cracked socket, the single electric outlet offered by the ancient high-ceilinged room.

Doubtful students suddenly felt compelled to take notes in the dim light provided by the irregularities of old-fashioned thick blinds that did not quite close completely.

"In the New World, in the Americas, from Alaska down to the tip of Tierra del Fuego, we only have well documented evidence that the first people lived here about 15,000–11,000 years ago. In contrast, people have been living in the Old World for 200,000 years or more—people in the sense of *Homo sapiens*."

"So what took them so long to get here?" a perplexed female voice asked.

"Please let me point out that your question contains a very telling assumption. You said, what took them so long to get here. The question is moot because these early peoples were not trying to get here. We're talking about the Paleolithic era—people were migratory. They hunted and collected their food every day. They followed their food resources, usually in seasonal patterns but within fairly local areas. If they moved at all, it was because they were successfully expanding in population. So it is a non-question. Let me explain, please.

"In archaeology, you have to ask the right questions before you can get any useful answers. That is why archaeologists dig—not to make discoveries, but to answer questions. Now, here's what I want you to do. Go home and try to think yourself back into the Paleolithic. Its 35,000 years ago, and mostly you hang out with your family and other close relatives. You get your food and shelter on a daily basis, and you have some free time, too. Everyone cooperates to survive. The point is that wherever you are, you are there. There is no place to try to get to. There is no notion of private property or ownership of land. Nobody needs to conquer anybody. There are no cities, no freeways, no clocks, and no rush. Think about it. It's a concept of life without measurements or urgencies."

"But they must have been pretty stupid back that long ago!" the young man with the beard, now nibbling his trowel, protested.

"Please think about that assumption! No, these were people just like you and me. If they were here today, they probably could program their DVRs. These were people with many skills and accomplishments. They met their needs as we meet ours. But they had something we might envy. They were already there no matter where they were! There's a lot to be learned from our prehistoric ancestors."

"But, frankly, tomorrow's another day." Alone in the classroom, Dr. Penny Pittmeyer finished her soda and allowed her eyes to glaze over as the forgotten Day-Glo-orange drop cards fluttered to the floor. She stared far back in time where she saw intelligent people living a simple life in peace—or so she hoped.

Article

Prepared by: Mari Pritchard Parker, *Pasadena City College* and Elvio Angeloni, *Pasadena City College*

The First Americans

Humans colonized the New World earlier than previously thought—a revelation that is forcing scientists to rethink long-standing ideas about these trailblazers.

HEATHER PRINGLE

Learning Outcomes

After reading this article, you will be able to:

- Evaluate the evidence with respect to when and how humans first entered the New World.
- Describe the kinds of hunting implements used by the first Americans.
- Summarize the genetic evidence for the origins of Native Americans.

In the sweltering heat of an early July afternoon, Michael R. Waters clambers down into a shadowy pit where a small hive of excavators edge their trowels into an ancient floodplain. A murmur rises from the crew, and one of the diggers gives Waters, an archaeologist at the Center for the Study of the First Americans at Texas A&M at the University, a dirt-smeared fragment of blue-gray stone called chert. Waters turns it over in his hand, then scrutinizes it under a magnifying loupe. The find, scarcely larger than a thumbnail, is part of an all-purpose cutting tool, an ice age equivalent of a box cutter. Tossed away long ago on this grassy Texas creek bank, it is one among thousands of artifacts here that are pushing back the history of humans in the New World and shining rare light on the earliest Americans.

Waters, a tall, rumpled man in his mid-fifties with intense blue eyes and a slow, cautious way of talking, does not look or sound like a maverick. But his work is helping to topple an enduring model for the peopling of the New World. For decades scientists thought the first Americans were Asian big-game hunters who tracked mammoths and other large prey eastward across a now submerged landmass known as Beringia that joined northern Asia to Alaska. Arriving in the Americas some 13,000 years ago, these colonists were said to have journeyed rapidly overland along an ice-free corridor that stretched from the Yukon to southern Alberta, leaving behind their distinctive stone tools across what is now the contiguous U.S. Archaeologists called these hunters the Clovis people, after a site near Clovis, N.M., where many of their tools came to light.

Over the past decade or so this Clovis First model has come under sharp attack as a result of new discoveries. In southern Chile, at a site known as Monte Verde, archaeologist Thomas D. Dillehay, now at Vanderbilt University, and his colleagues found traces of early Americans who slept in hide-covered tents and dined on seafood and a wild variety of potato 14,600 years ago, long before the appearance of Clovis hunters. Intrigued by the findings, some scientists began looking for similar evidence in North America. They found it: in Paisley Five Mile Point Caves in Oregon, for example, a team uncovered 14,400-year-old human feces flecked with seeds from desert parsley and other plants—not the kinds of comestibles that advocates of the big-game hunters scenario expected to find on the menu. "What we are seeing," says Dennis L. Jenkins, director of the Paisley Caves dig and an archaeologist at the Museum of Natural and Cultural History in Eugene, Ore., "is a broad-range foraging economy."

Now, along Buttermilk Creek, Waters and his team have made one of the most important finds yet: a mother lode of stone tools dating back a stunning 15,500 years ago. In all, the team has excavated more than 19,000 pre-Clovis artifacts—from small blades bearing tiny wear marks from cutting bone to a polished chunk of hematite, an iron mineral commonly used in the Paleolithic world for making a red pigment. Publicly unveiled this past spring, the site has yielded more pre-Clovis tools than all other such sites combined, and Waters has spared no expense in dating each layer multiple times. The work has impressed many experts. "It is easily the best evidence for pre-Clovis in North America," says Vance T. Holliday, an anthropologist and geoscientist at the University of Arizona.

Energized by such finds, archaeologists are now testing new models for the peopling of the New World. Drawing on evidence from a range of sciences—from genetics to geology—they are searching for answers to a host of pressing questions: Where did the earliest Americans come from more than 15,500 years ago? When exactly did they arrive, and what route did they take into the New World? For the first time in decades there is a heady whiff of discovery in the air. "We are now addressing the big issues," says James M. Adovasio, an archaeologist at Mercyhurst College. "We are looking at the circumstances of the dispersal of humans into the last great habitat on the planet."

Genetic Trails

The peopling of the New World, from the blustery cold of the Arctic to the sultry heat of the Amazon and the stormy winds of Tierra del Fuego, remains one of humanity's greatest achievements, a feat of endurance and adaptation not to be equaled, in the view of the famous 20th-century French archaeologist Francois Bordes, "until man lands on a planet belonging to another star." Yet archaeologists have long struggled to uncover the beginnings of this transcontinental adventure, given the daunting task of locating the early campsites of a tiny population of highly mobile hunters and gatherers in the vast northern wildernesses of North America and Asia. Over the past decade, however, geneticists have taken the search for the first Americans to the molecular level, finding new clues to where they hailed from and when they left their homeland in the DNA of indigenous peoples.

In more than a dozen studies geneticists examined modern and ancient DNA samples from Native Americans, looking for telltale genetic mutations or markers that define major human lineages known as haplogroups. They found that native peoples in the Americas stemmed from four major founding maternal haplogroups—A, B, C and D—and two major founding paternal haplogroups—C and Q. To find the probable source of these haplogroups, the teams then searched for human populations in the Old World whose genetic diversity encompassed all the lineages. Only the modern inhabitants of southern Siberia, from the Altai Mountains in the west to the Amur River in the east, matched this genetic profile, a finding that strongly indicates that the ancestors of the first Americans came from an East Asian homeland.

This evidence confirmed what most archaeologists suspected about the location of this homeland. It also strongly suggested that the timing proposed in the Clovis First scenario was wrong. Geneticists now calculate, based on mutation rates in human DNA, that the ancestors of the Native Americans parted from their kin in their East Asian homeland sometime between 25,000 and 15,000 years ago—a difficult time for a great northern migration. Huge glaciers capped the mountain valleys of northeastern Asia, at the same time massive ice sheets mantled most of Canada, New England and several northern states. Indeed, reconstructions of past climate based on data preserved in ice cores from Greenland and on measurements of past global sea levels show that these ice sheets reached their maximum extent in the last glacial period between at least 22,000 and 19,000 years ago. "But these folks were extraordinarily adept at moving over the landscape," says David Meltzer, an archaeologist at Southern Methodist University. "Their entire existence—and the existence of everyone they knew and the existence of their ancestors—was about adapting. They had a toolbox of tactics and strategies."

Dressed in warm, tailored hide garments stitched together with sinew and bone needles and armed with an expert knowledge of nature, the ancestors of the Paleo-Americans entered an Arctic world without parallel today. The ice sheets in northern Europe and North America had locked up vast quantities of water, lowering sea level by more than 100 meters and exposing the continental shelves of northeastern Asia and Alaska. These newly revealed lands, together with adjacent regions in Siberia, Alaska and northern Canada, formed a landmass that joined the Old World seamlessly to the New.

Known today as Beringia, this landmass would have made a welcoming way station for pre-Clovis migrants. The air masses that swept over it were so dry they brought little snowfall, preventing the growth of ice sheets. As a result, grasses, sedges and other cold-adapted plants thrived there, as shown by plant remains found preserved under a layer of volcanic ash in northwestern Alaska and in the frozen intestines of large herbivores that once grazed in Beringia. These plants formed an arid tundra-grassland, and there woolly mammoths weighing as much as nine tons grazed, as did giant ground sloths, steppe bison, musk ox and caribou. Genetic studies of modern Steller's sea lion populations suggest that this sea mammal likely hauled out on the rocks along Beringia's island-studded south shore. So the migrants may have had their pick not only of terrestrial mammals but also of seafaring ones.

Received wisdom holds that the trailblazers hurried across Beringia to reach warmer, more hospitable lands. Some researchers, however, think the journey could have been a more leisurely affair. The major genetic lineages of Native Americans possess many widespread founding haplotypes—combinations of closely linked DNA sequences on individual chromosomes that are often inherited together—that their closest Asian kin lack. This suggests the earliest Americans paused somewhere en route to the New World, evolving in isolation for thousands of years before entering the Americas. The most likely spot for this Kinetic incubator is Beringia. There the migrants could conceivably have been cut off from their Asian kin as the climate cooled some 22,000 years ago, forcing Siberian bands to retreat south.

Whether the migrants cooled their heels in Beringia, however, or somewhere else in northeastern Asia, people eventually began striking off farther east and south. A warming trend began slowly shrinking North America's ice sheets some 19,000 years ago, gradually creating two passable routes to the south and opening the possibility of multiple early migrations. According to several studies conducted over the past decade on the geographic distribution of genetic diversity in modern indigenous Americans, the earliest of these migrants started colonizing the New World between 18,000 and 15,000 years ago—a date that fits well with emerging archaeological evidence of pre-Clovis colonists. "At some point, these migrants surveyed the landscape and realized for the first time that smoke from all the other campfires was behind them, and ahead there was no smoke." Adovasio reflects. "And at that moment, they were literally strangers in a strange land."

A Coastal Route

Archaeologists take up the tale of the earliest Americans as these travelers pushed southward, exploring a wilderness untouched by humans. In an office decorated with prints and pictures of sharks and a poster of a traditional Clumash wood canoe, Jon M. Erlandson, an archaeologist at the University of Oregon, mulls over new evidence of their journey. Reed-thin, tousled and in his mid-fifties, Erlandson has spent much of his career digging at sites along the coast of California, becoming one of the foremost proponents of what is often called the coastal route theory. Whereas supporters of the Clovis First model envisioned humans reaching the Americas by trekking overland, Erlandson thinks the earliest trawlers arrived by sea, paddling small boats from East Asia to southern Beringia and down the western coast of the Americas. Now he and his colleague, Todd J. Braje of San Diego State University, have uncovered key new evidence of ancient mariners who set out in East Asia and ended their journey in Chile.

Scientists first began thinking about this coastal route in the late 1970s, when archaeologist Knut Fladmark, now a professor emeritus at Simon Fraser University in British Columbia, started examining geologic and pollen records to reconstruct ancient environments along Canada's western coast. At the time, most experts believed that the entire northwestern coast lay under thick ice until the end of the last glacial period. Analyses published in the 1960s and 1970s of ancient pollen from coastal bogs, however, showed that a coniferous forest thrived on Washington's Olympic Peninsula 13,000 years ago and that other green refugia dotted the coast. Early humans camping in these spots, Fladmark concluded, could have fueled up on seafood, from shellfish to migrating pink salmon. They may also have hunted waterfowl migrating along the Pacific flyway, as well as caribou and other handy land animals grazing in the larger refugia.

Archaeologists now know that much of the British Columbian coast was free of ice at least 16,000 years ago. Although they have yet to find any preserved boats in early American coastal sites, many researchers think such watercraft were probably available to these wayfarers: at least 45,000 years ago humans voyaged and island-hopped all the way from Asia to Australia. Traveling by water down the western coast of the New World would have been easier in many respects than trekking overland. "It's an environment that's relatively similar along a north-south transect, which makes it a path of least resistance," says Quentin Mackie, an archaeologist at the University of Victoria in British Columbia.

Still, finding campsites of early mariners has proved a tall order for scientists. As the ice sheets of the last glacial period thawed, the meltwater raised sea level, drowning ancient coastlines under meters of water. Last March, however, Erlandson and Braje detailed in the journal *Science* striking evidence of early seafarers at a newly discovered site on Santa Rosa Island located just off the southern California coast. Nearly 12,000 years ago Paleo American sailors crossed 10 kilometers of open water to reach Santa Rosa, a journey that would have required a boat.

The newly discovered site, known as CA-SRI-512W, lies near the mouth of an inland canyon and close to what might have been an ancient marsh. Erlandson and his team found human refuse buried in the sediments, including bird bones and charcoal the researchers radiocarbon-dated to 11,800 years ago.

Early coastal hunters had dined there on waterfowl and seabirds such as Canada geese and cormorants, as well as on pinnipeds, a group that encompasses seals and sea lions. The hunters also left behind traces of a distinctive technology: more than 50 dainty stemmed points that looked in outline like little brown Christmas trees. Such points may have tipped darts for hunting birds or small marine mammals. "They are just extremely thin and extremely well made," Erlandson says. Overall, their design and manufacture seemed very unlike the long, furrowed and sturdy-looking Clovis spearpoints used by big-game hunters on the mainland.

Curious about the origin of this coastal technology, Erlandson and Braje scoured published archaeological reports on other sites for clues. They discovered that excavators had dug up very similar stemmed points at ancient sites scattered around the northern rim of the Pacific Ocean. The earliest came from East Asia—the Korean peninsula, Japan and the Russian Far East—and all dated to around 15,000 years ago. Moreover, the farther one traveled away from there, the younger these weapons were, with 14,000-year-old stemmed points in Oregon and 12,000-year-old points on the Channel Islands, in Baja California and along coastal South America. Erlandson shakes his head in wonderment. "Some of the point assemblages in Japan are really similar to the ones in the Channel Islands," he says.

Erlandson and Braje now think this trail of technology marks out an early migration route along the northern Pacific Rim, a coastal highway loaded with food. Kelp, for example, flourishes in the cold, nutrient-rich waters there, forming coastal marine forests that harbor species ranging from rockfish to abalone to sea otters. Such marine forests would likely have thrived along Beringia's southern coast even during the last glacial period. Studies of ocean temperature some 18,000 years ago suggest that sea ice formed only in winter along Beringia's southern coast, and this seasonal deep freeze would not have eradicated the great marine forests. Kelp can survive under sea ice in a state akin to suspended animation for long months at a time, growing rapidly again when summer arrives and creating an abundant marine habitat. "And it's not just kelp that would have facilitated a coastal migration," Erlandson says. "There's an enormous amount of other resources in marine estuaries and in salmon streams." Indeed, edible species along the route today number in the hundreds, from cetaceans to seaweed.

Even so, Paleo-Americans exploring this rich coastal world were unlikely to have raced southward. Indeed, some researchers think they may have moved just a kilometer or so a year, as the migrants gradually expanded the southern boundaries of their hunting and gathering territory. "This wasn't a sprint down the coast," Erlandson concludes. "You had to have marriage partners because you were moving into unpopulated lands. So you had to maintain connections with people behind you."

An Inland Corridor

The western coast of the Americas was not the only available route for early colonists. Over the past five years a team of earth scientists and dating experts led by Kennedy Munyikwa, a geologist at Athabasca University in Alberta, has been reexamining another potential passageway, one that was widely championed by supporters of the Clovis First theory but that later fell out of favor after the discovery of pre-Clovis people at the site of Monte Verde near the Chilean coast. Known as the ice-free corridor, this mid-continental route formed after North America's largest ice sheet the Laurentide, began retreating eastward, separating from the Cordilleran ice sheet that blanketed the west, and after vast glacial lakes blocking the passageway drained, leaving dry land. The resulting corridor ran along the eastern flanks of the Rockies and extended nearly 1,900 kilometers, from Alaska to the lower 48 states.

The renewed interest in this route stems from new dates on the opening of the corridor that Munyikwa and his colleagues published in June in the journal *Quaternary Geochronology*. In the 1980s researchers at the Geological Survey of Canada dated its opening by radiocarbon-testing plant remains preserved in sediments along the route. Their findings indicated that the two colossal ice sheets parted company and that the glacial lakes drained around 13,000 years ago. This time frame fit well with the Clovis First scenario, although it ruled out the corridor as a migration route for earlier people.

Yet as Munyikwa examined these early studies for a project on ancient environment change, he saw serious problems. The radiocarbon dates were few in number, and some were clearly unreliable. Moreover, the dating of plants determined when vegetation had finally reestablished itself in the corridor, not when the ice had actually retreated and the lakes drained. So Munyikwa and his colleagues decided to redate the opening of the ice-free corridor by a technique known as optically stimulated luminescence (OSL). The team focused on a section of the corridor in northern Alberta, where large sand dunes—some exceeding 10 meters in height—had formed from windblown sediments after the Laurentide ice sheet retreated.

To obtain samples for dating, Munyikwa and his team cut pits into the tallest dunes in these fields. Then they hammered black plastic pipes horizontally into the walls of these pits. Capped on one end, the pipes filled with sand that had not been exposed to sunlight since the dunes accumulated. Next the team dated each sample by the OSL method, measuring the amount of energy from environmental radiation trapped in minerals such as feldspar in the samples. The results showed that the sand dunes formed between 14,000 and 15,000 years ago, a range that likely constitutes a minimum age for the opening of the corridor, Munyikwa says, because "it's possible that the dunes formed 1,000 years after the ice went away." Moreover, the corridor in northern Alberta stretched at least 400 kilometers across at this time and likely cradled few if any large meltwater lakes. The sand that accumulated in dunes, Munyikwa points out, came from dry lake bottoms.

The big question now is whether the entire corridor lay open during this period, particularly the section to the north. Munyikwa thinks it did. His team recently dated sand dunes farther north, along the Alberta-Northwest Territory border, with similar results. These data, Munyikwa says, fit current thinking about the Laurentide ice sheet. The general consensus among geologists, he notes, "is that the ice sheet retreated in a northeasterly direction as a wide front, as opposed to [moving] in discrete lobes. We envisage that the deglaciated land extended to the north." If so, explorers from Asia could have entered the corridor around 15,000 years ago, nearly 1,000 years after the route to the western coast opened.

The new OSL dates, says archaeologist Jack Ives of the University of Alberta in Edmonton, will prompt a fresh look at this corridor, rekindling a major debate over migration routes. "It is often alleged, in grave error, that the corridor region has been well investigated, when in fact it is vast, and we know little about it," Ives asserts. The oldest, broadly accepted evidence of humans in the northern corridor dates to some 12,000 years ago, but Ives thinks future archaeological surveying could well turn up much earlier sites. "I think if the coast was Highway 1, then the corridor was Highway 2," he quips.

Scoured by retreating ice and pierced by cold winds, the newly opened corridor would have seemed a formidable place to early travelers. Yet it is possible, argues Stuart J. Fiedel, an archaeologist at the Louis Berger Group in East Orange, N.J., that hunter-gatherers in Beringia decided to explore it after watching flocks of waterfowl head south in the fall and return in the spring. Food would have been scarce, Fiedel says, but the explorers may have hunted calorie-rich birds or larger game. Recent genetic data suggest that mountain sheep grazed in two refugia in the Yukon and northern British Columbia.

As an insurance policy, the travelers may have taken along man's best friend. Hunters in Siberia seem to have first domesticated wolves as early as 33,000 years ago, based on paleontological evidence. Fiedel thinks early dogs would have made invaluable hunting companions and pack animals on a journey through the corridor. In historic times, he notes, hunter-gatherers on the Great Plains placed pack saddles on dogs or hitched them to travoises to carry a variety of loads, from hides for bedding and shelter to food stores. Experiments have shown that dogs can haul about 27 kilograms, Fiedel says. Moreover, a study published in 1994 revealed that dogs carrying 13 kilograms of gear could travel as far as 27 kilometers a day, provided the temperature remained cool. If starvation threatened, the migrants could have eaten some of their dogs.

Fiedel has calculated that the colonists could have reached the southern end of the corridor in four months, traveling at a modest pace of 16 kilometers a day. As they left its stony bleakness behind, they would have laid eyes for the first time on a breathtaking abundance: warm, grassy plains filled with herds of mammoths, bison and horses; marshes and lakes dotted with waterfowl; oceans brimming with fish and marine mammals. It was a land empty of human rivals, a new world of possibilities.

Clovis Origins

In the shady air-conditioned house that serves as the field-camp headquarters at Buttermilk Creek, Waters lifts off the lid from a black box the size of a small laptop. In the kitchen, members of his crew chat and joke as they prepare lunch, but Waters seems oblivious to the patter. He quickly scans the contents of the box, picks up first one, then another of the 20 or so pre-Clovis stone tools lying inside. Fashioned from a lustrous local chert found near Buttermilk Creek, the blades and other tools are remarkably compact and lightweight, some measuring no more than a few centimeters in length. Such a tool kit, Waters says, would have been ideal for bands of early explorers, a people constantly on the move as they probed and investigated terra incognita.

In some of these tools—particularly the blades and bifaces—Waters also sees something else: a new clue to the origins of the Clovis people. Some 2,500 years after the pre-Clovis people here knapped blades and bifaces, Clovis hunters employed similar techniques across North America to make massive elongate blades, some reaching 21 centimeters or more in length. This technological continuity, Waters observes, hints strongly at a relationship between the two groups. Far from being migrants from Asia, the famous Clovis hunters may well have descended from bands such as the earliest hunters at Buttermilk Creek. "It looks as if they originated south of the ice sheet," he remarks.

What is beyond all doubt, however, is that the earliest Americans and their descendants were a resilient and resourceful people, trailblazers who settled the longest geographic expanse ever settled by humans. Braving the unknown, they adapted masterfully to a vast array of ecosystems on two continents. These early Americans deserve our admiration, says archaeologist David Anderson of the University of Tennessee. "I think they exemplify the spirit of survival and adventure that represents the very best of humanity."

Critical Thinking

1. What is the Clovis First model for the peopling of the New World?
2. What evidence challenges the Clovis First model?
3. What is the evidence for a coastal migration route through North America?
4. Why is there renewed interest in an inland corridor route?
5. How important were dogs to early hunters?

Create Central

www.mhhe.com/createcentral

Internet References

Anthropology, Archaeology, and American Indian Sites on the Internet
http://dizzy.library.arizona.edu/library/teams/sst/anthro

Society for American Archaeology
www.saa.org

USD Anthropology
www.usd.edu/anth

HEATHER PRINGLE is a Canadian science writer and a contributing editor to *Archaeology* magazine.

Pringle, Heather. From *Scientific American*, November, 2011. Copyright © 2011 by Scientific American, a division of Nature America, Inc. All rights reserved. Reprinted by permission.

Ancient Migration: Coming to America

For decades, scientists thought that the Clovis hunters were the first to cross the Arctic to America. They were wrong—and now they need a better theory.

ANDREW CURRY

Learning Outcomes

After reading this article, you will be able to:

- Describe the Clovis culture scenario as to how and when humans entered the New World.
- Discuss the archaeological evidence that contradicts the Clovis First scenario.
- Discuss the three competing notions as to how pre-Clovis peoples may have entered the New World.

The mastodon was old, its teeth worn to nubs. It was perfect prey for a band of hunters, wielding spears tipped with needle-sharp points made from bone. Sensing an easy target, they closed in for the kill.

Almost 14,000 years later, there is no way to tell how many hits it took to bring the beast to the ground near the coast of present-day Washington state. But at least one struck home, plunging through hide, fat and flesh to lodge in the mastodon's rib. The hunter who thrust the spear on that long-ago day didn't just bring down the mastodon; he also helped to kill off the reigning theory of how people got to the Americas.

For most of the past 50 years, archaeologists thought they knew how humans arrived in the New World. The story starts around the end of the last ice age, when sea levels were lower and big-game hunters living in eastern Siberia followed their prey across the Bering land bridge and into Alaska. As the ice caps in Canada receded and opened up a path southward, the colonists swept across the vast unpopulated continent. Archaeologists called these presumed pioneers the Clovis culture, after distinctive stone tools that were found at sites near Clovis, New Mexico, in the 1920s and 1930s.

As caches of Clovis tools were uncovered across North America over subsequent decades, nearly all archaeologists signed on to the idea that the Clovis people were the first Americans. Any evidence of humans in the New World before the Clovis time was dismissed, sometimes harshly. That was the case with the Washington-state mastodon kill, which was first described around 30 years ago[1] but then largely ignored.

Intense criticism also rained down on competing theories of how people arrived, such as the idea that early Americans might have skirted the coastline in boats, avoiding the Bering land bridge entirely. "I was once warned not to write about coastal migration in my dissertation. My adviser said I would ruin my career," says Jon Erlandson, an archaeologist at the University of Oregon in Eugene.

But findings over the past few years—and a re-examination of old ones, such as the mastodon rib—have shown conclusively that humans reached the Americas well before the Clovis people. That has sparked a surge of interest in the field, and opened it up to fresh ideas and approaches. Geneticists and archaeologists are collaborating to piece together who came first, when they arrived, whether they travelled by boat or by foot and how they fanned out across the New World.

To test their ideas, some researchers are examining new archaeological sites and reopening old ones. Others are sifting through the DNA of modern people and unearthing the remains of those buried millennia ago in search of genetic clues. "There's a powerful meshing of the archaeology we're pulling out of the ground with genetic evidence," says Michael Waters, a geographer at Texas A&M University in College Station.

Like those original Americans, researchers are exploring new frontiers, moving into fresh intellectual territory after a long period of stasis. "Clovis has been king for 50 years, and now we have to reimagine what the peopling of the New World looked like," Erlandson says. "If it wasn't Clovis, what was it?"

Overthrowing King Clovis

It took a chance finding halfway around the world to set this reappraisal in motion. In the late 1970s, Tom Dillehay, an archaeologist at Vanderbilt University in Nashville, Tennessee, uncovered the remains of a large campsite in southern Chile, close to the tip of South America. Radiocarbon dating of wood and other organic remains suggested that the site was around 14,600 years old, implying that humans made it from Alaska to Chile more than 1,000 years before the oldest known Clovis tools[2]. But because the remote site was so hard for most researchers to examine, it would take nearly 20 years for Dillehay to convince his colleagues.

The case for pre-Clovis Americans has now gained more support, including from analyses of ancient DNA. One of the first bits of genetic evidence came from preserved faeces, or coprolites, that had been discovered in a cave in south-central Oregon by Dennis Jenkins, an archaeologist at the University of Oregon. Radiocarbon dating showed that the coprolites are between 14,300 and 14,000 years old, and DNA analysis confirmed that they are from humans[3]. The recovered DNA even shared genetic mutations with modern Native Americans.

Since the coprolite evidence emerged, in 2008, ancient DNA has also been used to reconstruct that long-ago mastodon hunt. Radiocarbon studies in the 1970s had suggested that the mastodon pre-dated the Clovis people, but some researchers explained that away by arguing that the animal had died in an accident. However, DNA studies last year[4] showed that a fragment of bone embedded in the mastodon's rib had come from another mastodon—strong evidence that it was a spear point made by humans and not a shard that had chipped off a nearby bone in a fall.

The case against Clovis got another major boost last year, when an excavation in Texas unearthed stone tools that pre-dated Clovis-style artefacts by more than a millennium[5]. "We found a solid site with good context, good artefacts and solid dating," says Waters.

This slow avalanche of findings has all but buried the Clovis model—the problem now is what to replace it with. The abundant Clovis artefacts and sites discovered over the past century have set a high bar. Telling the story of the first Americans means coming up with a plausible explanation and definitive evidence to support it—a combination that researchers are struggling to achieve.

One idea they are exploring is that a small group of big-game hunters made it into the Western Hemisphere over land—but significantly earlier than previously thought. Another, more popular, theory argues that humans used boats to navigate along the coast of Siberia and across to the Americas.

There is also a controversial variant of the coastal migration model, put forward by archaeologists Dennis Stanford at the Smithsonian Institution in Washington DC and Bruce Bradley at the University of Exeter, UK. Called the Solutrean hypothesis, it suggests that coastal migration from Asia could have been supplemented by parallel migrations across the Atlantic, bringing stone-tool technologies from present-day Spain and southern Europe to eastern North America.

DNA studies argue strongly against this hypothesis, and it gets little support from researchers. But some are hesitant to reject the idea outright, recognizing that the community was once before too conservative. "That's what happened with the Clovis paradigm," says Dillehay.

To move the field forward, researchers are using as many types of data as possible. Some key clues have emerged from studies of population genetics, in which researchers tallied the number of differences between the genomes of modern Native Americans and those of people living in Asia today. They then used estimates of DNA mutation rates as a molecular clock to time how long the diversity took to develop. That provides an estimate for when people split from ancient Asian populations and migrated to the Americas.

Judging from the limited genetic diversity of modern Native Americans, Ripan Malhi, a geneticist at the University of Illinois at Urbana-Champaign, and others have argued that the founding population was small, perhaps just a few thousand hardy settlers. In a study of mitochondrial DNA from modern Native American and Asian populations, Malhi and his colleagues also found hints that the first American colonists paused on their way out of Asia[6], waiting out the peak of the last ice age on the exposed Bering land bridge for perhaps 5,000 years—long enough to become genetically distinct from other Asian populations. When the glaciers blocking their path into North America began to melt around 16,500 years ago, the Beringians made their way south over land or sea, passing those genetic differences on to their descendants in America.

Other researchers say that there is a major problem with relying on population genetics to answer questions about the peopling of the Americas. At least 80% of the New World's population was wiped out by disease, conflict or starvation after Europeans first arrived some five centuries ago. And the genes of many Native Americans today carry European and African markers, which confounds efforts to piece together the migration story. "If we look pre-contact, we're going to find a lot more indigenous diversity," says Malhi.

That means going back in time, by studying ancient genomes. "You're going to see a lot of ancient-DNA studies coming out, and that's going to tell a powerful story about the first Americans," says Waters.

The chances of finding well-preserved bones from the first Americans are slim, but valuable information can be pulled from DNA samples that fall in between then and now, argues Eske Willerslev, who studies ancient DNA at the University of Copenhagen. Willerslev and his colleague Thomas Gilbert proved that point in 2010, when they extracted the first complete ancient-human genome from a 4,000-year-old hank of hair found in Greenland that had languished for decades in a museum storeroom in Copenhagen. The DNA helped to show that there had been multiple waves of migration into Greenland, and that modern Greenlanders arrived more recently[7]. Now, Willerslev's lab is trying to extract similar information about population movements from ancient-human remains from sites all over the Americas.

Joining Forces

When paired with sequences from modern populations, ancient DNA can help to refine the calculations made by population geneticists and test the claims made by archaeologists. In 2008, Brian Kemp, now at Washington State University in Pullman, extracted mitochondrial DNA from a 10,300-year-old tooth found in On Your Knees Cave in Alaska. When he compared the DNA sequences with those from modern Native Americans, he found that the mutation rate was faster than previously thought[8]. The results, he says, effectively rule out the possibility that humans came to North America as early as 40,000 years ago—a date based on equivocal evidence from archaeological sites in the eastern United States. The finding also argues against the idea that people used boats before the thaw to go around the glaciers and come down the coast. Instead, the DNA evidence supports the consensus that people didn't migrate into the Americas—whether by boat or over land—until the end of the last glacial maximum, 16,500 years ago at most.

The DNA told researchers a few more things. The ancient man who died in that Alaskan cave had mitochondrial DNA most closely related to Native American groups living today along the west coast of North America. "Most of the people who descended from that type are still living near the coast," Kemp says. So the first wave of migrants probably came down the coast and then spread east from there, developing tiny variations in their DNA as they went, Kemp says.

Dennis O'Rourke, a geneticist at the University of Utah in Salt Lake City, is using similar comparisons to fill in the map of ancient migrations in the New World. In the past ten years, dozens of similar studies have established a clear trend—comparisons of DNA from modern people with ancient DNA have shown that the geographic distribution of genetic groups in the Americas has been stable for millennia. "The patterns must have been established more than 4,000 years ago," he says. That helps to constrain the timing of when people spread across the continent and when they stopped migrating, he says.

In Point Barrow, Alaska, O'Rourke recently began studying human remains from a cliff-top cemetery threatened by coastal erosion, where people have been buried for the past 1,000 years. By comparing the samples from ancient Alaskans to populations from Greenland, eastern Canada and elsewhere, O'Rourke hopes to learn more about the colonization of the Arctic, an environment similar to what the first Americans would have encountered towards the end of the last ice age.

O'Rourke's collaborators are also collecting DNA samples from Inupiat people in northern Alaska. By matching up the modern and ancient DNA sequences from that region, they hope to refine the genetic clock and improve estimates for when people arrived in the Americas. Similar work is going on at a cemetery on Prince Rupert Island off northern British Columbia, where local Tsimshian people are working with archaeologists to gather ancient and modern DNA evidence.

While geneticists open up intellectual frontiers, archaeologists are searching for ways to test the migration theories in the field. Direct evidence for coastal migration will be hard to come by, because a rise in the sea level since the end of the last ice age has flooded the ancient coastlines. But researchers are turning up indirect evidence in many locations. Last year, for example, Erlandson demonstrated that humans lived on California's Channel Islands as far back as 12,200 years ago[9], which shows that they must have mastered the use of boats before that time.

And at the Monte Verde site in Chile, researchers have found evidence that the ancient occupants were fans of seafood[10]. "Monte Verde has ten different species of seaweed at the site," Dillehay says. "Somebody was intimately familiar with seaweeds and the microhabitats where they could be found." That lends support to the idea that the earliest Americans were seafarers, he says.

Dillehay's recent findings, which came 30 years after the first excavations at Monte Verde, show that previously studied sites can become potential gold mines, says Waters. Because so many sites were either dismissed or forgotten during the 'Clovis-first' era, Waters says that "the field can really be pushed forward by going back and taking a look at sites that were put up on a shelf". He is already planning to reopen sites in Tennessee and Florida, where evidence of pre-Clovis mammoth hunting was uncovered in the 1980s and 1990s.

Geneticists and archaeologists agree that the death of the Clovis theory has injected the field with excitement and suspense. "There's a sense that there was something before Clovis," says Jenkins, whose coprolite study shook the field four years ago. "But what it was and how it led to the patterns that we see in North and South America—that's a whole new ball game."

Notes

1. Gustafson, C. E., Gilbow, D. & Daugherty, R. *Can. J. Archaeol.* **3,** 157–164 (1979).
2. Dillehay, T. D. *Monte Verde: A Late Pleistocene Settlement in Chile* Vol. 1 (Smithsonian Institution Press, 1989).
3. Gilbert, M. T. P. *et al. Science* **320,** 786–789 (2008).
4. Waters, M. R. *Science* **334,** 351–353 (2011).
5. Waters, M. R. *Science* **331,** 1599–1603 (2011).
6. Tamm, E. *et al. PLoS ONE* **2,** e829 (2007).
7. Rasmussen, M. *et al. Nature* **463,** 757–762 (2010).
8. Kemp, B. M. *et al. Am. J. Phys. Anthropol.* **132,** 605–621 (2007).
9. Erlandson, J. M. *et al. Science* **331,** 1181–1185 (2011).
10. Dillehay, T. D. *et al. Science* **320,** 784–786 (2008).

Critical Thinking

1. What evidence contradicts the long-held view that Clovis people were the first Americans?
2. What are the three competing ideas as to how pre-Clovis people arrived in the New World?
3. What is the DNA evidence as to the peopling of the New World?
4. How substantial is the evidence that the earliest Americans migrated along the coast?

Create Central

www.mhhe.com/createcentral

Internet References

Anthropology, Archaeology, and American Indian Sites on the Internet
　http://dizzy.library.arizona.edu/library/teams/sst/anthro
Society for American Archaeology
　www.saa.org
USD Anthropology
　www.usd.edu/anth

ANDREW CURRY is a freelance writer in Berlin.

Curry, Andrew. From *Nature*, May 2, 2012. Copyright © 2012 by Nature Publishing Group, a division of Macmillan Publishers Ltd. All rights reserved. Reprinted by permission via Rightslink.

Article

Prepared by: Mari Pritchard Parker, *Pasadena City College* and Elvio Angeloni, *Pasadena City College*

Beyond the Blue Horizon

How Ancient Voyagers Settled the Far-Flung Islands of the Pacific

ROFF SMITH

Learning Outcomes

After reading this article, you will be able to:

- Discuss the archaeological, genetic, and linguistic evidence for the origins of the people of the South Pacific.
- Discuss the issue as to whether the peopling of the South Pacific was accidental or by design.
- Summarize the "abundant leads" used by a seafaring people without navigational aids to find land over millions of square miles of ocean.

Much of the thrill of venturing to the far side of the world rests on the romance of difference. So one feels a certain sympathy for Captain James Cook on the day in 1778 that he "discovered" Hawaii. Then on his third expedition to the Pacific, the British navigator had explored scores of islands across the breadth of the sea, from lush New Zealand to the lonely wastes of Easter Island. This latest voyage had taken him thousands of miles north from the Society Islands to an archipelago so remote that even the old Polynesians back on Tahiti knew nothing about it. Imagine Cook's surprise, then, when the natives of Hawaii came paddling out in their canoes and greeted him in a familiar tongue, one he had heard on virtually every mote of inhabited land he had visited. Marveling at the ubiquity of this Pacific language and culture, he later wondered in his journal: "How shall we account for this Nation spreading itself so far over this Vast ocean?"

That question, and others that flow from it, has tantalized inquiring minds for centuries: Who were these amazing seafarers? Where did they come from, starting more than 3,000 years ago? And how could a Neolithic people with simple canoes and no navigation gear manage to find, let alone colonize, hundreds of far-flung island specks scattered across an ocean that spans nearly a third of the globe?

Answers have been slow in coming. But now a startling archaeological find on the island of Éfaté, in the Pacific nation of Vanuatu, has revealed an ancient seafaring people, the distant ancestors of today's Polynesians, taking their first steps into the unknown. The discoveries there have also opened a window into the shadowy world of those early voyagers.

At the same time, other pieces of this human puzzle are turning up in unlikely places. Climate data gleaned from slow-growing corals around the Pacific and from sediments in alpine lakes in South America may help explain how, more than a thousand years later, a second wave of seafarers beat their way across the entire Pacific.

On a lonely sun-drenched knoll on Éfaté, about half an hour's drive east of Port-Vila, the old colonial capital of Vanuatu, Matthew Spriggs is sitting on an upturned bucket, gently brushing away crumbs of dirt from a richly decorated piece of pottery unearthed only a few minutes earlier. "I've never seen anything like this," he says, admiring the intricate design. "Nobody has. This is unique." That description fits much of what is coming out of the ground here. "What we have is a first- or second-generation site containing the graves of some of the Pacific's first explorers," says Spriggs, professor of archaeology at the Australian National University and co-leader of an international team excavating the site. It came to light only by luck. A backhoe operator, digging up topsoil on the grounds of a derelict coconut plantation, scraped open a grave—the first of dozens in a burial ground some 3,000 years old. It is the oldest cemetery ever found in the Pacific islands, and it harbors the bones of an ancient people archaeologists call the Lapita, a label that derives from a beach in New Caledonia where a landmark cache of their pottery was found in the 1950s.

They were daring blue-water adventurers who roved the sea not just as explorers but also as pioneers, bringing along everything they would need to build new lives—their families and livestock, taro seedlings and stone tools. Within the span of a few centuries the Lapita stretched the boundaries of their world from the jungle-clad volcanoes of Papua New Guinea to the loneliest coral outliers of Tonga, at least 2,000 miles eastward in the Pacific. Along the way they explored millions of square miles of unknown sea, discovering and colonizing scores of tropical islands never before seen by human eyes: Vanuatu, New Caledonia, Fiji, Samoa.

It was their descendants, centuries later, who became the great Polynesian navigators we all tend to think of: the Tahitians and Hawaiians, the New Zealand Maori, and the curious people who erected those statues on Easter Island. But it was the Lapita who laid the foundation—who bequeathed to the islands the language, customs, and cultures that their more famous descendants carried around the Pacific.

While the Lapita left a glorious legacy, they also left precious few clues about themselves. What little is known or surmised about them has been pieced together from fragments of pottery, animal bones, obsidian flakes, and such oblique sources as comparative linguistics and geochemistry. Although their voyages can be traced back to the northern islands of Papua New Guinea, their language—variants of which are still spoken across the Pacific—came from Taiwan. And their peculiar style of pottery decoration, created by pressing a carved stamp into the clay, probably had its roots in the northern Philippines.

With the discovery of the Lapita cemetery on Éfaté, the volume of data available to researchers has expanded dramatically. The bones of at least 62 individuals have been uncovered so far—including old men, young women, even babies—and more skeletons are known to be in the ground.

Archaeologists were also thrilled to discover six complete Lapita pots; before this, only four had ever been found. Other discoveries included a burial urn with modeled birds arranged on the rim as though peering down at the human bones sealed inside. It's an important find, Spriggs says, for it conclusively identifies the remains as Lapita. "It would be hard for anyone to argue that these aren't Lapita when you have human bones enshrined inside what is unmistakably a Lapita urn."

Several lines of evidence also undergird Spriggs's conclusion that this was a community of pioneers making their first voyages into the remote reaches of Oceania. For one thing, the radiocarbon dating of bones and charcoal places them early in the Lapita expansion. For another, the chemical makeup of the obsidian flakes littering the site indicates that the rock wasn't local; instead it was imported from a large island in Papua New Guinea's Bismarck Archipelago, the springboard for the Lapita's thrust into the Pacific. This beautiful volcanic glass was fashioned into cutting and scraping tools, exactly the type of survival gear explorers would have packed into their canoes.

A particularly intriguing clue comes from chemical tests on the teeth of several skeletons. Then as now, the food and water you consume as a child deposits oxygen, carbon, strontium, and other elements in your still-forming adult teeth. The isotope signatures of these elements vary subtly from place to place, so that if you grow up in, say, Buffalo, New York, then spend your adult life in California, tests on the isotopes in your teeth will always reveal your eastern roots.

Isotope analysis indicates that several of the Lapita buried on Éfaté didn't spend their childhoods here but came from somewhere else. And while isotopes can't pinpoint their precise island of origin, this much is clear: At some point in their lives, these people left the villages of their birth and made a voyage by seagoing canoe, never to return.

DNA teased from these ancient bones may also help answer one of the most puzzling questions in Pacific anthropology: Did all Pacific islanders spring from one source or many? Was there only one outward migration from a single point in Asia, or several from different points? "This represents the best opportunity we've had yet," says Spriggs, "to find out who the Lapita actually were, where they came from, and who their closest descendants are today."

There is one stubborn question for which archaeology has yet to provide any answers: How did the Lapita accomplish the ancient equivalent of a moon landing, many times over? No one has found one of their canoes or any rigging, which could reveal how the canoes were sailed. Nor do the oral histories and traditions of later Polynesians offer any insights, for they segue into myth long before they reach as far back in time as the Lapita.

"All we can say for certain is that the Lapita had canoes that were capable of ocean voyages, and they had the ability to sail them," says Geoff Irwin, a professor of archaeology at the University of Auckland and an avid yachtsman. Those sailing skills, he says, were developed and passed down over thousands of years by earlier mariners who worked their way through the archipelagoes of the western Pacific making short crossings to islands within sight of each other. The real adventure didn't begin, however, until their Lapita descendants neared the end of the Solomons chain, for this was the edge of the world. The nearest landfall, the Santa Cruz Islands, is almost 230 miles away, and for at least 150 of those miles the Lapita sailors would have been out of sight of land, with empty horizons on every side.

Yet that passage, around 1200 B.C., was just the warm-up act, for Santa Cruz and Vanuatu were the Lapita's first and easiest discoveries. Reaching Fiji, as they did a century or so later, meant crossing more than 500 miles of ocean, pressing on day after day into the great blue void of the Pacific. What gave them the courage to launch out on such a risky voyage?

The Lapita's thrust into the Pacific was eastward, against the prevailing trade winds, Irwin notes. Those nagging headwinds, he argues, may have been the key to their success. "They could sail out for days into the unknown and reconnoiter, secure in the knowledge that if they didn't find anything, they could turn about and catch a swift ride home on the trade winds. It's what made the whole thing work."

Once out there, skilled seafarers would detect abundant leads to follow to land: seabirds and turtles, coconuts and twigs carried out to sea by the tides, and the afternoon pileup of clouds on the horizon that often betokens an island in the distance.

Some islands may have broadcast their presence with far less subtlety than a cloud bank. Some of the most violent eruptions anywhere on the planet during the past 10,000 years occurred in Melanesia, which sits nervously in one of the most explosive volcanic regions on Earth. Even less spectacular eruptions would have sent plumes of smoke billowing into the stratosphere and rained ash for hundreds of miles. It's possible that the Lapita saw these signs of distant islands and later sailed off in their direction, knowing they would find land.

For returning explorers, successful or not, the geography of their own archipelagoes provided a safety net to keep them from overshooting their home ports and sailing off into eternity. Vanuatu, for example, stretches more than 500 miles in a northwest-southeast trend, its scores of intervisible islands forming a backstop for mariners riding the trade winds home.

All this presupposes one essential detail, says Atholl Anderson, professor of prehistory at the Australian National University and, like Irwin, a keen yachtsman: that the Lapita had mastered the advanced art of tacking into the wind. "And there's no proof that they could do any such thing," Anderson says. "There has been this assumption that they must have done so, and people have built canoes to re-create those early voyages based on that assumption. But nobody has any idea what their canoes looked like or how they were rigged."

However they did it, the Lapita spread themselves a third of the way across the Pacific, then called it quits for reasons known only to them. Ahead lay the vast emptiness of the central Pacific, and perhaps they were too thinly stretched to venture farther. They probably never numbered more than a few thousand in total, and in their rapid migration eastward they encountered hundreds of islands—more than 300 in Fiji alone. Supplied with such an embarrassment of riches, they could settle down and enjoy what for a time were Earth's last Edens.

"It would have been absolutely amazing to have seen this place back then," says Stuart Bedford, an archaeologist from the Australian National University and co-leader, along with Matthew Spriggs, of the excavation on Éfaté. "These islands were far richer in biodiversity in those days than they are today." By way of illustration, he picks up a trochus shell the size of a dinner plate that was exposed in a test trench only that morning. "The reefs then were covered with thousands of these, each one a meal in itself. The seas were teeming with fish, and huge flightless birds could be found in the rain forest, virtually tame since they had never seen a human being. The Lapita would have thought they'd stumbled onto paradise."

As indeed it was. But theirs is a story of paradise found and lost, for although the Lapita were a Neolithic people, they had a modern capacity for overexploiting natural resources. Within a short span of time—a couple of generations, no more—those huge trochus shells vanished from the archaeological record. The plump flightless birds followed suit, as did a species of terrestrial crocodile. In all, it's estimated that more than a thousand species became extinct across the breadth of the Pacific islands after humans appeared on the scene.

Still, more than a millennium would pass before the Lapita's descendants, a people we now call the Polynesians, struck out in search of new territory. The pioneers who launched this second age of discovery some 1,200 or more years ago faced even greater challenges than their Lapita ancestors, for now they were sailing out beyond the island-stippled waters of Melanesia and western Polynesia and into the central Pacific, where distances are reckoned in thousands of miles, and tiny motes of islands are few and far between.

How difficult would it have been to find terra firma in all that watery wilderness? Consider this: When Magellan's fleet traversed the Pacific in 1520–21, sailing blind across an unknown sea, they went nearly four months without setting foot on land. (They missed the Society Islands, the Tuamotus, and the Marquesas, among other archipelagoes.) Many of the hapless sailors died of thirst, malnutrition, scurvy, and other diseases before the fleet reached the Philippines.

The early Polynesians found nearly everything there was to find, although it took them centuries to do so. Their feats of exploration are remembered and celebrated today at cultural festivals across the Pacific.

It is midafternoon, and a carnival atmosphere has settled over the beach at Matira Point on the island of Bora-Bora in French Polynesia. The air is fragrant with barbecue, and thousands of cheering spectators throng the shore to witness the grand finale of the Hawaiki Nui Va'a, a grueling, three-stage, 80-mile outrigger canoe race that virtually stops the nation.

"This is our heritage," says Manutea Owen, a former champion and a revered hero on his home island of Huahine. "Our people came from over the sea by canoe. Sometimes when I'm out there competing, I try to imagine what they must have endured and the adventures they had crossing those huge distances."

Imagination is now the only way one can conjure up those epic sea voyages. Like their Lapita ancestors, the earliest Polynesians left scanty artifacts of their seafaring life. Only a few pieces of one ancient canoe have ever been found, on Huahine in 1977. No surviving example of the great seagoing, sailing canoes thought to have borne the Polynesian pioneers has yet been discovered.

European explorers left the earliest descriptions of watercraft used by Pacific islanders. In the less isolated waters of Micronesia, they encountered sleek, lateen-rigged canoes, a style that may have filtered into the Pacific from China and the Arab world. But in the remote corners of Polynesia—Hawaii, the Marquesas, and New Zealand—the explorers saw only simple craft. Atholl Anderson suspects that these were the truly indigenous boats, the kind that, centuries earlier, carried Polynesian settlers to far islands.

Anderson also questions conventional wisdom about Polynesian seamanship, citing a later explorer, Captain Cook. While Cook was impressed with the speed of the Polynesian canoes—they could literally sail circles around his ships—he came to question the islanders' ability to make long, intentional sea voyages. He records an account of a group of Tahitians who, helpless in the face of a contrary wind and unable to set a course for home, drifted hundreds of miles off course and were marooned on Aitutaki, in what is now the Cook Islands.

Rather than give all the credit to human skill and daring, Anderson invokes the winds of chance. El Niño, the same climate disruption that affects the Pacific today, may have helped scatter the first settlers to the ends of the ocean, Anderson suggests. Climate data obtained from slow-growing corals around the Pacific and from lake-bed sediments in the Andes of South America point to a series of unusually frequent El Niños around the time of the Lapita expansion, and again between 1,600 and 1,200 years ago, when the second wave of pioneer navigators made their voyages farther east, to the remotest corners of the Pacific. By reversing the regular east-to-west flow of the trade winds for weeks at a time, these "super El Niños" might have sped the Pacific's ancient mariners on long, unplanned voyages far over the horizon.

The volley of El Niños that coincided with the second wave of voyages could have been key to launching Polynesians across the wide expanse of open water between Tonga, where the Lapita stopped, and the distant archipelagoes of eastern Polynesia. "Once they crossed that gap, they could island hop throughout the region, and from the Marquesas it's mostly downwind to Hawaii," Anderson says. It took another 400 years for mariners to reach Easter Island, which lies in the opposite direction—normally upwind. "Once again this was during a period of frequent El Nino activity."

Exactly how big a role El Niño played in dispersing humans across the Pacific is a matter of lively academic debate. Could lucky breaks and fickle winds really account for so wide a spread of people throughout the 65-million-square-mile vastness of the Pacific? By the time Europeans came on the scene, virtually every speck of habitable land, hundreds of islands and atolls in all, had already been discovered by native seafarers—who ultimately made it all the way to South America. Archaeologists in Chile recently found ancient chicken bones containing DNA that matches early Polynesian fowl.

Nor did they arrive as lone castaways who soon died out. They came to stay, in groups, with animals and crops from their former homes. "My sense is that there had to be something more at work here than canoes simply blown before a wind," says Irwin. He notes that the trade winds slacken during the summer monsoon, which might have allowed islanders to purposefully sail eastward. Moreover, says Irwin, "Sophisticated traditions of seafaring were planted in every island. Did they develop independently in all of those islands? If so, why do these traditions bear so many details in common?

"But whatever you believe, the really fascinating part of this story isn't the methods they used, but their motives. The Lapita, for example, didn't need to pick up and go; there was nothing forcing them, no overcrowded homeland.

"They went," he says, "because they wanted to go and see what was over the horizon."

Critical Thinking

1. What have been some of the tantalizing questions regarding the peopling of the Pacific?
2. Who were the Lapita? What did they accomplish and how?
3. What do we know about the origins of the Lapita and their culture and how do we know it?
4. What can we say about the obstacles facing Lapita expansion and how they may have overcome them? What does all of this "presuppose"?
5. How does the author describe the original biodiversity in the Pacific and what happened to it?
6. When did the second age of discovery occur and why were there even greater challenges?
7. What are the two basic ways to explain the later expansion?
8. How far does the expansion seem to have reached?

Create Central

www.mhhe.com/createcentral

Internet References

Archaeology and Anthropology: The Australian National University
http://online.anu.edu.au/AandA

ArchNet—WWW Virtual Library
http://archnet.asu.edu/archnet

Radiocarbon Dating for Archaeology
www.rlaha.ox.ac.uk/orau/index.html

Zeno's Forensic Page
http://forensic.to/forensic.html

ROFF SMITH's books include *Cold Beer and Crocodiles: A Bicycle Journey into Australia.*

Smith, Roff. From *National Geographic*, March, 2008. Copyright © 2008 by National Geographic Society. Reprinted by permission.

Article

Prepared by: Mari Pritchard Parker, *Pasadena City College* and
Elvio Angeloni, *Pasadena City College*

Prehistory *of* Warfare

Humans have been at each others' throats since the dawn of the species.

STEVEN A. LEBLANC

Learning Outcomes

After reading this article, you will be able to:

- Discuss the extent to which warfare has occurred in prehistoric societies.
- Explain the general causes of warfare among humans.
- Explain why warfare does not exist in some societies.

In the early 1970s, working in the El Morro Valley of west-central New Mexico, I encountered the remains of seven large prehistoric pueblos that had once housed upwards of a thousand people each. Surrounded by two-story-high walls, the villages were perched on steep-sided mesas, suggesting that their inhabitants built them with defense in mind. At the time, the possibility that warfare occurred among the Anasazi was of little interest to me and my colleagues. Rather, we were trying to figure out what the people in these 700-year-old communities farmed and hunted, the impact of climate change, and the nature of their social systems—not the possibility of violent conflict.

One of these pueblos, it turned out, had been burned to the ground; its people had clearly fled for their lives. Pottery and valuables had been left on the floors, and bushels of burned corn still lay in the storerooms. We eventually determined that this site had been abandoned, and that immediately afterward a fortress had been built nearby. Something catastrophic had occurred at this ancient Anasazi settlement, and the survivors had almost immediately, and at great speed, set about to prevent it from happening again.

Thirty years ago, archaeologists were certainly aware that violent, organized conflicts occurred in the prehistoric cultures they studied, but they considered these incidents almost irrelevant to our understanding of past events and people. Today, some of my colleagues are realizing that the evidence I helped uncover in the El Morro Valley is indicative warfare endemic throughout the entire Southwest, with its attendant massacres, population decline, and area abandonments that forever changed the Anasazi way of life.

When excavating eight-millennia-old farm villages in southeastern Turkey in 1970, I initially marveled how similar modern villages were to ancient ones, which were occupied at a time when an abundance of plants and animals made warfare quite unnecessary. Or so I thought. I knew we had discovered some plaster sling missiles (one of our workmen showed me how shepherds used slings to hurl stones at predators threatening their sheep). Such missiles were found at many of these sites, often in great quantities, and were clearly not intended for protecting flocks of sheep; they were exactly the same size and shape as later Greek and Roman sling stones used for warfare.

The so-called "donut stones" we had uncovered at these sites were assumed to be weights for digging sticks, presumably threaded on a pole to make it heavier for digging holes to plant crops. I failed to note how much they resembled the round stone heads attached to wooden clubs—maces—used in many places of the world exclusively for fighting and still used ceremonially to signify power. Thirty years ago, I was holding mace heads and sling missiles in my hands, unaware of their use as weapons of war.

We now know that defensive walls once ringed many villages of this era, as they did the Anasazi settlements. Rooms were massed together behind solid outside walls and were entered from the roof. Other sites had mud brick defensive walls, some with elaborately defended gates. Furthermore, many of these villages had been burned to the ground, their inhabitants massacred, as indicated by nearby mass graves.

Certainly for those civilizations that kept written records or had descriptive narrative art traditions, warfare is so clearly present that no one can deny it. Think of Homer's *Iliad* or the Vedas of South India, or scenes of prisoner sacrifice on Moche pottery. There is no reason to think that warfare played any less of a role in prehistoric societies for which we have no such records, whether they be hunter-gatherers or farmers. But most scholars studying these cultures still are not seeing it. They should assume warfare occurred among the people they study, just as they assume religion and art were a normal part of human culture. Then they could ask more interesting questions, such as: What form did warfare take? Can warfare explain some of the material found in the archaeological record? What were people fighting over and why did the conflicts end?

Today, some scholars know me as Dr. Warfare. To them, I have the annoying habit of asking un-politic questions about their research. I am the one who asks why the houses at a particular site were jammed so close together and many catastrophically burned. When I suggest that the houses were crowded behind defensive walls that were not found because no one was looking for them, I am not terribly appreciated. And I don't win any popularity contests when I suggest that twenty-mile-wide zones with no sites in them imply no-man's lands—clear evidence for warfare—to archaeologists who have explained a region's history without mention of conflict.

Scholars should assume warfare occurred among the people they study, just as they assume religion was a normal part of human culture. Then they would ask more interesting questions, such as: What form did warfare take? Why did people start and stop fighting?

Virtually all the basic textbooks on archaeology ignore the prevalence or significance of past warfare, which is usually not discussed until the formation of state-level civilizations such as ancient Sumer. Most texts either assume or actually state that for most of human history there was an abundance of available resources. There was no resource stress, and people had the means to control population, though how they accomplished this is never explained. The one archaeologist who has most explicitly railed against this hidden but pervasive attitude is Lawrence Keeley of the University of Illinois, who studies the earliest farmers in Western Europe. He has found ample evidence of warfare as farmers spread west, yet most of his colleagues still believe the expansion was peaceful and his evidence a minor aberration, as seen in the various papers in Barry Cunliffe's *The Oxford Illustrated Prehistory of Europe* (1994) or Douglas Price's *Europe's First Farmers* (2000). Keeley contends that "prehistorians have increasingly pacified the past," presuming peace or thinking up every possible alternative explanation for the evidence they cannot ignore. In his *War Before Civilization* (1996) he accused archaeologists of being in denial on the subject.

Witness archaeologist Lisa Valkenier suggesting in 1997 that hilltop constructions along the Peruvian coast are significant because peaks are sacred in Andean cosmology. Their enclosing walls and narrow guarded entries may have more to do with restricting access to the *huacas*, or sacred shrines, on top of the hills than protecting defenders and barring entry to any potential attackers. How else but by empathy can one formulate such an interpretation in an area with a long defensive wall and hundreds of defensively located fortresses, some still containing piles of sling missiles ready to be used; where a common artistic motif is the parading and execution of defeated enemies; where hundreds were sacrificed; and where there is ample evidence of conquest, no-man's lands, specialized weapons, and so on?

A talk I gave at the Mesa Verde National Park last summer, in which I pointed out that the over 700-year-old cliff dwellings were built in response to warfare, raised the hackles of National Park Service personnel unwilling to accept anything but the peaceful Anasazi message peddled by their superiors. In fact, in the classic book *Indians of Mesa Verde*, published in 1961 by the park service, author Don Watson first describes the Mesa Verde people as "peaceful farming Indians," and admits that the cliff dwellings had a defensive aspect, but since he had already decided that the inhabitants were peaceful, the threat must have been from a new enemy—marauding nomadic Indians. This, in spite of the fact that there is ample evidence of Southwestern warfare for more than a thousand years before the cliff dwellings were built, and there is no evidence for the intrusion of nomadic peoples at this time.

Of the hundreds of research projects in the Southwest, only one—led by Jonathan Haas and Winifred Creamer of the Field Museum and Northern Illinois University, respectively—deliberately set out to research prehistoric warfare. They demonstrated quite convincingly that the Arizona cliff dwellings of the Tsegi Canyon area (known best for Betatakin and Kiet Siel ruins) were defensive, and their locations were not selected for ideology or because they were breezier and cooler in summer and warmer in the winter, as was previously argued by almost all Southwestern archaeologists.

For most prehistoric cultures, one has to piece together the evidence for warfare from artifactual bits and pieces. Most human history involved foragers, and so they are particularly relevant. They too were not peaceful. We know from ethnography that the Inuit (Eskimo) and Australian Aborigines engaged in warfare. We've also discovered remains of prehistoric bone armor in the Arctic, and skeletal evidence of deadly blows to the head are well documented among the prehistoric Aborigines. Surprising to some is the skeletal evidence for warfare in prehistoric California, once thought of as a land of peaceful acorn gatherers. The prehistoric people who lived in southern California had the highest incident of warfare deaths known anywhere in the world. Thirty percent of a large sample of males dating to the first centuries A.D. had wounds or died violent deaths. About half that number of women had similar histories. When we remember that not all warfare deaths leave skeletal evidence, this is a staggering number.

There was nothing unique about the farmers of the Southwest. From the Neolithic farmers of the Middle East and Europe to the New Guinea highlanders in the twentieth century, tribally organized farmers probably had the most intense warfare of any type of society. Early villages in China, the Yucatán, present-day Pakistan, and Micronesia were well fortified. Ancient farmers in coastal Peru had plenty of forts. All Polynesian societies had warfare, from the smallest islands like Tikopia, to Tahiti, New Zealand (more than four thousand prehistoric forts), and Hawaii. No-man's lands separated farming settlements in Okinawa, Oaxaca, and the southeastern United

States. Such societies took trophy heads and cannibalized their enemies. Their skeletal remains show ample evidence of violent deaths. All well-studied prehistoric farming societies had warfare. They may have had intervals of peace, but over the span of hundreds of years there is plenty of evidence for real, deadly warfare.

When farmers initially took over the world, they did so as warriors, grabbing land as they spread out from the Levant through the Middle East into Europe, or from South China down through Southeast Asia. Later complex societies like the Maya, the Inca, the Sumerians, and the Hawaiians were no less belligerent. Here, conflict took on a new dimension. Fortresses, defensive walls hundreds of miles long, and weapons and armor expertly crafted by specialists all gave the warfare of these societies a heightened visibility.

> **Demonstrating the prevalence of warfare is not an end in itself. It is only the first step in understanding why there was so much of it, why it was "rational" for everyone to engage in it all the time. I believe the question of warfare links to the availability of resources.**

There is a danger in making too much of the increased visibility of warfare we see in these complex societies. This is especially true for societies with writing. When there are no texts, it is easy to see no warfare. But the opposite is true. As soon as societies can write, they write about warfare. It is not a case of literate societies having warfare for the first time, but their being able to write about what had been going on for a long time. Also, many of these literate societies link to European civilization in one way or another, and so this raises the specter of Europeans being warlike and spreading war to inherently peaceful people elsewhere, a patently false but prevalent notion. Viewing warfare from their perspective of literate societies tells us nothing about the thousands of years of human societies that were not civilizations—that is, almost all of human history. So we must not rely too much on the small time slice represented by literate societies if we want to understand warfare in the past.

The Maya were once considered a peaceful society led by scholarly priests. That all changed when the texts written by their leaders could be read, revealing a long history of warfare and conquest. Most Mayanists now accept that there was warfare, but many still resist dealing with its scale or implications. Was there population growth that resulted in resource depletion, as throughout the rest of the world? We would expect the Maya to have been fighting each other over valuable farmlands as a consequence, but Mayanist Linda Schele concluded in 1984 that "I do not think it [warfare] was territorial for the most part," this even though texts discuss conquest, and fortifications are present at sites like El Mirador, Calakmul, Tikal, Yaxuná, Uxmal, and many others from all time periods. Why fortify them, if no one wanted to capture them?

Today, more Maya archaeologists are looking at warfare in a systematic way, by mapping defensive features, finding images of destruction, and dating these events. A new breed of younger scholars is finding evidence of warfare throughout the Maya past. Where are the no-man's lands that almost always open up between competing states because they are too dangerous to live in? Warfare must have been intimately involved in the development of Maya civilization, and resource stress must have been widespread.

Demonstrating the prevalence of warfare is not an end in itself. It is only the first step in understanding why there was so much, why it was "rational" for everyone to engage in it all the time. I believe the question of warfare links to the availability of resources.

During the 1960s, I lived in Western Samoa as a Peace Corps volunteer on what seemed to be an idyllic South Pacific Island—exactly like those painted by Paul Gauguin. Breadfruit and coconut groves grew all around my village, and I resided in a thatched-roof house with no walls beneath a giant mango tree. If ever there was a Garden of Eden, this was it. I lived with a family headed by an extremely intelligent elderly chief named Sila. One day, Sila happened to mention that the island's trees did not bear fruit as they had when he was a child. He attributed the decline to the possibility that the presence of radio transmissions had affected production, since Western Samoa (now known as Samoa) had its own radio station by then. I suggested that what had changed was not that there was less fruit but that there were more mouths to feed. Upon reflection, Sila decided I was probably right. Being an astute manager, he was already taking the precaution of expanding his farm plots into some of the last remaining farmable land on the island, at considerable cost and effort, to ensure adequate food for his growing family. Sila was aware of his escalating provisioning problems but was not quite able to grasp the overall demographic situation. Why was this?

The simple answer is that the rate of population change in our small Samoan village was so gradual that during an adult life span growth was not dramatic enough to be fully comprehended. The same thing happens to us all the time. Communities grow and change composition, and often only after the process is well advanced do we recognize just how significant the changes have been—and we have the benefit of historic documents, old photographs, long life spans, and government census surveys. All human societies can grow substantially over time, and all did whenever resources permitted. The change may seem small in one person's lifetime, but over a couple of hundred years, populations can and do double, triple, or quadruple in size.

The consequences of these changes become evident only when there is a crisis. The same can be said for environmental changes. The forests of Central America were being denuded and encroached upon for many years, but it took Hurricane Mitch, which ravaged most of the region in late October 1998, to produce the dramatic flooding and devastation that fully demonstrated the magnitude of the problem: too many people cutting down the forest and farming steep hillsides to survive. The natural environment is resilient and at the same time delicate, as modern society keeps finding out. And it was just so in the past.

From foragers to farmers to more complex societies, when people no longer have resource stress they stop fighting. When climate greatly improves, warfare declines. The great towns of Chaco Canyon were built during an extended warm—and peaceful—period.

These observations about Mother Nature are incompatible with popular myths about peaceful people living in ecological balance with nature in the past. A peaceful past is possible only if you live in ecological balance. If you live in a Garden of Eden surrounded by plenty, why fight? By this logic, warfare is a sure thing when natural resources run dry. If someone as smart as Sila couldn't perceive population growth, and if humans all over Earth continue to degrade their environments, could people living in the past have been any different?

A study by Canadian social scientists Christina Mesquida and Neil Wiener has shown that the greater the proportion of a society is composed of unmarried young men, the greater the likelihood of war. Why such a correlation? It is not because the young men are not married; it is because they cannot get married. They are too poor to support wives and families. The idea that poverty breeds war is far from original. The reason poverty exists has remained the same since the beginning of time: humans have invariably overexploited their resources because they have always outgrown them.

There is another lesson from past warfare. It stops. From foragers to farmers, to more complex societies, when people no longer have resource stress they stop fighting. When the climate greatly improves, warfare declines. For example, in a variety of places the medieval warm interval of ca. 900–1100 improved farming conditions. The great towns of Chaco Canyon were built at this time, and it was the time of archaeologist Stephen Lekson's *Pax Chaco*—the longest period of peace in the Southwest. It is no accident that the era of Gothic cathedrals was a response to similar climate improvement. Another surprising fact is that the amount of warfare has declined over time. If we count the proportion of a society that died from warfare, and not the size of the armies, as the true measure of warfare, then we find that foragers and farmers have much higher death rates—often approaching 25 percent of the men—than more recent complex societies. No complex society, including modern states, ever approached this level of warfare.

If warfare has ultimately been a constant battle over scarce resources, then solving the resource problem will enable us to become better at ridding ourselves of conflict.

There have been several great "revolutions" in human history: control of fire, the acquisition of speech, the agricultural revolution, the development of complex societies. One of the most recent, the Industrial Revolution, has lowered the birth rate and increased available resources. History shows that peoples with strong animosities stop fighting after adequate resources are established and the benefits of cooperation recognized. The Hopi today are some of the most peaceful people on earth, yet their history is filled with warfare. The Gebusi of lowland New Guinea, the African !Kung Bushmen, the Mbuti Pygmies of central Africa, the Sanpoi and their neighbors of the southern Columbia River, and the Sirionno of Amazonia are all peoples who are noted for being peaceful, yet archaeology and historical accounts provide ample evidence of past warfare. Sometimes things changed in a generation; at other times it took longer. Adequate food and opportunity does not instantly translate into peace, but it will, given time.

The fact that it can take several generations or longer to establish peace between warring factions is little comfort for those engaged in the world's present conflicts. Add to this a recent change in the decision-making process that leads to war. In most traditional societies, be they forager bands, tribal farmers, or even complex chiefdoms, no individual held enough power to start a war on his own. A consensus was needed; pros and cons were carefully weighed and hotheads were not tolerated. The risks to all were too great. Moreover, failure of leadership was quickly recognized, and poor leaders were replaced. No Hitler or Saddam Hussein would have been tolerated. Past wars were necessary for survival, and therefore were rational; too often today this is not the case. We cannot go back to forager-band-type consensus, but the world must work harder at keeping single individuals from gaining the power to start wars. We know from archaeology that the amount of warfare has declined markedly over the course of human history and that peace can prevail under the right circumstances. In spite of the conflict we see around us, we are doing better, and there is less warfare in the world today than there ever has been. Ending it may be a slow process, but we are making headway.

Critical Thinking

1. Be familiar with the evidence cited by the author for prehistoric warfare.
2. What happened when farmers took over the world?
3. How did conflict take on a new dimension in more complex societies?
4. What is the relationship between literacy and our perception of warfare?
5. Did Europeans spread warfare to inherently peaceful people elsewhere?
6. What evidence is there for warfare among the Maya?
7. Why does the author think there is a link between warfare and the availability of resources?
8. When do the consequences of population growth become evident?
9. What did Christina Mesquida and Neil Wiener find with respect to the likelihood of warfare?
10. What is significant about the fact that warfare stops?
11. What is another "surprising fact"? Explain.
12. How does the author compare war in traditional societies versus today?

Create Central

www.mhhe.com/createcentral

Internet References

Library of Congress
www.loc.gov

Society for Historical Archaeology
www.sha.org

© 2003 by STEVEN A. LEBLANC. Portions of this article were taken from his book *Constant Battles*, published in April 2003 by St. Martin's Press. LeBlanc is director of collections at Harvard University's Peabody Museum of Archaeology and Ethnology. For further reading visit www.archaeology.org.

LeBlanc, Steven A. From *Archaeology*, May/June 2003, pp. 18–25. Copyright © 2003 by Steven A. LeBlanc. Reprinted by permission of the author.

Article

Prepared by: Mari Pritchard Parker, *Pasadena City College* and
Elvio Angeloni, *Pasadena City College*

Uncovering America's Pyramid Builders

KAREN WRIGHT

Learning Outcomes

After reading this article, you will be able to:

- Describe Cahokia as a complex, sophisticated society.
- Develop your own theory as to why the society of Cahokia existed.
- Discuss the various possible reasons for Cahokia's downfall.

When U.S. 40 reaches Collinsville, Illinois, the land is flat and open. Seedy storefronts line the highway: a pawnshop, a discount carpet warehouse, a taco joint, a bar. Only the Indian Mound Motel gives any hint that the road bisects something more than underdeveloped farmland. This is the Cahokia Mounds State Historic Site, a United Nations World Heritage Site on a par with the Great Wall of China, the Egyptian pyramids, and the Taj Mahal. The 4,000-acre complex preserves the remnants of the largest prehistoric settlement north of Mexico, a walled city that flourished on the floodplain of the Mississippi River 10 centuries ago. Covering an area more than five miles square, Cahokia dwarfs the ancient pueblos of New Mexico's Chaco Canyon and every other ruin left by the storied Anasazi of the American Southwest. Yet despite its size and importance, archaeologists still don't understand how this vast, lost culture began, how it ended, and what went on in between.

A thousand years ago, no one could have missed Cahokia—a complex, sophisticated society with an urban center, satellite villages, and as many as 50,000 people in all. Thatched-roof houses lined the central plazas. Merchants swapped copper, mica, and seashells from as far away as the Great Lakes and the Gulf of Mexico. Thousands of cooking fires burned night and day. And between A.D 1000 and 1300, Cahokians built more than 120 earthen mounds as landmarks, tombs, and ceremonial platforms. The largest of these monuments, now called Monks Mound, still dominates the site. It is a flat-topped pyramid of dirt that covers more than 14 acres and once supported a 5,000-square-foot temple. Monks Mound is bigger than any of the three great pyramids at Giza outside Cairo. "This is the third or fourth biggest pyramid in the world, in terms of volume," says archaeologist Tim Pauketat of the University of Illinois at Urbana-Champaign. It towers 100 feet over a 40-acre plaza that was surrounded by lesser mounds and a two-mile-long stockade. The monument was the crowning achievement of a mound-building culture that began thousands of years earlier and was never duplicated on this continent.

Why Cahokia crumbled and its people vanished is unknown. Malnutrition, overcrowding, a dwindling resource base, the raids of jealous trade partners—any or all of these reasons may have contributed to the city's demise. No one knows whether the populace cleared out all at once or dispersed gradually, but by A.D 1300 Cahokia was a ghost town. By the time Europeans arrived in the Mississippi bottomland, the region was only sparsely settled, and none of the native residents could recount what had happened there centuries before. So far, archaeologists have uncovered no evidence of invasion, rampant disease, overpopulation, deforestation, or any of the other hallmarks of the decline and fall of civilization. Cahokia abounds in artifacts, but archaeologists have not yet made sense of them in a meaningful way. "It actually becomes quite scary," says John Kelly of Washington University in St. Louis. "After a while you begin to realize that you're dealing with rituals that had a great deal of meaning 800 years ago and that you're kind of clueless."

Intellectual frustration is not the only reason for Cahokia's obscurity. Pauketat complains that the region is geographically challenged. It has the look and feel of a place "like Buffalo, except warmer," he says. Cahokia doesn't exactly lure others away from more exotic digs in Turkey, Mexico, or Peru, he says. "That's the problem with this site." Another reason for its lack of popularity is the ordinary, perishable building materials used by the residents. "Cahokians are discounted because they built with dirt—dirt and wood, things they valued," says Pauketat. "I get tired of hearing people say, 'We have civilization and you guys don't.'"

Meanwhile, developers see Cahokia as ripe for expansion; strip malls and subdivisions threaten on every side. "It's developing faster than we can survey," Pauketat says. "We don't know what we're losing out there." Although a good portion of the central city is now protected, archaeologists are discovering related sites throughout a six-county region on both sides of the nearby Mississippi—an area 3,600 miles square. Indeed, digs are under way in such unlikely places as a railroad yard eight miles west in East St. Louis, where a new bridge is scheduled. "If you want to find out the archaeology of an area," says Brad Koldehoff of the Illinois Department of Transportation's archaeology team, "build a road through it."

One morning last September, a warm red sun rose behind Monks Mound, inching above the level terrace where a tribal palace once stood, burning the mist off the flat green expanses of former plazas. To the west of the mound, in a circle more than 400 feet in diameter, several dozen cedar posts rise to the height of telephone poles. The woodhenge, as the structure is known, is a reconstruction of a series of circles found in the 1960s and '70s when excavations to build a mammoth cloverleaf joining three interstate highways unearthed the remains of several hundred houses and dozens of post pits. (The findings persuaded the Federal Highway Administration to relocate the cloverleaf a few miles north.)

At the autumnal equinox, the rising sun aligns exactly with one post when viewed from the center of the circle, just as it does at the spring equinox and the solstices. William Iseminger, assistant site manager for the Cahokia Mounds State Historic Society, takes these alignments as evidence that the posts may have functioned as a kind of calendar, marking the turn of the seasons. Other woodhenges may have been part of lesser mounds, but, says Iseminger, they are nearly impossible to find because the post pits are so far apart, and wood rarely survives centuries underground.

Many archaeologists point to the size and ambition of structures like the woodhenge as evidence of Cahokia's sophistication. The construction of Monks Mound, for example, used between 15 billion and 20 billion pounds of soil, which were lugged to the site in woven baskets that held 50 to 60 pounds of dirt each. Grading and draining the 40-acre plaza in front of it meant moving just as much earth. The stockade walls consumed 20,000 trees. Subsidiary mounds in the city "grid" seem to be placed according to a rational design. These accomplishments imply organized feats of labor and planning enacted by a central authority.

In many excavations, the number of artifacts and the amount of refuse indicate the population spiked sharply around A.D 1100, jumping from hundreds to perhaps tens of thousands of people. Large homes and mounds appeared where villages of small houses had existed just a generation before. In the mid-1990s, excavations by Pauketat, Kelly, and others showed that the hills east of Cahokia were far more populous than anyone had suspected. A wooded rise among farmhouses in the city of O'Fallon marks the site of an ancient acropolis that probably served more than 500 people. At a site south of O'Fallon, Pauketat found remnants of 80 houses, three temples, clay pots, hoe blades, ax heads, and carved redstone statues. On a tree-lined street in Lebanon, a flagpole is planted in the center of a former platform mound marking another temple center.

Based on these findings, Pauketat estimates that as many as 50,000 people may have lived in Cahokia's greater metropolitan area at the settlement's peak. They seem to have appeared as if from nowhere. "Cahokia had to be created by large-scale migration from other places," says Tom Emerson, director of the state transportation department's archaeological program. "Nobody can breed that fast."

Why did migrants come to Cahokia? Past theories suggested that the dual forces of nature and commerce drove the city's rapid growth. The fertile bottomland was ripe for cultivation by farmers skilled in raising corn, squash, and sunflowers. The nearby confluence of the Illinois, Missouri, and Mississippi rivers could have put Cahokia at the nexus of trade networks that spanned much of the continent. But American Indians had been building modest mounds in the Mississippi River valley since 3500 B.C.; they'd been growing corn with much the same tools for hundreds of years, and the rivers and flood-plains had been there for thousands. Economic and geographic felicities alone cannot account for the sudden concentration of people in the area at a particular moment.

Pauketat has come to believe that charismatic leaders created a dynamic social movement with Cahokia at the epicenter, luring inhabitants of far-flung communities away from their home-steads to the fast urban action. Pauketat resists the term *cult*, but it evokes the phenomenon he envisions. "There were certainly individuals who were movers and shakers, but they weren't consciously, deliberately exploiting people," he asserts.

"Cahokia is a political construct," Emerson adds. "It's not due to some massive change in subsistence, it's not archaeological, it's not technological. It's the kind of place that results from changes in how you conduct yourself socially and politically. What happened at Cahokia is politics, probably in the guise of religion."

Not all scholars see a burgeoning statehood in Cahokia's remains. Anthropologist George Milner of Pennsylvania State University believes there were at most 8,000 people at Cahokia, and he calculates that with even half that population one person per household working just a few weeks a year could have built Monks Mound. The construction would have proceeded at a desultory pace, he concedes; it may have required hundreds of years to complete. Only if the woodhenges and mounds were rapidly constructed would they require full-time laborers or engineers. And he is skeptical that the ecology of the region, abundant as it was, could have supported a community as vast as that supposed by Pauketat and others.

The trump card for Milner and other minimalists is the fact that, unlike the ancient Mesopotamians, Maya, Egyptians, and Chinese, Cahokians never developed a written counterpart to their spoken language. Writing is generally considered a prerequisite for the kind of record keeping typical of organized governments. (The names "Cahokia" and "Monks Mound" were applied long after the fact: Cahokia was the name of an Illini tribe that occupied the area in the 1600s, and Monks Mound was named for French Trappists who settled on one of its terraces in the 1800s.)

But champions of an advanced Cahokian civilization would rather make their case with numbers than with language anyway. Even Milner admits that if Cahokia was as populous or expansive as some claim, it would have exerted statelike control over its citizens. To support his theory, Pauketat is looking for evidence that the settlements outside of Cahokia follow a planned pattern—a support network of communities allied with the power center, perhaps communicating with the capital using runners and smoke signals. He found traces of buildings at the intersection of Routes 159 and 64, now home to a Toys 'R' Us and a Ramada Inn, and he believes they may have faced Cahokia, a six-hour walk away. That orientation would bolster his contention that the outlying villages were all part of one big polity.

Early in his career at the state department of transportation, Tom Emerson found an eight-inch statuette at the site of a temple two or three miles from Cahokia. Five pounds of distinctive redstone called flint clay had been carved into a kneeling female figure sinking a hoe into the back of a serpent. The serpent's tail climbs up the woman's back, bearing squash and gourds like a vine. The images echo familiar pre-Columbian themes of reproductive and agricultural fertility. As similar figures were discovered in the Cahokian environs, a pattern emerged. Around A.D 1100, Emerson says, the elite of Cahokia seem to have co-opted or codified the fertility symbol, raising it to an unprecedented stature that became a kind of brand identity for the budding metropolis. "They're taking a symbolism that exists across the entire hemisphere and selectively emphasizing parts of it to their own benefit," Emerson says.

Some archaeologists have taken the emphasis on the bucolic feminine as a sign that Cahokian society was peaceful, egalitarian, and possibly matriarchal. There is, in fact, no evidence that the city was ever invaded, and no indication of bellicose tendencies other than the robust stockade surrounding the city center. But Emerson warns against this interpretation. For one thing, he says, war wasn't necessary, because it would have been clear from the city's size alone that it could mount raiding parties with more members than the total of men, women, and children in any of the surrounding villages. "Nobody could stand against Cahokia. I don't know that they had to do much actual conflict. It was mostly intimidation."

Cahokia's downfall has been blamed on a variety of culprits. A corn-based, protein-poor diet might have sent urban dwellers west in search of buffalo. A centuries-long cold spell could have crippled the region's agricultural productivity. Deforestation of the uplands would have choked downstream water supplies with silt and exacerbated flooding. Or the cause could have been those same intangibles invoked by latter-day theorists to describe Cahokia's rise: a shift in belief systems or the balance of power. Certainly the sprawling pacts that Cahokian chiefs may have forged with nearby villages would have challenged any lasting centralization of power.

"The typical life history of a chiefdom is that it comes together, it has its heyday, and it falls apart, all within a couple of generations," says Emerson. "The interesting thing about Cahokia is that it managed to hang together. The fact that it didn't go on forever isn't unusual at all."

One of Cahokia's chiefs appears to be buried in Mound 72, which lies a half mile south of Monks Mound. It is a modest hillock by comparison, but the site holds far grimmer implications about Cahokian society. During excavations there in the late 1960s, Melvin Fowler of the University of Wisconsin at Milwaukee uncovered the remains of more than 250 people. One middle-aged male had been laid on a shelf of 20,000 seashell beads arranged in the shape of a bird. Near him were the bones of six other people, a cache of more than 800 flint arrowheads, a rolled-up sheet of copper, and several bushels of unprocessed mica—all seemingly placed in tribute to the Beaded Birdman.

In other parts of the mound, skeletons of more than 100 young women clearly indicate human sacrifice, and another grouping of four men with no hands or heads denotes the same. Another 40 bodies seemed to have been tossed into a grave haphazardly. Other mass burials in Mound 72 show varying degrees of respect and carelessness—and seem to reflect some sort of social hierarchy as yet undeciphered. Human sacrifice, for example, can be a sign of a coercive society or of a cult-like mentality. "Mound 72 is an ancient text with its own set of Rosetta stones and is slow to give up its secrets," Fowler wrote in *Cahokia,* a book he coauthored with Biloine Whiting Young.

The cause of Cahokia's demise is no more certain, but at least one expert links it to the Toltec civilization of south-central Mexico some 1,400 miles away. Although no Mexican artifacts have ever been found at Cahokia, similarities in the monumental and ornamental styles are conspicuous—and far from accidental, according to anthropologist Stephen Lekson of the University of Colorado at Boulder. Lekson and anthropologist Peter Peregrine of Lawrence University in Wisconsin believe that the mound cultures of the American East, the pueblo cultures of the American Southwest, and the pyramid cultures of the Mexican highlands were not only familiar but possibly even integrated with one another. There's plenty of evidence for such an exchange at Chaco Canyon, where copper bells, macaw feathers, pyrite mirrors, and other Mexican goods turn up. But Chaco was a wannabe compared with Cahokia—much smaller, far less populous, and without a centuries-long tradition preceding its development. Cahokia, with its central location, entrenched culture, and extensive trade network, didn't need Mexican trinkets to bolster its stature, Lekson says. "If someone from Cahokia showed up in any major town in Mexico, he'd be taken seriously," says Lekson. "But if someone from Chaco wandered in, they'd ask him if he had an appointment."

The Toltec, Chaco, and Cahokian societies all collapsed at very nearly the same moment, and Lekson believes that that, too, is no accident. Events in Mexico may have rippled up the Gulf Coast to the Mississippi and thence to Cahokia. "I'm not saying that Mexico is pulling everybody's strings," says Lekson. "But [the cultures] are more alike than not, and it's interesting to ask why."

Interesting as it might be, a continental perspective doesn't yield an explanation, because no one's sure what caused the Toltec regime to fall, either. It may be that if scientists ever determine why Cahokia fell, they may be able to help explain what happened elsewhere in the Americas. At present it's still anyone's guess. "We are telling stories that will fall apart in the future," says Pauketat. "But we can't ignore the evidence, either. You could make the mistake of saying this is a coercive society, based on Mound 72. Or you could look at the outlying villages and say, 'This is a peaceful community.' They must have *wanted* to build Cahokia. The truth may be somewhere in between. We don't really know what happened here."

Critical Thinking

1. Why is Cahokia on a par with the other World Heritage Sites?
2. What is it that archaeologists still don't understand about it?

3. Why does the author describe Cahokia as a "complex, sophisticated society" that "no one could have missed a thousand years ago"?
4. Why is it still unknown as to why Cahokia crumbled and its people vanished?
5. Why is it difficult to lure archaeologists there?
6. Why is economic development a concern?
7. What is the significance of the woodhenge?
8. What are the implications regarding the amount of work devoted to building Cahokia?
9. Why might migrants have come to Cahokia? Why are these theories insufficient, according to the author?
10. What do archaeologists Pauketat, Kelly, and Emerson suggest as an explanation? Why is George Milner skeptical of these views?
11. What "pattern emerged" with respect to the female figurines? How can this be variously interpreted?
12. What theories have been put forth regarding Cahokia's downfall?
13. What seems to be the significance of the burials?
14. Why does there seem to be a connection to the Toltecs of Mexico, which might help to explain Cahokia's downfall? Why would there still be no explanation even if there were a connection?
15. Why is it still as easy to say that Cahokia was peaceful as it is to say that it was a coercive society?

Create Central

www.mhhe.com/createcentral

Internet References

Cahokia Mounds
http://cahokiamounds.org

Society for American Archaeology
www.saa.org

Copyright © 2004 by Karen Wright. This article originally appeared in *Discover*.

Article

Prepared by: Mari Pritchard Parker, *Pasadena City College* and
Elvio Angeloni, *Pasadena City College*

A Coprological View of Ancestral Pueblo Cannibalism

Debate over a single fecal fossil offers a cautionary tale of the interplay between science and culture.

KARL J. REINHARD

Learning Outcomes

After reading this article, you will be able to:

- Discuss the importance of finding coprolites in an ancient archaeological site.
- Discuss the ways in which the Ancestral Pueblo people were adapted to their environment and whether or not their adaptation included cannibalism.
- Evaluate the pros and cons of Ancestral Pueblo cannibalism.

As the object of my scientific study, I've chosen coprolites. It's not a common choice, but to a paleonutritionist and archaeoparasitologist, a coprolite—a sample of ancient feces preserved by mineralization or simple drying—is a scientific bonanza. Analysis of coprolites can shed light on both the nutrition of and parasites found in prehistoric cultures. Dietary reconstructions from the analysis of coprolites can inform us about, for example, the origins of modern Native American diabetes. With regard to parasitology; coprolites hold information about the ancient emergence and spread of human infectious disease. Most sensational, however, is the recent role of coprolite analysis in debates about cannibalism.

Most Americans know the people who lived on the Colorado Plateau from 1200 B.C. onward as the Anasazi, a Navajo (or Dine) word. The modern Pueblo people in Arizona and New Mexico, who are their direct descendants, prefer the description Ancestral Pueblo or Old Ones. Because the image of this modern culture could be tainted by the characterization of their ancestors, it's especially important that archaeologists and physical anthropologists come to the correct conclusion about cannibalism. This is the story of my involvement in that effort.

When a coprolite arrived in my laboratory for analysis in 1997, I didn't imagine that it would become one of the most contentious finds in archaeological history. Banks Leonard, the Soil Systems archaeologist who directed excavation of the site at Cowboy Wash, Utah, explained to me that there was evidence of unusual dietary activity by the prehistoric individual who deposited the coprolite. He or she was possibly a cannibal.

I had been aware of the cannibalism controversy for a number of years, and I was interested in evaluating evidence of such activity. But from my scientific perspective, it was simply another sample that would provide a few more data points in my reconstruction of ancient diet from a part of the Ancestral Pueblo region that was unknown to me.

The appearance of the coprolite was unremarkable—in fact, it was actually a little disappointing. It looked like a plain cylinder of tan dirt with no obvious macrofossils or visible dietary inclusions. I have analyzed hundreds of Ancestral and pre-Ancestral Pueblo coprolites that were more interesting. Indeed, I have surveyed tens of thousands more that, to my experienced eye, held greater scientific promise. Yet this one coprolite, when news of it hit the media, undid 20 years of my research on the Ancestral Pueblo diet. On a broader scale, it caused the archaeological community to rethink our perception of the nature of this prehistoric culture and to question what is reasonable scientific proof.

Cannibalism, Without Question

In the arid environment of the U.S. Southwest, feces dried in ancient times provide a 9,000-year record of gastronomic traditions. This record allows me and a few other thick-skinned researchers to trace dietary history in the deserts. (I say "thick-skinned," because analysts generally don't last long in this specialty. Many have done one coprolite study, only to move on to a more socially acceptable archaeological specialty.)

From the mid-1980s to the mid-'90s, I had characterized the Ancestral Pueblo lifestyle as a combination of hunting and gathering mixed with agriculture based on the analysis of about 500 coprolites from half a dozen sites. Before me, Gary Fry, then at Youngstown State University, had come to the same conclusion in work he published during the '70s and '80s, based on the analysis of a large number of Ancestral Pueblo coprolites from many sites. These people were finely attuned to the diverse and complicated habitats of the Colorado Plateau for plant gathering, as well as for plant cultivation. The Ancestral Pueblo certainly ate meat—many kinds of meat—but never had there been any indication of cannibalism in any coprolite analysis from any site.

The evidence for cannibalism at Cowboy Wash has been widely published. A small number of people were undoubtedly killed, disarticulated and their flesh exposed to heat and boiling. This took place in a pit house typical of the Ancestral Pueblo circa 1200 A.D. At the time of the killings, the appearance of the pit house must have been appallingly gruesome. Human blood residue was found on stone tools, and I imagine that the disarticulation of the corpses must have left a horrifying splatter of blood around the room. But the most conclusive evidence of cannibalism did not come from the room where the corpses were dismembered. It came from a nearby room where someone had defecated on the hearth around the time that the killings took place. The feces was preserved as a coprolite and would turn out to be the conclusive evidence of cannibalism.

My analysis of the coprolite was not momentous. I could determine from its general morphology that it was indeed from a human being. However, the tiny fragment that I rehydrated and examined by several microscopic techniques contained none of the typical plant foods eaten by the Ancestral Pueblo. Background pollen of the sort that would have been inhaled or drunk was the only plant residue that I found. Thus, I concluded that the coprolite did not represent normal Ancestral Pueblo diet. It seemed to represent a purely meat meal, something that is unheard of from Ancestral Pueblo coprolite analyses.

After analyzing the Cowboy Wash coprolite, I took a half-year sabbatical as a Fulbright scholar in Brazil. When I returned, I learned that my analysis had been superseded by a new technology. Richard Marlar from the University of Colorado School of Medicine and colleagues had taken over direct analysis of the coprolite using an enzyme-linked immunosorbent assay to detect human myoglobin, and their work had confirmed and expanded my analysis. The coprolite was from a human who had eaten another human. The technical paper appeared in *Nature* and was followed by articles in the *New Yorker, Discover, Southwestern Lore* and the *Smithsonian*, among many others. The articles became the focus of a veritable explosion of media pieces in the press, on radio and television, and on the Internet, amounting to an absolute attack on Ancestral Pueblo culture.

Initially, I sat and watched the media feeding frenzy and Internet chat debates with a sense of awe and post-sabbatical detachment. My original report suggesting the coprolite was not of Ancestral Pueblo origin went largely unnoticed. The few journalists who did call me for an opinion proved uninterested in publishing it. In some cases it was too far to fly to Nebraska to film; in others my opinion didn't fit into the context of the debate. Well, I have looked at more Ancestral Pueblo feces than any other human being, and I do have an opinion: The Ancestral Pueblo were not cannibalistic. Cannibalism just doesn't make sense as a pattern of diet for people so exquisitely adapted to droughts by centuries of hunting-gathering traditions and agricultural innovation.

Then a media quote knocked me out of my stupor. Arizona State University anthropologist (emeritus) Christy G. Turner II, commenting in an interview about a book he co-authored on Ancestral Pueblo cannibalism, said, "I'm the guy who brought down the Anasazi." Perhaps to temper Turner's broad generalization, Brian Billman (a coauthor of the Marlar *Nature* paper) of the University of North Carolina at Chapel Hill, suggested that a period of drought brought on emergency conditions that resulted in cannibalism. Beyond the scientific quibbling about who ate whom and why, I am amazed at the vortex of debate around the Coyote Wash coprolite. The furor over that one coprolite represents a new way of thinking about the Ancestral Pueblo and archaeological evidence.

What Did the Ancestral Pueblo Eat?

To me, a specialist in Ancestral Pueblo diet, neither Turner's nor Billman's explanation made sense. So, in the years since the *Nature* paper appeared in 2000, I have renewed my analyses of Ancestral Pueblo coprolites to understand just what they did eat in times of drought. And let me say emphatically that Ancestral Pueblo coprolites are not composed of the flesh of their human victims. Some of their dietary practices were, perhaps, peculiar. I still recall in wonderment the inch-diameter deer vertebral centrum that I found in one sample. It was swallowed whole. The consumption of insects, snakes and lizards brought the Ancestral Pueblo notice in the children's book *It Was Disgusting and I Ate It*. But looking beyond such peculiarities, their diet was delightfully diverse and testifies to the human ability to survive in the most extreme environments. To me, diet is one of the most fundamental bases of civilization, and the Ancestral Pueblo possessed a complicated cuisine. They were gastronomically civilized.

Widespread analysis of coprolites by "paleoscatologists" began in the 1960s and culminated in the '70s and '80s when graduate students worked staunchly on their coprological theses and dissertations. From Washington State University to Northern Arizona University to Texas A & M and many more, Ancestral Pueblo coprolites were rehydrated, screened, centrifuged and analyzed. Richard Hevly, Glenna Williams-Dean, John Jones, Mark Stiger, Linda Scott-Cummings, Kate Aasen, Gary Fry, Karen Clary, Molly Toll and Vaughn Bryant, Jr., to name a few, joined me in puzzling over Ancestral Pueblo culinary habits. In their conscientious and rigorous research, the same general theme emerged. The Ancestral Pueblo were very well adapted to the environment, both in times of feast and in times of famine.

In general, the Ancestral Pueblo diet was the culmination of a long period of victual tradition that began around 9,000 years ago, when people on the Colorado Plateau gave up hunting big animals and started collecting plants and hunting smaller animals. Prickly pear cactus, yucca, grain from dropseed grass, seeds from goosefoot and foods from 15 other wild plants dominated pre-Ancestral Pueblo life. One of the truly interesting dietary patterns that emerged in the early time and continued through the Ancestral Pueblo culture was the consumption of pollen-rich foods. Cactus and yucca buds and other flowers were the sources of this pollen. Rabbit viscera probably provided a source of fungal spores of the genus *Endogane*, although I doubt that these people knew they were eating the spores when they ate the rabbits. The pre-Ancestral Pueblo people adapted to starvation from seasonal food shortages by eating yucca leaf bases and prickly pear pads and the few other plants that were available in such lean times.

Prey for the pre-Ancestral Pueblo people included small animals such as rabbits, lizards, mice and insects. In fact, most pre-Ancestral Pueblo coprolites contain the remains of small animals. My analysis of these remains shows that small animals, especially rabbits and mice, were a major source of protein in summer and winter, good times and bad.

The Ancestral Pueblo *per se* descended from this hunter-gatherer tradition. Coprolite analysis shows that they were largely vegetarian, and plant foods of some sort are present in every Ancestral Pueblo coprolite I have analyzed. But these later people also expanded on their predecessors' cuisine. They cultivated maize, squash and eventually beans. Yet they continued to collect a wide diversity of wild plants. They actually ate more species of wild plants—more than 50—than their ancestors who were totally dependent on wild species.

Adapting to the Environment

In 1992, I presented a series of hypotheses addressing why the Ancient Pueblo ate so many species of wild plants. Later, Mark Stiger of Western State College and I went to work on the problem using a statistical method that he devised. We determined that the Ancestral Pueblo encouraged the growth of edible weedy species in the disturbances caused by cultivation and village life. In doing so, they increased the spectrum of wild edible plants available to them, often using them to spice cultivated plants. Rocky Mountain beeweed, purslane and groundcherry were especially important in conjunction with maize. Corn smut was another important condiment. In fact, maize, purslane, beeweed and corn smut appear as the earliest components of a distinct cuisine in the earliest Ancestral Pueblo coprolites I have analyzed, from Turkey Pen Cave, Utah. These coprolites are about 1,500 years old. The maize-beeweed-corn smut-purslane association remained a central feature of Ancestral Pueblo cuisine at most sites to the latest periods of the culture. Importantly, they also ate wild plants to offset seasonal shortages, especially in winter when their stores of cultivated food were exhausted. Thus, retaining a diverse array of wild plants in the mix helped them adapt to food shortages.

Paul Minnis of the University of Oklahoma applied a different statistical test to address a different problem. He analyzed coprolite findings from Arizona, New Mexico, Utah and Colorado to see if people in different regions had distinct dietary traditions. Paul showed that the Ancient Pueblo adapted to the environmental variability of the Colorado Plateau by adjusting their agricultural, hunting and gathering habits to the natural resources available. Ancient Pueblo from Glen Canyon, Utah, had a slightly different dietary tradition from those of Inscription House, Arizona; those of Mesa Verde, Colorado; and those of Chaco Canyon, New Mexico. Later, in separate work, he identified how these people adapted to bad times. He found that the Ancestral Pueblo had "starvation foods," such as yucca and prickly pear, to get through poor times. These were a legacy from their hunter-gatherer ancestors.

Sometimes Ancestral Pueblo groups developed dietary traditions that required trade or foraging in areas remote from their home. Sara LeRoy-Toren, with the Lincoln High School Science Focus Program, and I are analyzing coprolites from Salmon Ruin, which was built along the San Juan River between the modern towns of Farmington and Bloomfield, New Mexico. It was abandoned by its original occupants and reoccupied by people from the San Juan River Valley. Our analysis is from the San Juan occupation, which was generally a time of abundance for both agriculture and gathered foods.

These coprolites reflect the Ancestral Pueblo tradition and contain juniper berries and cactus buds from areas local to the site, but they also contain piñon nuts that must have been harvested some miles away. We also calculated the number of pollen grains per gram of Salmon Ruin coprolites and found both maize and beeweed pollen in quantities as large as millions of grains per gram. Importantly, the maize pollen is shredded in a manner consistent with pollen eaten in corn meal, so maize was eaten both fresh off the cob and in the form of stored flour, although most of the macroscopic remains from Salmon Ruin are in the ground form.

One of my former graduate students, Dennis Danielson, now at the Central Identification Laboratory at the Joint POW/MIA Accounting Command, found phytoliths—microscopic crystals produced in plant cells—in the Salmon Ruin coprolites. More than half of the Salmon Ruin coprolites contain phytoliths from yucca-type plants and cactus, a legacy of pre-Ancestral Pueblo gathering adaptation to the desert. Denny eventually found phytoliths from these wild plants in coprolites from other Ancestral Pueblo sites. These gathered plants predominated in his analyses and reaffirmed that the Ancestral Pueblo could adapt to drought by turning to edible desert plants that were adapted to extremely dry conditions.

But were these plants actually what the Ancestral Pueblo ate in times of drought, rather than just a routine part of their diet? Denny and I analyzed coprolites from the last occupation of Antelope House in Canyon de Chelly, Arizona. All archaeological, climatological and biological analyses indicate that the last occupation was a time of ecological collapse. The level of anemia in skeletons from this time and region is the highest known among the Ancestral Pueblo. Archaeological surveys show that the mesas around the canyon were abandoned as people moved into the canyon to have access to water. The levels of parasitism, especially with crowd diseases, elevated; parasites were present in one-quarter of the 180 Antelope House coprolites I studied.

The coprolites at Antelope House record the adaptation to this environmental collapse and drought. Phytoliths from prickly pear and yucca leaf bases were present in 92 percent of the coprolites. The Ancestral Pueblo at Antelope House had clearly resorted to reliance on desert starvation foods. Yet their diet still lacked desperate monotony, as they ate wild plants from moist areas. Pollen occurs at concentrations in the hundreds of thousands to tens of millions of pollen grains per gram in the Antelope House coprolites. The main sources of pollen and spores were cattail, horsetail, beeweed and maize, but the diet at Antelope House included the greatest diversity of wild plants—27 species—ever recorded in Ancestral Pueblo coprolite studies. By contrast, only 16 wild species were identified in Salmon Ruin coprolites.

As for meat, my colleagues Mark Sutton, with California State University, Bakersfield, and Richard Marlar have found chemical signals in Ancestral Pueblo coprolites of bighorn sheep, rabbits, dogs and rodents. But as for cannibalism, Richard looked for human muscle indicators in the Salmon Ruin coprolites and found none. At Antelope House, Mark found protein residue of rabbit, rodents, dog, big horn sheep and pronghorn. There were also human protein residues present, but they were from intestinal cells shed by the body. The Ancestral Pueblo at Antelope House suffered parasitism from hookworms and hookworm-like organisms that would have resulted in excess shedding of intestinal cells. In fact, one Antelope House coprolite I analyzed was a mass of excreted parasitic worms mixed with seeds. Stable carbon and stable-nitrogen isotope analyses of the bones of these people from many sites indicate that, although they did eat meat, they were 70 percent herbivorous.

Every coprolite researcher who has worked with Ancestral Pueblo material has found animal bone. Kristin Sobolik of the University of Maine has shown that these people ate a particularly large number of lizard- and mouse-sized animals. This reliance on small animals was a remarkable adaptation to the Southwestern deserts, where small animals are most numerous and therefore a reliable source of protein—something the Ancestral Pueblo relied on feast or famine, just as their predecessors had.

Life on the Edge

Compared with other agricultural traditions I have studied in other parts of the world, the Ancestral Pueblo were rarely far from agricultural failure. My students and I have examined coprolites from the most primitive and advanced cultures in the Andes, from the earliest Chinchorros to the latest Incas. In the Andes, too, there is a long history of hunting and gathering that preceded agriculture. Once agriculture was established, however, 90 percent of the food species of Andean peoples were cultivated. This stands in meaningful contrast to the Ancestral Pueblo, whose food species remained predominantly wild. I think this is because they were on the very northern fringe of the region conducive to agriculture and couldn't rely on consistent productivity of their cultivated plots from year to year. Therefore, they maintained the hunter-gatherer dietary traditions to supplement, or replace if necessary, cultivated plants. Complete caloric dependence on cultivated plants, as took place in the Andes, was simply impossible for the Ancestral Pueblo.

Furthermore, these people often survived times of drought without cultural perturbations such as cannibalism. In my experience, the most poignant example of drought adaptation was seen in the analysis of a partially mummified child from Glen Canyon, Arizona. The child was buried during a long drought period, from 1210 to 1260 A.D. Archaeologist Steve Dominguez of the Midwest Archaeological Center directed the analysis of many specialists including myself and my students, Danielson and Kari Sandness. Burial offerings included a wide variety of ceramic, gourd and basketry artifacts. Compared with burial goods of other Ancestral Pueblo, these were consistent with those of average-status individuals. The drought did not disrupt the standard burial traditions for this three-to-four-year-old, yet x-rays showed that this child survived seven episodes of starvation. The cause of death is unknown for this otherwise healthy child.

Analysis of the intestinal contents of the child provided insights into adaptation to drought. About 20 coprolites were excavated, and all of them were composed of a wild grass known as "rice grass." In the absence of cultivated foods, the child was provided with an alternative, and equally nutritious, wild food. Dominguez summarized the findings from the research succinctly:

> Investigations in nearby areas indicate that this was a period of environmental degradation and that Anasazi populations may have experienced nutritional stress or other consequent forms of physiological stress. Studies of both prehistoric populations and living populations suggest that a number of methods were employed to support individuals through periods of stress, and to promote the well-being of the group.

Was the Cannibal Ancestral Pueblo?

Work by numerous investigators thus shows that the Ancestral Pueblo possessed remarkable ecological adaptability; if they resorted to cannibalism because of environmental stress, it was a highly atypical response. Further, burial excavations demonstrate that they maintained their traditions even in times of drought. Besides, beyond a single sample, hundreds of coprolite analyses find not even a hint of cannibalism. Overwhelmingly, the Ancestral Pueblo were primarily herbivorous. Why, then, does one coprolite from the northern reaches of the Ancestral Pueblo domain come to characterize an entire culture? A number of researchers were incredulous at the hysteria created by the Cowboy Wash cannibal coprolite. Vaughn Bryant, Jr., at Texas A & M, e-mailed his disbelief to our small specialist community. From his experience in the study of Western diets, cannibalism was simply not plausible. Karen Clary, with the University of Texas at Austin, also e-mailed her concerns with the findings as well as with the unbridled sensationalism.

Both coprolite and skeletal evidence examined by Utah State University bio-archaeologist Patricia Lambert do show that Ancestral Pueblo of Cowboy Wash were victims of violence and cannibalism—there's little question about it. But that doesn't mean that the cannibal(s) were Ancestral Pueblo. Mark

Sutton and I found that these people invariably ate plant foods when they ate meat; it was a feature of their cuisine. The complete lack of plant matter in the Cowboy Wash coprolite tells me that it was not from an individual who observed the Ancestral Pueblo dietary tradition. To date, none of the principal investigators involved in the Cowboy Wash analysis have implicated residents or even Ancestral Pueblo from another location as the perpetrators of the violence. In short, I don't know who killed and ate the residents of Cowboy Wash, but I am sure the cannibal wasn't an Ancestral Pueblo.

The Peaceful People Concept

Christy Turner's quote in the popular media puzzled me. Why would anyone want to bring down an ancient culture, especially Turner, whose work is characterized by attention to detail, meticulous analytical procedures and, most of all, accumulation of mountains of data to support his conclusions? One of my most striking memories of any scientist was an afternoon chat I had with Turner regarding his work with dental traits to trace migrations to the New World. His office was packed with neat columns of computer printouts from data collected from thousands of skulls. That same afternoon, the conversation turned to his study of cannibalism. I asked him specifics about his methods and found that he approached this area of research with the same exhaustive thoroughness he applied to his dental work. At no time did he indicate that he intended to "bring down the Anasazi."

Then I read the book that Turner cowrote, *Man Corn,* and I realized that it was not the Ancestral Pueblo culture that he brought down. He was after our archaeological biases in how we reconstruct the nature of Ancestral Pueblo culture. To understand how that one coprolite came to be considered ironclad evidence of cannibalism among the Ancestral Pueblo, it's necessary to understand how these people have been characterized by anthropologists and archaeologists at various times over the past 50 or so years.

The view of the Ancestral Pueblo as peaceful people took root in the 1960s and '70s. Earlier work had shown that violence, and perhaps even cannibalism, had taken place among the Ancestral Pueblo. But in the '60s and '70s—a time of social volatility, seemingly suffused in the violence of combat and revolt—modern American culture was searching for examples of nonviolent social systems. Academia sought out paradigms of peacefulness from other regions, other times and even other species. The Ancestral Pueblo became one of those "paragons of peace," as did the San Bushmen and wild chimpanzees. Elizabeth Marshall Thomas published her book about the bushmen, *The Harmless People,* in 1959, and anthropologists took to highlighting the nonviolence of hunter-gatherers. This was when the "New Archaeology" emerged as a replacement for previous approaches. Students were discouraged from reading archaeological research that dated from before 1960; thus the earlier work that described evidence of violence was ignored.

Excavations during the 1970s were very counter-cultural in appearance and philosophy. Scholarly excavation camps often had the flavor of hippie communes. In that atmosphere, evidence of violence was largely dismissed both in the field and during the analysis phase. I recall participating in three excavations in which houses had burned and people perished within them. This seemed like pretty good evidence that all was not tranquil with the peaceful people, but such fires were explained as accidental. Once, when we discovered arrow points in a skeleton in a burned house, the evidence of violence was not deemed conclusive because the arrow points had not penetrated bone. At the time, I wondered whether we were being a little too quick to dismiss the possibility of violence; the alternative was that these people were remarkably negligent with their hearths and weapons. I began to think of the Ancestral Pueblo as peaceful but fatally accident prone.

Those claiming evidence of cannibalism among ancient American cultures were excluded from presenting their findings at the Pecos Conference, the regional meeting for Southwestern archaeologists. This caused quite a furor. A symposium on the subject of violence and cannibalism had been scheduled for the meeting, and the participants arrived, but the symposium was canceled at the last minute. In 20 years of participating in scientific meetings, this is the only instance I can recall of a scheduled event being canceled for purely political reasons.

In the '80s and '90s, the paragons of peaceful society began to fall—and fall in a big way. First, violence was acknowledged among the Maya, held as the Mesoamerican counterweight to the undoubtedly violent and cannibalistic Aztec prior to ascendance of the peaceful people. Violence and cannibalism were then documented among wild chimpanzees, the behavioral analogues to ancestral human beings. The evidence of conflict among the Ancestral Pueblo became so overwhelming that it was the focus of a 1995 Society of American Archaeology symposium, the proceedings of which were published in the book, *Deciphering Anasazi Violence*. The Ancestral Pueblo cannibalism argument was formalized in University of California, Berkeley anthropologist Tim White's 1992 book *Prehistoric Cannibalism at Mancos 5Mtumr2346*. In each case, physical anthropology alone, or in combination with scientific archaeology, brought down the peaceful paradigm with the weight of scientific evidence. Turner produced much of that evidence.

Cannibalism at Other Sites?

In *Man Corn,* Turner carefully stated that he thought the Ancestral Pueblo were victims of terrorism imposed on them by a more violent and cannibalistic culture. The book reviews skeletal evidence of violence at more than 76 sites in the Ancestral Pueblo region. He believes that violence and cannibalism were introduced by migrants from central Mexico, where there is a long tradition of violence, human sacrifice and cannibalism.

Of the sites Turner discusses, I have first-hand experience with one, Salmon Ruin, where I spent three seasons excavating and later reconstructing the parasite ecology and diet of this large pueblo's occupants as part of my thesis and dissertation research. He focuses on a high structure called a kiva at the center of the three-story pueblo. Initially it was thought that the bodies of two adults and 35 children were burned in the tower kiva. His analysis indicates that these bodies were disarticulated and cannibalized. However, there are other interpretations.

In 1977, I discussed the tower kiva finds with the excavation director, the late Cynthia Irwin-Williams, who was then with Eastern New Mexico State University. She believed that the children were sent to the highest place in the pueblo with two adults when the structure caught fire. As the fire went out of control, they were trapped there.

Another explanation was offered to me by Larry Baker, director of the Salmon Ruin Museum. He told me that a new analysis of the bones showed that the people in the tower kiva were long dead when their bodies burned. Furthermore, there is evidence in the burned bones that the bodies had at least partly decomposed. It may be that the bodies were placed in the tower as part of a mortuary custom after the pueblo was abandoned. When the pueblo burned, so did the bodies.

More recently, Nancy Akins, with the Museum of New Mexico, reanalyzed the human remains and stratigraphy of the tower kiva. She found that only 20 children and 4 adults were represented. Some of the bodies were deliberately cremated and others partially burned. Some remains showed that the bodies were dry before they were burned. This analysis suggests a complex series of mortuary events preceding the burning of the tower kiva and surrounding rooms. Analysis of the stratigraphy shows that they were not burned simultaneously but were deposited in different episodes. In this view, the evidence suggests a previously unknown mortuary practice rather than trauma and cannibalism.

I conclude that when analyzing the remains of the Ancestral Pueblo, it is important to consider that recent work shows that their mortuary practices were more complicated than we previously thought—and that complex mortuary practices should come as no surprise and constitute ambiguous evidence. Prehistoric people in Chile, the Chinchorros, not only disarticulated the dead, but also rearticulated the cleaned bones in vegetation and clay "statues." In Nebraska, disarticulation and burning of bones was done as a part of mortuary ritual. Closer to the Ancestral Pueblo, the Sinagua culture of central Arizona cremated their dead. Thus disarticulated skeletal remains and burning fall short of proving cannibalism.

What We Can Learn

Because the members of extinct cultures cannot speak for themselves, the nature of cultural reconstruction easily becomes colored by the projections of the archaeological community and the inclination of the media to oversimplify or even sensationalize. The Ancestral Pueblo, once thought to be peaceful, have now become, especially in the lay mind, violent cannibals. Neither depiction is fair. They had a level of violence typical of most human populations—present but not excessive. Is that really so surprising?

Perhaps more astonishing is how unquestioning our culture can be in tearing down its icons. Much as we scientists may prefer to stick to the field or the laboratory, shunning the bright lights, we bear a responsibility to present our data in a way that reduces the opportunity for exaggeration. Our findings must be qualified in the context of alternative explanations. As such, the Cowboy Wash coprolite offers us a cautionary tale.

Bibliography

Billman, B. R., P. M. Lambert and L. B. Leonard. 2000. Cannibalism, warfare, and drought in the Mesa Verde Region during the Twelfth Century A.D. *American Antiquity* 65:145–178.

Bryant, V. M., Jr., and G. Williams-Dean. 1975. The coprolites of man. *Scientific American* 232:100–109.

Dongoske, K. K., D. L. Martin and T. J. Ferguson. 2000. Critique of the claim of cannibalism at Cowboy Wash. *American Antiquity* 65:179–190.

Fry, G. F. 1980. Prehistoric diet and parasites in the desert west of North America. In: *Early Native Americans*, ed. F. L. Browman. The Hague: Mouton Press, pp. 325–339.

Fry, G. F., and H. J. Hall. 1986. Human coprolites. In: *Archaeological Investigations at Antelope House*, ed. D. P. Morris. Washington, D. C.: U.S. Government Printing Office, pp. 165–188.

Lambert, P. M., L. B. Leonard, B. R. Billman, R. A. Marlar, M. E. Newman and K. J. Reinhard. 2000. Response to the critique of the claim of cannibalism at Cowboy Wash. *American Antiquity* 65:397–406.

Marlar, R., B. Billman, B. Leonard, P. Lambert and K. Reinhard. 2000. Fecal evidence of cannibalism. *Southwestern Lore* 4:14–22.

Reinhard, K. J. 1992. Patterns of diet, parasitism, anemia in prehistoric west North American. In: *Diet, Demography, and Disease: Changing Perspectives on Anemia*, ed. P. Stuart-Macadann and S. Kent. New York: Aldine de Gruyter, pp. 219–258.

Reinhard, K. J., and V. M. Bryant, Jr. 1992a. Coprolite analysis: A biological perspective on archaeology. In: *Advances in Archaeological Method and Theory 4*, ed. M. D. Schiffer. Tucson: University of Arizona Press, pp. 245–288.

Reinhard, K. J., and D. R. Danielson. 2005. Pervasiveness of phytoliths in prehistoric southwestern diet and implications for regional and temporal trends for dental mircowear. *Journal of Archaeological Science* 32:981–988.

Scott, L. 1979. Dietary inferences from Hoy House coprolites: A palynological interpretation. *The Kiva* 44:257–281.

Sobolik, K. 1993. Direct evidence for the importance of small animals to prehistoric diets: A review of coprolite studies. *North American Archaeologist* 14:227–243.

Sutton, M. Q., and K. J. Reinhard, 1995. Cluster analysis of coprolites from Antelope House:. Implications for Anasazi diet and culture. *Journal of Archaeological Science* 22:741–750.

Critical Thinking

1. What is a coprolite? What can we learn from analyses of coprolites?

2. What is the evidence for cannibalism at Cowboy Wash? What did the author's analysis of the coprolite show?

3. What part of the author's report went largely unnoticed by the media? What is the author's opinion about Ancestral Pueblo cannibalism?

4. How does the author describe the Ancestral Pueblo diet?

5. How were "starvation foods" important?

6. How does the author describe the health and diet of the Ancestral Pueblo at the time of the last occupation in Canyon de Chelly? What about cannibalism at this time?

7. How does the author compare and contrast Ancestral Pueblo agriculture with that of the Andes?
8. How did the analysis of the partially mummified child serve as an example of drought adaptation?
9. How does the author answer the question of cannibalism among the Ancestral Pueblo people?
10. How did the author come to understand the Christy Turner intention to "bring down the Anasazi"?
11. Be familiar with the rise and fall of the "peaceful people" concept.
12. How might disarticulated bones be interpreted in other ways than as cannibalism?

Create Central

www.mhhe.com/createcentral

Internet References

Anthropology, Archaeology, and American Indian Sites on the Internet
http://dizzy.library.arizona.edu/library/teams/sst/anthro

Society for American Archaeology
www.saa.org

Zeno's Forensic Page
http://forensic.to/forensic.html

KARL J. REINHARD is a professor in the School of Natural Resources at the University of Nebraska and a Fulbright Commission Senior Specialist in Archaeology for 2004–2009. The main focus of his career since earning his PhD. from Texas A&M has been to find explanations for modern patterns of disease in the archaeological and historic record. He also developed a new specialization called archaeoparasitology, which attempts to understand the evolution of parasitic disease.

Reinhard, Karl J. From *American Scientist*, May/June 2006, pp. 254–261. Copyright © 2006 by American Scientist, magazine of Sigma Xi, The Scientific Research Society. Reprinted by permission.

Article

Prepared by: Mari Pritchard Parker, *Pasadena City College* and Elvio Angeloni, *Pasadena City College*

Beer and Bling in Iron Age Europe

If you wanted to get ahead in Iron-Age Central Europe you would use a strategy that still works today—dress to impress and throw parties with free alcohol.

Learning Outcomes

After reading this article, you will be able to:

- Discuss the relationship between beverage choice and social status among the ancient Celts.
- Discuss the relationship between clothing and social status among the ancient Celts.

Pre-Roman Celtic people practiced what archaeologist Bettina Arnold calls "competitive feasting," in which people vying for social and political status tried to outdo one another through power partying. Artifacts recovered from two 2,600-year-old Celtic burial mounds in southwest Germany, including items for personal adornment and vessels for alcohol, offer a glimpse of how these people lived in a time before written records were kept.

That was the aim of the more than 10-year research project, says Arnold, anthropology professor at the University of Wisconsin-Milwaukee and co-director of a field excavation at the Heuneburg hillfort in the German state of Baden-Wurttemberg. The work was partially funded by the National Geographic Society and Arnold collaborated with the State Monuments Office in Tübingen, Germany.

In fact, based on the drinking vessels found in graves near the hillfort settlement and other imported objects, archaeologists have concluded the central European Celts were trading with people from around the Mediterranean.

Bräu or Mead?

"Beer was the barbarian's beverage, while wine was more for the elite, especially if you lived near a trade route," says Kevin Cullen, an archaeology project associate at Discovery World in Milwaukee and a former graduate student of Arnold's.

Since grapes had not yet been introduced to central Europe, imported grape wine would indicated the most social status.

The Celts also made their own honey-based wine, or mead, flavored with herbs and flowers, that would have been more expensive than beer, but less so than grape wine.

They also made a wheat or barley ale without hops that could be mixed with mead or consumed on its own, but that had to be consumed very soon after being made. "Keltenbräu," is an example of such an ale. It would have been a dark, roasted ale with a smoky flavor.

To the upper-class, the quantity of alcohol consumed was as important as the quality. Arnold excavated at least one fully intact cauldron used for serving alcoholic beverages in one of the graves at Heuneburg. But it's hard to top the recovery of nine drinking horns—including one that held 10 pints—at a single chieftain's grave in nearby Hochdorf in the 1970s.

Dapper Dudes and Biker Chicks

In addition to their fondness for alcohol, Celtic populations from this period were said by the Greeks and Romans to favor flashy ornament and brightly striped and checked fabrics, says Arnold. The claim has always been difficult to confirm, however, since cloth and leather are perishable.

The Heuneburg mounds yielded evidence of both, even though no bones remain due to acidic soil. But the team of archaeologists were able to reconstruct elements of dress and ornamentation using new technology.

Rather than attempt to excavate fragile metal remains, such as hairpins, jewelry, weapons and clothing fasteners, Arnold and her colleagues encased blocks of earth containing the objects in plaster, then put the sealed bundles through a computerized tomography, or CT, scanner.

"We found fabulous leather belts in some of the high-status women's graves, with thousands of tiny bronze staples attached to the leather that would have taken hours to make," she says. "I call them the Iron-Age Harley-Davidson biker chicks." Images show such fine detail, the archaeologists theorize that some of the items were not just for fashion.

"You could tell whether someone was male, female, a child, married, occupied a certain role in society and much more from what they were wearing."

The pins that secured a veil to a woman's head, for example, also appear to symbolize marital status and perhaps motherhood. Other adornment was gender-specific—bracelets worn on the left arm were found in men's graves, but bracelets worn on both arms and neck rings were found only in graves of women.

Surprisingly, it was the metal implements in close contact with linen and wool textiles in the graves that provided a chance for their preservation. Bits of fabric clinging to metal allowed the archaeologists to use microscopic inspection to recreate the colors and patterns used.

"When you can actually reconstruct the costume," says Arnold, "all of a sudden these people are 'there'—in three dimensions. They have faces. They can almost be said to have personalities at that point."

Critical Thinking

1. What was "competitive feasting" among the pre-Roman Celtic people?
2. What were the status differences in drinking behavior? In wearing apparel?

Create Central

www.mhhe.com/createcentral

Internet References

GMU Anthropology Department
www.gmu.edu/departments/anthro

Radiocarbon Dating for Archaeology
www.rlaha.ox.ac.uk/orau/index.html

Society for Historical Archaeology
www.sha.org

From *Science Daily*, March 19, 2012. Copyright © 2012 by Newswise. Reprinted by permission.

Woman the Toolmaker

A day in the life of an Ethiopian woman who scrapes hides the old-fashioned way.

STEVEN A. BRANDT AND KATHRYN WEEDMAN

Learning Outcomes

After reading this article, you will be able to:

- Discuss the ways in which Konso hide workers are unique as toolmakers.
- Discuss the social and economic roles and the social standing of hide workers among the Konso.

On the edge of the western escarpment of the Ethiopian Rift Valley, we sit in awe, not of the surrounding environment—some of the world's most spectacular scenery—but of an elderly woman deftly manufacturing stone scrapers as she prepares food, answers an inquisitive child, and chats with a neighbor. She smiles at us, amused and honored by our barrage of questions and our filming of her activities.

In our world of electronic and digital gadgetry, it is surprising to meet someone who uses stone tools in their everyday life. Yet, over the past three decades, researchers have identified a handful of ethnic groups in Ethiopia's southern highlands whose artisans live by making stone scrapers and processing animal hides.

In 1995, with colleagues from Ethiopia's Authority for Research and Conservation of Cultural Heritage and the University of Florida, we surveyed the highlands and, much to our surprise, identified hundreds of stone tool makers in ten different ethnic groups.

The Konso, one group we surveyed, grow millet and other crops on terraces and raise livestock that provide the skins for the hide workers. While hide working in virtually all of the other groups is conducted by men who learn from their fathers, among the Konso the hide workers are women, taught by their mothers or other female relatives.

In archaeological writings, scholarly and popular, stone toolmaking has generally been presented as a male activity; *Man the Toolmaker* is the title of one classic work. This is despite the fact that Australian Aboriginal, North American Inuit (Eskimo), and Siberian women, among others, have been reported in recent times to have made flaked-stone artifacts. The Konso hide workers are probably the only women in the world still making stone tools on a regular basis. They provide a unique opportunity for ethnoarchaeology, the study of the material remains of contemporary peoples. In the past two summers, our team returned to study the women hide workers, following them with our notebooks and cameras, and observing them as they went through their daily lives.

One Konso woman we studied is Sokate, a respected and energetic grandmother now in her 70s. Our many questions amuse Sokate, but she is polite and patient with us. When we ask why only 31 of the 119 Konso hide workers are men, she can only laugh and say that hide working has always been women's work.

After an early morning rain, Sokate strides through her village's terraced millet fields to the same riverbed in which her mother and grandmother searched for chert, a flakeable stone similar to flint. She uses a digging stick to pry stones loose. After almost an hour, Sokate picks up a small nodule of chert. She places it on a large, flat basalt rock. Lifting another large piece of basalt, she brings it down onto the nodule several times, striking off many pieces. Sokate selects ten of the flakes and places them into the top ruffle of her skirt, folding it into her waistband. She also tucks in three pieces of usable quartz, found with the aid of accompanying children.

Returning home, Sokate is greeted by children, goats, and chickens. She picks up the iron tip of a hoe, and, sitting on a goat hide in front of her house, strikes flakes off a chert nodule she collected earlier. She then picks up a wooden bowl filled with scraper components—wooden handles, used stone scrapers, small, unused flakes—and puts the new chert and quartz flakes in it. Moving to the hearth area in front of her house, she takes a flake from the bowl. Resting the flake directly along the edge of a large basalt block that serves as a hearthstone and an anvil, she strikes the flake's edges with the hoe tip, shaping it into a scraper that will fit into the socket of the wooden handle. Although she has access to iron, Sokate tells us that she prefers using stone because it is sharper, more controllable, and easier to resharpen than iron, or even glass. But not all Konso hide workers share her opinion, and in fact, there are now only 21 of them who still use stone regularly.

She places the handle, passed down to her from her mother, into the ashes of the hearth, warming the acacia tree gum (mastic) that holds the scraper in its socket. When the mastic becomes pliable, Sokate pulls the old, used-up scraper out of the socket, then places the end of the handle back into the ashes. After a few minutes, she takes it out and removes some of the old mastic with a stick. On an earthenware sherd, she mixes fresh resin she collected earlier in the day with ashes and heats it. Winding it onto a stick, she drips it into the socket. Sokate then puts a new scraper into the socket, patting the resin down around it with her index finger, making certain that it is set at the proper 90-degree angle to the haft.

Local farmers and other artisans bring Sokate hides to scrape, paying her with grain or money. This morning she is going to scrape a cow hide, Sokate brushes it with a mixture of water and juice from the enset plant, or false banana. If the hide is too dry, removing the fat from its inner side is difficult. After the hide is saturated, she latches one end of it to a tree or post so the hide is slightly above the ground. Squatting or kneeling, she holds the hide taut with her feet to facilitate scraping it. Then with both hands holding the wooden handle, she scrapes the cow hide in long strokes, using a "pull" motion. Goat hides are laid flat on the ground with Sokate sitting with one leg on top of the hide and the other underneath to keep it taut. She scrapes a goat hide with short strokes and a "push" motion away from her body, giving better control of the scraper with the thin goat skin.

Sokate removes the fatty inner layer, shaving off long strips in a rhythmic motion. When the edge of her tool becomes dull, usually after about 60 strokes, she resharpens it. Most of the small chips she removes from the scraper to resharpen it fall into a wooden bowl or gourd. Her barefoot grandchildren periodically dump the sharp chips onto the communal trash pile just outside the village. Sokate uses the scraper until it becomes too dull for scraping and too small to resharpen further. She'll wear out two or three scraping a single cattle hide, one or two for a goat hide.

Many hide-working activities take place in Konso compounds, which are often surrounded by stone walls. A broken pot on the roof indicates the father of a household is a first-born son, a person of higher status.

After Sokate scrapes the hide, she spreads a reddish, oily paste of ground castor beans and pieces of red ocher over it. She then folds the hide over and works the mixture into it. After a few days, the skin is soft. Cow hides are then made into bedding, sandals, straps, belts, and musical instruments, while goat hides are made into bags and (now much more rarely) clothing. During harvest time, the demand for goat hides increases because more bags are needed to carry agricultural goods. Sokate then sends her granddaughter to tell the hide's owner that it is ready.

Sokate and the other Ethiopian hide workers say they are proud of their profession, as they play important economic and social roles within their villages. In addition to hide working, they may also be responsible for announcing births, deaths, and meetings, and for performing puberty initiation ceremonies and other ritual activities. Despite the usefulness of their craft and other duties in the community, Konso hide workers and other artisans, such as ironsmiths and potters, have low social status. Farmers hold them in low esteem and consider them polluted, probably because their crafts involve contact with items that are thought to be impure, like the skins of dead animals. They cannot marry outside of their artisan group, usually cannot own land, and are often excluded from political and judicial life.

Clearly, the Konso hide workers are a rich source of information from which we can address a range of questions: Can excavations of abandoned hide worker compounds provide insights into the identification of social inequality and ranking? How and in what social contexts is stone toolmaking learned? Can we differentiate women's activities from men's on the basis of stone tools?

There is a sense of urgency in our work. Many of the hide workers are elderly and have not taught their children their craft; the influx of plastic bags and Western furnishings have greatly reduced demand for their products. And many of the hide workers have abandoned the use of stone in favor of bottle glass: why hike two hours for chert when you can just walk down the road and pick up pieces of glass? We want to complete our study of the Konso hide workers as soon as possible and begin studying other groups in southern Ethiopia whose hide workers are still using flaked stone, for after 2.5 million years of stone tool use and probably more than 100,000 years of scraping hides with stone, humanity's first and longest-lasting cultural tradition is rapidly being lost.

Critical Thinking

1. How extensive is stone toolmaking today in Ethiopia?
2. In what way are the Konso hide workers unique? Have there been other such cases?
3. Why does Sokate prefer tools made of stone rather than iron?
4. For what purposes does Sokate scrape hides?
5. What social and economic roles do the hide scrapers play? What is their social standing in the community and why? What restrictions have been placed upon them?
6. Why does the author say "there is a sense of urgency about our work"?

Create Central

www.mhhe.com/createcentral

Internet References

Anthropology Resources on the Internet
www.socsciresearch.com/r7.html

Smithsonian Institution Website
www.si.edu

STEVEN A. BRANDT and KATHRYN WEEDMAN are in the department of anthropology at the University of Florida, Gainesville. Their work is supported by funds from the National Science Foundation.

Brandt, Steven A.; Weedman, Kathryn. From *Archaeology*, September/October 2002. Copyright © 2002 by Archaeological Institute of America. Reprinted by permission of *Archaeology Magazine*. www.archaeology.org

Article

Prepared by: Mari Pritchard Parker, *Pasadena City College* and
Elvio Angeloni, *Pasadena City College*

Bushmen

JOHN YELLEN

Learning Outcomes

After reading this article, you will be able to:

- Show how the use of taphonomy in archaeological investigation can reveal details of the past.
- Describe and explain how and why the Bushmen's life style changed in recent decades.

I followed Dau, kept his slim brown back directly in front of me, as we broke suddenly free from the dense Kalahari bush and crossed through the low wire fence that separated Botswana from Namibia to the West. For that moment while Dau held the smooth wires apart for me, we were out in the open, in the full hot light of the sun and then we entered the shadows, the tangled thickets of arrow grass and thorn bush and mongongo trees once again. As soon as the bush began to close in around us again, I quickly became disoriented, Dau's back my only reference point.

Even then, in that first month of 1968, while my desert boots retained their luster, I knew enough to walk behind, not next to Dau. I had expected the Kalahari Desert to be bare open sand. I had imagined myself looking out over vast stretches that swept across to the horizon. But to my surprise, I found that the dunes were covered with trees and that during the rains the grasses grew high over my head. The bare sand, where I could see it, was littered with leaves, and over these the living trees and brush threw a dappled pattern of sunlight and shade. To look in the far distance and maintain a sense of direction, to narrow my focus and pick a way between the acacia bushes and their thorns, and then to look down, just in front of my feet to search out menacing shapes, was too much for me. Already, in that first month, the Bushmen had shown me a puff adder coiled motionless by the base of an acacia tree, but not until Cumsa the Hunter came up close to it, ready to strike it with his spear, could I finally see what all those hands were pointing at.

As Dau walked, I tried to follow his lead. To my discomfort I knew that many of these bushes had thorns—the Kalahari cloaks itself in thorns—some hidden close to the ground just high enough to rake across my ankles and draw blood when I pushed through, others long and straight and white so they reflected the sun. That morning, just before the border fence, my concentration had lagged and I found myself entangled in wait-a-bit thorns that curved backwards up the branch. So I stopped and this short, brown-skinned Bushman pushed me gently backwards to release the tension, then worked the branch, thorn by thorn from my shirt and my skin.

In the mid-1960s, the South African government had decided to accurately survey the Botswana border, mark it with five-strand fence, and cut a thin firebreak on either side. At intervals they constructed survey towers, strange skeletal affairs, like oil drilling rigs, their tops poking well above the highest mongongo trees. It was to one of these that Dau led me across the border, through the midday sun. Although he would not climb it himself, since it was a white man's tower, he assumed I would. I followed his finger, his chain of logic as I started rather hesitantly up the rusted rungs. I cleared the arrow grass, the acacia bushes, finally the broad leafy crowns of the mongongo nut trees. Just short of the top I stopped and sat, hooked my feet beneath the rung below, and wrapped my arms around the metal edges of the sides.

For a month now I had copied the maps—the lines and the circles the !Kung tribesmen had drawn with their fingers in the sand. I had listened and tried to transcribe names of those places, so unintelligible with their clicks, their rising and falling tones. I had walked with Dau and the others to some of those places, to small camps near ephemeral water holes, but on the ground it was too confusing, the changes in altitude and vegetation too subtle, the sun too nearly overhead to provide any sense of where I was or from where I had come.

For the first time from the tower, I could see an order to the landscape. From up there on the tower, I could see that long thin border scar, could trace it off to the horizon to both the north and south. But beyond that, no evidence, not the slightest sign of a human hand. The Bushmen camps were too few in number, too small and well-hidden in the grass and bush to be visible from here. Likewise, the camp where we anthropologists lived, off to the east at the Dobe waterhole, that also was too small to see.

As Dau had intended, from my perch on that tower I learned a lot. At least now I could use the dunes, the shallow valleys, to know whether I was walking east and west or north and south.

In those first years with the Dobe Bushmen, I did gain at least a partial understanding of that land. And I learned to recognize many of those places, the ones that rate no name at all

Bushmen by John Yellen

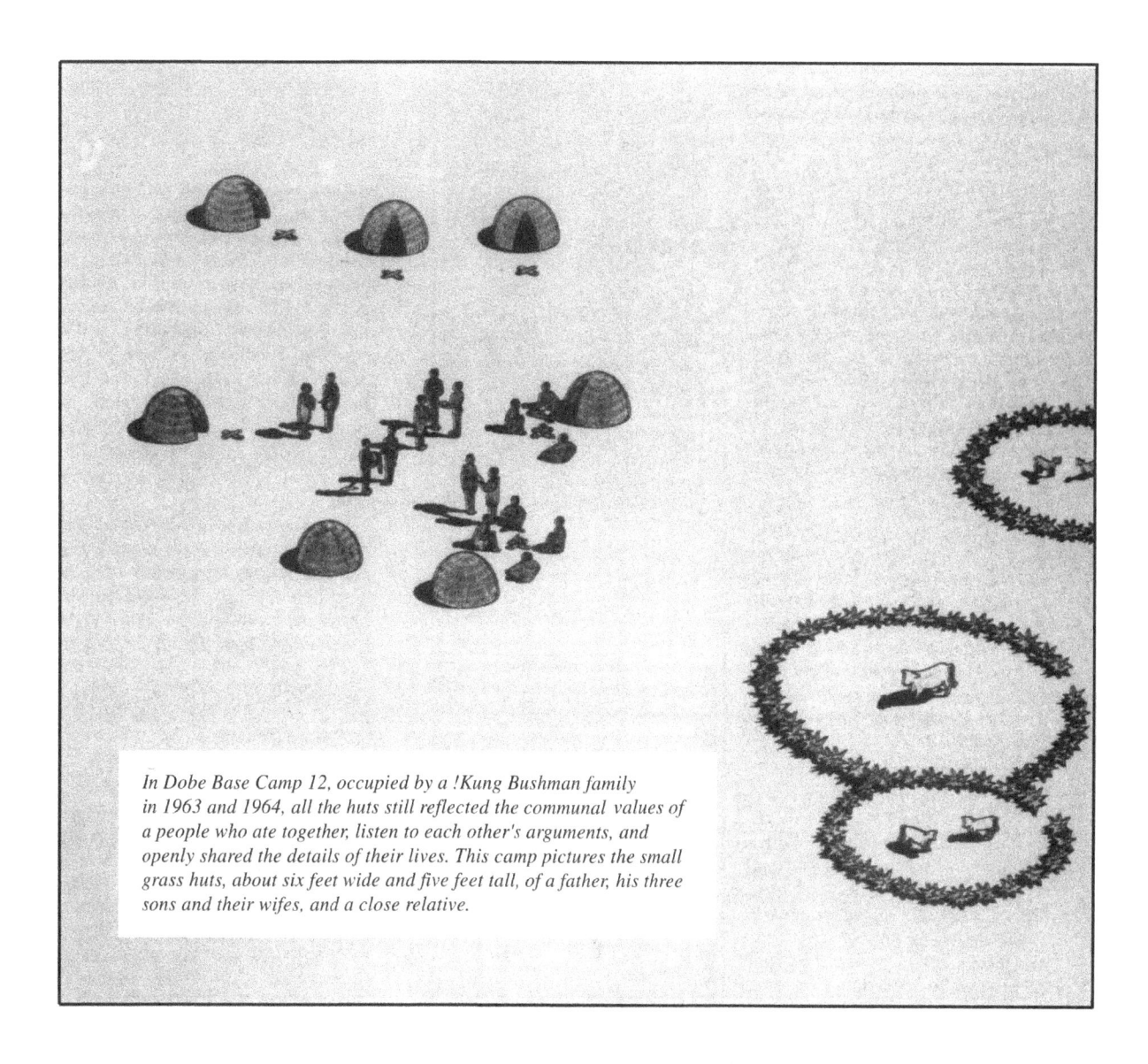

In Dobe Base Camp 12, occupied by a !Kung Bushman family in 1963 and 1964, all the huts still reflected the communal values of a people who ate together, listen to each other's arguments, and openly shared the details of their lives. This camp pictures the small grass huts, about six feet wide and five feet tall, of a father, his three sons and their wifes, and a close relative.

but are marked only by events—brief, ephemeral happenings that leave no mark on the land. I learned to walk with the Bushmen back from a hunt or a trip for honey or spear-shaft wood and listen. They talked, chattered almost constantly, decorating the bus, these no-name places as they went, putting ornaments of experience on them: "See that tree there, John? That's where we stopped, my brother and I, long before he was married, when he killed a kudu, a big female. We stopped under that tree, hung the meat up there and rested in the shade. But the flies were so bad, the biting flies, that we couldn't stay for long."

It took me a long time to realize that this chatter was not chatter at all, to understand that those remarks were gifts, a private map shared only among a few, an overlay crammed with fine, spidery writing on top of the base map with its named waterholes and large valleys, a map for friends to read. Dau would see a porcupine burrow, tiny, hidden in the vastness of the bush. And at night he could sit by the fire and move the others from point to point across the landscape to that small opening in the ground.

But as an archeologist, I had a task to do—to name those places and to discover what life had been like there in the past. "This place has a name now," I told Dau when I went back in 1976. Not the chicken camp, because when I was there I kept 15 chickens, or the cobra camp, for the cobra we killed one morning among the nesting hens, but Dobe Base Camp 18. Eighteen because it's the eighteenth of these old abandoned camps I've followed you to in the last three days. See? That's what goes into this ledger, this fat bound book in waterproof ballpoint ink. We could get a reflector in here—a big piece of tin like some metal off a roof and get some satellite or a plane to photograph it. We could tell just where it is then, could mark it on one of those large aerial maps down to the nearest meter if we wanted.

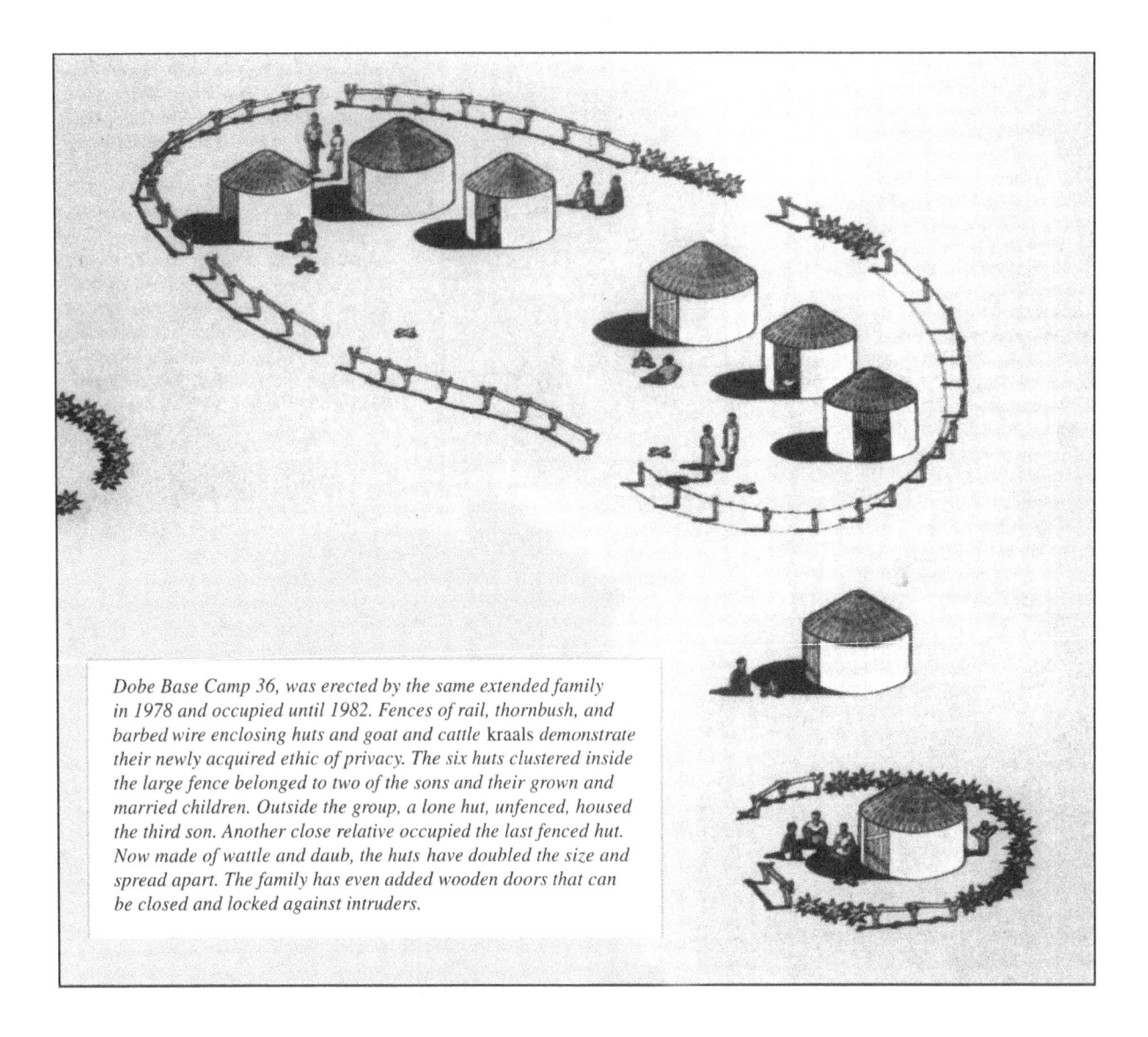

Dobe Base Camp 36, was erected by the same extended family in 1978 and occupied until 1982. Fences of rail, thornbush, and barbed wire enclosing huts and goat and cattle kraals *demonstrate their newly acquired ethic of privacy. The six huts clustered inside the large fence belonged to two of the sons and their grown and married children. Outside the group, a lone hut, unfenced, housed the third son. Another close relative occupied the last fenced hut. Now made of wattle and daub, the huts have doubled the size and spread apart. The family has even added wooden doors that can be closed and locked against intruders.*

We came back to these camps, these abandoned places on the ground, not once but month after month for the better part of a year. Not just Dau and myself but a whole crew of us, eight Bushmen and I, to dig, to look down into the ground. We started before the sun was too high up in the sky, and later Dau and I sat in the shade sipping thick, rich tea. I asked questions and he talked.

"One day when I was living here, I shot a kudu: an adult female. Hit it with one arrow in the flank. But it went too far and we never found it. Then another day my brother hit a wildebeest, another adult female and that one we got. We carried it back to camp here and ate it."

"What other meat did you eat here, Dau?"

"One, no two, steenbok, it was."

1948: 28 years ago by my counting was when Dau, his brothers, his family were here. How could he remember the detail? This man sat in the shade and recalled trivial events that have repeated themselves in more or less the same way at so many places over the last three decades.

We dug day after day in the old camps—and found what Dau said we should. Bones, decomposing, but still identifiable: bones of wildebeest and steenbok among the charcoal and mongongo nut shells.

We dug our squares, sifting through the sand for bones. And when I dumped the bones, the odd ostrich eggshell bead, the other bits and pieces out onto the bridge table to sort, so much of what my eyes and ears told me was confirmed in this most tangible form. If excavation in one square revealed the bones of a wildebeest or kudi or other large antelope, then the others would contain them as well. In an environment as unpredictable as the Kalahari, where the game was hard to find and the probability of failure high, survival depended on sharing, on spreading the risk. And the bones, distributed almost evenly around the individual family hearths confirmed that. What also

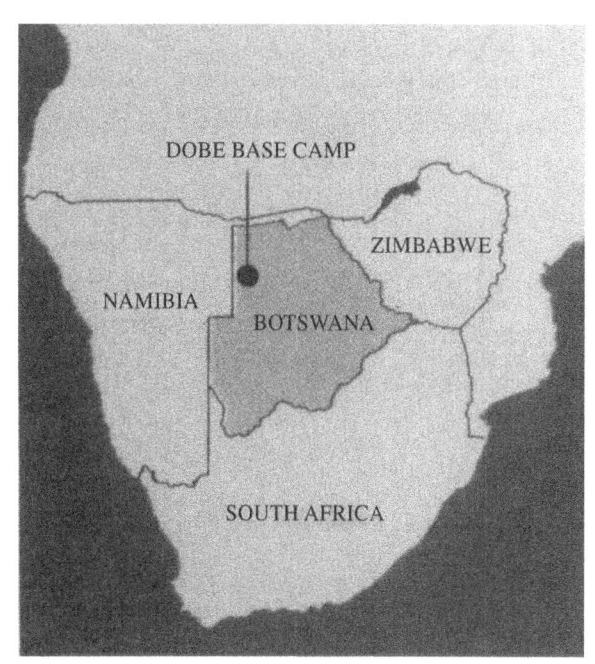

© J. Wisenbaugh

impressed me was how little else other than the bones there was. Most archeological sites contain a broad range of debris. But in those years the Bushmen owned so little. Two spears or wooden digging sticks or strings of ostrich eggshell beads were of no more use than one. Better to share, to give away meat or extra belongings and through such gifts create a web of debts, of obligations that some day would be repaid. In 1948, even in 1965, to accumulate material goods made no sense.

When it was hot, which was most of the year, I arranged the bridge table and two chairs in a patch of nearby shade. We sat there with the bound black and red ledger and dumped the bones in a heap in the center of the table, then sorted them out. I did the easy stuff, separated out the turtle shells, the bird bones, set each in a small pile around the table's edge. Dau did the harder part, separated the steenbok from the duiker, the wildebeest from kudu, held small splintered bone fragments and turned them over and over in his hands. We went through the piles then, one by one, moved each in its turn to the center of the table, sorted them into finer categories, body part by body part, bone by bone. Cryptic notes, bits of data that accumulated page by page. The bones with their sand and grit were transformed into numbers in rows and columns, classes and subclasses which would, I hoped, emerge from some computer to reveal a grander order, a design, an underlying truth.

Taphonomy: That's the proper term for it. The study of burial and preservation. Archeologists dig lots of bones out of the ground, not just from recent places such as these but from sites that span the millions of years of mankind's existence. On the basis of the bones, we try to learn about those ancient people. We try to reconstruct their diet, figure out how the animals were hunted, how they were killed, butchered, and shared.

What appealed to me about the Dobe situation, why I followed Dau, walked out his youth and his early manhood back and forth around the waterhole was the neat, almost laboratory situation Dobe offered. A natural experiment. I could go to a modern camp, collect those discarded food bones even before the jackals and hyenas had gotten to them, examine and count them, watch the pattern emerge. What happened then to the bones after they'd been trampled, picked over, rained on, lain in the ground for five years? Five years ago? Dobe Base Camp 21, 1971. I could go there, dig up a sample and find out.

What went on farther and farther back in time? Is there a pattern? Try eight years ago. 1968, DBC 18. We could go there to the cobra camp and see. Thirty-four years ago? The camp where Tsaa with the beautiful wife was born. One can watch, can see how things fall apart, can make graphs, curves, shoot them back, watch them arc backwards beyond Dau, beyond Dau's father, back into the true archeological past.

We dug our way through the DBCs, back into the early 1940s, listening day after day to the South African soap operas on the short-wave radio, and our consumption of plastic bags went down and down. Slim pickings in the bone department. And the bones we did find tended to be rotten: They fragmented, fell apart in the sieve.

So we left the 1940s, collapsed the bridge table and the folding chairs and went to that site that played such a crucial role for anthropologists: DBC 12, the 1963 camp where those old myths about hunters and gatherers came up against the hard rock of truth.

They built this camp just after Richard Lee, the pioneer, arrived. They lived there through the winter and hunted warthog with spears and a pack of dogs so good they remember each by name to this day. Richard lived there with them. He watched them—what they did, what they ate, weighed food on his small scale slung with a rope from an acacia tree. He weighed people, sat in camp day after day with his notebook and his wristwatch and scale. He recorded times: when each person left camp in the morning, when each returned for the day.

In this small remnant group, one of the last in the world still living by hunting and gathering, it should be possible, he believed, to see a reflection, a faint glimmer of the distant universal past of all humanity, a common condition that had continued for millions and millions of years. He went there because of that and for that reason, later on, the rest of us followed him.

What he found in that desert camp, that dry, hard land, set the anthropological world back on its collective ear. What his scale and his wristwatch and his systematic scribbles showed was that we were fooled, that we had it all wrong. To be a hunter and gatherer wasn't that bad after all. They didn't work that hard, even in this land of thorns: For an adult, it came to less time than a nine-to-five office worker puts in on the job. They lived a long time, too, didn't wear out and die young but old-looking, as we had always thought. Even in this camp, the camp with the good hunting dogs, it was plants, not meat, which provided the staff of life. Women walked through the nut groves and collected nuts with their toes, dug in the molapos and sang to each other through the bush. Unlike the game, which spooked so easily and followed the unpredictable rains, the nuts, roots, and berries were dependable, there in plenty, there for the picking. Another distinguished anthropologist, Marshall Sahlins, termed those DBC 12 people "the original affluent society"—something quite different from the traditional conception of hunting and gathering as a mean, hard existence half a step ahead of starvation and doom.

Over the years that name has held—but life in the Kalahari has changed. That kind of camp, with all the bones and mongongo nuts and dogs, is no more.

By the mid-1970s, things were different at Dobe. Diane Gelburd, another of the anthropologists out there then, only needed to look around her to see how the Bushman lifestyle had changed from the way Richard recorded it, from how Sahlins described it. But what had changed the people at DBC 12 who believed that property should be commonly held and shared? What had altered their system of values? That same winter Diane decided to find out.

She devised a simple measure of acculturation that used pictures cut from magazines: an airplane, a sewing machine, a gold mine in South Africa. (Almost no one got the gold mine right.) That was the most enjoyable part of the study. They all liked to look at pictures, to guess.

Then she turned from what people knew to what they believed. She wanted to rank them along a scale, from traditional to acculturated. So again she asked questions:

"Will your children be tattooed?"

To women: "If you were having a difficult childbirth and a white doctor were there, would you ask for assistance?"

To men: "If someone asked you for permission to marry your daughter would you demand (the traditional) bride service?"

Another question so stereotyped that in our own society one would be too embarrassed to ask it: "Would you let your child marry someone from another tribe—a Tswana or a Herero—a white person?"

First knowledge, then belief, and finally material culture. She did the less sensitive questions first. "Do you have a field? What do you grow? What kind of animals do you have? How many of what?" Then came the hard part: She needed to see what people actually owned. I tagged along with her one day and remember the whispers inside one dark mud hut. Trunks were unlocked and hurriedly unpacked away from the entrance to shield them from sight. A blanket spread out on a trunk revealed the secret wealth that belied their statements: "Me? I have nothing." In the semidarkness she made her inventory. Then the trunks were hastily repacked and relocked with relief.

She went through the data, looked at those lists of belongings, itemized them in computer printouts. Here's a man who still hunts. The printout shows it. He has a bow and quiver and arrows on which the poison is kept fresh. He has a spear and snares for birds. He has a small steenbok skin bag, a traditional carryall that rests neatly under his arm.

He also has 19 goats and two donkeys, bought from the Herero or Tswana, who now get Dobe Bushmen to help plant their fields and herd their cows. They pay in livestock, hand-me-down clothing, blankets, and sometimes cash. He has three large metal trunks crammed full: One is packed to the top with shoes, shirts, and pants, most well-worn. He has two large linen mosquito nets, 10 tin cups, and a metal file. He has ropes of beads: strand upon strand—over 200 in all, pounds of small colored glass beads made in Czechoslovakia that I had bought in Johannesburg years earlier. He has four large iron pots and a five-gallon plastic jerry can. He has a plow, a gift from the anthropologists. He has a bridle and bit, light blankets, a large tin basin. He has six pieces of silverware, a mirror and hairbrush, two billycans. His wife and his children together couldn't carry all that. The trunks are too heavy and too large for one person to carry so you would have to have two people for each. What about the plow, those heavy iron pots? Quite a job to carry those through bush, through the thick thorns.

But here is the surprising part. Talk to that man. Read the printout. See what he knows, what he believes. It isn't surprising that he speaks the Herero language and Setswana fluently or that he has worked for the Herero, the anthropologists. Nothing startling there. A budding Dobe capitalist. But then comes the shock: He espouses the traditional values.

"Bushmen share things, John. We share things and depend on each other, help each other out. That's what makes us different from the black people."

But the same person, his back to the door, opens his trunks, unlocks them one by one, lays out the blankets, the beads, then quickly closes each before he opens the next.

Multiply that. Make a whole village of people like that, and you can see the cumulative effect: You can actually measure it. As time goes on, as people come to own more possessions; the huts move farther and farther apart.

In the old days a camp was cosy, intimate and close. You could sit there by one fire and look into the other grass huts, see what the other people were doing, what they were making or eating. You heard the conversations, the arguments and banter.

We ask them why the new pattern?

Says Dau: "It's because of the livestock that we put our huts this way. They can eat the grass from the roofs and the sides of our houses. So we have to build fences to keep them away and to do that, you must have room between the huts."

I look up from the fire, glance around the camp, say nothing. No fences there. Not a single one around any of the huts, although I concede that one day they probably will build them. But why construct a lot of separate small fences, one around each hut? Why not clump the huts together the way they did in the old days and make a single large fence around the lot? Certainly a more efficient approach. Why worry about fences now in any case? The only exposed grass is on the roofs, protected by straight mud walls and nothing short of an elephant or giraffe could eat it.

Xashe's answer is different. Another brief reply. An attempt to dispose of the subject politely but quickly. "It's fire, John. That's what we're worried about. If we put our houses too close together, if one catches fire, the others will burn as well. We don't want one fire to burn all our houses down. That's why we build them so far apart."

But why worry about fire now? What about in the old days when the huts were so close, cheek by jowl? Why is it that when the huts were really vulnerable, when they were built entirely of dried grass, you didn't worry about fires then?

You read Diane's interviews and look at those lists of how much people own. You see those shielded mud huts with doors spaced, so far apart. You also listen to the people you like and trust. People who always have been honest with you. You hear their explanations and realize the evasions are not for you but for themselves. You see things they can't. But nothing can be done. It would be ludicrous to tell these brothers: "Don't you see, my friends, the lack of concordance between your values and the changing reality of your world?"

Now, years after the DBC study, I sit with data spread out before me and it is so clear. Richard's camp in 1963: just grass huts, a hearth in front of each. Huts and hearths in a circle, nothing more. 1968: more of the same. The following year though the first *kraal* appears, just a small thorn enclosure, some acacia bushes cut and dragged haphazardly together for their first few goats. It's set apart way out behind the circle of huts. On one goes, from plot to plot, following the pattern from year to year. The huts change from grass to mud. They become larger, more solidly built. Goats, a few at first, then more of them. So you build a fence around your house to keep them away from the grass roofs. The *kraals* grow larger, move in closer to be incorporated finally into the circle of huts itself. The huts become spaced farther and farther apart, seemingly repelled over time, one from the next. People, families move farther apart.

The bones tell the same story. 1947: All the bones from wild animals, game caught in snares or shot with poisoned arrows—game taken from the bush. By 1964 a few goat bones, a cow bone or two, but not many. Less than 20 percent of the total. Look then at the early 1970s and watch the line on the graph climb slowly upwards—by 1976 over 80 percent from domesticated stock.

But what explains the shattering of this society? Why is this hunting and gathering way of life, so resilient in the face of uncertainty, falling apart? It hasn't been a direct force—a war, the ravages of disease. It is the internal conflicts, the tensions, the inconsistencies, the impossibility of reconciling such different views of the world.

At Dobe it is happening to them all together. All of the huts have moved farther apart in lockstep, which makes it harder for them to see how incompatible the old system is with the new. But Rakudu, a Bushman who lived at the Mahopa waterhole eight miles down the valley from Dobe, was a step ahead of the rest. He experienced, before the rest of them, their collective fate.

When I was at the Cobra Camp in 1969, Rakudu lived down near Mahopa, off on his own, a mile or so away from the pastoral Herero villages. He had two hats and a very deep bass voice, both so strange, so out of place in a Bushman. He was a comical sort of man with the hats and that voice and a large Adam's apple that bobbed up and down.

The one hat must have been a leftover from the German-Herero wars because no one in Botswana wore a hat like that—a real pith helmet with a solid top and rounded brim. It had been cared for over the years because, although soiled and faded, it still retained the original strap that tucks beneath the chin. The second hat was also unique—a World War I aviator's hat, one of those leather sacks that fits tightly over the head and buckles under the chin. Only the goggles were missing.

I should have seen then how out of place the ownership of two hats was in that hunter-gatherer world. Give two hats like that to any of the others and one would have been given away on the spot. A month or two later, the other would become a gift as well. Moving goods as gifts and favors along that chain of human ties. That was the way to maintain those links, to keep them strong.

When I went to Rakudu's village and realized what he was up to, I could see that he was one of a kind. The mud-walled huts in his village made it look like a Herero village—not a grass hut in sight. And when I came, Rakudu pulled out a hand-carved wood and leather chair and set it in the shade. This village was different from any of the Bushman camps I had seen. Mud huts set out in a circle, real clay storage bins to hold the corn—not platforms in a tree—and *kraals* for lots of goats and donkeys. He had a large field, too, several years before the first one appeared at Dobe.

Why shouldn't Bushmen do it—build their own villages, model their subsistence after the Herero? To plant a field, to tend goats, to build mud-walled houses like that was not hard to do. Work for the Herero a while and get an axe, accumulate the nucleus of a herd, buy or borrow the seeds. That year the rains were long and heavy. The sand held the water and the crickets and the birds didn't come. So the harvest was good, and I could sit there in the carved chair and look at Rakudu's herd of goats and their young ones and admire him for his industry, for what he had done.

Only a year later I saw him and his eldest son just outside the Cobra Camp. I went over and sat in the sand and listened to the negotiations for the marriage Rakudu was trying to arrange. His son's most recent wife had run away, and Rakudu was discussing a union between his son and Dau the Elder's oldest daughter who was just approaching marriageable age. They talked about names and Dau the Elder explained why the marriage couldn't take place. It was clear that the objection was trivial, that he was making an excuse. Even I could see that his explanation was a face-saving gesture to make the refusal easier for all of them.

Later I asked Dau the Elder why he did it. It seemed like a good deal to me. "Rakudu has all that wealth, those goats and field. I'd think that you would be anxious to be linked with a family like that. Look at all you have to gain. Is the son difficult? Did he beat his last wife?"

"She left because she was embarrassed. The wife before her ran away for the same reason and so did the younger brother's wife," he said. "Both brothers treated their wives well. The problem wasn't that. It was when the wives' relatives came. That's when it became so hard for the women because Rakudu and his sons are such stingy men. They wouldn't give anything away, wouldn't share anything with them. Rakudu has a big herd just like the Herero, and he wouldn't kill goats for them to eat."

Not the way Bushmen should act toward relatives, not by the traditional value system at least. Sharing, the most deeply held Bushman belief, and that man with the two hats wouldn't go along. Herero are different. You can't expect them to act properly, to show what is only common decency; you must take them as they are. But someone like Rakudu, a Bushman, should know better than that. So the wives walked out and left for good.

But Rakudu understood what was happening, how he was trapped—and he tried to respond. If you can't kill too many goats from the herd that has become essential to you, perhaps you can find something else of value to give away. Rakudu thought he had an answer.

He raised tobacco in one section of his field. Tobacco, a plant not really adapted to a place like the northern Kalahari, has to be weeded, watered by hand, and paid special care. Rakudu did that and for one year at least harvested a tobacco crop.

Bushmen crave tobacco and Rakudu hoped he had found a solution—that they would accept tobacco in place of goats, in place of mealie meal. A good try. Perhaps the only one open to him. But, as it turned out, not good enough. Rakudu's son could not find a wife.

Ironic that a culture can die yet not a single person perish. A sense of identity, of a shared set of rules, of participation in a single destiny binds individuals together into a tribe or cultural group. Let that survive long enough, let the participants pass this sense through enough generations, one to the next, create enough debris, and they will find their way into the archeological record, into the study of cultures remembered only by their traces left on the land.

Rakudu bought out. He, his wife, and his two sons sold their goats for cash, took the money and walked west, across the border scar that the South Africans had cut, through the smooth fence wire and down the hard calcrete road beyond. They became wards of the Afrikaaners, were lost to their own culture, let their fate pass into hands other than their own. At Chum kwe, the mission station across the border 34 miles to the west, they were given numbers and the right to stand in line with the others and have mealie meal and other of life's physical essentials handed out to them. As wards of the state, that became their right. When the problems, the contradictions of your life are insoluble, a paternalistic hand provides one easy out.

Dau stayed at Dobe. Drive there today and you can find his mud-walled hut just by the waterhole. But he understands: He has married off his daughter, his first-born girl to a wealthy Chum kwe man who drives a tractor—an old man, more than twice her age, and by traditional Bushmen standards not an appropriate match. Given the chance, one by one, the others will do the same.

Critical Thinking

1. Describe the nature of the Bushmen's map of their territory and how the author came to learn it.
2. What did the author learn at the 1948 camp site?
3. What is "taphonomy" and what can be learned from it?
4. In what sense were the Dobe offering a "natural experiment"?
5. In what respects did we "have it all wrong" about hunters and gatherers?
6. How does the author describe the changes in Bushmen lifestyle over time? How does the author explain them and with what evidence?

Create Central

www.mhhe.com/createcentral

Internet References

Archaeology Links (NC)
www.arch.dcr.state.nc.us/links.htm#stuff

Society for Historical Archaeology
www.sha.org

JOHN YELLEN, director of the anthropology program at the National Science Foundation, has returned to the Kalahari four times since 1968.

Yellen, John. From *Science Magazine*, May 1985. Copyright © 1985 by John Yellen. Reprinted by permission of the author.

Unit 3

UNIT

Prepared by: Mari Pritchard Parker, *Pasadena City College* and Elvio Angeloni, *Pasadena City College*

Techniques in Archaeology

Archaeology has evolved significantly from being an exercise in separating the remains of past human behavior from the "dirt." And as such, archaeology in turn employs a diversified group of highly sophisticated techniques. Digging in itself has gone through its own evolution of techniques, ranging from the wild thrashings of Heinrich Schielmann to the obsessive, military-like precise technique of Sir Mortimer Wheeler. Archaeology continues to expand the use of a multidisciplinary approach, and is therefore incorporating more techniques that will prove to enlighten us about our human past.

The most well-known technique to be developed in archaeology was radiocarbon dating. This provides archaeologists with one of their most valuable means of establishing the age of archaeological materials. This technique was a major revolution in archaeology, and was developed by W. F. Libby at UCLA in 1949. It has enabled archaeologists, for the first time (in all of history and prehistory) to have an empirical means of determining the age of archaeological sites in terms of absolute years. This dating technique is based on the principle of radioactive decay in which unstable radioactive isotopes transform into stable elements at a constant rate. In order to qualify their accuracy, dates are presented with a standard statistical margin of error. Great care is taken with respect to any factors that may skew the results of materials being dated. It can date materials as far back as 45,000 B.P. (before present). The word "present" was designated to be 1950 C.E. As the technique is perfected, it may be able to date organic matter of even earlier times. Radiocarbon dating is limited to the dating of organic materials. It cannot directly date such things as stone tools, but it may do so indirectly by dating the layer in which the tools were deposited. Other new, cleverly devised radiometric techniques are being developed to suit specific conditions to date archaeological remains by association.

The preservation of archaeological materials is dependent upon many variables. These include the original material of the artifact and the conditions of the site in which it is preserved. For example, a nineteenth-century adobe mission on the Mojave Desert in California may be so weathered as to be unrecognizable. This is due to the fact that extreme temperatures, varying from very hot to very cold, typical of a low-desert region, tend to rapidly destroy any kind of organic matter. On the other hand, consistently wet or consistently dry conditions tend to preserve organic matter in a relatively pristine state for a long period of time. Thus, human remains tend to be well preserved in bogs—as in Denmark and in the arid coastal deserts of Peru. In Denmark, the conditions are constantly moist. In the coastal deserts of Peru, the conditions remain dry. Therefore, archaeological material may be preserved for many thousands of years.

Since the discovery of radiocarbon dating, numerous other techniques have been invented that have their applications to archaeology to further clarify dates, preserve, and in general, add to the ability of archaeologists to do cultural historical reconstruction. Discussed in this section are some of the extraordinary applications of such varied hard sciences. We can now describe sites in terms of time-space systemics and virtual reality in a way that exceeds recent science fiction. Remote sensing devices from outer space allow sites to be reconstructed without invasive excavation. There are even sensing devices that can, from an airplane, "see" through the rainforest canopy to find previously hidden Mayan settlements. It seems that nothing will escape detection by future archaeologists.

Archaeologists sometimes rely on the use of forensic specialists to present images of the past that we could never before see. Used in conjunction with the exponential knowledge from DNA analysis, our images of the past became as detailed as that captured on a digital camera. Unglazed cooking pots have been tested to yield information on prehistoric diets through molecular analysis. Because clams add a tiny layer of carbonate each day and each layer reflects the weather conditions at the time, we can now tell what kind of day a clam had 350 million years ago. By inference, of course, we can also tell what was happening to the human environments in more recent times.

In spite of the ever-increasing sophistication of tools available to the archaeologist, the simple time-tested technique of archaeological surveying still helps reconstruct sites, again without invasive excavation. The future of archaeology will increasingly depend on techniques to maximize preservation of sites and minimize archaeological excavation.

Article

Prepared by: Mari Pritchard Parker, *Pasadena City College* and
Elvio Angeloni, *Pasadena City College*

Lasers in the Jungle

Airborne sensors reveal a vast Maya landscape.

ARLEN F. CHASE, DIANE Z. CHASE, AND JOHN F. WEISHAMPEL

Learning Outcomes

After reading this article, you will be able to:

- Summarize the advances made in techniques to date archaeological sites in the last 50 years.
- Discuss the use of laser technology in identifying Mayan archaeological sites in the rainforest.

Even when one is almost directly on top of them, many Maya sites are impossible to see. In the jungle, small palms and brush can spring to 14 feet high in a year, filling the space between towering cedar, mahogany, ramon, and ceiba trees. When we *can* find large Maya sites, we cannot easily map them because it is expensive and labor-intensive. Even modern electronic distance meters have limited functionality; if we can't see through the trees, neither can they. So we cut paths with machetes, scramble through thick underbrush, and wonder what we might be missing. The ability to see through this dense, steamy jungle has long been the dream of Maya archaeologists.

These difficulties have led us to underestimate the accomplishments and ingenuity of the ancient Maya. There is little agreement among archaeologists over just how big some Maya cities were, how many people lived in them, or how intensively their residents modified the landscape. It often appears that sites in more easily studied areas of the world—plains, sparse forests, or areas cleared in modern times—are larger and more complex than their tropical forest counterparts. Does this impression reflect the inability of ancient humans to create large, sustainable settlements in the tropics, or is it the result of incomplete investigations, hampered by the complications of working in a rainforest?

For more than 25 years, we—a multidisciplinary team from the University of Central Florida—have struggled to document the jungle-covered archaeological remains at Caracol in western Belize. Caracol was occupied from 600 B.C. to A.D 900 by a population that we believe peaked with at least 115,000 inhabitants. A system of radial roads, or causeways, links different parts of the site across most of Belize's lush Vaca Plateau.

We have mapped, using traditional on-the-ground techniques, approximately 9 square miles of settlement, 1.3 square miles of terracing, and 25 miles of causeways. We have also studied the buildings and pyramids of the site's center, as well as 118 residential groups that consist of rubble foundations and stone buildings arranged around a central plaza. Our work so far clearly establishes Caracol as the largest known archaeological site in the southern Maya lowlands, but reconnaissance and scouting suggest that the city was even larger than was previously thought. Despite the quantity of data we have, there are still lingering questions about the site's true size and population, and about the density of the terrace systems that the ancient Maya constructed for agriculture. To answer these difficult questions without spending another 25 years in the field, we clearly needed a new strategy—a way to "see" through the dense forest covering the archaeological remains.

For the last three decades archaeologists all over the world have been using space-based imaging tools to better understand ancient landscape and settlement patterns. Like their colleagues, Maya archaeologists have turned to these techniques to overcome the complications of working beneath a forest canopy—but often with little success. Generally, we have only been able to see archaeological features that extend above the canopy, are in areas devoid of vegetation, or disrupt the forest in a bold way. Even large pyramids can escape the eye in the sky. A newer remote-sensing technology called LiDAR (Light Detection and Ranging), operated from a plane rather than a satellite, has helped us penetrate the jungle of Caracol and promises to revolutionize our understanding of Maya civilization. (Laser-based on-the-ground scanning, featured in "The Past in High-Def," May/June 2009, is also gaining traction in the archaeological world.)

In addition to a detailed study of existing satellite imagery, the Caracol remote-sensing project, funded by NASA, was designed to determine if LiDAR can be used to see below the forest canopy to provide images of a complete ancient Maya landscape. It was even more successful than we had hoped. Just a few days of flyovers and three weeks of processing yielded a far superior picture of Caracol than on-the-ground mapping ever had.

Airborne LiDAR works by sending out billions of laser pulses from a plane—in this case one operated by the National

Science Foundation-supported National Center for Airborne Laser Mapping—half a mile above the canopy. Carefully calibrated sensors measure the pulses that bounce back. Initially, the lasers are refracted by the tops of trees, producing a detailed record of the forest cover. But treetops are porous, so some photons penetrate deeper, while others reach all the way to the ground and reflect back from the underlying surface terrain—and any buildings or ancient structures on it. The result is an accurate, three-dimensional map of both the forest canopy and the ground elevation beneath it. For looking at Maya sites, it was important to take the measurements at the end of the dry season, when the forest is the most depleted. This laser-sensing technology is not by itself new, but has been refined—we used a significantly advanced airborne laser swath mapping (ALSM) system that swept across a 1,500-foot-wide area with each pass of the plane. The Caracol data represent the first time that the ALSM technology has been applied across an extensive region in the Maya area, and the results were stunning.

Seemingly without effort, the system produced a detailed view of nearly 80 square miles—only 13 percent of which had previously been mapped—revealing topography, ancient structures, causeways, and agricultural terraces. The data show the full extent of Caracol, how the settlement was structured, and how the ancient Maya radically modified their landscape to create a sustainable urban environment, challenging long-held assumptions about the development of civilization in the tropics.

The LiDAR data confirm that Caracol was a low-density agricultural city encompassing some 70 square miles. Our previous on-the-ground work had documented multiple causeways, but the LiDAR images revealed 11 new ones and 5 new causeway termini (concentrations of buildings at the ends of roads), revealing the site's entire communication and transportation infrastructure at its height during the Late Classic Period (A.D 550–900). Equally important, the LiDAR images clearly show unmodified hills and valleys at the edges of the surveyed area, indicating the limits of the site and providing hints about why the Maya of Caracol settled where they did and how the city expanded over time.

The study clearly confirms our earlier population estimates for Caracol, and also documents the extent to which the people of the city modified the land to feed themselves. We were particularly impressed with LiDAR's ability to reveal Caracol's agricultural terraces. We had documented these structures in on-the-ground surveys, but it was near-impossible to imagine the extent of the modified landscape. The remote-sensing data show that almost all of the Caracol landscape had been altered; soil- and water-conserving terraces cover entire valleys and hills, making it clear that agricultural production and sustainability were critical to the ancient Maya. Airborne LiDAR is clearly the tool that Maya archaeologists have been waiting for.

LiDAR results dwarf what was possible before, even through long-term archaeological projects, such as those at Tikal in Guatemala and Calakmul in Mexico, but the technology has drawbacks. It may not record the remains of completely perishable structures, which may leave only a few lines of stone, though our results suggest it can distinguish features less than a foot high. On-the-ground confirmation, traditional mapping, and excavation are still necessary to add information about how buildings were used, details, and dating. But because LiDAR covers large areas so efficiently, it could ultimately replace traditional mapping in tropical rainforests, and drive new archaeological research by revealing unusual settlement patterns and identifying new locales for on-the-ground work. At Caracol, for example, we found previously unknown clusters of complex architecture that are not directly tied to the Late Classic causeway system. Possibly areas of craft or pottery production or the remains of earlier settlements, these are prime targets for future archaeological investigation.

Understanding the scale of a modified Maya landscape will also help us compare the Maya with other ancient civilizations more effectively. Remote-sensing techniques used in the Amazon Basin and Southeast Asia have revolutionized our thinking about ancient cultures there. Satellite imaging, combined with on-the-ground GPS mapping, for example, demonstrated that complex and populous societies occupied the Amazonian rainforest before European contact. And at Angkor in Cambodia, remote sensing helped delineate a metropolitan area that covers nearly 400 square miles and led to new interpretations of the site's complex water systems and eventual abandonment. At Caracol, we see a large, low-density, agricultural city that thrived in a tropical environment. But where the people of Angkor made extensive and difficult-to-maintain hydrological changes to grow enough food to feed themselves, Caracol's inhabitants focused on the intensive creation of sustainable terraced fields. These terraces not only controlled water flow during the rainy season, which reduced erosion, but also retained water longer. Using the terraces, the ancient Maya could produce multiple harvests of maize, beans, squash, and other crops in a single year, and nutrients could be replenished by fertilizing the earth with night soil and compost. Combined with the appropriate spacing of settlements and reservoirs, the recycling of garbage, and a causeway system to communicate and distribute resources, the agricultural terrace system was designed to work with its environment—and support the daily needs of more than 100,000 city dwellers.

For too long, Maya archaeologists have been blinded by the jungle, able only to sample once-wondrous cities and speculate about vanished people. The airborne LiDAR data will help us finally dispel preconceived notions about ancient tropical civilizations—that they were limited in size and sophistication—by letting us peer through the trees. In a broader sense, we will even be able to connect sites with one another and detect political boundaries to reconstruct ancient tropical polities in full. Imagine being able to see and map the entire Maya world—its fields and pyramids, its houses and trade routes, its interactions and conflicts. But that is in the future. For now, it is enough to be able to see the entire urban landscape of one ancient Maya city, and know that palm fronds and tangled forest will no longer obscure our view of the past.

Critical Thinking

1. What have been some of the difficulties in finding and mapping Maya sites? What have been the consequences of such difficulties for archaeologists?

2. What has the multidisciplinary team been able to accomplish over the past 25 years at Caracol and how?
3. What have been some of the "lingering questions" and what has been needed to answer them?
4. Why have space-based imaging tools been of limited use?
5. How do the laser-sensing systems work and how have they improved upon the archaeological findings at Caracol?
6. What are the drawbacks of the new technology? What are some of its potential benefits?
7. How have remote-sensing techniques revolutionized our thinking about ancient cultures in the Amazon Basin and in Southeast Asia?
8. How does the author contrast the agriculture of Caracol with that of Angkor? What were some of the benefits of the Caracol system?
9. What does the author see as the future for Maya archaeologists?

Create Central

www.mhhe.com/createcentral

Internet References

GIS and Remote Sensing for Archaeology: Burgundy, France
Maya Archaeology Initiative
http://mayaarchaeology.org
Society for American Archaeology
www.saa.org
Society for Archaeological Sciences
www.socarchsci.org

Chase et al., Arlen. From *Archaeology*, July/August 2010. Copyright © 2010 by Archaeological Institute of America. Reprinted by permission of *Archaeology Magazine*. www.archaeology.org

Article

Prepared by: Mari Pritchard Parker, *Pasadena City College* and
Elvio Angeloni, *Pasadena City College*

Archaeology of Titanic

It has been 100 years since it sank, and 27 years since it was rediscovered. Now the wreck of *Titanic* has finally become what it was always meant to be: an archaeological site.

JAMES P. DELGADO

Learning Outcomes

After reading this article, you will be able to:

- Discuss the latest technological advances in locating and investigating underwater archaeological sites.
- Evaluate the pros and cons of extracting artifacts from the wreckage of the *Titanic*.

At the bottom of the ocean, centuries pass with little occurring in the way of incident. But on April 15, 1912, deep in the Atlantic, 375 miles southeast of Halifax, Nova Scotia, that changed. A massive steel structure, after falling for more than two miles, hit the silt and drove into thick clay beneath. Silt bloomed as the sound of the impact reverberated in the darkness. Other pieces of the world's largest passenger steamship followed like a heavy rain. The bow came in fast, nose first, plowing a deep furrow into the clay. Over the next several hours, fragments of the hull, dishes, machinery, and linoleum tiles—and the remains of people—settled across miles of seabed. What had once been a floating city was fragmented and scattered two and a half miles down. More than 1,500 people lost their lives.

Slowly but inexorably, the processes of the deep sea went to work. Marine organisms and acidic clay consumed wood and other organic material, including human remains. Bacteria colonized and began to eat away at the steel, leaving behind tendrils and puddles of red, orange, and yellow byproducts. The ship's crisp angles blurred and the proud name on the bow, *Titanic*, dissolved. Silt slowly accumulated on intact paneling, doors still on their hinges, and a metal bed frame with a nightgown draped over it. In 1912, Thomas Hardy imagined, in a poem lamenting *Titanic*, "Over the mirrors meant/To glass the opulent/The sea-worm crawls—grotesque, slimed, dumb, indifferent." Intact compartments and cabins that had once been filled with air, light, and passengers were full of water pressurized to 6,000 pounds per square inch and seemingly alien life.

Over decades, the wreck became a haven for deep-sea creatures such as ghost crabs, crinoids, and worms—a series of "reefs" in what had once been a deep-sea desert.

Seventy-three years after the sinking, in the early morning of September 1, 1985, *Argo,* an unmanned deep-sea vehicle, disturbed the darkness for the first time. *Argo,* carrying video cameras and sonar, was towed at the end of miles of coaxial cable by the Woods Hole Oceanographic Institution (WHOI) ship *Knorr. Argo* sent back to the ship grainy, real-time images from the deep—the first the world had seen of *Titanic* since black-and-white photographs depicted it departing the Irish coast in 1912. Humans first visited the wreck the following year in the research submersible *Alvin,* peering out of small portholes. In 1987, another submersible, *Nautile,* glided over the site, and with a robotic arm carefully picked up the first of 1,800 artifacts it would recover from the mud during that expedition.

Since then, a new era has dawned in our quest to study the past that lies at the bottom of the ocean. In 2010 two highly sophisticated robotic vehicles systematically crisscrossed the seabed on their own, with high-resolution sonar and camera systems, creating the first comprehensive map of the *Titanic* site. Another robot, at the end of a fiber-optic cable, sent to the surface live, full-color, 3-D images, allowing scientists to virtually walk the decks of the ship. This latest research effort, of which I was a part, represents a paradigm shift in underwater archaeology. For the first time, *Titanic* can be treated and explored like any other underwater site—even extreme depth is no longer an obstacle to archaeology. Thanks to rapid technological advances and interdisciplinary work, archaeologists have a whole new perspective on sites such as *Titanic,* and new questions to ask, questions we never could have dreamed of when underwater archaeology began just 50 years ago.

Around the time that deep-sea technology was first developing, so was underwater archaeology. Its specific techniques and methods began to emerge in the late 1950s, through pioneers such as Jacques Yves Cousteau,

Frederic Dumas, Peter Throckmorton, Honor Frost, and George Bass. Their work culminated in Bass' first complete underwater excavation of a shipwreck—a Bronze Age vessel at Cape Gelidonya, Turkey—in 1960. When asked by colleagues whether "proper" archaeology could be done underwater, Bass said that archaeology was archaeology, regardless of where it was performed. Since then, thousands of underwater archaeological sites, from shipwrecks to prehistoric sites to submerged cities, have been located, documented, and excavated. And advanced diving, especially mixed-gas technology, has allowed divers to go deeper and stay longer, without the muddling effects of pressurized air on the brain. However, deep sites still lay beyond the reach of divers.

Ironically, the first steps in expanding underwater archaeology to the depths were propelled by the *Titanic* disaster itself, as the first sonar systems were developed and tested after the sinking to locate and avoid icebergs. This technology improved through the two world wars and into the Cold War, moving into deeper waters, until its most dramatic discovery to date—*Titanic*. But even in 1985, the idea that *Titanic* could be explored, photographed, and mapped like an archaeological site seemed like the stuff of science fiction.

The introduction of the global positioning system (GPS) was the next big step, providing a platform on which to integrate sonar data with increasingly sophisticated maps and satellite imagery. Better robotic systems also evolved, as well as manned submersibles that could travel even deeper than *Titanic*. But the submersibles are hardly the same as diving on a site. They are built on Cold War technology, with tiny crew compartments surrounded by life support, thrusters, batteries, lights, cameras, and sonar systems. Lying face down, neck craned upward in the cold, dark capsules, scientists peer through small portholes and rely on deployed instruments and mechanical arms to interact with the environment outside.

My first submersible dive was in 2000, in a Russian *Mir*-class sub, to assess the wreck and cultural tourism at the *Titanic* site. I was struck by both the extreme conditions and the incredible skill that these unsung pilots need to safely launch, dive, navigate, and ascend. As submersible pilot Paul-Henry Nargeolet of the salvage and exhibition company RMS *Titanic* Inc. noted, those missions to *Titanic* were merely glimpses through a "keyhole." I spent my submersible dive with my forehead pressed for hours against the cold steel of a *Mir* hull to stare through four-inch-thick Plexiglas—I know exactly what he means. Each of those dives added incrementally to our knowledge of *Titanic*, but the ability to do a basic detailed survey, map with accuracy, and measure—let alone impose the archaeological discipline of a grid and units, as one would on a divable underwater site—remained elusive.

After my 2000 visit to *Titanic*, I wrote in *Archaeology* magazine:

> *We see scoop marks that show where selected pieces have been plucked from clusters of artifacts—no grids, no scientific sampling—simply for their display or monetary value. What is happening here, two-and-one-half miles down and out of sight of much of the world, is not archaeology. . . . In short, other than the well-known intact bow section and the stern and the sub pilots' recollections, no detailed "road map," let alone a highly detailed archaeological site plan, exists.*

Photos of *Titanic* had been taken and artifacts collected, but none of these activities reflected the process by which we apply scientific methods to the study of the past. To actually study the wreck, and the lives of the people on the ship, we would need a detailed site map that we could visit again and again, with ever-more sophisticated questions. Could such a map be created not only for the largest features—the bow and stern sections—but also for artifacts ranging from boilers and hull sections, down to a teacup, bottle, or button? Could we catalog the site's smallest constituents in a nondestructive way? Could we discern the site formation process—determine exactly how the pieces of the ship and its contents came to their resting places? And did the salvage of artifacts from the site compromise its archaeological integrity and render archaeological technique and method moot? The 2010 *Titanic* expedition, led by David Gallo of WHOI, set out to answer these questions and establish that archaeological science beyond mere observation could be conducted at crushing depths.

Following the discovery of the wreck in 1985, there were opposing views on what should be done with it. In the United States, Congress passed the RMS Titanic Memorial Act at the urging of oceanographer Robert Ballard, who led the expedition that discovered the wreck. It recommended that the site be left untouched as a memorial. But because *Titanic* rests in international waters, it was under no nation's jurisdiction—under admiralty law, *Titanic* was open to anyone with the right equipment and technical expertise to reach it. The act also gave the National Oceanic and Atmospheric Administration (NOAA), working with the Department of State, the task of negotiating an international agreement on *Titanic* and developing guidelines for appropriate activities on the site, a process that took a decade and a half.

As this discussion was taking place, beginning in 1987, a private American company formed by investors and known as Titanic Ventures Limited Partnership (now Premier Exhibitions, with the *Titanic* artifacts handled by subsidiary RMS *Titanic* Inc.), began diving to the wreck with codiscoverers IFREMER, France's deep-sea agency, to recover artifacts and photograph the ship. Working from submersibles, over seven expeditions between 1987 and 2004, RMS Titanic Inc. ultimately raised some 5,000 artifacts, with the aim of displaying them for profit. Their activities were controversial. In 1987, the *London Daily Express* called the recovery dives "Vandalism for Profit." A 1988 editorial in *Discover* magazine was titled, "We All Loot in a Yellow Submarine." Guest columnists squared off in the pages of *USA Today*: "Salvaging Artifacts Is an Insult to the Dead" versus "Salvaging Artifacts Brings the Legend to Life." Public opinion remains divided. While newspaper columnists, cartoonists, and archaeologists decried the practice, countless people have lined up to visit RMS *Titanic* Inc.'s touring artifact exhibitions.

The furor over the recovery of artifacts from *Titanic* is understandable. The greater concerns for archaeology, however, are how and why the artifacts were removed, and what would become of them. Were they being appropriately conserved, cataloged, and researched? Would they ultimately go under the hammer at auction, artifact by artifact? The legal history of *Titanic* and RMS Titanic Inc. is long and complex. The U.S. District Court in Norfolk, Virginia, which for two decades has overseen the salvage company's activities under admiralty law, decided a number of these questions. Rulings by the court have limited recovery to artifacts scattered outside the intact bow and stern sections. At one stage, RMS Titanic Inc. sued the Departments of State and Commerce unsuccessfully to stop publication of the International Agreement on *Titanic* guidelines. Most recently the court awarded RMS Titanic Inc. title to the 5,000 artifacts, with the stipulation that the company follow international standards for conservation, treatment, and display of the collection. Furthermore, any sale of the artifacts would be subject to review by the court, and allowed only if the collection stays together and is maintained for public display and study.

Amid the years of legal battles and publicity, in 1997 I participated in an independent review of the work that had been done on the *Titanic* site for the International Congress of Maritime Museums. The review was prompted by concerns of the international museum and archaeological communities over the impending display of recovered *Titanic* artifacts at the National Maritime Museum in Greenwich, England. Larry Murphy of the National Park Service, Roger Knight of the National Maritime Museum, and I were surprised to learn that though RMS *Titanic* Inc.'s artifact recoveries had been selective—for iconic, intact, and, at times, random artifacts—they had been conducted with great skill. The recoveries had been documented by video, and additional data existed, we were told, to create a map of where the artifacts had come from.

RMS Titanic Inc. had also conducted studies in 1996 of the wreck and its environment, such as a sonar survey through the mud to assess now-buried damage to the hull that may be from the iceberg impact, and an ongoing assessment of the biological corrosion by microbiologist Roy Cullimore and his colleagues to determine how long *Titanic* would remain intact. Ballard and NOAA also jointly examined the site and the remains of the bow and stern, and film director James Cameron explored the interior, revealing much about the ship and what happened inside it the evening that it sank.

Much data had been gathered since *Titanic*'s rediscovery, but the scope of the entire site remained largely unknown—we had no detailed knowledge of the whole, and didn't even know how large it was. The "keyhole" views of the wreck had not described or defined the scattered field of artifacts, for example. Understanding *Titanic* from these efforts was like driving through a city at night, in a rainstorm, peering through a portion of the windshield, and trying to piece together in your mind's eye what the headlights revealed around each corner. But by 2010, with the latest technology and the right team, a comprehensive, finely detailed site map was finally in reach. A decade after my first visit to *Titanic* in 2000, I returned with the best-equipped and most experienced group of scientists and technicians ever assembled for such a project.

The result was a multiagency expedition, including WHOI, the Waitt Institute, Phoenix International, NOAA, and the National Park Service, that would develop a detailed archaeological site plan and report. The new effort also includes a *Titanic* Advisory Council to review proposals to work on the site in accordance with UNESCO and U.S. historic preservation law and practice. Other recommendations include a voluntary exclusion zone around the wreck site where ships would not discharge waste of any sort (modern garbage is indeed present on the site) and designated areas where submersibles visiting the wreck would enter and exit the archaeological area. This last point is important—25 years of dives have littered the wreck site with the dive weights each sub drops to ascend to the surface.

RMS Titanic Inc. paid for the expedition, which included many staunch critics (some directly involved in the litigation) of the prior handling of the *Titanic* wreck—myself among them. Such a collaboration was simply unimaginable to many people right up until the mission's launch in the research ship *Jean Charcot* from St. John's, Newfoundland, in August 2010.

Rather than peering at *Titanic* as if through a rain-splattered windshield at night, we now have an elevated view of the "city," with the clarity and detail of a slow, low-altitude flight at noon. This is possible because of the latest robotic technology, deployed in the 2010 expedition—two autonomous underwater vehicles (AUVs) and a remotely operated vehicle (ROV). The AUV team, including Mike Dessner and Andy Sherrell of the Waitt Institute, and Greg Packard, Mike Purcell, and Jim Partan of WHOI, operated and maintained the AUVs. At 12.5 feet long and 28 inches in diameter, they look like fat, yellow torpedoes. Weighing one ton and costing nearly three million dollars each, they can dive to almost 20,000 feet and run for up to 22 hours autonomously at depth, following preprogrammed courses at speeds of up to five knots. They carry a variety of instruments, including high-resolution multi-beam profiling sonar; dual-frequency side-scan sonar; sub-bottom profiling sonar; an automatic digital camera with strobe; conductivity, depth, and temperature sensors; and collision avoidance software. One of the scientists on the expedition joked that if you are not there to pick the AUVs up when they surface, they have the ability to call your cellphone to ask for a ride. Once retrieved, they provide terabytes of data from the ocean floor. (After our expedition, they were deployed on another mission, classified at the time: the successful location of the wreckage of Air France flight 447 in the South Atlantic.)

The other robot was an ROV, *Remora*, a refrigerator-sized frame covered with crush-proof foam, cables, thrusters, deep-sea lights, and high-definition cameras from WHOI's Advanced Imaging and Visualization Laboratory (AIVL). Rated to dive to 20,000 feet, *Remora*, operated by Tim Weller and Bradley Gillis of Phoenix International, was tethered to the ship by more than 12,400 feet of fiber-optic cable and driven by joystick. Two levels above the main deck of *Jean Charcot*, in a darkened compartment of the ship's laboratory, the AIVL team conducted systematic sonar and digital imaging of the bow, stern, and other major sections of *Titanic*. Wearing bulky black plastic glasses, we watched large screens and saw *Titanic*, brightly lit and in 3-D, and relayed directions to the ROV's pilot—stop, a little to port, turn 10 degrees—for hours. I was struck by how much more insight—digitally documented in high definition, with remarkable precision and clarity—we were gaining compared with being down there in a manned submersible. The lights, literally and figuratively, were on for the first time. Previously, the results of work on the wreck had to be carefully pieced together, at times by hand, to provide glimpses of certain artifacts and features. Now, the entire wreck site became accessible, down to a teacup or wine bottle or crabs crawling along the hull.

Our data acquisition complete, the processing of this information is ongoing. AIVL's William Lange (a member of the original *Titanic* discovery team) and his visualization team, including 3-D specialist Evan Kovacs, are merging all this optical and sonar data together into a detailed, comprehensive baseline map of the wreck, built on a GIS database developed by the National Park Service's David Conlin, co-principal archaeologist on the expedition (with me). Science begins with measurement. Understanding the relationships between features and objects on the seafloor is key to deciphering how the site was created on April 15, 1912.

With the new site map, we are able to virtually "fly in" on the wreck, dropping into the water anywhere in a roughly three-by-five-mile area that encompasses the full extent of the wreck, and get a view of anything, from the large intact portions of the ship down to the most current-scattered pieces of coal, dishes, and deck tiles. Digitally, we can move in closer to any portion of *Titanic*—now sectioned into grid units like a proper archaeological site—including a small area that holds the greatest concentration of features. There, close to the intact but mangled stern, is a collection of pieces of hull, machinery, superstructure, and other artifacts known for decades as the "debris field." We have now started referring to it as the "artifact field"—more than 60 major features and tens of thousands of artifacts in a non-random pattern—where we are both plotting relationships between objects and studying the features on a pair of shoes.

We have begun the task of identifying features, artifacts, and their contexts, especially with the help of *Titanic* expert Bill Sauder. I have known of Sauder's scholarship for years, so I was not surprised by the depth of his knowledge. But I was amazed all the same when he meticulously explained how a battered feature on the seabed was one of the revolving doors from *Titanic*'s first-class smoking room, and as he identified the half-intact oval domed skylight from one of the ship's two grand staircases.

Returning virtually to the wreck again and again like this is critical to any scientific approach. Rather than seeing *Titanic* through a keyhole, we can interrogate the entire thing and ask fresh questions of it.

The archaeological methods now being applied to *Titanic* have given us clear insights into the site formation process, specifically how *Titanic* broke apart and fell, and how the bow plowed into the mud at an angle. We can see how the stern sank, along with broken sections of the hull, including a cluster of boilers. We can delineate where heavier objects landed and blew away silt, and at the bow we can see how the hull dug in, flexed, and sprang back, leaving a knife-sharp edge in the mud even a century later. We have also plotted pairs of shoes, laced and tied, next to disturbed mud—places where victims came to rest.

Some of the site formation processes were known or surmised before. As early as 1986, Lange, with Ballard and Al Uchupi of WHOI, worked with images from *Argo* to begin to map around *Titanic*'s stern and hypothesize about patterns of the fallen artifacts. Others, including a 2005 television documentary crew working with experts, developed new theories on how *Titanic* came apart. And Cameron's expeditions sent small robots deep into the bow that yielded detailed information on the sinking and the exceptional levels of preservation inside the wreck. A variety of further expeditions, including two by NOAA in 2003–2004, had surveyed, generated partial photomosaics, and continued to assess the bacteriological consumption of *Titanic*'s steel.

The 2010 expedition brought these efforts together with a new base of solid data, a grid, assigned units, and feature numbers, providing a new perspective on how *Titanic* went from ship to shipwreck, and how it continues to change over time. The new map revealed to us that the scattered features and artifacts do not represent everything that once lay inside or on the ship. Rather than streaming like comet tails from the bow and stern as the ship sank, most contents of the artifact field come from the full disintegration of a section of the ship—some 70 feet of *Titanic*'s 882-foot length that branched up and out between two of the deck funnels. Broken pieces of the hull from that section were accompanied by two of the reciprocating engine cylinders, the five boilers from the number one boiler room, 51 tons of coal (of 1,000 or more tons on board), and four tons of coke. This segment also included the contents of the Verandah Café, the Palm Court, the aft end of the First Class Lounge, and a group of first-, second-, and third-class cabins, as well as the galleys and pantries, sculleries, wine room, barber shop, smoking room, hospital, cold storage rooms, silverware locker, and baker's shop. Among these items on the seafloor are also pieces swept from the deck, such as the funnels, the davits used to launch lifeboats, and the remains of the bridge. There is a lot of material down there and reflected on the site map, but it represents just a tiny fraction of the presumed millions of artifacts. The artifacts salvaged between 1987 and 2004 do not represent even 1 percent of that total.

Where is everything else? Still inside. Cameron's explorations of the bow interior revealed cabins complete with furniture, cupboards stacked with dishes, painted wooden paneling, and hanging light fixtures. Cargo and luggage, including the packed bags of passengers, remain in the hold, and the mailroom, visible through a hole that opened in the hull when it flexed and broke on impact with the seabed, has stacks of mailbags. We believe that, while badly mangled, the stern also retains intact cabins. *Titanic* was a floating microcosm of society, a city short-lived and dramatically terminated that carried both the rich traveling for pleasure and immigrants seeking new lives in the United States or Canada. Each cabin, trunk, suitcase, valise, grip, and mailbag is itself both archive and memorial.

RMS Titanic Inc. recovered a few scattered bags from the ship, and the clothing, correspondence, and personal effects inside them demonstrated exceptional levels of preservation. These bags speak evocatively about the people who packed them, many of whom are known only as initials and a last name on a manifest. By the time this story hits newsstands and mailboxes, the bags, the rest of RMS *Titanic* Inc.'s collection, and the company's documentation on the site will have, pending court approval, a new steward. Hopefully further study of this collection will continue to tell the story of what we now know to be one of the great human migrations, the nineteenth- and twentieth-century maritime trail from Europe to America.

It is clear that *Titanic,* though well-studied, has so much more to teach us. We have yet to conduct detailed oceanographic studies to assess the wreck's effects on the surrounding deep-sea environment, and what currents, oxygen levels, temperature, and marine organisms are precisely doing to *Titanic.* Those processes are as important to the future of *Titanic* as is our dedication to preserving and learning from the site. *Titanic* still awaits a solid, comprehensive research and management plan, as well as what I see as the most appropriate home for its salvaged artifacts, a public *Titanic* museum. There are no plans for such an initiative at the moment, but those artifacts are as close as we will ever get to the people who were caught up in that night's events a century ago. Ultimately, archaeology's role in *Titanic*'s story will be to move beyond April 15, 1912, and deeper into the society that produced *Titanic,* populated its cabins, and looked to the ship as a voyage to the future. Answers will be elusive, but we're now better equipped than ever before to ask those questions.

Critical Thinking

1. What kinds of technology are being used to locate archaeological sites underwater?
2. How has technology been expanded to carry out archaeology to the depths of the *Titanic?*
3. In what ways has the *Titanic* become a proper archaeological site?
4. How do you assess the pros and cons of extracting artifacts from the wreckage of the *Titanic?*

Create Central

www.mhhe.com/createcentral

Internet References

Smithsonian Institution Website
www.si.edu

Society for Historical Archaeology
www.sha.org

The New York Times
www.nytimes.com

JAMES P. DELGADO is the Director of Maritime Heritage for the National Oceanic and Atmospheric Administration's Office of National Marine Sanctuaries.

Delgado, James P. From *Archaeology*, May/June 2012, pp. 35–40. Copyright © 2012 by Archaeological Institute of America. Reprinted by permission of *Archaeology Magazine*. www.archaeology.org

Article

Prepared by: Mari Pritchard Parker, *Pasadena City College* and
Elvio Angeloni, *Pasadena City College*

Mayas Mastered Rubber Long before Goodyear

They used various formulas to make bouncy balls, glue and even resilient rubber sandals, a study finds.

THOMAS H. MAUGH II

Learning Outcomes

After reading this article, you will be able to:

- Discuss the vulcanization process used by the ancient Mayans in making rubber products.
- Recount the Mayan uses of rubber.

Hundreds and perhaps even thousands of years before Charles Goodyear discovered the vulcanization process that made commercial rubber viable, Mesoamerican peoples were carrying out a similar process to produce rubber artifacts for a broad variety of uses, two MIT researchers have found.

By varying the amount of materials they added to raw rubber, Mesoamericans were able to produce bouncy rubber balls for the Mayas' ceremonial games, resilient rubber sandals and sticky material used to glue implements to handles, the research shows.

The researchers "have compiled a compelling case that ancient Mesoamerican peoples were the first polymer scientists, exerting substantial control over the mechanical properties of rubber for various applications," said materials scientist John McCloy of the Pacific Northwest National Laboratory, who was not involved in the research.

Ancient rubber footwear has not been found at archaeological sites, but written records of the Spanish conquistadores indicate that the indigenous peoples wore them. Archaeologists have found rubber balls, bands, statues and adhesives.

Rubber is a latex material produced from the sap of a variety of trees. Mesoamericans got it from what is now known as the Panama rubber tree, *Castilla elastica*. But the rubber produced as the sap dries is sticky and, ultimately, brittle.

The current research derives from a simple question asked by then-MIT-undergraduate Michael J. Tarkanian in a freshman archaeology class in 1996: How did the Maya produce bouncy rubber balls from this material?

Intrigued, the course's teacher, materials scientist Dorothy Hosler, did some quick research and "a few days later, she e-mailed me and said no one has ever answered the question," Tarkanian said in a telephone interview.

That kicked off what has so far been a 14-year collaboration between the two scientists.

Thorough study of written records of the Spanish conquerors indicated that the Maya made their balls by mixing the latex with juice from the morning glory, *Ipomoea alba,* a vine that grows throughout the region. In 1999, Hosler and Tarkanian reported that they could make bouncy rubber balls by mixing equal amounts of latex and morning glory juice and heating them.

"But doing the work, I noticed that different ratios [of the two ingredients] produced different properties," Tarkanian said.

Ultimately, as they will report in a forthcoming issue of the journal *Latin American Antiquity,* they found different formulas that provided different characteristics. A 50-50 mixture produced a bouncy rubber ball, for example, while adding one part morning glory to three parts latex produced a strong, durable material suitable for sandals.

Adding no morning glory produces a material that is a good adhesive. In the paper, they characterize for the first time the physical and chemical properties of each form.

The oldest known rubber balls from the region date to 1600 B.C., suggesting that the indigenous peoples possessed this knowledge at least that far back. By the time the Spaniards arrived in the 16th century, Tarkanian said, "there was a large rubber industry in the region," producing 16,000 rubber balls each year and large numbers of rubber statues, sandals, bands and other products.

Most of these were produced in outlying areas and shipped to Tikal, the Maya capital, as tax payments.

Around 1839, American inventor Charles Goodyear came up with the vulcanization process, in which latex from the Brazilian rubber tree is heated with sulfur. The sulfur causes the polymer chains of the latex to become cross-linked, making them stronger, more durable and more elastic.

The morning glory juice has sulfur-containing amino acids that apparently do much the same thing, Tarkanian said. The density of cross-links is much greater in the vulcanized rubber, however.

Tarkanian and Hosler have not yet identified a unique chemical signature of their lab-produced material that can be compared directly to archaeological samples—a process that is complicated by the tendency of rubbers to deteriorate over long periods. But they have noted that certain proteins in the raw latex are removed during their manufacturing process. Analysis of some ancient artifacts indicates the same proteins are missing there as well.

Archaeologist Frances Berdan of CSU San Bernardino said in a statement that the work has implications well beyond rubber. "There are other areas of production where the pre-Hispanic peoples cleverly combined materials to achieve enhanced products," she said.

The MIT work should encourage researchers to investigate these other areas as well, she said.

Critical Thinking

1. What was the process used by Mesoamericans to produce rubber and to what uses did they put it?
2. What is the archaeological and historical evidence for such uses?
3. Be familiar with the various materials and processes that were probably used to fashion the various products and their uses.
4. When were the first rubber balls produced?
5. Be familiar with the vulcanization process developed by Charles Goodyear and its similarity to the ancient Mesoamerican process.

Create Central

www.mhhe.com/createcentral

Internet References

Maya Archaeology Initiative
http://mayaarchaeology.org

Society for American Archaeology
www.saa.org

Society for Archaeological Sciences
www.socarchsci.org

Maugh II, Thomas H. From *Los Angeles Times*, by Maugh II, Thomas H., May 31, 2010. Copyright © 2010 by The Los Angeles Times. All rights reserved. Used with permission of LA Times Reprints.

Article

Prepared by: Mari Pritchard Parker, *Pasadena City College* and
Elvio Angeloni, *Pasadena City College*

Profile of an Anthropologist: No Bone Unturned

PATRICK HUYGHE

Learning Outcomes

After reading this article, you will be able to:

- Using examples, show how forensic anthropology can contribute to airline safety and human rights work.
- Discuss "osteobiography" in terms of what it can tell us about a person's life and death.

The research of some physical anthropologists and archaeologists involves the discovery and analysis of old bones (as well as artifacts and other remains). Most often these bones represent only part of a skeleton or maybe the mixture of parts of several skeletons. Often these remains are smashed, burned, or partially destroyed. Over the years, physical anthropologists have developed a remarkable repertoire of skills and techniques for teasing the greatest possible amount of information out of sparse material remains.

Although originally developed for basic research, the methods of physical anthropology can be directly applied to contemporary human problems.... In this profile, we look briefly at the career of Clyde C. Snow, a physical anthropologist who has put these skills to work in a number of different settings....

As you read this selection, ask yourself the following questions:

- Given what you know of physical anthropology, what sort of work would a physical anthropologist do for the Federal Aviation Administration?
- What is anthropometry? *How might anthropometric surveys of pilots and passengers help in the design of aircraft equipment?*
- What is forensic anthropology? *How can a biological anthropologist be an expert witness in legal proceedings?*

Clyde Snow is never in a hurry. He knows he's late. He's always late. For Snow, being late is part of the job. In fact, he doesn't usually begin to work until death has stripped some poor individual to the bone, and no one—neither the local homicide detectives nor the pathologists—can figure out who once gave identity to the skeletonized remains. No one, that is, except a shrewd, laconic, 60-year-old forensic anthropologist.

Snow strolls into the Cook County Medical Examiner's Office in Chicago on this brisk October morning wearing a pair of Lucchese cowboy boots and a three-piece pin-striped suit. Waiting for him in autopsy room 160 are a bunch of naked skeletons found in Illinois, Wisconsin, and Minnesota since his last visit. Snow, a native Texan who now lives in rural Oklahoma, makes the trip up to Chicago some six times a year. The first case on his agenda is a pale brown skull found in the garbage of an abandoned building once occupied by a Chicago cosmetics company.

Snow turns the skull over slowly in his hands, a cigarette dangling from his fingers. One often does. Snow does not seem overly concerned about mortality, though its tragedy surrounds him daily.

"There's some trauma here," he says, examining a rough edge at the lower back of the skull. He points out the area to Jim Elliott, a homicide detective with the Chicago police. "This looks like a chopping blow by a heavy bladed instrument. Almost like a decapitation." In a place where the whining of bone saws drifts through hallways and the sweet-sour smell of death hangs in the air, the word surprises no one.

Snow begins thinking aloud. "I think what we're looking at here is a female, or maybe a small male, about thirty to forty years old. Probably Asian." He turns the skull upside down, pointing out the degree of wear on the teeth. "This was somebody who lived on a really rough diet. We don't normally find this kind of dental wear in a modern Western population."

"How long has it been around?" Elliott asks.

Snow raises the skull up to his nose. "It doesn't have any decompositional odors," he says. He pokes a finger in the skull's nooks and crannies. "There's no soft tissue left. It's good and dry. And it doesn't show signs of having been buried. I would say that this has been lying around in an attic or a box for years. It feels like a souvenir skull," says Snow.

Souvenir skulls, usually those of Japanese soldiers, were popular with U.S. troops serving in the Pacific during World

War II; there was also a trade in skulls during the Vietnam War years. On closer inspection, though, Snow begins to wonder about the skull's Asian origins—the broad nasal aperture and the jutting forth of the upper-tooth-bearing part of the face suggest Melanesian features. Sifting through the objects found in the abandoned building with the skull, he finds several looseleaf albums of 35-millimeter transparencies documenting life among the highland tribes of New Guinea. The slides, shot by an anthropologist, include graphic scenes of ritual warfare. The skull, Snow concludes, is more likely to be a trophy from one of these tribal battles than the result of a local Chicago homicide.

"So you'd treat it like found property?" Elliott asks finally. "Like somebody's garage-sale property?"

"Exactly," says Snow.

Clyde Snow is perhaps the world's most sought-after forensic anthropologist. People have been calling upon him to identify skeletons for more than a quarter of a century. Every year he's involved in some 75 cases of identification, most of them without fanfare. "He's an old scudder who doesn't have to blow his own whistle," says Walter Birkby, a forensic anthropologist at the University of Arizona. "He know's he's good."

Yet over the years Snow's work has turned him into something of an unlikely celebrity. He has been called upon to identify the remains of the Nazi war criminal Josef Mengele, reconstruct the face of the Egyptian boy-king Tutankhamen, confirm the authenticity of the body autopsied as that of President John F. Kennedy, and examine the skeletal remains of General Custer's men at the battlefield of the Little Bighorn. He has also been involved in the grim task of identifying the bodies in some of the United States' worst airline accidents.

Such is his legend that cases are sometimes attributed to him in which he played no part. He did not, as *The New York Times* reported, identify the remains of the crew of the *Challenger* disaster. But the man is often the equal of his myth. For the past four years, setting his personal safety aside, Snow has spent much of his time in Argentina, searching for the graves and identities of some of the thousands who "disappeared" between 1976 and 1983, during Argentina's military regime.

Snow did not set out to rescue the dead from oblivion. For almost two decades, until 1979, he was a physical anthropologist at the Civil Aeromedical Institute, part of the Federal Aviation Administration in Oklahoma City. Snow's job was to help engineers improve aircraft design and safety features by providing them with data on the human frame.

One study, he recalls, was initiated in response to complaints from a flight attendants' organization. An analysis of accident patterns had revealed that inadequate restraints on flight attendants' jump seats were leading to deaths and injuries and that aircraft doors weighing several hundred pounds were impeding evacuation efforts. Snow points out that ensuring the survival of passengers in emergencies is largely the flight attendants' responsibility. "If they are injured or killed in a crash, you're going to find a lot of dead passengers."

Reasoning that equipment might be improved if engineers had more data on the size and strength of those who use it, Snow undertook a study that required meticulous measurement. When his report was issued in 1975, Senator William Proxmire was outraged that $57,800 of the taxpayers' money had been spent to caliper 423 airline stewardesses from head to toe. Yet the study, which received one of the senator's dubious Golden Fleece Awards, was firmly supported by both the FAA and the Association of Flight Attendants. "I can't imagine," says Snow with obvious delight, "how much coffee Proxmire got spilled on him in the next few months."

It was during his tenure at the FAA that he developed an interest in forensic work. Over the years the Oklahoma police frequently consulted the physical anthropologist for help in identifying crime victims. "The FAA figured it was a kind of community service to let me work on these cases," he says.

The experience also helped to prepare him for the grim task of identifying the victims of air disasters. In December 1972, when a United Airlines plane crashed outside Chicago, killing 43 of the 61 people aboard (including the wife of Watergate conspirator Howard Hunt, who was found with $10,000 in her purse), Snow was brought in to help examine the bodies. That same year, with Snow's help, forensic anthropology was recognized as a specialty by the American Academy of Forensic Sciences. "It got a lot of anthropologists interested in forensics," he says, "and it made a lot of pathologists out there aware that there were anthropologists who could help them."

Each nameless skeleton poses a unique mystery for Snow. But some, like the second case awaiting him back in the autopsy room at the Cook County morgue, are more challenging than others. This one is a real chiller. In a large cardboard box lies a jumble of bones along with a tattered leg from a pair of blue jeans, a sock shrunk tightly around the bones of a foot, a pair of Nike running shoes without shoelaces, and, inside the hood of a blue windbreaker, a mass of stringy, blood-caked hair. The remains were discovered frozen in ice about 20 miles outside Milwaukee. A rusted bicycle was found lying close by. Paul Hibbard, chief deputy medical examiner for Waukesha County, who brought the skeleton to Chicago, says no one has been reported missing.

Snow lifts the bones out of the box and begins reconstructing the skeleton on an autopsy table. "There are two hundred six bones and thirty-two teeth in the human body," he says, "and each has a story to tell." Because bone is dynamic, living tissue, many of life's significant events—injuries, illness, childbearing—leave their mark on the body's internal framework. Put together the stories told by these bones, he says, and what you have is a person's "osteobiography."

Snow begins by determining the sex of the skeleton, which is not always obvious. He tells the story of a skeleton that was brought to his FAA office in the late 1970s. It had been found along with some women's clothes and a purse in a local back lot, and the police had assumed that it was female. But when Snow examined the bones, he realized that "at six foot three, she would have probably have been the tallest female in Oklahoma."

Then Snow recalled that six months earlier the custodian in his building had suddenly not shown up for work. The man's supervisor later mentioned to Snow, "You know, one of these days when they find Ronnie, he's going to be dressed as a woman." Ronnie, it turned out, was a weekend transvestite.

A copy of his dental records later confirmed that the skeleton in women's clothing was indeed Snow's janitor.

The Wisconsin bike rider is also male. Snow picks out two large bones that look something like twisted oysters—the innominates, or hipbones, which along with the sacrum, or lower backbone, form the pelvis. This pelvis is narrow and steep-walled like a male's, not broad and shallow like a female's. And the sciatic notch (the V-shaped space where the sciatic nerve passes through the hipbone) is narrow, as is normal in a male. Snow can also determine a skeleton's sex by checking the size of the mastoid processes (the bony knobs at the base of the skull) and the prominence of the brow ridge, or by measuring the head of an available limb bone, which is typically broader in males.

From an examination of the skull he concludes that the bike rider is "predominantly Caucasoid." A score of bony traits help the forensic anthropologist assign a skeleton to one of the three major racial groups: Negroid, Caucasoid, or Mongoloid. Snow notes that the ridge of the boy's nose is high and salient, as it is in whites. In Negroids and Mongoloids (which include American Indians as well as most Asians) the nose tends to be broad in relation to its height. However, the boy's nasal margins are somewhat smoothed down, usually a Mongoloid feature. "Possibly a bit of American Indian admixture," says Snow. "Do you have Indians in your area?" Hibbard nods.

Age is next. Snow takes the skull and turns it upside down, pointing out the basilar joint, the junction between the two major bones that form the underside of the skull. In a child the joint would still be open to allow room for growth, but here the joint has fused—something that usually happens in the late teen years. On the other hand, he says, pointing to the zigzagging lines on the dome of the skull, the cranial sutures are open. The cranial sutures, which join the bones of the braincase, begin to fuse and disappear in the mid-twenties.

Next Snow picks up a femur and looks for signs of growth at the point where the shaft meets the knobbed end. The thin plates of cartilage—areas of incomplete calcification—that are visible at this point suggest that the boy hadn't yet attained his full height. Snow double-checks with an examination of the pubic symphysis, the joint where the two hipbones meet. The ridges in this area, which fill in and smooth over in adulthood, are still clearly marked. He concludes that the skeleton is that of a boy between 15 and 20 years old.

"One of the things you learn is to be pretty conservative," says Snow. "It's very impressive when you tell the police, 'This person is eighteen years old,' and he turns out to be eighteen. The problem is, if the person is fifteen you've blown it—you probably won't find him. Looking for a missing person is like trying to catch fish. Better get a big net and do your own sorting."

Snow then picks up a leg bone, measures it with a set of calipers, and enters the data into a portable computer. Using the known correlation between the height and length of the long limb bones, he quickly estimates the boy's height. "He's five foot six and a half to five foot eleven," says Snow. "Medium build, not excessively muscular, judging from the muscle attachments that we see." He points to the grainy ridges that appear where muscle attaches itself to the bone. The most prominent attachments show up on the teenager's right arm bone, indicating right-handedness.

Then Snow examines the ribs one by one for signs of injury. He finds no stab wounds, cuts, or bullet holes, here or elsewhere on the skeleton. He picks up the hyoid bone from the boy's throat and looks for the tell-tale fracture signs that would suggest the boy was strangled. But, to Snow's frustration, he can find no obvious cause of death. In hopes of identifying the missing teenager, he suggests sending the skull, hair, and boy's description to Betty Pat Gatliff, a medical illustrator and sculptor in Oklahoma who does facial reconstructions.

Six weeks later photographs of the boy's likeness appear in the *Milwaukee Sentinel*. "If you persist long enough," says Snow, "eighty-five to ninety percent of the cases eventually get positively identified, but it can take anywhere from a few weeks to a few years."

Snow and Gatliff have collaborated many times, but never with more glitz than in 1983, when Snow was commissioned by Patrick Barry, a Miami orthopedic surgeon and amateur Egyptologist, to reconstruct the face of the Egyptian boy-king Tutankhamen. Normally a facial reconstruction begins with a skull, but since Tutankhamen's 3,000-year-old remains were in Egypt, Snow had to make do with the skull measurements from a 1925 postmortem and X-rays taken in 1975. A plaster model of the skull was made, and on the basis on Snow's report—"his skull is Caucasoid with some Negroid admixtures"—Gatliff put a face on it. What did Tutankhamen look like? Very much like the gold mask on his sarcophagus, says Snow, confirming that it was, indeed, his portrait.

Many cite Snow's use of facial reconstructions as one of his most important contributions to the field. Snow, typically self-effacing, says that Gatliff "does all the work." The identification of skeletal remains, he stresses, is often a collaboration between pathologists, odontologists, radiologists, and medical artists using a variety of forensic techniques.

One of Snow's last tasks at the FAA was to help identify the dead from the worst airline accident in U.S. history. On May 25, 1979, a DC-10 crashed shortly after takeoff from Chicago's O'Hare Airport, killing 273 people. The task facing Snow and more than a dozen forensic specialists was horrific. "No one ever sat down and counted," says Snow, "but we estimated ten thousand to twelve thousand pieces or parts of bodies." Nearly 80 percent of the victims were identified on the basis of dental evidence and fingerprints. Snow and forensic radiologist John Fitzpatrick later managed to identify two dozen others by comparing postmortem X-rays with X-rays taken during the victim's lifetime.

Next to dental records, such X-ray comparisons are the most common way of obtaining positive identifications. In 1978, when a congressional committee reviewed the evidence on John F. Kennedy's assassination, Snow used X-rays to show that the body autopsied at Bethesda Naval Hospital was indeed that of the late president and had not—as some conspiracy theorists believed—been switched.

The issue was resolved on the evidence of Kennedy's "sinus print," the scalloplike pattern on the upper margins of the sinuses that is visible in X-rays of the forehead. So characteristic is a person's sinus print that courts throughout the world accept the matching of antemortem and postmortem X-rays of the sinuses as positive identification.

Yet another technique in the forensic specialist's repertoire is photo superposition. Snow used it in 1977 to help identify the mummy of a famous Oklahoma outlaw named Elmer J. McCurdy, who was killed by a posse after holding up a train in 1911. For years the mummy had been exhibited as a "dummy" in a California funhouse—until it was found to have a real human skeleton inside it. Ownership of the mummy was eventually traced back to a funeral parlor in Oklahoma, where McCurdy had been embalmed and exhibited as "the bandit who wouldn't give up."

Using two video cameras and an image processor, Snow superposed the mummy's profile on a photograph of McCurdy that was taken shortly after his death. When displayed on a single monitor, the two coincided to a remarkable degree. Convinced by the evidence, Thomas Noguchi, then Los Angeles County coroner, signed McCurdy's death certificate ("Last known occupation: Train robber") and allowed the outlaw's bones to be returned to Oklahoma for a decent burial.

It was this technique that also allowed forensic scientists to identify the remains of the Nazi "Angel of Death," Josef Mengele, in the summer of 1985. A team of investigators, including Snow and West German forensic anthropologist Richard Helmer, flew to Brazil after an Austrian couple claimed that Mengele lay buried in a grave on a São Paulo hillside. Tests revealed that the stature, age, and hair color of the unearthed skeleton were consistent with information in Mengele's SS files; yet without X-rays or dental records, the scientists still lacked conclusive evidence. When an image of the reconstructed skull was superposed on 1930s photographs of Mengele, however, the match was eerily compelling. All doubts were removed a few months later when Mengele's dental X-rays were tracked down.

In 1979 Snow retired from the FAA to the rolling hills of Norman, Oklahoma, where he and his wife, Jerry, live in a sprawling, early-1960s ranch house. Unlike his 50 or so fellow forensic anthropologists, most of whom are tied to academic positions, Snow is free to pursue his consultancy work full-time. Judging from the number of miles that he logs in the average month, Snow is clearly not ready to retire for good.

His recent projects include a reexamination of the skeletal remains found at the site of the Battle of the Little Bighorn, where more than a century ago Custer and his 210 men were killed by Sioux and Cheyenne warriors. Although most of the enlisted men's remains were moved to a mass grave in 1881, an excavation of the battlefield in the past few years uncovered an additional 375 bones and 36 teeth. Snow, teaming up again with Fitzpatrick, determined that these remains belonged to 34 individuals.

The historical accounts of Custer's desperate last stand are vividly confirmed by their findings. Snow identified one skeleton as that of a soldier between the ages of 19 and 23 who weighed around 150 pounds and stood about five foot eight. He'd sustained gunshot wounds to his chest and left forearm. Heavy blows to his head had fractured his skull and sheared off his teeth. Gashed thigh bones indicated that his body was later dismembered with an ax or hatchet.

Given the condition and number of the bodies, Snow seriously questions the accuracy of the identifications made by the original nineteenth-century burial crews. He doubts, for example, that the skeleton buried at West Point is General Custer's.

For the last four years Snow has devoted much of his time to helping two countries come to terms with the horrors of a much more recent past. As part of a group sponsored by the American Association for the Advancement of Science, he has been helping the Argentinian National Commission on Disappeared Persons to determine the fate of some of those who vanished during their country's harsh military rule: between 1976 and 1983 at least 10,000 people were systematically swept off the streets by roving death squads to be tortured, killed, and buried in unmarked graves. In December 1986, at the invitation of the Aquino government's Human Rights Commission, Snow also spent several weeks training Philippine scientists to investigate the disappearances that occurred under the Marcos regime.

But it is in Argentina where Snow has done the bulk of his human-rights work. He has spent more than 27 months in and around Buenos Aires, first training a small group of local medical and anthropology students in the techniques of forensic investigation, and later helping them carefully exhume and examine scores of the *desaparecidos,* or disappeared ones.

Only 25 victims have so far been positively identified. But the evidence has helped convict seven junta members and other high-ranking military and police officers. The idea is not necessarily to identify all 10,000 of the missing, says Snow. "If you have a colonel who ran a detention center where maybe five hundred people were killed, you don't have to nail them with five hundred deaths. Just one or two should be sufficient to get him convicted." Forensic evidence from Snow's team may be used to prosecute several other military officers, including General Suarez Mason. Mason is the former commander of the I Army Corps in Buenos Aires and is believed to be responsible for thousands of disappearances. He was recently extradited from San Francisco back to Argentina, where he is expected to stand trial this winter [1988].

The investigations have been hampered by a frustrating lack of antemortem information. In 1984, when commission lawyers took depositions from relatives and friends of the disappeared, they often failed to obtain such basic information as the victim's height, weight, or hair color. Nor did they ask for the missing person's X-rays (which in Argentina are given to the patient) or the address of the victim's dentist. The problem was compounded by the inexperience of those who carried out the first mass exhumations prior to Snow's arrival. Many of the skeletons were inadvertently destroyed by bulldozers as they were brought up.

Every unearthed skeleton that shows signs of gunfire, however, helps to erode the claim once made by many in the Argentinian military that most of the *desaparecidos* are alive and well and living in Mexico City, Madrid, or Paris. Snow recalls the case of a 17-year-old boy named Gabriel Dunayavich, who disappeared in the summer of 1976. He was walking home from a movie with his girlfriend when a Ford Falcon with no license plates snatched him off the street. The police later found his body and that of another boy and girl dumped by the roadside on the outskirts of Buenos Aires. The police went through the motions of an investigation, taking photographs and doing an autopsy, then buried the three teenagers in an unmarked grave.

A decade later Snow, with the help of the boy's family, traced the autopsy reports, the police photographs, and the grave of the three youngsters. Each of them had four or five closely spaced bullet wounds in the upper chest—the signature, says Snow, of an automatic weapon. Two also had wounds on their arms from bullets that had entered behind the elbow and exited from the forearm.

"That means they were conscious when they were shot," says Snow. "When a gun was pointed at them, they naturally raised their arm." It's details like these that help to authenticate the last moments of the victims and bring a dimension of reality to the judges and jury.

Each time Snow returns from Argentina he says that this will be the last time. A few months later he is back in Buenos Aires. "There's always more work to do," he says. It is, he admits quietly, "terrible work."

"These were such brutal, cold-blooded crimes," he says. "The people who committed them not only murdered; they had a system to eliminate all trace that their victims even existed."

Snow will not let them obliterate their crimes so conveniently. "There are human-rights violations going on all around the world," he says. "But to me murder is murder, regardless of the motive. I hope that we are sending a message to governments who murder in the name of politics that they can be held to account."

Critical Thinking

1. Using Clyde Snow as an example, what does a forensic anthropologist do? How was he instrumental in improving aircraft design and safety?
2. What is "osteobiography"?
3. How does Snow determine the various characteristics of an individual from the skeleton?
4. What conclusions did Clyde Snow draw from his reexamination of the skeletal remains at the Battle of the Little Bighorn?
5. What kind of human rights work has Snow done? How have the investigations been hampered? What findings did he come to?

Create Central

www.mhhe.com/createcentral

Internet References

Smithsonian Institution Website
www.si.edu

Society for Archaeological Sciences
www.socarchsci.org

Society for Historical Archaeology
www.sha.org

Zeno's Forensic Page
http://forensic.to/forensic.html

Huyghe, Patrick. From *Discover*, December 1988. Copyright © 1988 by Patrick Huyghe. Reprinted by permission of the author.

Article

Prepared by: Mari Pritchard Parker, *Pasadena City College* and
Elvio Angeloni, *Pasadena City College*

Interbreeding with Neanderthals

Telltale evidence of ancient liaisons with Neanderthals and other extinct human relatives can be found in the DNA of billions of people.

CARL ZIMMER

Learning Outcomes

After reading this article, you will be able to:

- Discuss the "out-of-Africa" model of modern human origins and whether or not they interbred with Neanderthals.
- Discuss what happened to the Neanderthals.

David Reich, a geneticist at the Harvard Medical School, has redrawn our species's family tree. And today, in his office overlooking Avenue Louis Pasteur in Boston, he picks up a blue marker, walks up to a blank white wall, and shows the result to me. He starts with a pair of lines—one for humans and one for Neanderthals—that split off from a common ancestor no more than 700,000 years ago. The human branch divides into lineages of Africans, Asians, and Europeans, and then into twigs for smaller groups like the people of New Guinea or the residents of the remote Andaman Islands in the Indian Ocean. Reich also creates a branch off the Neanderthal line for the Denisovans, a paleolithic lineage geneticists discovered only a few years ago.

All well and good. This is the sort of picture you'd expect if we and our humanlike relatives diverged neatly through evolution. It looks a lot like the tree of life that Darwin included in *The Origin of Species*. But then Reich violates his tree. Instead of making new branches, he starts linking branches together. He inscribes a line that links the Neanderthal lineage to the Europeans and Asians. He joins the Denisovan line and the one leading to the people of New Guinea. He crisscrosses the tree again and again, joining the branches into a thicket of grafts.

Reich steps back and looks over his creation. He has a high forehead, a peregrine profile, and a very soft voice. "So," he says quietly, "it's a little bit complicated."

That's putting it mildly. Over the past 15 years, Reich has developed a toolbox of sophisticated statistical methods to extract history out of our DNA. And with those methods he has revealed scandalous liaisons dating back tens of thousands of years. Some 200,000 years ago, our ancestors evolved in East Africa. They spread throughout the rest of the continent and then moved out into Asia and Europe. As they journeyed along coastlines and over mountains, they encountered Neanderthals and other human relatives. And at least once in a while, they had sex.

We don't know the prurient details of those encounters, although it is possible that someday Reich and other scientists will be able to fill in a few of them. But the work Reich has done already leaves no doubt that interbreeding was a major feature of human evolution. Billions of people carry sizable chunks of DNA from Neanderthals and other archaic human relatives. Some of those genes may play important roles in our health today.

"We've been mixing quite often with distant relatives in our history," Reich says. In fact, he expects much more evidence of interbreeding to surface. There may be other, undiscovered humanlike beings lurking in our genomes.

Reich's wall, in other words, is about to get a lot messier.

New Revelations from DNA

When Reich entered college, in 1992, most of what scientists knew about human evolution came from fossils. The emerging consensus was that *Homo sapiens* evolved only in Africa. Humans then migrated to the other continents, where they lived for a time alongside humanlike relatives known as hominins.

Paleoanthropologists who supported this "out-of-Africa" model argued that Neanderthals, although they ranged over much of Europe, did not give rise to today's Europeans. Instead, they evolved separately from an ancient hominin and then, about 30,000 years ago, disappeared. Today's Europeans are not latter-day Neanderthals but African immigrants.

A new way to dig up human history emerged and bolstered this perspective. Geneticists learned how to sequence small fragments of DNA and compare the versions of those fragments from different individuals. In the mid-1980s, the late geneticist Allan Wilson and molecular geneticist Rebecca Cann gathered samples of genes from people belonging to a wide range of ethnic groups. They zeroed in on the DNA found in sausage-shaped structures in the cell, known as mitochondria.

Mitochondrial DNA is unusual in that it is passed down virtually unchanged from mothers to their children. When a woman's mitochondrial DNA mutates, all of her children will inherit the change, creating a genetic marker in her descendants.

The results of the new genetic studies strongly supported the out-of-Africa model. Cann and Wilson took advantage of the fact that mitochondrial DNA mutates at a relatively steady rate over the centuries. By tallying up the mutations in the mitochondrial DNA in various human populations, therefore, they could estimate how long they had been diverging from each other. They found that all the different mitochondrial DNA in living humans descended from a common ancestor who lived in Africa about 200,000 years ago, a woman who was nicknamed "mitochondrial Eve."

"I was very much a part of that tradition," says Reich, who arrived at the University of Oxford to earn his PhD. in genetics several years after Cann and Wilson published their results. Reich began learning how to analyze human DNA to learn more about how humans emerged from Africa. The research was interesting, but he wasn't sure yet that he wanted to be a scientist.

In the summer of 1997, he took a break from the lab bench to try his hand at journalism, writing a short article for *The Economist* about the findings of Svante Pääbo, a geneticist in Leipzig, Germany, at the Max Planck Institute for Evolutionary Anthropology. Pääbo's team had just extracted DNA from a 40,000-year-old Neanderthal fossil. "That was the only story I ever wrote," Reich says. He chose a good subject. It was one of the most important achievements in the study of human evolution.

The researchers had ground up a peppercorn-size chip of bone from a Neanderthal humerus. They doused it in chemicals that drew away all the molecules except any DNA it might hold. It did hold a lot of DNA, and most of that genetic material belonged to the bacteria that had inhabited its pores. After setting aside the microbial DNA, the Max Planck researchers were left with 379 base pairs of mitochondrial Neanderthal DNA. "I thought it was totally the most amazing stuff in the world," Reich says.

Pääbo and his colleagues compared the Neanderthal DNA to the same stretch of DNA from human mitochondria, as well as to equivalent chimpanzee DNA. The Neanderthal DNA was more similar to human than to chimp. But it was still quite different from the gene fragments of Asian, African, and European humans, which were all very similar to one another.

This result seemed to confirm the out-of-Africa model. If Neanderthals were the ancestors of living humans, then you'd expect their mitochondrial DNA to be more like that of Europeans. As Reich wrote in his article, Pääbo's study suggested that no Neanderthal DNA was present in living humans.

But Pääbo was examining just a minuscule portion of the Neanderthal genome. Reich would later help Pääbo study its entirety, and the full story would turn out to be far more complicated. "I guess not only Svante turned out to be wrong, but I did, too," Reich reflects.

Detecting Ancient Relations

After his try at writing, Reich decided that he preferred science after all and went back to the bench. And it was then that his research made a decisive shift. At the time, most geneticists were looking for ways to reconstruct the history of distinct populations. They wanted to trace the expansion of Celts into Great Britain, for example, or track Native Americans back to their closest relatives in Siberia. But Reich was curious about what happened when these groups came into contact with each other. Even though they would probably remain mostly separate, some individuals might interbreed. Reich wondered if he could look at the genomes of living humans and find evidence of those ancient liaisons.

Detecting these signs is not easy. Imagine that two people from very distant parts of the world—a woman from Spain, say, and a man from Polynesia—get married and have a girl. She is born with 23 pairs of chromosomes: one set from her mother and one from her father. Her mother's chromosomes are loaded with genetic markers that pinpoint her Spanish heritage. Likewise, her father's DNA is unmistakably Polynesian. But as the girl's own eggs develop, her DNA gets mixed up. In the cells that give rise to an egg, a Spanish chromosome will pair up with its Polynesian counterpart. Segments of the chromosomes switch places. Each egg ends up with a new, hybrid chromosome. Now imagine that the girl grows up and marries a Spanish man. The DNA of her children will be only one quarter Polynesian, and the Polynesian DNA will be chopped up into even smaller segments. As the generations pass, the signs of interbreeding get even fainter.

Despite the challenge, Reich thought that detecting interbreeding could be important. It could expose some of humanity's hidden history, or even shed light on why people are susceptible to certain diseases. When Reich arrived at Harvard Medical School, he began a study on prostate cancer that proved the value of this type of analysis by revealing the genes that make certain men more likely to develop such cancers. "Prostate cancer occurs 1.5 to 2 times more often in African American men than in European men," Reich says. "We were able to find the reason why."

To do so, Reich had to reconstruct the genetic history of African Americans, who came to the United States as slaves beginning in the 17th century. White owners sometimes had sex with their slaves and fathered children, thereby introducing European genes into the African American population. Freed slaves also had children with Native Americans and Latinos. As a result, African Americans today may have up to 80 percent European DNA.

Reich and his colleagues inspected the DNA of 1,597 African American men with prostate cancer. They surveyed around 1,300 short segments scattered through the men's genomes and compared them with the same locations in the genomes of men from Europe, Asia, and Africa. They were able to determine which continent each segment in each African American man's genome had come from.

Reich and his colleagues found seven genetic risk factors, which together constituted a hot spot of cancer risk. African

American men who had the European version of all seven of the markers were no more likely to get prostate cancer than Europeans were; the African versions, though, were associated with elevated risk. The seven sites appear to control a gene involved in cell division. Mutations to those sites lead to cells' multiplying too quickly.

Interbreeding in the United States took place over just the past few centuries. For his next project, Reich took on a much bigger challenge: the entire ethnic history of India. Today 1.21 billion people live in India. Their cultural variety is staggering: The country is home to 2,000 ethnic groups, and every Indian banknote has to have its value printed in 15 languages.

Reich wanted to see if the DNA of Indians contained clues about their origins as a people. Did they all descend from the same founding population, or could he tease apart DNA passed down from different ancestral groups?

He collaborated with scientists from the Centre for Cellular and Molecular Biology in Hyderabad to analyze the DNA of 132 Indians. Their subjects represented 25 ethnic groups, ranging from the Kashmiri Pandit, who live near the base of the Himalayas, to the Kurumba, who inhabit the southern tip of India. In each person's DNA, the scientists surveyed 560,000 sites, comparing each site in each Indian. The researchers also compared the data with that of groups of people outside India, including Europeans and Africans.

Reich and his colleagues programmed a computer to carry out a thorough analysis of these tens of millions of data points. The computer then created a range of possible genealogical trees and measured how well each tree could explain the genetic variations found across India. In 2009 the scientists reported that Indians can trace much of their DNA to just two ancestral populations.

"It's a mixture between populations that are as different from each other as East Asians are from Europeans," Reich says.

One population came from the same stock as the people of the Andaman Islands in the Indian Ocean. They arrived on the Indian subcontinent perhaps 40,000 years ago, and their descendants made up most of the population of India until maybe a few thousand years ago. Then a second group, closely related to the ancestors of Europeans, appeared on the subcontinent. When the two groups made contact, they began to intermarry, mixing their genes together. In some ethnic groups, their DNA is now almost entirely blended. But in the far north and south of the subcontinent, the genes have mixed far less.

This discovery impressed Reich with the importance of interbreeding in human history. "You might think we're living in special times now," he says. "But we've been mixing quite often with distant relatives in our history." And the statistical methods that Reich and his colleagues designed to probe the history of India proved crucial for his project deciphering the far earlier relationship of humans and Neanderthals.

Ever since Reich wrote his article about Neanderthal DNA back in 1997, Pääbo had been pushing to get more of their genes. By 2010 he and his colleagues had created a rough draft of the entire Neanderthal genome, comprising over 60 percent of its more than 3 billion base pairs. Pääbo could now return to the question of how Neanderthals and humans were related, with thousands of times more data. But in order to make sense of the huge amount of DNA he had, he needed to work with people who were experts on how the relationships between populations can be gleaned from DNA—people like Reich.

"For our community it was always the great question, what the history of Neanderthal and modern human interactions was," Reich says. "And the data Pääbo was gathering was a great way to get into it."

The Neanderthal within Us

Reich and his colleagues began analyzing Pääbo's Neanderthal genome in 2007. They worked their way through the DNA in much the same way they had looked at the genes of Indians. They compared each site in the Neanderthal genome to the corresponding site in the genomes of humans, as well as the genome of a chimpanzee. Once more, they tried to work out the most likely evolutionary history that would explain the evidence.

"We were assuming Neanderthals and humans had not mixed," Reich says. After all, that's what Pääbo had initially found in 1997, looking at a tiny snip of mitochondrial DNA. And when he was able to look at larger pieces of mitochondrial DNA, he got the same result.

Most of the Neanderthal genes Reich and his colleagues looked at again supported Pääbo's earlier research. In other words, all the human versions resembled each other more than any of them resembled the Neanderthal version. But then their computers began to spit out some strange results. Chunks of Neanderthal DNA turned out to be more similar to the corresponding chunks of Europeans and Asians than they were to African DNA. On the other hand, in no case did Africans and Neanderthals share similar versions of a gene, to the exclusion of other humans. Was it possible that Europeans and Asians had a little Neanderthal DNA after all?

"We were suspicious of the result," Reich says. "We found signals of mixture and then worked very hard to make them go away."

He tried for a year, to no avail. Finally, Reich and his colleagues had no choice but to conclude that Neanderthals had mated with humans. They estimated that the DNA of living Asians and Europeans was (on average) 2.5 percent Neanderthal. They had to reject a pure version of the out-of-Africa model. Instead, their model was closer to out-of-Africa-and-get-to-know-some-Neanderthals-very-well.

The patterns Reich and his colleagues identified can help narrow down when and where the interbreeding took place. Since Africans do not carry Neanderthal DNA, it would appear Neanderthals bred only with the ancestors of Europeans and Asians. One possibility is that when humans emerged out of Africa some 50,000 or more years ago, they encountered Neanderthals in the Near East. Once humans and Neanderthals mated, the humans continued to expand into Europe and Asia, taking Neanderthal genes with them. Another possibility is that the interbreeding came later. Neanderthals lived across a vast range, from Spain to Russia. As humans came into contact with Neanderthals, they might have mated in several places.

Humans and Neanderthals did not merge into a single people, however; the 2.5 percent of Neanderthal DNA found in

Asians and Europeans is a very small fraction. Mathias Currat and Laurent Excoffier, two Swiss geneticists, studied how much interbreeding would be necessary to end up with so little Neanderthal DNA in humans today. All it would take, they concluded, would be for a Neanderthal and a human to create a child once every 30 years. "It's not surprising to me," Reich says of that finding. "Humans don't mix easily across group boundaries. People tend to mix with people who look like them, who speak their language."

Beyond these rough outlines, the story quickly gets foggy. Clearly the hybrid children from these interbreedings had to have been accepted into human cultures. But we can't say whether these couplings happened as rapes during violent battles between humans and Neanderthals or when individual Neanderthals were welcomed into human society.

Reich hopes to find more clues to bring the story into better focus. One question he wants to address is how genes flowed from Neanderthals into humans. Were human males mating with Neanderthal females, or vice versa?

"There is actually a real chance of studying the directionality of gene flow," Reich says. Females have two X chromosomes, while males have one X and one Y. If Neanderthal females mated with male humans, he notes, they would provide an X chromosome to all of their children. If Neanderthal males were involved, they would be able to provide an X to their daughters but none to their sons. If Reich were to find an unusually low amount of Neanderthal DNA on the X chromosome compared with the other chromosomes, it might be a clue that Neanderthal males impregnated human females. A high ratio would point the other way, to Neanderthal great-great-grandmothers. "We are looking hard at this," he says.

Other Distant Relatives

One evening in 2010, Reich was having dinner with Pääbo and some colleagues in a Leipzig beer garden. They were finishing up their work on the Neanderthal genome. Now Pääbo had more news for Reich. He believed he had found DNA in another extinct hominin.

Pääbo had been collaborating with Russian paleoanthropologists who were excavating fossils in a cave in Siberia called Denisova. The cavern was loaded with petrified remains that had been laid down over thousands of years. Some appeared to be Neanderthal. Some seemed human. The Russians shipped bone samples to Germany, where Pääbo's postdoc, Johannes Krause, began grinding them to search for DNA. Most held nothing but bacterial genes. But then Krause looked at the tip of a pinkie bone that belonged to a girl who died more than 50,000 years ago, and everything changed.

The specimen was packed with DNA. When Krause sequenced a small sample, he could immediately see it was not quite human and not quite Neanderthal. It belonged to some other hominin unknown to science. Pääbo and his colleagues dubbed the long-gone girl the Denisovan.

Reich immediately jumped into the project. He and his colleagues applied the same methods to the new genome as they had to Neanderthal DNA. Overall, the Denisovan genes were closest to the Neanderthals, but the genome had many mutations not found in either humans or Neanderthals. Denisovan ancestors apparently had diverged from the ancestors of Neanderthals somewhat more recently than the split between Neanderthals and modern human beings.

It is possible that their common ancestor emigrated from Africa many hundreds of thousands of years ago, leaving our own ancestors behind on that continent. The ancestors of Neanderthals headed north and as far west as Europe. The Denisovans' ancestors, meanwhile, headed east and survived long enough to at least leave that pinkie bone in the Siberian cave. The Denisovan girl's genes give us a few clues to what she might have looked like. She had gene variants that would have given her dark skin, brown eyes, and brown hair, for example. At some point after 50,000 years ago, the Denisovans vanished, just like their Neanderthal cousins.

Knowing that Neanderthals and humans had interbred, Reich and his colleagues looked carefully for Denisovan DNA in the genomes of living humans. They found it in genomes from two populations, one from New Guinea and another from the nearby island of Bougainville. As much as 5 percent of their DNA came from the vanished Denisovans.

This result was dramatically different from the findings in their Neanderthal study. It prompted Reich and his colleagues to make a much broader survey of human DNA. They could not find a trace of Denisovan DNA in Africans. Nor could they find it in Europeans, nor in mainland Asians. But they did find vestiges in the genomes of Australian Aborigines. In the Philippines they also found it in people called Mamanwa. These short, dark-skinned tribespeople have long intrigued anthropologists, since they seem so unlike most residents of the western Pacific.

"It was so striking that we thought it must be a mistake at first. But it's a really distinct, consistent, overwhelming pattern. The only way to explain this is by gene exchange," Reich says. "The Denisovan group probably was spread out over thousands and thousands of miles," extending from the tundra of Siberia in the north all the way down to the steamy jungles of southeast Asia—a bigger range than Neanderthals'.

Ancient DNA, Modern Health

By the time the Neanderthals and Denisovans encountered modern humans, their genes had been evolving separately for hundreds of thousands of years. Yet it's possible their DNA is still influencing the health of billions of people today. It's possible that some of their genes caused harm when they were combined with human DNA, raising the risk of certain diseases or reducing a person's fertility.

On the other hand, some of the foreign DNA may have benefited us. In August 2011, Peter Parham of Stanford University and his colleagues found that the Neanderthal and Denisovan versions of some immune system genes are now remarkably widespread. They can be found in Europe, Asia, and even the Pacific islands. Their prevalence suggests that they may have provided some disease-fighting advantage.

Reich is not ready to take a firm stand on how our Neanderthal or Denisovan DNA is affecting our health. The draft genomes of Neanderthals and Denisovans still have too many gaps and errors to allow for that sort of certainty. But he is open to the possibility that some of their genes were favored by natural selection in humans. "These were people coming out of Africa, and they had to cope with environments to which Neanderthals and Denisovans were already adapted."

Fortunately, Reich says, we can do more than just speculate about why a particular piece of Neanderthal or Denisovan DNA is still in our genomes. "You could associate it to people's traits," he says. Are people with a particular chunk of Neanderthal DNA faster runners than people without it? Are people with a particular chunk of Denisovan DNA better at logic puzzles? "It's an experiment you can actually do."

For Reich, the revelations from the Neanderthal and Denisovan genomes are probably just the beginning of a new understanding of our evolution. He would not be surprised if the genome of yet another ancient hominin comes to light in our DNA. "Why not? It doesn't seem unlikely at this point," he says.

One place where such evidence might turn up is in Africa. Michael Hammer, a geneticist at the University of Arizona, and his colleagues have found hints of a new hominin by looking at the DNA of Africans. They found snippets, about 2 percent of the genome in total, that seem out of place in human DNA. The best explanation is that this is the result of another archaic human who interbred with Africans about 35,000 years ago, Hammer argues.

To confirm such findings, scientists will need to find more ancient genomes, and Reich thinks they will. "I'm optimistic," he says. "The world is full of things like Denisova Cave. There must be thousands of other bones out there."

Critical Thinking

1. What does our species' "family tree" look like, according to David Reich? What has happened in the past 200,000 years to account for this?
2. What was originally claimed by the "out-of-Africa" model? How did the study of mitochondrial DNA support this view? How and why did Pääbo's Neanderthal fossil seem to support this view?
3. How is it possible to detect interbreeding between distinct human populations and when such interbreeding occurred?
4. Using the example of prostate cancer among African Americans, how is it possible to determine genetic risk and disease?
5. Using India as an example, how can DNA be used to determine the origins of a people?
6. How much interbreeding between modern humans and Neanderthals would it take to account for the Neanderthal DNA in modern populations?
7. How might we determine the male-female directionality of the gene flow?
8. How has DNA helped us to a better understanding of human migration throughout the world and the role of past interbreeding of human populations, including the Neanderthals?
9. How might some of the "foreign DNA" have benefited us, according to the author?

Create Central

www.mhhe.com/createcentral

Internet References

Fossil Hominids FAQ
  www.talkorigins.org/faqs/homs
Long Foreground: Human Prehistory
  www.public.wsu.edu/gened/learn-modules/top_longfor/timeline/00...
Max Planck Institute for Evolutionary Biology
  www.evolbio.mpg.de/2169/en

CARL ZIMMER is an award-winning biology writer and regular Discover contributor. He is the author of *The Tangled Bank: An Introduction to Evolution.*

Zimmer, Carl. From *Discover*, vol. 34, no. 2, March, 2013, pp. 38–44. Copyright © 2013 by Discover Media. All rights reserved. Reprinted by permission via PARS International and protected by the copyright laws of the United States. The printing, copying, redistribution, or retransmission of this content without express written permission is prohibited.

Unit 4

UNIT

Prepared by: Mari Pritchard Parker, *Pasadena City College* and
Elvio Angeloni, *Pasadena City College*

Prehistoric Archaeology

One of the most intriguing aspects of archaeology has to do with human beginnings. As Chris Stringer has observed, "our species' origins have been a source of fascination for millennia and account for the huge range of creation myths that are recorded in different cultures." The search for clues as to where we come from and how we came to be as we are goes to the heart of what archaeology in particular and anthropology in general are all about. Just as cultural anthropologists seek to understand contemporary cultures as a means for gaining insights into our own way of life and biological anthropologists probe into our evolutionary past in order to comprehend our biological present, so archaeologists seek to understand the material remains of past cultures in order to reconstruct the pathways to the here and now.

But archaeologists are just as involved as paleoanthropologists in seeking to understand who we are in terms of what we once were. Much of what archaeologists do relates to the biological, anatomical, and genetic aspects of our evolutionary development. Yes, there are the bones to be studied as a way of reconstructing our anatomical and biological evolutionary past (which require archaeological techniques to recover by the way), but alongside them are often the remains of artifacts, ranging from crude stone tools of 2 million years ago to some of the most incredibly beautiful artwork in the painted caves of southern France, much of which would be worthy of inclusion in the Louvre. After all, it is the archaeological evidence that provides us with the all-important cultural context, which has enabled our species to survive and develop to the point where we are today.

Unfortunately, nothing about our past is as simple, tangible, and straightforward as the purveyors of "bones and stones" would like to have it. There are interpretations to be made, biases to overcome and differences in perspectives to be resolved. Prehistoric archaeology is appropriately rifled with controversy, conflict, and calumny. But archaeology, after all, is a science and, as in all of the sciences, new evidence raises new questions, resolves old ones and shakes things up even more.

So, what are we to make of all these claims? To those sitting on the sidelines, the controversies can be exciting, confusing, exasperating, or a combination of all of the these. To those scientists working in the thick of it, that's archaeology!

Article

Prepared by: Mari Pritchard Parker, *Pasadena City College* and
Elvio Angeloni, *Pasadena City College*

Human Evolution: The Long, Winding Road to Modern Man

CHRIS STRINGER

Learning Outcomes

After reading this article, you will be able to:

- Discuss the features of modern *Homo sapiens* and the evidence for where they evolved.
- Discuss whether modern humans replaced archaic *Homo sapiens* or mated with them.

Our species' origins have been a source of fascination for millennia and account for the huge range of creation myths that are recorded in different cultures. Linnaeus, that great classifier of living things, gave us our biological name *Homo sapiens* (meaning "wise man") and our high rounded skulls certainly make us distinctive, as do our small brow ridges and chins. However, we are also remarkable for our language, art and complex technology.

The question is: where did these features evolve? Where can humanity place its homeland? In terms of our earliest ancestors, the answer is generally agreed to be Africa. It was here that our first ape-like ancestors began to make their homes on the savannah. However, a fierce debate has continued about whether it was also the ultimate birthplace of our own species.

Forty years ago, no one believed that modern humans could have originated in Africa. In some cases this idea was based on fading racist agendas. For example, in 1962, the American anthropologist Carleton Coon claimed that "If Africa was the cradle of mankind, it was only an indifferent kindergarten. Europe and Asia were our principal schools."

Part of the confusion was due to the lack of well-dated fossil and archaeological evidence. In the intervening years, however, I have been privileged to be involved in helping to accumulate data—fossil, chronological, archaeological and genetic—that show our species did have a recent African origin. But as the latest evidence shows, this origin was complex and in my new book, *The Origin of Our Species,* I try to make it clear what it means to be human and change perceptions about our origins.

I had been fascinated by ancient humans called Neanderthals even as a 10-year-old, and in 1971, as a 23-year-old student, I left London on a four-month research trip to museums and institutes in 10 European countries to gather data on the shapes of skulls of Neanderthals and of their modern-looking successors in Europe, the Cro-Magnons. My purpose was to test the then popular theory which held that Neanderthals and people like them in each region of the ancient world were the ancestors of people in those same regions today. I had only a modest grant, and so I drove my old car, sleeping in it, camping or staying in youth hostels—in Belgium I even spent one night in a shelter for the homeless. I survived border confrontations and two robberies, but by the end of my 5,000-mile trip I had collected one of the largest data sets of Neanderthal and early modern skull measurements assembled up to that time.

Over the next three years I added data on other ancient and modern samples, and the results were clear: Neanderthals had evolved their own special characteristics, and did not look like ancestors for the Cro-Magnons or for any modern people. The issue was: where had our species evolved? In 1974 I was unable to say, but taking up a research post at the Natural History Museum meant I could continue the quest.

My research uncovered clues, however, and over the next decade my work—along with that of a few others—focused on Africa as the most likely homeland of our species. We remained an isolated minority until 1987, when the paper "Mitochondrial DNA and Human Evolution," was published by Rebecca Cann, Mark Stoneking and Allan Wilson. It put modern human origins on the front pages of newspapers all over the world for the first time for it showed that a tiny and peculiar part of our genome, inherited only through mothers and daughters, derived from an African ancestor about 200,000 years ago. This woman became known as Mitochondrial Eve. A furor followed, as anthropologists rowed over the implications for human evolution.

After that, the "out of Africa" theory—or as I prefer to call it "the recent African origin" model for our origins—really took off. My version depicted the following background. The ancient species *Homo erectus* survived in East Asia and Indonesia but evolved into *Homo heidelbergensis* in Europe and Africa. (This last species had been named from a 600,000-year-old jawbone found in Germany in 1907.) Then, about 400,000 years ago, *H. heidelbergensis* underwent an evolutionary split: north of the Mediterranean it developed into the Neanderthals, while to the south, in Africa, it became us, modern humans.

Finally, about 60,000 years ago *Homo sapiens* began to leave Africa and by 40,000 years ago, with the advantages of more complex tools and behaviours, spread into Asia and Europe, where we replaced the Neanderthals and all the other archaic people outside of Africa. In other words, under our skins, we are all Africans.

Not every scientist agreed, however. One group continued to support the idea of multiregional evolution, an updated version of ideas from the 1930s. It envisaged deep parallel lines of evolution in each inhabited region of Africa, Europe, Asia and Australasia, stretching from local variants of *H. erectus* right through to living people in the same areas today. These lines did not diverge through time, since they were glued together by interbreeding across the ancient world, so modern features could gradually evolve, spread and accumulate, alongside long-term regional differences in things like the shape of the face and the size of the nose.

A different model, known as the assimilation model, took the new fossil and genetic data on board and gave Africa a key role in the evolution of modern features. However, this model envisaged a much more gradual spread of those features from Africa than did mine. Neanderthals and archaic people like them were assimilated through widespread interbreeding. Thus the evolutionary establishment of modern features was a blending process rather than a rapid replacement.

So who was right? Genetic data continued to accumulate through the 1990s in support of the recent African origin model, both from recent human populations and Neanderthal fossils. Recent massive improvements in recovery and analysis of ancient DNA have produced even more information, some of it very surprising. Fossil fragments from Croatia have yielded up a nearly entire Neanderthal genome, providing rich data that promise insights into their biology—from eye colour and hair type through to skull shape and brain functions. These latest results have largely confirmed a separation from our lineage about 350,000 years ago. But when the new Neanderthal genome was compared in detail with modern humans from different continents, the results produced an intriguing twist to our evolutionary story: the genomes of people from Europe, China and New Guinea lay slightly closer to the Neanderthal sequence than did those of Africans. Thus if you are European, Asian or New Guinean, you could have 2.5% of Neanderthal DNA in your genetic make-up.

The most likely explanation for this discovery is that the ancestors of today's Europeans, Asians and New Guineans interbred with Neanderthals (or at least with a population that had a component of Neanderthal genes) in North Africa, Arabia or the Middle East, as they exited Africa about 60,000 years ago. That ancient human exodus may have involved only a few thousand people, so it would have taken the absorption of only a few Neanderthals into a group of *H. sapiens* for the genetic effect—greatly magnified as modern human numbers exploded—to be felt tens of thousands of years later.

The breakthrough in reconstructing a Neanderthal genome has been mirrored across Asia in equally remarkable work on the human group that has become known as the "Denisovans." A fossil finger bone, about 40,000 years old, found in Denisova Cave, Siberia, together with a huge molar tooth, could not be assigned to a particular human species, though it has also had much of its genome reconstructed. This has revealed a previously unrecognised Asian offshoot of the Neanderthal line, but again with a twist. These Denisovans are also related to one group of living humans—the Melanesians of southeast Asia (and probably their Australian neighbours too). These groups also carry about 5% of Denisovan DNA from another interbreeding event that must have happened as their ancestors passed through southern Asia over 40,000 years ago.

So where does this added complexity and evidence of interbreeding with Neanderthals and Denisovans leave my favoured Recent African Origins model? Has it been disproved in favour of the multiregional model, as some have claimed? I don't think so. As we have seen, back in 1970, no scientists held the view that Africa was the evolutionary home of modern humans; the region was considered backward and largely irrelevant, with the pendulum of scientific opinion strongly swinging towards non-African and Neanderthal ancestry models. Twenty years later, the pendulum was starting to move in favour of our African origins, as fossil evidence began to be reinforced by the clear signals of mitochondrial DNA. The pendulum swung even further with growing fossil, archaeological and genetic data in the 1990s.

Now, the advent of huge amounts of DNA data, including the Neanderthal and Denisovan genomes, has halted and even reversed that pendulum swing, away from absolute replacement. Instead we are looking at a mixed replacement-hybridisation or "leaky replacement" model. This dynamism is what makes studying human evolution so fascinating. Science is not about being right or wrong, but about gradually approaching truth about the natural world.

The big picture is that we are still predominantly of recent African origin (more than 90% of our genetic ancestry). But is there a special reason for this observation? Overall, the pre-eminence of Africa in the story of our origins does not involve a special evolutionary pathway but is a question of the continent's consistently large habitable areas which gave greater opportunities for morphological and behavioural variations, and for genetic and behavioural innovations to develop and be conserved. "Modernity" was not a package that had an origin in one African time, place and population, but was a composite whose elements appeared at different times and places, and then gradually coalesced to assume the form we recognise today.

My studies have led me to a greater recognition in recent human evolution of the forces of demography (the need for large populations and social networks to make progress), drift and contingency (chance events), and cultural rather than natural selection than I had considered before. It seems that cultural "progress" was a stop-start affair for much of our evolution, until human groups were large, had long-lived individuals, and wide social networks, all helping to maximise the chances that innovations would survive and accumulate.

Linnaeus said of *Homo sapiens* "know thyself." Knowing ourselves means a recognition that becoming modern is the path we perceive when looking back on our own evolutionary history. That history seems special to us, of course, because we owe our very existence to it. Those figures of human species (usually males, who become increasingly hairless and light-skinned) marching boldly across the page have illustrated our evolution in many popular articles, but they have wrongly enshrined the view that evolution was simply a progression leading to us, its pinnacle and final achievement.

Nothing could be further from the truth. There were plenty of other paths that could have been taken; many would have led to no humans at all, others to extinction, and yet others to a different version of "modernity." We can inhabit only one version of being human—the only version that survives today—but what is fascinating is that palaeoanthropology shows us those other paths to becoming human, their successes and their eventual demise, whether through failure or just sheer bad luck.

Sometimes the difference between failure and success in evolution is a narrow one. We are certainly on a knife-edge now, as we confront an overpopulated planet and the prospect of global climate change on a scale that humans have never faced before. Let's hope our species is up to the challenge.

Critical Thinking

1. What are the features of our species that make us distinctive and remarkable?
2. Where did our species evolve? What has the "fierce debate" been about?
3. What was the belief forty years ago and why?
4. As a student, what theory did the author test and how? What were his results? How did mitochondrial DNA confirm this?
5. What was the author's version of the "out of Africa" theory?
6. What was the "multiregional view"? The "assimilation model"?
7. What has recent genetic data shown about the separation of our species from Neanderthals? What is the "intriguing twist"?
8. What is the most likely explanation for this discovery, according to the author?
9. How has the breakthrough in reconstructing a Neanderthal genome been mirrored across Asia and what have been the results?
10. What is the "leaky replacement" model?
11. What is the "big picture," according to the author?
12. How and why was Africa conducive to the development of our "modernity"?
13. When and why did cultural "progress" cease to be a stop-start affair for our species?
14. Why does the author take issue with the view that evolution was simply a progression leading to us?

Create Central

www.mhhe.com/createcentral

Internet References

Bradshaw Foundation
www.bradshawfoundation.com/clottes/index.php
Department of Human Evolution/Max Planck Institute
www.eva.mpg.de/evolution
Fossil Hominids FAQ
www.talkorigins.org/faqs/homs
Long Foreground: Human Prehistory
Turkana Basin Institute
www.turkanabasin.org

PROFESSOR CHRIS STRINGER is the research leader in human origins at the Natural History Museum, London.

Stringer, Chris. From *The Guardian*, June 18, 2011. Copyright © 2011 by Guardian News & Media Ltd. Reprinted by permission.

Article

Prepared by: Mari Pritchard Parker, *Pasadena City College* and
Elvio Angeloni, *Pasadena City College*

When the Sea Saved Humanity

Shortly after Homo sapiens arose, harsh climate conditions nearly extinguished our species. Recent finds suggest that the small population that gave rise to all humans alive today survived by exploiting a unique combination of resources along the southern coast of Africa.

CURTIS W. MAREAN

Learning Outcomes

After reading this article, you will be able to:

- Discuss the environmental conditions that almost drove humanity to extinction.
- Discuss the survival skills that enabled our species to avoid extinction over 100,000 years ago.

With the global population of humans currently approaching seven billion, it is difficult to imagine that *Homo sapiens* was once an endangered species. Yet studies of the DNA of modern-day people indicate that, once upon a time, our ancestors did in fact undergo a dramatic population decline. Although scientists lack a precise timeline for the origin and near extinction of our species, we can surmise from the fossil record that our forebears arose throughout Africa shortly before 195,000 years ago. Back then the climate was mild and food was plentiful; life was good. But around 195,000 years ago, conditions began to deteriorate. The planet entered a long glacial stage known as Marine Isotope Stage 6 (MIS6) that lasted until roughly 123,000 years ago.

A detailed record of Africa's environmental conditions during glacial stage 6 does not exist, but based on more recent, better-known glacial stages, climatologists surmise that it was almost certainly cool and arid and that its deserts were probably significantly expanded relative to their modern extents. Much of the landmass would have been uninhabitable. While the planet was in the grip of this icy regime, the number of people plummeted perilously—from more than 10,000 breeding individuals to just hundreds. Estimates of exactly when this bottleneck occurred and how small the population became vague among generic studies, but all of them indicate that everyone alive today is descended from a small population that lived in one region of Africa sometime during this global cooling phase.

I began my career as an archaeologist working in East Africa and studying the origin of modern humans. But my interests began to shift when I learned of the population bottleneck that geneticists had started talking about in the early 1990s. Humans today exhibit very low genetic diversity relative to many other species with much smaller population sizes and geographic ranges—a phenomenon best explained by the occurrence of a population crash in early *H. sapiens*. Where, I wondered, did our ancestors manage to survive during the climate catastrophe? Only a handful of regions could have had the natural resources to support hunter-gatherers. Paleoanthropologists argue vociferously over which of these areas was the ideal spot. The southern coast of Africa, rich in shellfish and edible plants year-round, seemed to me as if it would have been a particularly good refuge in tough times. So, in 1991, I decided I would go there and look for sites with remains dating to glacial stage 6.

My search within that coastal area was not random. I had to find a shelter close enough to the ancient coastline to provide easy access to shellfish and elevated enough that its archaeological deposits would not have been washed away 123,000 years ago when the climate warmed and sea levels surged. In 1999 my South African colleague Peter Nilssen and I decided to investigate some caves he had spotted at a place called Pinnacle Point, a promontory near the town of Mossel Bay that juts into the Indian Ocean. Scrambling down the sheer cliff face, we came across a cave that looked particularly promising—one known simply as PP13B. Erosion of the sedimentary deposits located near the mouth of the cave had exposed clear layers of archaeological remains, including hearths and stone tools. Even better, a sand dune and a layer of stalagmite capped these remnants of human activity, suggesting that they were quite old. By all appearances, we had hit the jackpot. The following year, after a local ostrich farmer built us a 180-step wooden staircase to allow safer access to the site, we began to dig.

Since then, my team's excavations at PP13B and other nearby sites have recovered a remarkable record of the activities undertaken by the people who inhabited this area between approximately 164,000 and 35,000 years ago, hence during the bottleneck and after the population began to recover. The deposits in these caves, combined with analyses of the ancient environment there, have enabled us to piece together a plausible account of how the prehistoric residents of Pinnacle Point eked out a living during a grim climate crisis. The remains also debunk the abiding notion that cognitive modernity evolved long after anatomical modernity: evidence of behavioral sophistication abounds in even the oldest archaeological levels at PP13B. This advanced intellect no doubt contributed significantly to the survival of the species, enabling our forebears to take advantage of the resources available on the coast.

While elsewhere on the continent populations of *H. sapiens* died out as cold and drought claimed the animals and plants they hunted and gathered, the lucky denizens of Pinnacle Point were feasting on the seafood and carbohydrate-rich plants that proliferated there despite the hostile climate. As glacial stage 6 cycled through its relatively warmer and colder phases, the seas rose and fell, and the ancient coastline advanced and retreated. But so long as people tracked the shore, they had access to an enviable bounty.

A Coastal Cornucopia

From a survival standpoint, what makes the southern edge of Africa attractive is its unique combination of plants and animals. There a thin strip of land containing the highest diversity of flora for its size in the world hugs the shoreline. Known as the Cape Floral Region, this 90,000-square-kilometer strip contains an astonishing 9,000 plant species, some 64 percent of which live only there. Indeed, the famous Table Mountain that rises above Cape Town in the heart of the Cape Floral Region has more species of plants than does the entire U.K. Of the vegetation groups that occur in this realm, the two most extensive are the fynbos and the renosterveld, which consist largely of shrubs. To a human forager equipped with a digging stick, they offer a valuable commodity: the plants in these groups produce the world's greatest diversity of geophytes—underground energy-storage organs, such as tubers, bulbs and corms.

Geophytes are an important food source for modern-day hunter-gatherers for several reasons. They contain high amounts of carbohydrate; they attain their peak carbohydrate content reliably at certain times of year; and, unlike aboveground fruits, nuts and seeds, they have few predators. The bulbs and corms that dominate the Cape Floral Region are additionally appealing because in contrast to the many geophytes that are highly fibrous, they are low in fiber relative to the amount of energy-rich carbohydrates they) contain, making them more easily digested by children. (Cooking further enhances their digestibility.) And because geophytes are adaptations to dry conditions, they would have been readily available during arid glacial phases.

The southern coast also has an excellent source of protein to offer, despite not being a prime hunting ground for large mammals. Just offshore, the collision of nutrient-rich cold waters from the Benguela upwelling and the warm Agulhas current creates a mix of cold and warm eddies along the southern coast. This varied ocean environment nurtures diverse and dense beds of shellfish in the rocky intertidal zones and sandy beaches.

Shellfish are a very high quality source of protein and omega-3 fatty acids. And as with geophytes, glacial cooling does not depress their numbers. Rather, lower ocean temperatures result in a greater abundance of shellfish.

Survival Skills

With its combination of calorically dense, nutrient-rich protein from the shellfish and low-fiber, energy-laden carbs from the geophytes, the southern coast would have provided an ideal diet for early modern humans during glacial stage 6. Furthermore, women could obtain both these resources on their own, freeing them from relying on men to provision them and their children with high-quality food. We have yet to unearth proof that the occupants of PP13B were eating geophytes—sites this old rarely preserve organic remains—although younger sites in the area contain extensive evidence of geophyte consumption. But we have found clear evidence that they were dining on shellfish. Studies of the shells found at the site conducted by Antonieta Jerardino of the University of Barcelona show that people were gathering brown mussels and local sea snails called alikreukel from the seashore. They also ate marine mammals such as seals and whales on occasion.

Previously the oldest known examples of humans systematically using marine resources dated to less than 120,000 years ago. But dating analyses performed by Miryam Bar-Matthews of the Geological Survey of Israel and Zenobia Jacobs of University of Wollongong in Australia have revealed that the PP13B people lived off the sea far earlier than that: as we reported in 2007 in the journal *Nature*, marine foraging there dates back to a stunning 164,000 years ago. By 110,000 years ago the menu had expanded to include species such as limpets and sand mussels.

This kind of foraging is harder than it might seem. The mussels, limpets and sea snails live on the rocks in the treacherous intertidal zone, where an incoming swell could easily knock over a hapless collector. Along the southern coast, safe harvesting with sufficiently high returns is only possible during low spring tides, when the sun and moon align, exerting their maximum gravitational force on the ebb and flow of the water. Because the tides are linked to the phases of the moon, advancing by 50 minutes a day, I surmise that the people who lived at PP13B—which 164,000 years ago was located much farther inland, two to five kilometers from the water, because of lower sea levels—scheduled their trips to the shore using a lunar calendar of sorts, just as modern coastal people have done for ages.

Harvesting shellfish is not the only advanced behavior in evidence at Pinnacle Point as early as 164,000 years ago. Among the stone tools are significant numbers of "bladelets"—tiny flakes twice as long as they are wide—that are too small to wield by hand. Instead they must have been attached to shafts of wood and used as projectile weapons. Composite toolmaking is indicative of considerable technological know-how, and the bladelets at PP13B are among the oldest examples of it. But we soon learned that these tiny implements were even more complex than we thought.

Most of the stone tools found at coastal South African archaeological sites are made from a type of stone called quartzite.

This coarse-grained rock is great for making large flakes, but it is difficult to shape into small, refined tools. To manufacture the bladelets, people used fine-grained rock called silcrete. There was something odd about the archaeological silcrete, though, as observed by Kyle S. Brown of the Institute of Human Origins at Arizona State University, an expert stone tool flaker on my team. After years of collecting silcrete from all over the coast, Brown determined that in its raw form the rock never has the lustrous red and gray coloring seen in the silcrete implements at Pinnacle Point and elsewhere. Furthermore, the raw silcrete is virtually impossible to shape into bladelets. Where, we wondered, did the toolmakers find their superior silcrete?

A possible answer to this question came from Pinnacle Point Cave 5-6, where one day in 2008 we found a large piece of silcrete embedded in ash. It had the same color and luster seen in the silcrete found at other archaeological deposits in the region. Given the association of the stone with the ash, we asked ourselves whether the ancient toolmakers might have exposed the silcrete to fire to make it easier to work with—a strategy that has been documented in ethnographic accounts of native North Americans and Australians. To find out, Brown carefully "cooked" some raw silcrete and then attempted to knap it. It flaked wonderfully, and the flaked surfaces shone with the same luster seen in the artifacts from our sites. We thus concluded that the Stone Age silcrete was also heat treated.

We faced an uphill battle to convince our colleagues of this remarkable claim, however. It was archaeology gospel that the Solutrean people in France invented heat treatment about 20,000 years ago, using it to make their beautiful tools. To bolster our case, we used three independent techniques. Chantal Tribolo of the University of Bordeaux performed what is called thermoluminescence analysis to determine whether the silcrete tools from Pinnacle Point were intentionally heated. Then Andy Merries of the University of New South Wales in Australia employed magnetic susceptibility, which looks for changes in the ability of rock to be magnetized—another indicator of heat exposure among iron-rich rocks. Finally, Brown used a gloss meter to measure the luster that develops after heating and flaking and compare it with the luster on the tools he made. Our results, detailed last year in the journal *Science,* showed that intentional heat treatment was a dominant technology at Pinnacle Point by 72,000 years ago and that people there employed it intermittently as far back as 164,000 years ago.

The process of treating by heat testifies to two uniquely modern human cognitive abilities. First, people recognized that they could substantially alter a raw material to make it useful—in this case, engineering the properties of stone by heating it, thereby turning a poor-quality rock into high-quality raw material. Second, they could invent and execute a long chain of processes. The making of silcrete blades requires a complex series of carefully designed steps: building a sand pit to insulate the silcrete, bringing the heat slowly up to 350 degrees Celsius, holding the temperature steady and then dropping it down slowly. Creating and carrying out the sequence and passing technologies down from generation to generation probably required language. Once established, these abilities no doubt helped our ancestors outcompete the archaic human species they encountered once they dispersed from Africa. In particular, the complex pyrotechnology detected at Pinnacle Point would have given early modern humans a distinct advantage as they entered the cold lands of the Neandertals, who seem to have lacked this technique.

Smart from the Start

In addition to being technologically savvy, the prehistoric denizens of Pinnacle Point had an artistic side. In the oldest layers of the PP13B sequence, my team has unearthed dozens of pieces of red ochre (iron oxide) that were variously carved and ground to create a fine powder that was probably mixed with a binder such as animal fat to make paint that could be applied to the body or other surfaces. Such decorations typically encode information about social identity or other important aspects of culture—that is, they are symbolic. Many of my colleagues and I think that this ochre constitutes the earliest unequivocal example of symbolic behavior on record and pushes the origin of such practices back by tens of thousands of years. Evidence of symbolic-activities also appears later in the sequence. Deposits dating to around 110,00 years ago include both red ochre and seashells that were clearly collected for their aesthetic appeal, because by the time they washed ashore from their deepwater home, any flesh would have been long gone. I think these decorative seashells, along with the evidence for marine foraging, signal that people had, for the first time, begun to embed in their worldview and rituals a clear commitment to the sea.

The precocious expressions of both symbolism and sophisticated technology at Pinnacle Point have major implications for understanding the origin of our species. Fossils from Ethiopia show that anatomically modern humans had evolved by at least 195,000 years ago. The emergence of the modern mind, however, is more difficult to establish. Paleoanthropologists use various proxies in the archaeological record to try to identify the presence and scope of cognitive modernity. Artifacts made using technologies that require outside-the-box connections of seemingly unrelated phenomena and long chains of production—like heat treatment of rock for tool manufacture are one proxy. Evidence of art or other symbolic activities is another, as is the tracking of time through proxies such as lunar phases. For years the earliest examples of these behaviors were all found in Europe and dated to after 40,000 years ago. Based on that record, researchers concluded that there was a long lag between the origin of our species and the emergence of our peerless creativity.

But over the past 10 years archaeologists working at a number of sites in South Africa have found examples of sophisticated behaviors that predate by a long shot their counterparts in Europe. For instance, archaeologist Ian Watts, who works in South Africa, has described hundreds to thousands of pieces of worked and unworked ochre at sites dating as far back as 120,000 years ago. Interestingly, this ochre, as well as the pieces at Pinnacle Point, tends to be red despite the fact that local sources of the mineral exhibit a range of hues, suggesting that humans were preferentially curating the red pieces—perhaps associating the color with menstruation and fertility. Jocelyn A. Bernatchez, a PhD. student at Arizona State, thinks that many of these ochre pieces may have been yellow originally and then heat-treated to turn them red. And at Blombos Cave, located about 100 kilometers west of Pinnacle Point, Christopher S. Henshilwood of the University of Bergen in Norway has discovered pieces of ochre with systematic engravings, beads made of snail shells and refined bone tools, all of which date to around 71,000 years ago [see "The Morning of the Modern Mind," by Kate Wong; SCIENTIFIC AMERICAN, June 2005]. These sites, along with those at Pinnacle Point, belie the claim that modern cognition evolved late in our lineage and suggest instead that our species had this faculty at its inception.

I suspect that a driving force in the evolution of this complex cognition was strong long-term selection acting to enhance our ancestors' ability to mentally map the location and seasonal variation of many species of plants in arid environments and to convey this accumulated knowledge to offspring and other group members. This capacity laid the foundation for many other advances, such as the ability to grasp the link between the phases of the moon and the tides and to learn to schedule their shellfish-hunting trips to the shore accordingly. Together the readily available shellfish and geophytes provided a high-quality diet that allowed people to become less nomadic, increased their birth rates and reduced their child mortality. The larger group sizes that resulted from these changes would have promoted symbolic behavior and technological complexity as people endeavored to express their social identity and build on one another's technologies, explaining why we see such sophisticated practices at PP13B.

Follow the Sea

PP13B preserves a long record of changing occupations that, in combination with the detailed records of local climate and environmental change my team has obtained, is revealing how our ancestors used the cave and the coast over millennia. Modeling the paleocoastline over time, Erich C. Fisher of the University of Florida has shown that the conditions changed quickly and dramatically, thanks to a long, wide, gently sloping continental shelf off the coast of South Africa called the Agulhas bank. During glacial periods, when sea levels fell, significant amounts of this shelf would have been exposed, putting considerable distance—up to 95 kilometers—between Pinnacle Point and the ocean. When the climate warmed and sea levels rose, the water advanced over the Agulhas bank again, and the caves were seaside once more.

Judging from rainfall and vegetation patterns evident in records from stalagmites spanning the time between 350,000 and 50,000 years ago, we see that the fynbos probably followed the retreating coast out onto the now submerged continental shelf and back again, keeping the geophytes and shellfish in close proximity. As for the people, during these periods of low population density they were free to target the best part of the landscape, and that was the intersection of the geophytes and shellfish—so I suspect they followed the sea. The tracking of resources would explain why PP13B appears to have been occupied intermittently.

Our excavations at PP13B have intercepted the people who may very well be the ancestors of everyone on the planet as they shadowed the shifting shoreline. Yet if I am correct about these people and their connection to the coast, the richest record of the progenitor population lies underwater on the Agulhas bank. There it will remain for the near future, guarded by great white sharks and dangerous currents. We can still test the hypothesis that humans followed the sea by examining sites on the current coast such as PP13B and another site we are excavating called PP5-6. But we can also study locations where the continental shelf drops steeply and the coast was always near—investigations that my colleagues and I are currently initiating.

The genetic, fossil and archaeological records are reasonably concordant in suggesting that the first substantial and prolonged wave of modern human migration out of Africa occurred around 50,000 years ago. But questions about the events leading up to that exodus remain. We still do not know, for example, whether at the end of glacial stage 6 there was just one population of H. sapiens left in Africa or whether there were several, with just one ultimately giving rise to everyone alive today. Such unknowns are providing my team and others with a very clear and exciting research direction for the foreseeable future: our fieldwork needs to target the other potential progenitor zones in Africa during that glacial period and expand our knowledge of the climate conditions just before that stage. We need to flesh out the story of these people who eventually pushed out of their refuge, filled up the African continent and went on to conquer the world.

Critical Thinking

1. How does the author describe the deteriorating environmental conditions for our ancestors during the Marine Isotope Stage 6 and why does he think the population plummeted to dangerously low levels?
2. What were the environmental circumstances and the survival skills that enabled our species to avoid extinction?

Create Central

www.mhhe.com/createcentral

Internet References

Archaeology Links (NC)
www.arch.dcr.state.nc.us/links.htm#stuff

Department of Human Evolution/Max Planck Institute
www.eva.mpg.de/evolution

Society for Historical Archaeology
www.sha.org

CURTIS W. MAREAN is a professor at the School of Human Evolution and Social Change at Arizona State University and a member of the Institute of Human Origins. He studies the origins of modern humans, the prehistory of Africa, paleoclimates and paleoenvironments, and animal bones from archaeological sites. Marean is particularly interested in human occupation of coastal ecosystems. He is the principal investigator for the South African Coast Paleoclimate, Paleoenvironment, Paleoecology, Paleoanthropology (SACP4) project, funded by the National Science Foundation.

Marean, Curtis W. From Scientific American, vol. 303, no. 2, August, 2010, pp. 54–61. Copyright © 2010 by Scientific American, a division of Nature America, Inc. All rights reserved. Reprinted by permission.

Article

Prepared by: Mari Pritchard Parker, *Pasadena City College* and Elvio Angeloni, *Pasadena City College*

A New View of the Birth of *Homo sapiens*

New genomic data are settling an old argument about how our species evolved.

Ann Gibbons

Learning Outcomes

After reading this article, you will be able to:

- Discuss when, where, and how modern humans evolved.
- Discuss whether the modern humans that came out of Africa replaced archaic *Homo sapiens* or mated with them.

For 27 years, Chris Stringer and Milford Wolpoff have been at odds about where and how our species was born. Stringer, a paleoanthropologist at the Natural History Museum in London, held that modern humans came out of Africa, spread around the world, and replaced, rather than mated with, the archaic humans they met. But Wolpoff, of the University of Michigan, Ann Arbor, argued that a single, worldwide species of human, including archaic forms outside of Africa, met, mingled and had offspring, and so produced *Homo sapiens*. The battle has been long and bitter: When reviewing a manuscript in the 1980s, Wolpoff scribbled "Stringer's desperate argument" under a chart; in a 1996 book, Stringer wrote that "attention to inconvenient details has never been part of the Wolpoff style." At one tense meeting, the pair presented opposing views in rival sessions on the same day—and Wolpoff didn't invite Stringer to the meeting's press conference. "It was difficult for a long time," recalls Stringer.

Then, in the past year, geneticists announced the nearly complete nuclear genomes of two different archaic humans: Neandertals, and their enigmatic eastern cousins from southern Siberia. These data provide a much higher resolution view of our past, much as a new telescope allows astronomers to see farther back in time in the universe. When compared with the genomes of living people, the ancient genomes allow anthropologists to thoroughly test the competing models of human origins for the first time.

The DNA data suggest not one but at least two instances of interbreeding between archaic and modern humans, raising the question of whether *H. sapiens* at that point was a distinct species (see box, The Species Problem). And so they appear to refute the complete replacement aspect of the Out of Africa model. "[Modern humans] are certainly coming out of Africa, but we're finding evidence of low levels of admixture wherever you look," says evolutionary geneticist Michael Hammer of the University of Arizona in Tucson. Stringer admits: "The story has undoubtedly got a whole lot more complicated."

But the genomic data don't prove the classic multiregionalism model correct either. They suggest only a small amount of interbreeding, presumably at the margins where invading moderns met archaic groups that were the worldwide descendants of *H. erectus,* the human ancestor that left Africa 1.8 million years ago. "I have lately taken to talking about the best model as replacement with hybridization, ... [or] 'leaky replacement,'" says paleogeneticist Svante Pääbo of the Max Planck Institute for Evolutionary Anthropology in Leipzig, lead author of the two nuclear genome studies.

The new picture most resembles so-called assimilation models, which got relatively little attention over the years. "This means so much," says Fred Smith of Illinois State University in Normal, who proposed such a model. "I just thought 'Hallelujah! No matter what anybody else says, I was as close to correct as anybody.'"

Evolving Models

Stringer and others first proposed Africa as the birthplace of modern humans back in the mid-1980s. The same year, researchers published a landmark study that traced the maternally inherited mitochondrial DNA (mtDNA) of all living people to a female ancestor that lived in Africa about 200,000 years ago, dubbed mitochondrial Eve. She caught the attention of the popular press, landing on the cover of *Newsweek* and *Time.*

Additional studies of living people—from Y chromosomes to snippets of nuclear DNA to the entire mtDNA genome—consistently found that Africans were the most diverse genetically. This suggests that modern humans arose in Africa, where they had more time to accumulate mutations than on other continents (*Science,* 17 November 2006, p. 1068). Meanwhile, ancient DNA technology also took off. Pääbo's group sequenced first a few bits of Neandertal mitochondrial DNA in

The Species Problem

Our ancestors had sex with at least two kinds of archaic humans at two different times and places—and those liaisons produced surviving children, according to the latest ancient DNA research (see main text). But were the participants in these prehistoric encounters members of separate species? Doesn't a species, by definition, breed only with others of that species?

These are the questions paleogeneticist Svante Pääbo dodged twice last year. His team published two papers proposing that both Neandertals and mysterious humans from Denisova Cave in Siberia interbred with ancient modern humans. But the researchers avoided the thorny question of species designation and simply referred to Neandertals, Denisovans, and modern humans as "populations." "I think discussion of what is a species and what is a subspecies is a sterile academic endeavor," says Pääbo, who works at the Max Planck Institute for Evolutionary Anthropology in Leipzig, Germany.

The question of how to define a species has divided researchers for centuries. Darwin's words in *On the Origin of Species* still hold: "No one definition has satisfied all naturalists." However, many scientists use the biological species concept proposed by Ernst Mayr: "groups of actually or potentially interbreeding natural populations, which are reproductively isolated from other such groups."

The draft versions of the Neandertal and Denisovan nuclear genomes show low levels of interbreeding between each of them and modern humans. Apply Mayr's definition strictly, and all three must be considered *Homo sapiens*. "They mated with each other. We'll call them the same species," says molecular anthropologist John Hawks of the University of Wisconsin, Madison.

But that's a minority view among paleoanthropologists. Many consider Neandertals a species separate from modern humans because the anatomical and developmental differences are "an order of magnitude higher than anything we can observe between extant human populations," says Jean-Jacques Hublin, a co-author of Pääbo's at Max Planck. In the real world, he says, Mayr's concept doesn't hold up: "There are about 330 closely related species of mammals that interbreed, and at least a third of them can produce fertile hybrids."

There's also no agreed-upon yardstick for how much morphologic or genetic difference separates species. That's why Pääbo's team avoided the species question a second time with respect to the Denisovans. These hominins are known only from a scrap of bone, a single tooth, and their DNA. They are genetically closest to Neandertals. The genetic distance between Denisovans and Neandertals, in fact, is only 9% larger than that between a living Frenchman and a living San Bushman in Africa, both of whom belong to *H. sapiens*. But so far Neandertals seem to have low genetic diversity, based on the DNA of six Neandertals from Russia to Spain. To Pääbo's team, that makes the difference from the Denisovans significant.

Also, the Denisovan tooth doesn't look much like that of a Neandertal. So the team considers them a distinct population but declined to name a new species. "Why take a stand on it when it will only lead to discussions and no one will have the final word?" asks Pääbo.

—A.G.

1997, then the entire mitochondrial genomes of several Neandertals—and found them to be distinct from those of living people. So ancient DNA, too, argued against the idea of mixing between Neandertals and moderns. Over the years the replacement model became the leading theory, with only a stubborn few, including Wolpoff, holding to multiregionalism.

Yet there were a few dissenting notes. A few studies of individual genes found evidence of migration from Asia into Africa, rather than vice versa. Population geneticists warned that complete replacement was unlikely, given the distribution of alleles in living humans. And a few paleoanthropologists proposed middle-of-the-road models. Smith, a former student of Wolpoff's, suggested that most of our ancestors arose in Africa but interbred with local populations as they spread out around the globe, with archaic people contributing to about 10% of living people's genomes. At the University of Hamburg in Germany, Gunter Brauer similarly proposed replacement with hybridization, but with a trivial amount of interbreeding. But neither model got much traction; they were either ignored or lumped in with multiregionalism. "Assimilation got kicked so much," recalls Smith.

Over time, the two more extreme models moved toward the middle, with most multiregionalists recognizing that the chief ancestors of modern humans arose in Africa. "The broad line of evolution is pretty clear: Our ancestors came out of Africa," says biological anthropologist John Relethford of the State University of New York College at Oneonta. "But what happens next is kind of complex."

Genes from the Past

Then in May 2010 came the Neandertals' complete nuclear genome, sequenced from the bones of three female Neandertals who lived in Croatia more than 38,000 years ago. Pääbo's international team found that a small amount—1% to 4%—of the nuclear DNA of Europeans and Asians, but not of Africans, can be traced to Neandertals. The most likely model to explain this, Pääbo says, was that early modern humans arose in Africa but interbred with Neandertals in the Middle East or Arabia before spreading into Asia and Europe, about 50,000 to 80,000 years ago (*Science*, 7 May 2010, pp. 680, 710).

Seven months later, on 23 December, the team published in *Nature* the complete nuclear genome of a girl's pinky finger from Denisova Cave in the Altai Mountains of southern Siberia. To their surprise, the genome was neither a Neandertal's nor a modern human's, yet the girl was alive at the same time, dating to at least 30,000 years ago and probably older than 50,000 years. Her DNA was most like a Neandertal's, but her people were a distinct group that had long been separated from Neandertals.

By comparing parts of the Denisovan genome directly with the same segments of DNA in 53 populations of living people, the team found that the Denisovans shared 4% to 6% of their DNA with Melanesians from Papua New Guinea and the Bougainville Islands. Those segments were not found in Neandertals or other living humans.

The most likely scenario for how all this happened is that after Neandertal and Denisovan populations split about 200,000 years ago, modern humans interbred with Neandertals as they left Africa in the past 100,000 years. Thus Neandertals left their mark in the genomes of living Asians and Europeans, says co-author Montgomery Slatkin, a population geneticist at the University of California, Berkeley. Later, a subset of this group of moderns—who carried some Neandertal DNA—headed east toward Melanesia and interbred with the Denisovans in Asia on the way. As a result, Melanesians inherited DNA from both Neandertals and Denisovans, with as much as 8% of their DNA coming from archaic people, says co-author David Reich, a population geneticist at Harvard Medical School in Boston.

This means *H. sapiens* mixed it up with at least two different archaic peoples, in at least two distinct times and places. To some, that's starting to sound a lot like multiregionalism. "It's hard to explain how good I feel about this," says Wolpoff, who says that seeing complete replacement falsified twice in 1 year was beyond his wildest expectations. "It was a good year."

And yet the interbreeding with archaic humans seems limited—from 1% to 8% of some living people's genomes. Stringer and many others don't consider it full-scale multiregional continuity. "I think interbreeding was at a low level," says Slatkin, who says that if there had been a great deal of admixture, the genetic data would have revealed it already. Low levels of interbreeding suggest that either archaic people mated with moderns only rarely—or their hybrid offspring had low fitness and so produced few viable offspring, says population geneticist Laurent Excoffier of the University of Bern in Switzerland.

In any case, Reich notes that at least 90% of our genomes are inherited from African ancestors who replaced the archaic people on other continents but hybridized with them around the margins. And that scenario most closely backs the assimilation models proposed by Smith and Brauer.

Of course, it's possible that future data will overturn today's "leaky replacement" model. Slatkin says he cannot rule out an alternative explanation for the data: The "archaic" DNA thought to have come from mating with Neandertals could instead stem from a very ancient ancestor that we shared with Neandertals. Most modern humans retained those archaic sequences, but Africans lost them. But Slatkin says this "doesn't seem very plausible," because it requires modern human populations with the archaic DNA and those without

it to have been partially isolated from each other in Africa for hundreds of thousands of years. And it seems even less probable that Melanesians and Denisovans are the only groups that retained a second set of archaic DNA motifs from a common ancestor shared by all modern humans, Neandertals and Denisovans. If those explanations do prove true, replacement would not be falsified.

In the wake of the big genome studies, other researchers such as Hammer are scrutinizing DNA from more living humans to further test the model. Researchers are also trying to pinpoint when admixture happened, which has significant consequences. At just what point did we evolve from archaic humans to become "modern" humans? "There are still archaic [genetic] features floating around until amazingly recently, until 40,000 years ago," says Hammer. He wonders whether the process of becoming modern took longer and was more complex than once thought. "There's no line you can draw and say everything after this is modern. That's the elephant in the room."

Meanwhile, paleoanthropologists are searching for fossils in Asia that might belong to the enigmatic Denisovan population—and might yield more ancient DNA. Paleoanthropologist Russell Ciochon of the University of Iowa in Iowa City and Wolpoff say there are several known, ambiguous fossils in Asia that might be candidates for early Denisovans. "I believe things were going on in Asia that we just don't know about," says Ciochon. "Before this paper on the Denisovans, we didn't have any insight into this. Now, with this nuclear genome, I find myself talking about 'the Denisovans.' It's already had an impact."

As for Stringer and Wolpoff, both now in their 60s, their battle has mellowed. Their views, while still distinct, have converged somewhat, and they shared a beer at a Neandertal meeting last year. "The reason we get on well now," says Stringer, "is we both think we've been proved right."

Critical Thinking

1. Discuss the evidence for the "replacement model" and the "multiregional model" for the origins of modern humans.
2. What evidence is there for a "leaky replacement model"?
3. What is the "species problem" and how does it relate to an understanding of modern human origins?

Create Central

www.mhhe.com/createcentral

Internet References

Fossil Hominids FAQ
    www.talkorigins.org/faqs/homs
How Humans Evolved
    www.wwnorton.com/college/anthro/bioanth
Max Planck Institute for Evolutionary Biology
    http://wwwstaff.eva.mpg.de/~paabo

Gibbons, Ann. From *Science Magazine*, January 28, 2011, pp. 392–394. Copyright © 2011 by American Association for the Advancement of Science. Reprinted by permission via Rightslink. www.sciencemag.org

Article

Prepared by: Mari Pritchard Parker, *Pasadena City College* and
Elvio Angeloni, *Pasadena City College*

Refuting a Myth about Human Origins

Homo sapiens emerged once, not as modern-looking people first and as modern-behaving people later.

JOHN J. SHEA

Learning Outcomes

After reading this article, you will be able to:

- Discuss the phrase, "Upper Paleolithic Revolution" in terms of what it proposed and what evidence now challenges the notion.
- Discuss the evidence for looking at artifacts as byproducts of behavioral strategies rather than as expressions of evolutionary states.

For decades, archeologists have believed that modern behaviors emerged among *Homo sapiens* tens of thousands of years after our species first evolved. Archaeologists disagreed over whether this process was gradual or swift, but they assumed that *Homo sapiens* once lived who were very different from us. These people were not "behaviorally modern," meaning they did not routinely use art, symbols and rituals; they did not systematically collect small animals, fish, shellfish and other difficult-to-procure foods; they did not use complex technologies: Traps, nets, projectile weapons and watercraft were unknown to them.

Premodern humans—often described as "archaic *Homo sapiens*"—were thought to have lived in small, vulnerable groups of closely related individuals. They were believed to have been equipped only with simple tools and were likely heavily dependent on hunting large game. Individuals in such groups would have been much less insulated from environmental stresses than are modern humans. In Thomas Hobbes's words, their lives were "solitary, nasty, brutish and short." If you need a mental image here, close your eyes and conjure a picture of a stereotypical caveman. But archaeological evidence now shows that some of the behaviors associated with modern humans, most importantly our capacity for wide behavioral variability, actually did occur among people who lived very long ago, particularly in Africa. And a conviction is growing among some archaeologists that there was no sweeping transformation to "behavioral modernity" in our species' recent past.

As Misia Landau argued nearly a quarter of a century ago in the essay "Human Evolution as Narrative" (*American Scientist*, May–June 1984), prescientific traditions of narrative explanation long encouraged scientists to envision key changes in human evolution as holistic transformations. The idea of an archaic-to-modern human transition in *Homo sapiens* arises, in part, from this narrative tradition. All this makes for a satisfying story, but it is not a realistic framework for understanding the actual, complex and contingent course of human evolution. Most evolutionary changes are relatively minor things whose consequences play out incrementally over thousands of generations.

In order to better understand human prehistory, I recommend another approach, one that focuses on behavioral variability. This trait, easily observed among recent humans, is becoming more apparent in the archaeological record for early *Homo sapiens*. Prehistoric people lived in different ways in different places at different times. We must seek out and explain those differences, for, in evolution, only differences matter. Thinking about prehistoric human behavioral variability in terms of various adaptive strategies offers an attractive way to explain these differences. But first, we need to discard an incorrect and outdated idea about human evolution, the belief that prehistoric *Homo sapiens* can be divided into "archaic" and "modern" humans.

An Idea Is Born

Archaeology's concept of archaic versus modern humans developed as prehistoric archaeological research spread from Europe to other regions. The study of prehistoric people began in Europe during the 19th century in scientific societies, museums and universities. By the 1920s, discoveries made at a number of European archaeological sites had prompted a consensus about the Paleolithic Period, which is now dated from 12,000 to nearly 2.6 million years ago. Archaeologists divided this period into Lower (oldest), Middle, and Upper (youngest) Paleolithic phases. Distinctive stone-tool assemblages—or "industries"—characterized each phase. Archaeologists identified these industries by the presence of diagnostic artifact types, such as Acheulian hand axes (Lower Paleolithic), Mousterian scrapers made of Levallois flakes (Middle Paleolithic), and Aurignacian prismatic blades and carved antler points (Upper Paleolithic). The fact that tools from more recent industries were lighter, smaller and more heavily modified suggested there was a trend toward greater technological and cultural sophistication in the Paleolithic sequence. European Upper Paleolithic industries were associated exclusively with *Homo sapiens* fossils and Lower and Middle Paleolithic industries were associated with earlier hominins (*Homo heidelbergensis* and *Homo neanderthalensis*). This supported the idea that there were important evolutionary differences between modern *Homo sapiens* and earlier archaic hominins.

Early Upper Paleolithic contexts in Europe preserve evidence for prismatic blade production, carved bone tools, projectile weaponry, complex hearths, personal adornments, art, long-distance trade, mortuary rituals, architecture, food storage and specialized big-game hunting, as well as systematic exploitation of smaller prey and aquatic resources. Furthermore, the variability of these behaviors within the Upper Paleolithic is much greater than that seen in earlier periods. In much the same way that anthropologists have documented cultural variability among recent humans, archaeologists can easily tell whether a particular carved bone point or bone bead is from a site in Spain, France or Germany. Not surprisingly, most prehistorians accept that the archaeology of the Upper Paleolithic is, in effect, "the archaeology of us."

Lower and Middle Paleolithic stone tools and other artifacts found in Europe and elsewhere vary within a narrow range of simple forms. Properly equipped and motivated modern-day flintknappers (people who make stone tools) can turn out replicas of any of these tools in minutes, if not seconds. Many of the differences among Lower and Middle Paleolithic artifacts simply reflect variation in rock types and the extent to which tools were resharpened. Geographic and chronological differences among Middle and Lower Paleolithic tools mostly involve differences in relative frequencies of these simple tool types. Nearly the same range of Lower and Middle Paleolithic stone tool types are found throughout much of Europe, Africa and Asia.

The differences between the Lower/Middle and Upper Paleolithic records in Europe are so pronounced that from the 1970s onward prehistorians have described the transition between them as "The Upper Paleolithic Revolution." This regional phenomenon went global in the late 1980s after a conference at Cambridge University entitled "The Human Revolution." This revolution was portrayed as a watershed event that set recent modern humans apart from their archaic predecessors and from other hominins, such as *Homo neanderthalensis*. The causes of this assumed transformation were hotly debated. Scientists such as Richard Klein attributed the changes to the FOXP2 polymorphism, the so-called language gene. But the polymorphism was eventually discovered in Neanderthal DNA too. Many researchers—such as Christopher Henshilwood of the University of Witwatersrand, Curtis Marean of Arizona State University, Paul Mellars of the University of Cambridge, April Nowell of the University of Victoria and Phil Chase of the University of Pennsylvania—continue to see symbolic behavior as a crucial component of behavioral modernity. Yet as João Zilhão of the University of Bristol and Francesco d'Errico of the University of Bordeaux have argued, finds of mineral pigments, perforated beads, burials and artifact-style variation associated with Neanderthals challenge the hypothesis that symbol use, or anything else for that matter, was responsible for a quality of behavioral modernity unique to *Homo sapiens*.

The Missing Revolution

In fact, fossil evidence threatening the Upper Paleolithic revolution hypothesis emerged many decades ago. At about the same time the Paleolithic framework was developed during the 1920s and 1930s, European-trained archaeologists began searching for human fossils and artifacts in the Near East, Africa and Asia. Expatriate and colonial archaeologists such as Dorothy Garrod and Louis Leakey expected that the European archaeological record worked as a global model for human evolution and used the European Paleolithic framework to organize their observations abroad. Very quickly, however, they discovered a mismatch between their expectations and reality when *Homo sapiens* remains outside Europe were found with Lower or Middle Paleolithic artifacts. Archaeologists started assuming then that the remains dated to periods just before the Upper Paleolithic revolution. But in fact, those discoveries, as well as more recent finds, challenge the notion that the revolution ever occurred.

In Europe, the oldest *Homo sapiens* fossils date to only 35,000 years ago. But studies of genetic variation among living humans suggest that our species emerged in Africa as long as 200,000 years ago. Scientists have recovered *Homo sapiens* fossils in contexts dating to 165,000 to 195,000 years ago in Ethiopia's Lower Omo Valley and Middle Awash Valley. Evidence is clear that early humans dispersed out of Africa to southern Asia before 40,000 years ago. Similar modern-looking human fossils found in the Skhul and Qafzeh caves in Israel date to 80,000 to 120,000 years ago. *Homo sapiens* fossils dating to 100,000 years ago have been recovered from Zhiren Cave in China. In Australia, evidence for a human presence dates to at least 42,000 years ago. Nothing like a human revolution precedes *Homo sapiens*' first appearances in any of these regions. And all these *Homo sapiens* fossils were found with either Lower or Middle Paleolithic stone tool industries.

There are differences between the skeletons of these early *Homo sapiens* and Upper Paleolithic Europeans. The best-documented differences involve variation in skull shape. Yet, as Daniel Lieberman of Harvard University writes in the recently published *The Evolution of the Human Head*, we are just beginning to understand the genetic and behavioral basis for variation in human skulls. It makes no sense whatsoever to draw major evolutionary distinctions among humans based on skull shape unless we understand the underlying sources of cranial variation. There is no simple morphological dividing line among these fossil skulls. Most fossils combine "primitive" (ancestral) characteristics as well as "derived" (recently evolved) ones. Even if physical anthropologists divided prehistoric humans into archaic and modern groups, it would be foolish for archaeologists to invoke this difference as an explanation for anything unless we knew how specific skeletal differences related to specific aspects of behavior preserved in the archaeological record.

Early *Homo sapiens* fossils in Africa and Asia are associated with "precocious," or unexpectedly early evidence for modern behaviors such as those seen in the European Upper Paleolithic. They include intensive fish and shellfish exploitation, the production of complex projectile weapons, the use of symbols in the form of mineral pigments and perforated shells, and even rare burials with grave goods in them. But as Erella Hovers and Anna Belfer-Cohen of The Hebrew University of Jerusalem argued in a chapter of *Transitions Before the Transition,* "Now You See It, Now You Don't—Modern Human Behavior in the Middle Paleolithic," much of this evidence is recursive. It is not a consistent feature of the archaeological record. Evidence for one or more of these modern behaviors appears at a few sites or for a few thousand years in one region or another, and then it vanishes. If behavioral modernity were both a derived condition and a landmark development in the course of human history, one would hardly expect it to disappear for prolonged periods in our species' evolutionary history.

For me, the most surprising aspect about the debate regarding when *Homo sapiens* became human is that archaeologists have not tested the core hypothesis that there were significant behavioral differences between the earliest and more recent members of our species. Because modernity is a typological category, it is not easy to test this hypothesis. One is either behaviorally modern or not. And, not all groups classified as behaviorally modern have left clear and unambiguous evidence for that modernity at all times and in all contexts. For example, expedient and opportunistic flintknapping of river pebbles and cobbles by living humans often creates stone tools indistinguishable from the pebble tools knapped by *Homo habilis* or *Homo erectus.* This similarity reflects the nature of the tool-making strategies, techniques and raw materials, not the evolutionary equivalence of the toolmakers. Thus, the archaeological record abounds in possibilities of false-negative findings about prehistoric human behavioral modernity.

This issue caught my interest in 2002 while I was excavating 195,000-year-old archaeological sites associated with early *Homo sapiens* fossils in the Lower Omo River Valley Kibish Formation in Ethiopia. I am an archaeologist, but I am also a flintknapper. Nothing about the stone tools from Omo Kibish struck me as archaic or primitive. (When I teach flintknapping at my university, I have ample opportunity to see what happens when people with rudimentary skills try to knap stone and how those skills vary with experience and motivation.) The Omo Kibish tools showed that their makers had great versatility in effectively knapping a wide range of rock types. This set me to thinking: Have we been asking the wrong questions about early humans' behavior?

A Better Way

Documenting and analyzing behavioral variability is a more theoretically sound approach to studying differences among prehistoric people than searching for the transition to behavioral modernity. Nearly everything humans do, we do in more than one identifiably different way. As Richard Potts of the Smithsonian Institution argued in *Humanity's Descent* in 1996, our species' capacity for wide behavioral variability appears to be uniquely derived. No other animal has as wide a behavioral repertoire as *Homo sapiens* does. And variability can be investigated empirically, quantitatively, and with fewer problems than occur in ranking prehistoric people in terms of their modernity.

One way to gauge early *Homo sapiens'* behavioral variability is to compare their lithic technologies. Lithics, or stone tools, are nearly indestructible and are found everywhere hominins lived in Pleistocene times. Stone tools do not tell us everything we might wish to know about prehistoric human behavior, but they are no less subject to the selective pressures that create variation in other types of archaeological evidence. Lithic artifacts made by recent humans are more complex and variable than those associated with early hominins. Early Paleolithic stone tools are more complex and variable than those made by nonhuman primates. Thus, there is reason to expect that analysis of these tools will produce a valid signal about early *Homo sapiens'* capacity for behavioral variability. Eastern Africa is an especially good place in which to compare early and later *Homo sapiens'* stone technology because that region preserves our species' longest continuous archaeological record. Restricting this comparison to eastern Africa minimizes the complicating effects of geographic constraints on stone-tool technology.

One of the most popular ways of describing variation among stone-tool industries is a framework that the British archaeologist Grahame Clark proposed in *World Prehistory: A New Synthesis* (1969). This framework describes lithic technological variability in terms of five modes of core technology. (In flintknapping, "cores" are the rocks from which flakes are struck, with the flakes later developed into various kinds of tools.) Variation in core technology is thought to reflect differences in ecological adaptations. Clark's framework is a crude instrument, but it can be made into a reasonably sensitive register of technological variability if we simply note which of these modes are represented in each of a series of lithic assemblages. When it is applied to sites in eastern Africa dating 284,000 to 6,000 years ago, a more complex view of prehistoric life there emerges. One does not see a steady accumulation of novel core technologies since our species first appeared or anything like a "revolution." Instead one sees a persistent pattern of wide technological variability.

What does this variability mean? Archaeologists' understanding of lithic technology continues to grow, from experiments, from studies of recent stone-tool-using groups and from contextual clues in the archaeological record. Our understanding is far from perfect, but we do know enough to make some plausible interpretations. Pebble-core reduction (mode 1 in Clark's framework), in which toolmakers strike flakes opportunistically from rounded pebbles or cobbles, is the simplest way to obtain a cutting edge from stone. Stone tools are still made this way in rural parts of eastern Africa. Its ubiquity in the archaeological assemblages probably reflects a stable strategy of coping expediently with unpredictable needs for cutting edges.

Large bifacial core tools (mode 2) are thought to have been dual-purpose tools. Their heft and long ratting edges make them effective in heavy-duty tasks, such as woodworking or the butchering of large animal carcasses. Thinner flakes knapped from bifacial core tools can be used for lighter-duty cutting or retouched into more functionally specialized forms. In recent archaeological contexts, large bifacial cutting tools are often correlated with people who moved their residences frequently, whereas expedient pebble cores are correlated with more lengthy occupations. High topographic relief and wide seasonal variation in rainfall make residential stability a difficult thing for even recent eastern African pastoralist groups to achieve. The persistence of this technology may reflect relatively high residential mobility among prehistoric eastern Africans.

The behavioral correlates of Levallois prepared-core technology (mode 3) are less clear, if only because the term encompasses so many different core-knapping strategies. Some archaeologists see Levallois prepared cores as reflecting knappers' efforts to obtain desired tool shapes, or to produce relatively broad and thin flakes that efficiently recover cutting edge. These hypotheses are not mutually exclusive, and in the long run, each of them probably explains some part of why people made such cores in eastern Africa for a very long time.

Prismatic-blade core technology (mode 4) involves detaching long rectangular flakes one after another from a cone-shaped core. The most widely repeated hypothesis about the appeal of prismatic-blade production is that it produces greater amounts of ratting edge per unit mass of stone than other strategies. However, recent experiments by Metin Eren at Southern Methodist University and his colleagues have shown that this hypothesis is wrong. A far more likely appeal of this strategy is that the blades' morphological consistency makes them easier to attach to a handle. Attaching a stone tool to a handle vastly increases leverage and mechanical efficiency, but it also restricts the range of tool movement and limits the portion of the tool that can be resharpened. The comings and goings of blade core technology in eastern Africa probably reflect a complex interplay of these strategic considerations.

Differing amounts of geometric microlithic technology (mode 5) are preserved in the most ancient and most recent assemblages in the east African sample. Geometric microliths are small tools made by segmenting blades or flakes and shaping them into triangles, rectangles, crescents and other geometric forms by blunting one or more of their edges. Too small to have been useful while hand-held, geometric microliths were almost certainly used as hafted tools. They are easy to attach to handles, making them suitable for use as projectile armatures, woodworking tools and aids to preparing plant foods. Archaeologists view microlithic stone-tool technology as a strategy for optimizing versatility and minimizing risk. Microlithic technologies first appear and proliferate among African and Eurasian human populations from about 50,000 years ago to around 10,000 years ago. This was a period of hypervariable climate, and it makes a certain amount of sense that humans at that time devised versatile and efficiently transportable stone tools. If, for example, climate change required people to frequently shift from hunting game to reaping grasses and back again, using microlith-barbed arrows and microlith-edged sickles would allow them to do this efficiently, without any major change to their technological strategies. Because microlithic tooks are small, they preserve high ratios of cutting edge to mass. This means that if climate shifts required more seasonal migrations, individuals transporting microliths would be carrying the most cutting edge per unit mass of stone. Variability in the use of microlithic technology in eastern Africa probably reflects strategic responses to environmental unpredictability along with efforts to cope with increased subsistence risk by optimizing versatility in stone-tool technology.

How do the differences between earlier and later eastern African core technologies compare to variation among recent stone-tool-using humans? The range of variability in recent human stone-tool technology is greater than that in the eastern African sample. All five of Clark's modes are to be found among the lithic technology of recent humans. Yet some technologies are not represented in the African sample. For example, more than 30,000 years ago in Australia, and later elsewhere, people began grinding and polishing the edges of stone tools. Such grinding and polishing reduces friction during work, making cutting tools more efficient to use and resharpen. In the New World, ancestral Native American flintknappers deployed a wide range of bifacial-core technologies fundamentally different from those seen in eastern Africa. They used these tools in contexts ranging from hunter-gatherer campsites on the Great Plains to Mesoamerican city-states like Teotihuacan. Differences in recent stone-tool technology reflect variability in adaptive strategies. No anthropologists in their right minds would attribute this variability to evolutionary differences among recent humans. If this kind of explanation makes so little sense in the present, what possible value can it have for explaining past behavioral variability among *Homo sapiens*?

The lithic evidence reviewed here challenges the hypothesis that there were significant behavioral differences between the earliest and more recent members of our species in eastern Africa. Obviously, there is more to human behavioral variability than what is reflected in stone tools. Using Clark's technological modes to capture that variability, as described here, is just a first step. But it is a step forward. This emphasis on variability will gain strength if and when it is supported by more detailed analyses of the stone tools and by other archaeological evidence.

Abandoning a Myth

One could view these findings as just another case of precocious modern behavior by early *Homo sapiens* in Africa, but I think they have a larger lesson to teach us. After all, something is only precocious if it is unexpected. The hypothesis that there were skeletally modern-looking humans whose behavioral capacities differed significantly from our own is not supported by uniformitarian principles (explanations of the past based on studies of the present), by evolutionary theory or by archaeological evidence. There are no known populations of *Homo sapiens* with biologically constrained capacities for behavioral variability. Generations of anthropologists have sought in vain for such primitive people in every corner of the world and have consistently failed to find them. The parsimonious interpretation of this failure is that such humans do not exist.

Nor is there any reason to believe that behaviorally archaic *Homo sapiens* ever did exist. If there ever were significant numbers of *Homo sapiens* individuals with cognitive limitations on their capacity for behavioral variability, natural selection by intraspecific competition and predation would have quickly and ruthlessly winnowed them out. In the unforgiving Pleistocene environments in which our species evolved, reproductive isolation was the penalty for stupidity, and lions and wolves were its cure. In other words: No villages, no village idiots. If any such cognitive "winner take all" wipeout event ever happened, it was probably among earlier hominins (*Homo ergaster/erectus* or *Homo heidelbergensis*) or during the evolutionary differentiation of our species from these hominin ancestors.

Dividing *Homo sapiens* into modern and archaic or pre-modern categories and invoking the evolution of behavioral modernity to explain the difference has never been a good idea. Like the now-discredited scientific concept of race, it reflects hierarchical and typological thinking about human variability that has no place in a truly scientific anthropology. Indeed, the concept of behavioral modernity can be said to be worse than wrong, because it is an obstacle to understanding. Time, energy and research funds that could have been spent investigating the sources of variability in particular behavioral strategies and testing hypotheses about them have been wasted arguing about behavioral modernity.

Anthropology has already faced this error. Writing in the early 20th century, the American ethnologist Franz Boas railed against evolutionary anthropologists who ranked living human societies along an evolutionary scale from primitive to advanced. His arguments found an enthusiastic reception among his colleagues, and they remain basic principles of anthropology to this day. A similar change is needed in the archaeology of human origins. We need to stop looking at artifacts as expressions of evolutionary states and start looking at them as byproducts of behavioral strategies.

The differences we discover among those strategies will lead us to new and very different kinds of questions than those we have asked thus far. For instance, do similar environmental circumstances elicit different ranges of behavioral variability? Are there differences in the stability of particular behavioral strategies? Are certain strategies uniquely associated with particular hominin species, and if so, why? By focusing on behavioral variability, archaeologists will move toward a more scientific approach to human-origins research. The concept of behavioral modernity, in contrast, gets us nowhere.

Even today, a caveman remains the popular image of what a prehistoric person looked like. This individual usually is shown with enlarged eyebrows, a projecting face, long hair and a beard. The stereotypical caveman is inarticulate and dim-witted, and possesses a limited capacity for innovation. In 2006, GEICO commercials put an ironic twist on this image. Their cavemen were more intelligent, articulate, creative and culturally sophisticated than many "modern" people. In a striking case of life imitating art, recent archaeological discoveries are overturning long-standing misconceptions about early human behavior.

Bibliography

Bar-Yosef, O. 2002. The Upper Paleolithic revolution. *Annual Review of Anthropology* 31:363–393.

Clark, G. 1969. *World Prehistory: A New Synthesis*. Cambridge: Cambridge University Press.

Klein, R. G. 2009. *The Human Career*, third edition. Chicago: University of Chicago Press.

Landau, M. L. 1984. Human evolution as narrative. *American Scientist* 72:262–268.

McBrearty, S., and A. S. Brooks. 2000. The revolution that wasn't: A new interpretation of the origin of modern human behavior. *Journal of Human Evolution* 39:453–563.

Mellars, P., and C. Stringer. 1989. *The Human Revolution: Behavioural and Biological Perspectives on the Origins of Modern Humans*. Edinburgh: Edinburgh University Press.

Nowell, A. 2010. Defining behavioral modernity in the context of Neandertal and anatomically modern human populations. *Annual Review of Anthropology* 39:437–452.

Potts, R. 1998. Variability selection and hominid evolution. *Evolutionary Anthropology* 7(3):81–96.

Shea, J. J. 2008. The Middle Stone Age archaeology of the Lower Omo Valley Kibish Formation: Excavations, lithic assemblages, and inferred patterns of early *Homo sapiens* behavior. *Journal of Human Evolution* 55(3):448–485.

Shea, J. J. 2011. *Homo sapiens* is as *Homo sapiens* was: Behavioral variability versus "behavioral modernity" in Paleolithic archaeology. *Current Anthropology* 52(1):1–35.

Critical Thinking

1. What is meant by "behaviorally modern" in the context of this article and how were "pre-modern" people presumed to live by most archeologists?

2. How did archeologists perceive the technological stages of the Paleolithic period and their associations with fossil hominin remains?

3. What is meant by the "Upper Paleolithic Revolution" and how is it explained? What kinds of finds associated with Neanderthals challenge this view?

4. In what sense and where has there been a "mismatch" between the fossil record and archeologists' expectations?

5. What is the problem with associating cranial variation among early humans with actual behavior?

6. What are some of the specific kinds of modern behavior found among early modern humans in Africa and Asia? What is the significance of the fact that these behaviors are "not a consistent feature of the archeological record"?

7. Why is it difficult to test the core hypothesis about the presumed relationship between modern technology and modern-looking *Homo sapiens*?

8. What alternative approach does the author propose? Why is eastern Africa an especially good place to compare early and later *Homo sapiens*' technology?

9. Be familiar with Graham Clarke's five modes of core technology and the benefits of each.

10. Why is it that the range of variability in recent human stone tools is greater than that found in just the east African sample?

How does this help to invalidate the assumption that stone tool variation in the fossil record reflects stages of human evolution?

11. Why does the author say, "We need to stop looking at artifacts as expressions of evolutionary states and start looking at them as byproducts of behavioral strategies"?

Create Central

www.mhhe.com/createcentral

Internet References

About.com Archeology
http://archaeology.about.com

American Anthropologist Association
www.aaanet.org

Department of Human Evolution/Max Planck Institute
www.eva.mpg.de/evolution

How Humans Evolved
www.wwnorton.com/college/anthro/bioanth

Society for Historical Archaelogy
www.sha.org

JOHN J. SHEA is a professor of anthropology at Stony Brook University and a research associate with the Turkana Basin Institute in Kenya. He earned his PhD at Harvard University in 1991 and has conducted research in Israel, Jordan, Ethiopia, Eritrea, Kenya, and Tanzania. Two of his key scientific articles are "The origins of lithic projectile point technology: Evidence from Africa, the Levant, and Europe" (*Journal of Archaeological Science*, 2006) and "Stone age visiting cards revisited: A strategic perspective on the lithic technology of early hominin dispersal" (*Vertebrate Paleobiology and Paleoanthropology*, 2010). His forthcoming book will be titled *Paleolithic and Neolithic Stone Tools of the Near East: A Guide*. Shea is a professional flintknapper whose work appears in numerous documentaries and in exhibits at the Smithsonian Institution and the American Museum of Natural History.

Shea, John J. From *American Scientist*, March/April 2011, pp. 128–135. Copyright © 2011 by American Scientist, magazine of Sigma Xi, The Scientific Research Society. Reprinted by permission.

Rethinking the Hobbits of Indonesia

KATE WONG

Learning Outcomes

After reading this article, you will be able to:

- Describe the two positions regarding the "Hobbit," as either a stage of hominin evolution or as deformed modern human.
- Explain how the *H. floresiensis* came to be where it was found, assuming that it represents a hominin evolutionary branch.

New analyses reveal the mini human species to be even stranger than previously thought and hint that major tenets of human evolution need revision.

In 2004 a team of Australian and Indonesian scientists who had been excavating a cave called Liang Bua on the Indonesian island of Flores announced that they had unearthed something extraordinary: a partial skeleton of an adult human female who would have stood just over a meter tall and who had a brain a third as large as our own. The specimen, known to scientists as LB1, quickly received a fanciful nickname—the hobbit, after writer J.R.R. Tolkien's fictional creatures. The team proposed that LB1 and the other fragmentary remains they recovered represent a previously unknown human species, *Homo floresiensis*. Their best guess was that *H. floresiensis* was a descendant of *H. erectus*—the first species known to have colonized outside of Africa. The creature evolved its small size, they surmised, as a response to the limited resources available on its island home—a phenomenon that had previously been documented in other mammals, but never humans.

The finding jolted the paleoanthropological community. Not only was *H. floresiensis* being held up as the first example of a human following the so-called island rule, but it also seemed to reverse a trend toward ever larger brain size over the course of human evolution. Furthermore, the same deposits in which the small-bodied, small-brained individuals were found also yielded stone tools for hunting and butchering animals, as well as remainders of fires for cooking them—rather advanced behaviors for a creature with a brain the size of a chimpanzee's. And astonishingly, LB1 lived just 18,000 years ago—thousands of years after our other late-surviving relatives, the Neandertals and *H. erectus*, disappeared [see "The Littlest Human," by Kate Wong; *Scientific American*, February 2005].

Skeptics were quick to dismiss LB1 as nothing more than a modern human with a disease that stunted her growth. And since the announcement of the discovery, they have proposed a number of possible conditions to explain the specimen's peculiar features, from cretinism to Laron syndrome, a genetic disease that causes insensitivity to growth hormone. Their arguments have failed to convince the hobbit proponents, however, who have countered each diagnosis with evidence to the contrary.

A Perplexing Pastiche

Nevertheless, new analyses are causing even the proponents to rethink important aspects of the original interpretation of the discovery. The recent findings are also forcing paleoanthropologists to reconsider established views of such watershed moments in human evolution as the initial migration out of Africa by hominins (the group that includes all the creatures in the human line since it branched away from chimps).

Perhaps the most startling realization to emerge from the latest studies is how very primitive LB1's body is in many respects. (To date, excavators have recovered the bones of an estimated 14 individuals from the site, but LB1 remains the most complete specimen by far.) From the outset, the specimen has invited comparisons to the 3.2-million-year-old Lucy—the best-known representative of a human ancestor called *Australopithecus afarensis*—because they were about the same height and had similarly small brains. But it turns out LB1 has much more than size in common with Lucy and other pre-erectus hominins. And a number of her features are downright apelike.

A particularly striking example of the bizarre morphology of the hobbits surfaced this past May, when researchers led by William L. Jungers of Stony Brook University published their analysis of LB1's foot. The foot has a few modern features—for instance, the big toe is aligned with the other toes, as opposed to splaying out to the side as it does in apes and australopithecines. But by and large, it is old-fashioned. Measuring around 20 centimeters in length, LB1's foot is 70 percent as long as her short thighbone, a ratio unheard of for a member of the human family. The foot of a modern human, in contrast, is on average 55 percent as long as the femur. The closest match to LB1 in this regard, aside from, perhaps, the large-footed hobbits of Tolkien's imagination, is a bonobo. Furthermore, LB1's big toe is short, her other toes are long and slightly curved, and her foot lacks a proper arch—all primitive traits.

"A foot like this one has never been seen before in the human fossil record," Jungers declared in a statement released to the press. It would not have made running easy. Characteristics of the pelvis, leg and foot make clear that the hobbits walked upright. But with their short legs and relatively long feet, they would have had to use a high-stepping gait to avoid dragging their toes on the ground. Thus, although they could probably sprint short distances—say, to avoid becoming dinner for one of the Komodo dragons that patrolled Flores—they would not have won any marathons.

If the foot were the only part of the hobbit to exhibit such primitive traits, scientists might have an easier time upholding the idea that *H. floresiensis* is a dwarfed descendant of *H. erectus* and just chalking the foot morphology up to an evolutionary reversal that occurred as a consequence of dwarfing. But the fact is that archaic features are found throughout the entire skeleton of LB1. A bone in the wrist called the trapezoid, which in our own species is shaped like a boot, is instead shaped like a pyramid, as it is in apes; the clavicle is short and quite curved, in contrast to the longer, straighter clavicle that occurs in hominins of modern body form; the pelvis is basin-shaped, as in australopithecines, rather than funnel-shaped, as in *H. erectus* and other later *Homo* species. The list goes on.

Indeed, from the neck down LB1 looks more like Lucy and the other australopithecines than *Homo*. But then there is the complicated matter of her skull. Although it encased a grapefruit-size brain measuring just 417 cubic centimeters—a volume within the range of chimpanzees and australopithecines—other cranial features, such as the narrow nose and prominent brow arches over each eye socket, mark LB1 as a member of our genus, *Homo*.

Primitive Roots

Fossils that combine *Homo*-like skull characteristics with primitive traits in the trunk and limbs are not unprecedented. The earliest members of our genus, such as *H. habilis*, also exhibit a hodgepodge of old and new. Thus, as details of the hobbits' postcranial skeletons have emerged, researchers have increasingly wondered whether the little Floresians might belong to a primitive *Homo* species, rather than having descended from *H. erectus*, which scientists believe had modern body proportions.

A new analysis conducted by doctoral candidate Debbie Argue of the Australian National University in Canberra and her colleagues bolsters this view. To tackle the problem of how the hobbits are related to other members of the human family, the team employed cladistics—a method that looks at shared, novel traits to work out relationships among organisms—comparing anatomical characteristics of LB1 to those of other members of the human family, as well as apes.

In a paper in press at the *Journal of Human Evolution*, Argue and her collaborators report that their results suggest two possible positions for the *H. floresiensis* branch of the hominin family tree. The first is that *H. floresiensis* evolved after a hominin called *H. rudolfensis*, which arose some 2.3 million years ago but before *H. habilis*, which appeared roughly two million years ago. The second is that it emerged after *H. habilis* but still well before *H. erectus*, which arose around 1.8 million years ago. More important, Argue's team found no support for a close relationship between *H. floresiensis* and *H. erectus*, thereby dealing a blow to the theory that the hobbits were the product of island dwarfing of *H. erectus*. (The study also rejected the hypothesis that hobbits belong to our own species.)

If the hobbits are a very early species of *Homo* that predates *H. erectus*, that positioning on the family tree would go a long way toward accounting for LB1's tiny brain, because the earliest members of our genus had significantly less gray matter than the average *H. erectus* possessed. But Argue's findings do not solve the brain problem entirely. LB1 aside, the smallest known noggin in the genus *Homo* is a *H. habilis* specimen with an estimated cranial capacity of 509 cubic centimeters. LB1's brain was some 20 percent smaller than that.

Could island dwarfing still have played a role in determining the size of the hobbit's brain?

When the discovery team first attributed LB1's wee brain to this phenomenon, critics complained that her brain was far smaller than it should be for a hominin of her body size, based on known scaling relationships. Mammals that undergo dwarfing typically exhibit only moderate reduction in brain size. But study results released this past May suggest that dwarfing of mammals on islands may present a special case. Eleanor Weston and Adrian Lister of the Natural History Museum in London found that in several species of fossil hippopotamus that became dwarfed on the African island nation of Madagascar, brain size shrank significantly more than predicted by standard scaling models. Based on their hippo model, the study authors contend, even an ancestor the size of *H. erectus* could conceivably attain the brain and body proportions of LB1 through island dwarfing.

The work on hippos has impressed researchers such as Harvard University's Daniel Lieberman. In a commentary accompanying Weston and Lister's report in *Nature*, Lieberman wrote that their findings "come to the rescue" in terms of explaining how *H. floresiensis* got such a small brain.

Although some specialists favor the original interpretation of the hobbits, Mike Morwood of the University of Wollongong in Australia, who helps to coordinate the Liang Bua project, now thinks the ancestors of LB1 and the gang were early members of *Homo* who were already small—much smaller than even the tiniest known *H. erectus* individuals—when they arrived on Flores and then "maybe underwent a little insular dwarfing" once they got there.

Artifacts left behind by the hobbits support the claim that *H. floresiensis* is a very primitive hominin. Early reports on the initial discovery focused on the few stone tools found in the hobbit levels at Liang Bua that were surprisingly sophisticated for a such a small-brained creature—an observation that skeptics highlighted to support their contention that the hobbits were modern humans, not a new species. But subsequent analyses led by Mark W. Moore of the University of New England in Australia and Adam R. Brumm of the University of Cambridge have revealed the hobbit toolkit to be overall quite basic and in line with the implements produced by other small-brained hominins. The advanced appearance of a handful of the hobbit tools at Liang Bua, Moore and Brumm concluded, was produced by chance, which is not unexpected considering that the hobbits manufactured thousands of implements.

To make their tools, the hobbits removed large flakes from rocks outside the cave and then struck smaller flakes off the large flakes inside the cave, employing the same simple stone-working techniques favored by humans at another site on Flores 50 kilometers east of Liang Bua called Mata Menge 880,000 years ago—long before modern humans showed up on the island. (The identity of the Mata Menge toolmakers is unknown, because no human remains have turned up there yet, but they conceivably could be the ancestors of the diminutive residents of Liang Bua.) Furthermore, the Liang Bua and Mata Menge tools bear a striking resemblance to artifacts from Olduvai Gorge in Tanzania that date to between 1.2 million and 1.9 million years ago and were probably manufactured by *H. habilis*.

Tiny Trailblazer

In some ways, the latest theory about the enigmatic Flores bones is even more revolutionary than the original claim. "The possibility that a very primitive member of the genus *Homo* left Africa, perhaps roughly two million years ago, and that a descendant population persisted until only several thousand years ago, is one of the more provocative hypotheses to have emerged in paleoanthropology during the past few years," reflects David S. Strait of the University at Albany. Scientists have long believed that *H. erectus* was the first member of the human family to march out of the natal continent and colonize new lands, because that is the hominin whose remains appear outside of Africa earliest in the fossil record. In explanation, it was proposed that humans needed to evolve large brains and long striding limbs and to invent sophisticated technology before they could finally leave their homeland.

Today the oldest unequivocal evidence of humans outside of Africa comes from the Republic of Georgia, where researchers have recovered *H. erectus* remains dating to 1.78 million years ago [see "Stranger in a New Land," by Kate Wong; *Scientific American*, November 2003]. The discovery of the Georgian remains dispelled that notion of a brawny trailblazer with a tricked-out toolkit, because they were on the small side for *H. erectus*, and they made Oldowan tools, rather than the advanced, so-called Acheulean implements experts expected the first pioneers to make. Nevertheless, they were *H. erectus*.

But if proponents of the new view of hobbits are right, the first intercontinental migrations were undertaken hundreds of thousands of years earlier than that—and by a fundamentally different kind of human, one that arguably had more in common with primitive little Lucy than the colonizer paleoanthropologists had envisioned. This scenario implies that scientists could conceivably locate a long-lost chapter of human prehistory in the form of a two-million-year record of this primitive pioneer stretching between Africa and Southeast Asia if they look in the right places.

This suggestion does not sit well with some researchers. "The further back we try to push the divergence of the Flores [hominin], the more difficult it becomes to explain why a [hominin] lineage that must have originated in Africa has left only one trace on the tiny island of Flores," comments primate evolution expert Robert Martin of the Field Museum in Chicago. Martin remains unconvinced that *H. floresiensis* is a legitimate new species. In his view, the possibility that LB1—the only hobbit whose brain size is known—was a modern human with an as yet unidentified disorder that gave rise to a small brain has not been ruled out. The question, he says, is whether such a condition can also explain the australopithecine-like body of LB1.

In the meantime, many scientists are welcoming the shake-up. LB1 is "a hominin that no one would be saying anything about if we found it in Africa two million years ago," asserts Matthew W. Tocheri of the Smithsonian Institution, who has analyzed the wrist bones of the hobbits. "The problem is that we're finding it in Indonesia in essentially modern times." The good news, he adds, is that it suggests more such finds remain to be recovered.

"Given how little we know about the Asian hominin record, there is plenty of room for surprises," observes

---

Digging for Hobbits

Field Notes

Liang Bua is a large limestone cave located in the lush highlands of western Flores. Beyond the remains of some 14 hobbits, excavations there have yielded thousands of stone tools, as well as the bones of Komodo dragons, elephant-like stegodonts, giant rats and a carnivorous bird that stood some three meters high. The hobbits seem to have occupied the cave from around 100,000 to 17,000 years ago. They may have been drawn to Liang Bua because of its proximity to the Wae Racang River, which would have attracted thirsty prey animals. Researchers are now looking for clues to why, after persisting for so long, the hobbits eventually vanished. They are also eager to recover a second small skull. Such a find would establish that LB1 and the other specimens do indeed represent a new species and are not just the remains of diseased modern humans. Bones and teeth containing DNA suitable for analysis would be likewise informative.

Sick Human Hypotheses

Scientists who doubt that LB1 belongs to a new human species argue that she is simply a modern human with a disease resulting in a small body and small brain. Those who think LB1 does represent a new species, however, have presented anatomical evidence against each of the proposed diagnoses, several of which are listed below.

- Laron syndrome, a genetic disease that causes insensitivity to growth hormone.
- Myxoedematous endemic cretinism, a condition that arises from prenatal nutritional deficiencies that hinder the thyroid.
- Microcephalic osteodysplastic primordial dwarfism type II, a genetic disorder whose victims have small bodies and small brains but nearly normal intelligence.

A Mysterious Mosaic

The Evidence
To date, excavators have recovered the remains of about 14 individuals from Liang Bua, a cave site on Flores. The most complete specimen is a nearly complete skeleton called LB1 that dates to 18,000 years ago. Some of its characteristics call to mind those of apes and of australopithecines such as the 3.2-million-year-old Lucy. Other traits, however, are in keeping with those of our own genus, *Homo*. This mélange of primitive features and modern ones has made it difficult to figure out where on the human family tree the hobbits belong.

Homo traits

Thick braincase
Small teeth
Short face

Ape and australopithecine traits

Robust lower jaw
Broad, flaring pelvis
Short thighbone
Short shinbone

BRAIN is the size of a chimpanzee's. But a virtual reconstruction—generated from CT scans of the interior of the braincase—indicates that despite its small size, the organ had a number of advanced features, including an enlarged Broadmann area 10, a part of the brain that has been theorized to play a role in complex cognitive activities. Such features may help explain how a creature with a brain the size of a chimp's was able to make stone tools.

WRIST resembles ape. Of particular called the trapezoid, which has a pyramidal form. Modern humans, in contrast, have a trapezoid shaped like a boot, which facilitates tool manufacture and use by better distributing forces across the hand.

FOOT is exceptionally long compared with the short leg. This relative foot length is comparable to that seen in bonobos, and it suggests the hobbits were inefficient runners. Other apelike traits include long, curved toes and the absence of an arch. Yet the big toe aligns with the rest of the toes, among other modern characteristics.

Did *Homo sapiens* Copy Hobbits?

Analysis of hobbit implements spanning the time from 95,000 to 17,000 years ago indicates that the tiny toolmakers used the same so-called Oldowan techniques that human ancestors in Africa employed nearly two million years ago. The hobbits combined these techniques in distinctive ways, however—a tradition that the modern humans who inhabited Liang Bua starting 11,000 years ago followed, too. This finding raises the intriguing possibility that the two species made contact and that *H. sapiens* copied the hobbits' style of tool manufacture, rather than the other way around.

The Hobbits' Roots

Findings
Researchers originally believed that LB1 and the other hobbits, formally known as *Homo floresiensis*, were descendants of a human ancestor with essentially modern body proportions known as *H. erectus* that shrank dramatically in response to the limited resources available on their island home. But a new analysis suggests *H. floresiensis* is significantly more primitive than *H. erectus* and evolved either right after one of the earliest known members of our genus, *H. habilis* or right before it. Either way, the study implies that *H. floresiensis* evolved in Africa, along with the other early *Homo* species, and was already fairly small when the species reached Flores, although it may have undergone some dwarfing when it got there.

Blazing a Trail

The textbook account of human origins holds that *H. erectus* was the first human ancestor to wander out of Africa and colonize distant lands around 1.8 million years ago. But the evidence from Flores suggests that an older, more primitive forebear was the original pioneer, one who ventured away from the natal continent perhaps around two million years ago. If so, then paleoanthropologists may have missed a significant chunk of the human fossil record spanning nearly two million years and stretching from Africa to Southeast Asia.

Already hobbit hunter Mike Morwood is looking for more remains of *H. floresiensis* and its ancestors at two sites on Sulawesi. And he thinks further excavation at Niah cave in north Borneo could produce evidence of hominins much older than the ones at Liang Bua. The mainland will be harder to comb, because rocks of the right age are rarely exposed there.

Robin W. Dennell of the University of Sheffield in England. Dennell has postulated that even the australopithecines might have left Africa, because the grasslands they had colonized in Africa by three million years ago extended into Asia. "What we need, of course, are more discoveries—from Flores, neighboring islands such as Sulawesi, mainland Southeast Asia or anywhere else in Asia," he says.

Morwood, for his part, is attempting to do just that. In addition to the work at Liang Bua and Mata Menge, he is helping to coordinate two projects on Sulawesi. And he is eyeing Borneo, too. Searching the mainland for the ancestors of the Liang Bua hobbits will be difficult, however, because rocks of the right age are rarely exposed in this part of the world. But with stakes this high, such challenges are unlikely to prevent intrepid fossil hunters from trying. "If we don't find something in the next

15 years or so in that part of the world, I might start wondering whether we got this wrong," Tocheri reflects. "The predictions are that we should find a whole bunch more."

More to Explore

The Primitive Wrist of *Homo floresiensis* and Its Implications for Hominin Evolution. Matthew W. Tocheri et al. in *Science*, Vol. 317, pages 1743–1745; September 21, 2007.

A New Human: The Startling Discovery and Strange Story of the "Hobbits" of Flores, Indonesia. Mike Morwood and Penny van Oosterzee. *Smithsonian*, 2007.

The Foot of *Homo floresiensis*. W. L. Jungers et al. in *Nature*, Vol. 459, pages 81–84; May 7, 2009.

Homo floresiensis and the African Oldowan. Mark W. Moore and Adam R. Brumm in *Interdisciplinary Approaches to the Oldowan*. Edited by Erella Hovers and David R. Braun. Springer, 2009.

Homo floresiensis: A Cladistic Analysis. Debbie Argue et al. in *Journal of Human Evolution* (in press).

LB1's Virtual Endocast, Microcephaly and Hominin Brain Evolution. Dean Falk et al. in *Journal of Human Evolution* (in press).

Critical Thinking

1. Based upon the initial description of *Homo floresiensis*, what was the discoverers' "best guess" about why it looked the way it did?
2. Why did it jolt the anthropological community?
3. How did the skeptics respond?
4. What is it about the foot that is "bizarre"? How would running have been affected?
5. What are some of the other archaic features of the skeleton? What marks it as a member of our genus, *Homo*?
6. What are the two possible positions offered by Debbie Argue and her colleagues? What would this mean with respect to the idea that *H. floresiensis* is a descendant of *H. erectus* and is the result of island dwarfing? In what sense could island dwarfing still play a role and why?
7. What do the artifacts indicate with respect to the claim that *H. floresiensis* is a very primitive hominin? How are the few "sophisticated" tools to be explained?
8. If *H. floresiensis* is a very primitive hominin, how would this idea be even more revolutionary than the original claim?
9. What is the oldest unequivocal evidence of humans outside of Africa? What notion does it dispel and why?
10. What does the new scenario mean and what does it imply? Why does this suggestion not "sit well with some researchers"?
11. What is primate evolution expert Robert Martin's view? What does it perhaps not explain?
12. Why does Robin W. Dennell think that even some australopithecines might have left Africa? What is needed to shed light on the issue? What are the predictions?

Create Central

www.mhhe.com/createcentral

Internet References

Australian Museum
http://australianmuseum.net.au

Department of Human Evolution/Max Planck Institute
www.eva.mpg.de/evolution

How Humans Evolved
www.wwnorton.com/college/anthro/bioanth

Smithsonian Institution Website
www.si.edu

Wong, Kate. From *Scientific American*, November 2009. Copyright © 2009 by Scientific American, a division of Nature America, Inc. All rights reserved. Reprinted by permission.

Article

Prepared by: Mari Pritchard Parker, *Pasadena City College* and
Elvio Angeloni, *Pasadena City College*

Putting Stonehenge in Its Place

WILLIAM UNDERHILL

Learning Outcomes

After reading this article, you will be able to:

- Explain why Stonehenge is now seen as part of a much wider ritual landscape.
- Discuss the possible ritual functions of Stonehenge.

With the click of a mouse, archaeologist Vince Gaffney proudly summons up a vision of an ancient landscape. Amid the clutter of his office at the University of Birmingham in England, the 52-year-old professor of landscape archaeology is displaying early results of a virtual excavation at Britain's best-known prehistoric monument. On the screen: a giant ring of wood posts that may have stood roughly 1,000 yards northwest of Stonehenge, a timber twin of its grander neighbor. In 2010 Gaffney began a three-year project heading an international team that will probe the surrounding countryside in one more attempt to unravel the site's mysteries, this time with the aid of the very latest technology. The first reward came quickly. Within just two weeks the team, armed with high-powered magnetometers and ground-penetrating radar, discovered traces of that putative timber ring—possibly the most important find on the site in half a century.

Gaffney's is one of many recent discoveries that have scientists rethinking Stonehenge. The recovery of new materials, along with the reanalysis of earlier finds using modern archaeological techniques, has led to a steady flow of new information. Advances in carbon dating mean experts can provide a more accurate chronology. More sophisticated chemical analysis of human remains allows archaeologists to identify the likely origin of the earliest visitors to the site. The pace is quickening. Radar devices can turn out data at a rate inconceivable even a few years ago. (Gaffney's equipment collected as much data in two days at Stonehenge as he managed in three years at a previous site.) And with more data come fresh ideas. New evidence is now emerging to bolster a front-running theory: Stonehenge never stood in majestic isolation. Says Gaffney: "It was just part of a much wider ritual landscape."

An Enduring Enigma

Scholars have been struggling to unscramble the significance of Stonehenge since the 17th century. Almost every generation has thrown up its own solutions to the big questions of who built the monument, how and why. At different times, its function has been described as an astronomical observatory, a burial place for the great, a temple for Druid priests of the Iron Age, and more. Before scientists assigned credit for its construction to Neolithic humans, the list of possible builders included the Romans, the Danes and Merlin the magician.

Trouble is, telltale signs of the builders are frustratingly scarce—a smattering of charcoal from their fires, stone chippings, cattle bones, arrowheads and the occasional antler pick. All that is known for certain is a broad outline of the chronology. A circular ditch and bank, possibly surrounding a circle of timber posts, appeared around 3,000 B.C., and over the next 1,000 years the monument gradually took its final shape. On the outside: a ring of sarsens—huge blocks of sandstone probably dragged to the site from quarries in the Marlborough Downs 18 miles away. On the inside: arrangements of smaller bluestones, somehow transported 150 miles from the mountains of southern Wales, and one more horseshoe of giant sarsen slabs. The placement of the stones appears to have been significant, aligning the central axis with the rising sun at dawn on the summer solstice and sunset at midwinter.

Since the construction, much has happened to confuse the archaeologist's task. Stonehenge's early builders appear to have changed the arrangement of the bluestones. Some have vanished altogether. Today only around half of the total— originally 80 or so—remain. The messy habits of the 20th century have not helped. Gaffney's magnetometers pick up the debris—scraps of metal and bottle tops—dropped by the crowds at the music festivals of the 1970s and 1980s. That is not to mention the spectral outline of trenches dug when the land was used as a military training ground in World War I or the problems caused by the casual approach of the earliest archaeologists who allowed evidence to disappear. The designation of Stonehenge as a World Heritage Site in 1986 helped to protect the monument and its environs, but it also limited the scope for archaeological digging.

Cradle to Grave

The idea of Stonehenge as the focal point of a much wider ritual landscape is not new—one glance at a map shows a rich scattering of tombs, some predating Stonehenge, across the surrounding countryside. And aerial photography revealed the site of a timber henge called Woodhenge as far back as 1925. But slowly the evidence is accumulating that allows archaeologists to speculate on how the ceremonies that governed life and death might have fitted together.

A few years before Gaffney's team picked up the latest circle of timber posts, other excavations in the greater Stonehenge area had already begun to yield hints of a bigger picture. In 2007 archaeologist Mike Parker Pearson of the University of Sheffield in England and his team from the Stonehenge Riverside Project, which includes some of the country's leading archaeologists, announced discovery of the remains of a vast prehistoric settlement, possibly the largest in Britain, at Durrington Walls, a massive man-made enclosure just two miles northeast of the monument itself. The smart application of soil chemistry—think nitrogen or phosphorus levels—yielded a mass of information about how its residents might have organized their homes, from where the cooking took place to where they slept. (Bed-wetting babies leave their mark even after millennia through traces of urine.) And hyperaccurate carbon dating suggested that the village was occupied for less than 45 years, leading Parker Pearson and his collaborators to speculate that this was where the builders of Stonehenge once lived, moving on after their work was complete.

Just as important, the team had excavated traces of another henge, prior to Gaffney's: a concentric ring of timber posts dubbed the Southern Circle that was apparently aligned to mark sunset at the summer solstice—the mirror image of the arrangement at Stonehenge. Parker Pearson posits that Stonehenge had its own wood counterpart, the two monuments forming a single spectacular ceremonial site linked to the worship of the ancestors and the sun. "This is evidence that clarifies the site's true purpose," he asserts. "We have found that Stonehenge was just half of a larger complex."

Each half, he believes, had its own symbolic role. Most likely, the great ring at Stonehenge represented the domain of the dead, a lasting monument to the ancestors, whereas the Southern Circle was the opposite: a secular place where the living came first as builders of the stone circle and later for seasonal celebrations. Inspiration for this interpretation came partly from a colleague of Parker Pearson's from Madagascar who saw similarities with practices at home where wood dwellings are matched by stone buildings for the dead. Tests on animal bones found at Durrington Walls offer some backing for the theory, suggesting that cattle were brought from many miles away in southern England, perhaps to be eaten at ritual feasts. Further evidence came in 2009, when the Stonehenge Riverside Project uncovered the site of a circle of 25 bluestones two miles from the monument (and the same distance from Durrington Walls), beside the river Avon—a site quickly dubbed Bluehenge. The stone slabs were gone, possibly taken to Stonehenge itself, but left behind were fragments of the distinctive blue rock and, more important, traces of charcoal suggesting the structure was erected around 5,000 years ago. Perhaps, Parker Pearson surmises, Bluehenge was a place of cremation, a sacred site where the dead began the final journey to Stonehenge.

Certainly the bluestones held a special meaning for Neolithic humans—why else would they have stood at the very center of Stonehenge protected by the bigger sarsen monoliths?—and one more theory now places them at the heart of the entire Stonehenge story while also assigning yet another role to Stonehenge. Evidence collected in a 2008 dig at Stonehenge itself—the first within the circle for 40 years—supports the idea that Stonehenge was mainly a place of healing, a destination for the sick who traveled hundreds of miles in the hope of a cure. "Like a great medieval cathedral, all sorts of things would have happened at Stonehenge, but its principal draw was as a sacred place of healing," asserts Timothy Darvill of Bournemouth University in England, who conducted the 2008 excavation with Geoff Wainwright, former president of the Society of Antiquaries in London.

Curative Powers

Darvill and Wainwright's theory could help explain the stupendous efforts undertaken to transport the massive slabs of bluestone—each weighing up to four tons—some 150 miles from their source in the Preseli Hills in South Wales all the way to southern England. (Not so difficult as it might seem: a team of students demonstrated last fall how the slabs might have been rolled across the ground on small stone balls. Experts devised the test after finding such balls close to a similar stone circle in Scotland.) It could also explain why so many of the milestones are now missing. In the course of his 2008 excavation, Darvill found plenty of tiny flakes apparently deliberately chipped off the larger blocks, perhaps for use as talismans. Maybe whole stones were shipped off for use elsewhere.

But the dead, not the stones, provide the most telling support for Stonehenge's past as a prehistoric equivalent of Lourdes, the Catholic shrine in France famed for its supposedly miraculous healings. In 2002 archaeologists excavating a building site three miles from Stonehenge at Amesbury reported that they had turned up the grave of a Bronze Age male, buried around 2,300 B.C., with a rich assortment of treasures. Studies of the skeleton, dubbed the Amesbury Archer for the archery gear that accompanied his remains, showed he had lost one knee, and infection had entered his bones. And intriguingly, analyses of his tooth chemistry revealed a blend of strontium isotopes that suggested his original home was far away in the Alps (tooth enamel forms in a child's earliest years, storing a chemical record of where an individual was raised). Maybe he had crossed to England seeking a cure or at least relief from pain at the already fabled Stonehenge. Indeed, excavations at many of the tombs buried nearby have turned up remains of individuals who seem to have suffered serious injury. One likely interpretation is that the Amesbury Archer was one of a stream of visitors hoping for relief at Stonehenge.

Recent isotope analysis of tooth enamel from a grave found in nearby Boscombe in 2003 suggests that the archer was not the only visitor from afar. Seven of the grave's occupants may have spent part of their early lives in Wales, the source of the bluestones. And last year Jane Evans of the British Geological Survey reported that similar tests on the remains of a teenager discovered nearby in 2005 appear to suggest that he came from a warmer, Mediterranean climate, although there are still question marks over the interpretation of the data.

The Lourdes theory, like all Stonehenge theories, has it doubters. The strongest argument against it is that there is insufficient evidence to back the idea that a disproportionate number of human remains found in the area show signs of trauma. Substantiating that point would require a far larger sample of bones. Yet even if further discoveries do indeed bolster the Lourdes hypothesis, they will not necessarily weaken Parker Pearson's case, because the theories are not mutually incompatible. No doubt over the course of 5,000 years people used the site for different purposes and regarded it in different ways.

Despite all the new finds, much about Stonehenge remains a mystery. The peoples of the Stone Age have left scant clues as to their beliefs or how they lived their lives. But archaeologists, equipped with new technology, will not abandon the challenge. This year English Heritage, the state body that controls the site, hopes to conduct a laser scan of the stones, searching for telltale scratch marks and graffiti. And Parker Pearson is analyzing animal bones found at Durrington Walls as part of the Feeding Stonehenge project, looking exactly at how the people who built the stone circle lived, what they ate and where they came from. Meanwhile Gaffney's own high-tech trawl, covering more than five square miles, will in time yield the first comprehensive picture of what lies underneath the soil. More revelations seem certain to come. Stonehenge, Gaffney says, appears to be part of a "complex multitude of monuments." Complex but perhaps not impervious to scientific scrutiny.

Critical Thinking

1. How are technological advances enhancing our understanding of Stonehenge?
2. How has Stonehenge been variously explained in the past?
3. What do we know for certain?
4. What has happened to confuse the archaeologists' task?
5. What evidence is there that Stonehenge was the focal point of a much wider ritual landscape?
6. How does Parker Pearson interpret the symbolism of Stonehenge and what is his evidence?
7. What evidence is there that Stonehenge was a place for healing, a prehistoric equivalent of Lourdes?

Create Central

www.mhhe.com/createcentral

Internet References

Current Archaeology
www.archaeology.co.uk

Radiocarbon Dating for Archaeology
www.rlaha.ox.ac.uk/orau/index.html

Society for Historical Archaeology
www.sha.org

WILLIAM UNDERHILL is a journalist living in England. He has contributed to a wide range of newspapers and magazines, including *Newsweek*, the *Economist*, the *Guardian* and the *Daily Telegraph*. He has a particular enthusiasm for British history.

Underhill, William. From *Scientific American*, March 2011. Copyright © 2011 by Scientific American, a division of Nature America, Inc. All rights reserved. Reprinted by permission.

Article

Prepared by: Mari Pritchard Parker, *Pasadena City College* and
Elvio Angeloni, *Pasadena City College*

The First Vikings

Two remarkable ships may show that the Viking storm was brewing long before their assault on England and the continent.

ANDREW CURRY

Learning Outcomes

After reading this article, you will be able to:

- Discuss the Salme archaeological site as evidence for Viking origins and territorial expansion.
- Discuss the Salme ship burials as representative of the Viking social order and militarism.

According to historians, the Viking Age began on June 8, A.D. 793, at an island monastery off the coast of northern England. A contemporary chronicle recorded the moment with a brief entry: "The ravages of heathen men miserably destroyed God's church on Lindisfarne, with plunder and slaughter." The "heathen men" were Vikings, fierce warriors who sailed from Scandinavia and bore down on their prey in Europe and beyond in sleek, fast-sailing ships. In the centuries that followed, the Vikings' vessels carried them deep into Russia and as far south as Constantinople, Sicily, and possibly even North Africa. They organized flotillas capable of carrying warriors across vast distances, and terrorized the English, Irish, and French coasts with lightning-fast raids. Exploratory voyages to the west took them all the way to North America.

The Vikings' explosion across Europe and Asia and into the Americas was the result of the right combination of tools, technology, adventurousness, and ferocity. They came to be known as an unstoppable force capable of raiding and trading on four continents, yet our understanding of what led up to that June day on Lindisfarne is surprisingly shaky. A recent discovery on a remote Baltic island is beginning to change that. Two ships filled with slain warriors uncovered on the Estonian island of Saaremaa may help archaeologists and historians understand how the Vikings' warships evolved from short-range, rowed craft to sailing ships; where the first warriors came from; and how their battle tactics developed. "We all agree these burials are Scandinavian in origin," says Marge Konsa, an archaeologist at the University of Tartu. "This is our first taste of the Viking era."

Between them, the two boats contain the remains of dozens of men. Seven lay haphazardly in the smaller of the two boats, which was found first. Nearby, in the larger vessel, 33 men were buried in a neat pile, stacked like wood, together with their weapons and animals. The site seems to be a hastily arranged mass grave, the final resting place for Scandinavian warriors killed in an ill-fated raid on Saaremaa, or perhaps waylaid on a remote beach by rivals. The archaeologists believe the men died in a battle sometime between 700 and 750; perhaps almost as much as a century before the Viking Age officially began. This was an era scholars call the Vendel period, a transitional time not previously known for far-reaching voyages—or even for sails. The two boats themselves bear witness to the tremendous technological transformations in the eighth-century Baltic.

In 2008, workers digging trenches for electrical cables in the tiny island town of Salme uncovered human bones and a variety of odd objects that they unceremoniously piled next to their trench. Local authorities at first assumed the remains belonged to a luckless WWII soldier, until Konsa arrived and recognized a spearhead and carved-bone gaming pieces among the artifacts, clear signs the remains belonged to someone from a much earlier conflict. Together with a small team, Konsa dug a little deeper and soon found traces of a boat's hull. Nearly all of the craft's timber had rotted away, leaving behind only discolorations in the soil. But 275 of the iron rivets holding the boat together remained in place, allowing the researchers to reconstruct the outlines of the 38-foot-long craft.

Soon Konsa realized she had found something unique for this place and period. "This isn't a fishing boat, it's a war boat," Konsa says. "It's quite fast and narrow, and also quite light." Based on radiocarbon dating of tiny fragments of boat timbers, Konsa estimates the vessel was built between 650 and 700, and perhaps repaired and patched for decades before making its final voyage. It had no sail, and would have been rowed for short stretches along the Baltic coast, or between islands to make the journey from Scandinavia to the seafarers' hunting grounds farther east. From bones found inside the boat, Konsa pieced together the remains of the seven men, all between the ages of 18 and 45. She also found knives, whetstones, and a bone comb among the remains. The craft was a remarkable find—the first such boat ever recovered in Estonia, complete with the bodies of its slain crew.

Two years later, Jüri Peets, an archaeologist at the University of Tallinn, uncovered evidence of another, far larger and more technologically sophisticated craft just 100 feet away from the first boat. Soon workmen were ripping up a nearby road to reveal the vessel they dubbed Salme 2—the smaller boat would later be called Salme 1. The Vikings' tremendous geographic reach, from Nova Scotia to Constantinople, was made possible by their mastery of the ocean, particularly the sail. However, archaeologically speaking, there's not a great deal of evidence for sailing in the Baltic until roughly 820, when researchers think a 60-foot-long vessel, called the Oseberg ship, was built. Discovered in 1904, the Oseberg ship was used for the burial of a high-ranking Viking woman in what is today Norway.

The Salme site may change all that, pushing the first evidence for sailing back a century or more. Though, again, most of the wood had disappeared, by measuring the position of the more than 1,200 nails and rivets and carefully looking at soil where the wood had rotted, Peets concluded that Salme 2 was about 55 feet long and 10 feet wide. The craft had a keel, an element critical to keeping a sailing ship upright in the water. Peets believes clusters of iron and wood near the center of the boat and pieces of cloth recovered from the soil are indications of a mast and sail.

If he is right, Salme 2 is the oldest sailing vessel ever found in the Baltic. And other scholars are inclined to agree. "I would think that the big Salme boat would be the perfect place to find the first example of a sail before the Viking Age," says Jan Bill, an archaeologist and specialist in Viking ships at the University of Oslo. "It's the size of vessel," says Bill, "where a sail would make a lot of sense." Salme 2, built, sailed, and beached a half-century or more before the first raids on England heralded the dawn of the Viking Age, was, for all intents and purposes, a Viking ship. The Salme 2 vessel was certainly capable of crossing the open sea between the Swedish coast and Saaremaa, a distance of about 100 miles. The vessel also shows that the key technology of the Viking Age took shape at least decades, and maybe almost a whole century, before 793.

Like its nearby sister vessel, Salme 2 brought a crew with it when it was buried. "Three days after we started digging, a sword was discovered, and after some days skeletons in rows began to appear," says Ragnar Saage, a graduate student who worked with Peets on the excavation. It took two summers of painstaking work to excavate all the bodies: 33 in all, stacked neatly four deep. "We couldn't believe our eyes," says Saage. "It was a strange feeling to dig this kind of site."

Taken together, the two ships represent a tantalizing mystery. Peets and Konsa agree the vessels were probably buried at the same time, as part of the same event. Based on the boats' construction and the artifacts and remains found inside, the archaeologists believe the dead men were Scandinavian, probably from what is today Sweden, 150 miles away across the Baltic Sea. But what were they doing in Estonia? And why didn't they make it home?

Peets, who finished excavating the larger ship, Salme 2, in September 2012, has gathered enough information to sketch out what might have happened. Lured across the sea by booty, to collect tribute from the locals, or to settle a grudge, a mighty raiding party met a formidable foe on this isolated beach. After a struggle, one side's survivors—there's no way to tell if they were the winners or the losers—gathered the bodies together and ceremonially destroyed their fallen comrades' swords by burning, and then bending or breaking them.

The surviving warriors then had enough time to pull at least two of their ships 70 yards up the gently sloping beach. The 33 men of Salme 2, all of whom were vigorous, healthy adult men of fighting age, were then buried inside. This was done with obvious care and respect. "The skeletons were covered with shields, like a blanket," says Saage. (The 15 shields have long since rotted away, but their bronze bosses and fragments of their handles remain.) The men were buried with their belongings, including everything from weaponry to elk-horn combs, joints of sheep and cow, and even the remains of dogs and a hawk. "Every time I tried to clean the skeletons or bring up bodies, I found more artifacts and swords," says Raili Allmae, the forensic anthropologist in charge of excavating the site's human remains. Fragments of textile, perhaps bits of a sail used as a shroud to cover the pile of bodies before sand was laid on top, were also recovered from among the bones. The condition and placement of the warriors in the smaller ship are harder to explain. Konsa used a program designed to help reconstruct crime scenes to piece together the men's original locations. Some had been slumped in pairs or alone and some were leaning up against the inside of the hull in a sitting position. And these men are much less richly equipped than those found nearby.

While boat burials are familiar from both written sagas and archaeological finds in England, Sweden, and Norway, both the Salme ship burials are exceptional. Boat graves were almost always solo affairs, with a king or lord buried alone under a large earthen mound that covered the entire vessel. And no boat graves had ever been found this far east. The Salme boats are evidence that these later practices probably evolved over centuries, another thread connecting the Vendel period to the Vikings. "These burials correspond to medieval written descriptions of how you would bury warriors who died abroad," says Bill. "It's extremely interesting to see something very similar taking place in the pre-Viking period. Perhaps it tells us where those stories are coming from."

Yet to trained eyes the burials bore indications of a rush job. Only the bodies in each ship were covered with sand, perhaps to discourage scavenging animals from disturbing them. Men moving rocks with their hands and scooping sand with their helmets could have done the job in a few hours. "It is an amazing find," says John Ljungkvist, an expert in Iron Age burials at Uppsala University in Sweden. "It seems like a post-battlefield burial, but carries a lot of elements of a boat burial. They don't have the time or the logistics to do a regular boat burial, and instead have to make a mass grave."

The job done, the two boats and their cargo of corpses were then abandoned on the beach. Peets and Konsa think a heavy fall or winter storm might have washed up enough sand and gravel to partially fill in and cover the crafts. Over the next 1,300 years, the area's coastline receded, leaving the boat graves buried more than 200 yards from the sea and 12 feet above the waterline.

The bodies themselves are already proving a rich source of information, drawing clear connections between the Vendel era and the aggression that would soon emerge as a Viking hallmark. Given the Vikings' bloodthirsty reputation, surprisingly little is known about warfare leading up to the Viking era. "A mass grave from this period is unique," says Ljungkvist. "We don't have physical evidence of warfare and raiding, so that is very special." By looking at the bodies, archaeologists can tell a great deal about how they died and how such raiding parties might have been organized.

It's a key question. Scholars have long debated why the Vikings expanded as rapidly and aggressively as they did—and why the Viking raids on western Europe didn't happen earlier. The theories range from climate change, with a warm period in Europe around 800 creating overpopulation that forced young men to seek their fortune elsewhere, to a coincidence of greed, wanderlust, and the technology to make long-distance raids possible.

The Salme finds suggest that the historical view of the Viking Age as a sudden phenomenon needs a radical adjustment. It's clear from the remains that Scandinavian princes were organizing war parties decades or more before the fateful 793 raid on Lindisfarne: Though the men were interred en masse, the Salme sailing party was far from egalitarian. The weapons paint a picture of warriors led by a rich warlord or chieftain and a handful of well-equipped lieutenants. Even the stack of bodies on Salme 2 was hierarchical. Five men with double-edged swords and elaborately decorated hilts were buried on top. At the bottom, the bodies were buried with simple, single-edged iron blades. "These were some noblemen with their retinue," Peets says. "The more elaborate swords are clearly connected to people of higher status." One of the uppermost skeletons even had an elaborately decorated walrus-ivory gaming piece—perhaps the "king"—in his mouth. A jeweled sword hilt, the finest of the 40 blades in the burial, was found nearby. It's possible the men found in Salme 1 were from the bottom of the social ladder. Konsa thinks they may have been servants or lower-class "support staff," and buried with less care, and fewer grave goods, far away from the warriors and aristocrats of Salme 2.

To find out who these men were and where they came from, archaeologists are looking at the skeletons themselves. Since Peets finished excavating Salme 2 in fall 2012, the remains of the slain warriors have come to rest at the University of Tallinn's Institute of History, a centuries-old stone building on a narrow side street in the Estonian capital's medieval center. Neatly arranged in dozens of white cardboard boxes, they line one wall of a lab on the institute's top floor, accessible via a groaning, creaking Soviet-era elevator. Forensic anthropologist Allmae has spent the last two years trying to untangle the story of the yellowed bones she pulls from the boxes.

Allmae has ample reason to think the men were felled in a fierce battle. Lying on a steel lab table is a humerus, or upper arm bone. Lining it up against her own arm, she demonstrates how the man probably raised his right hand over his head to ward off sword blows—to no avail. Deep chop marks cut clean through the bone. Another warrior's skull was cut straight through. "Somebody chopped off the top of his head," Allmae says. "I also suppose it was done with a sword—two strokes." Only five of the 40 skeletons have clear cut marks on their bones, which she says isn't unusual for mass graves—there are lots of ways to die in battle, after all. "There were also arrowheads in the body or in the pelvic area that could have been deadly but not touched the bones," Allmae adds. Bloody flesh wounds that didn't connect with bone could also have felled the men without leaving a lasting trace.

Unlike many battlefield graves, and different from the treatment of the seven men found in the first ship, the Salme 2 bodies seem to have been laid to rest with some thought to the afterlife. The man with the severed arm was found with the rest of his limb carefully arranged in its proper place. Allmae's analysis shows that this would have been an intimidating crew, especially in eighth-century Europe. The average height was 5'10", and several of the men might have been well over six feet tall. Some of the bones bear signs of old wounds, suggesting these were veterans of more than one scrap. Based on the style of the swords, arrowheads, and other weapons, in addition to the objects found in the graves and especially the boats themselves, Peets and Konsa are already certain that the men were from Scandinavia. "These were very typical swords for Scandinavian warriors," Peets says. More clues may come from the chemical composition of the bones. Allmae plans to use a technique called isotopic analysis that matches chemical signatures in the bones to trace elements in water to help pin down where the men might have grown up.

For all the information the team has gathered from the excavation, there are some questions the dead men simply can't answer. It's clear there was a battle, but who was fighting whom? A saga written in 1225 tells of a Swedish noble named Yngvar who met his end while raiding in Estonia around 600. "The men of Estland came down from the interior with a great army, and there was a battle; but the army of the country was so brave that the Swedes could not withstand them, and King Yngvar fell, and his people fled," the saga reads. "He was buried close to the seashore under a mound in Estland; and after this defeat the Swedes returned home." It's tempting—but ultimately impossible—to tie the Salme boats to Yngvar's legendary expedition. "We shouldn't use historical material to put a story behind the archaeological finds," Konsa warns. "It's dangerous to look for Yngvar in the Salme boats, but Salme confirms that the events in the saga might have happened."

Saaremaa would have been a strange place for a raid. As far as we know from historical sources, Viking raids were usually aimed at population centers or rich, isolated monasteries—high-value targets, in other words. Did these proto-Vikings have similar goals in sight? The Estonian team can't say. Nothing of the kind is known from this part of Estonia. The 1,200-square-mile island of Saaremaa is better known for bitter tank battles between Soviet and German troops during WWII than for Vendel-era sword fights, and decades of excavations around the island have turned up little in the immediate vicinity of the burials. "Saaremaa's a pretty big island, but we don't have any known settlements or graves from the period in the vicinity of the boat finds," Saage says. "The closest are about 12 miles away."

If the battle was a raid on a village, or a military clash with locals, the visitors may have won a costly victory. "They must have had some control of the battleground—not necessarily won, but enough time to make the boat graves," says Saage. But the fact that the dead men and their grave goods were left untouched long enough for storms to cover them with sand suggests the area was abandoned after the fight.

Perhaps the men were fighting other Scandinavians. Konsa found arrowheads where the outside of the smaller ship's hull would have been, as though arrows were embedded in the wood. "Maybe the battle had already begun out at sea," she says, before fighting continued on the beach. Could rival warlords have been duking it out on an isolated shore, carrying on a feud begun back home? Or was this the final resting place of the fabled Yngvar, brought low by fierce local fighters? We'll never know the whole story. But the remains of these bold, unlucky adventurers are enough to sketch out a powerful scene of a voyage gone badly wrong, and a warlord slain while leading his men into battle on a far-off shore.

Critical Thinking

1. What was the "Viking Age" as it came to be known?
2. What is the significance of the Vendel period?
3. What indications are there at the Salme site of a mast and sail?
4. How do the archaeologists interpret the site?
5. What makes this boat burial exceptional?
6. Why does the burial seem like a "rush job"?
7. Why is it clear that princes were organizing a war party and that the war party was far from egalitarian?
8. Why is there ample reason to think the men were felled in a fierce battle?
9. Why does it seem that the Salme 2 bodies were laid to rest with some thought to the afterlife?
10. In what respects was this an "intimidating crew"?

Create Central

www.mhhe.com/createcentral

Internet References

Archaeology Magazine
www.archaeology.org

Society for Historical Archaeology
www.sha.org

Zeno's Forensic Page
http://forensic.to/forensic.html

Andrew Curry is a contributing editor at *Archaeology*.

Curry, Andrew. From *Archaeology*, June 10, 2013. Copyright © 2013 by Archaeological Institute of America. Reprinted by permission of *Archaeology Magazine*. www.archaeology.org

Unit 5

UNIT

Prepared by: Mari Pritchard Parker, *Pasadena City College* and
Elvio Angeloni, *Pasadena City College*

Historical Archaeology

So just what is historical archaeology and what is the time frame being studied? Well, that is often dependent on what continent the archeologist is working on. While the dominant definition could be stated as "the study of people with a written record," for many—particularly those working in the Americas—it is defined as "the study of the spread of European colonization throughout the world." In the new world, historical archaeologists work on a broad range of topics, such as early European settlement and its effects on Native American peoples, as well as the spread of the frontier and later urbanization and industrialization. Historic archaeologists investigate remains left on both the land and underwater. They work at a variety of sites such as shipwrecks, southern plantations, abandoned mining localities, and ghost towns. Historical archaeology is practiced by a wide range of scholars with research interests representing the disciplines of anthropology, history, geography, and folklore. They work both with the physical remains left behind and the documented record of these sites. Historical archaeologists often look for the common, everyday life of the past—the "fabric of the past"—and seek to understand the broader historical development of their own and other societies. The common thread among historical archaeologists is that they study the material remains of past societies that also left behind some other form of historical evidence.

Let us now work through the following exercise to help us understand the process of their investigations. How many times have you misplaced your car keys? Locked yourself out of the house? Lost your wallet? Your address book? Eye glasses? Sometimes these artifacts are recovered and brought back into the historical present. Sometimes they are lost forever, becoming part of the garbage of an extinct culture. Have you ever noticed that lost things, when found, are always in the last place you look? Is this a law of science? Be skeptical. Here is an opportunity to practice historical archaeology. You may wish to try this puzzler in order to practice thinking like an archaeologist. The incident recounted here is true. Only the names, dates, and places are changed to protect the privacy of the famous personages involved in this highly-charged mystery.

Problem: Dr. Wheeler, a British archaeologist at a large university left his office on Friday December 17, 2003, around 10 p.m. on a cold Friday evening. This was his last night to be at the university because he would not be back again until after the holidays.

Right before he left his office, he placed a thin, reddish, three-ring notebook in an unlocked cupboard.

Dr. Wheeler then proceeded to go directly to his designated campus parking space, got into his Mini Cooper S, and drove directly to his flat in Marshalltown Goldens. When he arrived home, he went straightaway to his study. He remained at his flat with his family and never left his flat during the entire holiday. Dr. Wheeler had a jolly good holiday with his family and he thought nothing more of his notebook until the university resumed its session on Wednesday, January 5, 2004, at the beginning of the New Year.

Upon returning to his office, Dr. Wheeler could not find his notebook in the cupboard, and he became very agitated. He chased his assistant, Miss Mortimer, around the office, wielding a wicked looking Acheulean hand ax. Poor Miss Mortimer claimed that she had no knowledge of the whereabouts of the notebook.

But Dr. Wheeler had always suspected that Miss Mortimer pinched pens and pencils from his desk, so, naturally. . . . but Miss Mortimer protested so earnestly that Dr. Wheeler eventually settled in, had a cup of tea, and decided that perhaps he had absentmindedly taken the notebook home after all.

However, a thorough search of his flat indicated that the notebook was clearly not there. It was lost! Dr. Wheeler had almost lost himself when his wife, Sophia, caught him excavating her rose garden in the vain hope that Tut, the family dog, had buried the lost article there. It was a professor's nightmare; the notebook contained the only copy of all his class records for the entire term. What could he do? He knew he was in danger of being fired for incompetence.

So, Dr. Wheeler approached the problem in the manner of a proper, eccentric archaeologist. He had another cup of tea and generated several hypotheses about where his notebook might have gone, but to no avail!

His notebook was still missing. However, being a good archaeologist, he kept on generating hypotheses. But his notebook was not to be found. Then he began to wonder if maybe the post-processualists weren't right after all!

Dr. Wheeler was at his wits' end when, pure happenstance intervened, as it often does in archaeology. You just get lucky sometimes. Everyone does. His faithful assistant Miss Mortimer received a phone call on January 9, 2004, from a woman who had found the missing notebook on the evening of December 31, 2003. The helpful lady found his notebook in a gutter! To be precise, she found it in a family neighborhood located on the corner of Olduvai Drive and East Turkana Avenue in Hadar Heights, about a mile away from the university. Please note that this area is in the opposite direction from Dr. Wheeler's flat in Marshalltown Goldens. The notebook was wet and muddy, and furthermore, it was wedged down into a gutter grill in the street.

Greatly relieved, the next day, January 10, 2004, Dr. Wheeler had Miss Mortimer run over to the kind woman's flat. It was in this mysterious way that he recovered his class records. Dr. Wheeler was so delighted that when Miss Mortimer returned with the notebook, he invited her to sit and join him for a pot of tea (which was not his habit, being a misogynist). Yet, Dr. Wheeler was not satisfied with merely recovering his notebook. He was curious to know what had happened to it and why!

He continued to generate ever more sophisticated hypotheses to solve the mystery.

Challenge to the Student

Try to place yourself in Dr. Wheeler's position. Attempt to generate your own hypotheses as to the whereabouts of the lost notebook from the night of Friday, December 17, 2003, to the time of its return on January 10, 2004.

How do you go about doing this? First, review everything you "believe" to be true. Be very careful and skeptical about what is true and what is not. Then convert this into your original database. From that point, again set up more hypotheses and/or make alternative hypotheses until you arrive at the simplest possible explanation. The simplest possible explanation is most likely to be the correct answer. Support your answer with your database.

Pretend that you are doing historical archaeology. Ask your living informant(s) for information first. What could you ask Dr. Wheeler? You could ask, "Did you go back to the lavatory before you left the building on December 17, 2003? Are you sure as to where your motorcar was parked or could you be mistaken? What was the weather like? Was it raining? Is it possible that you in fact stopped and talked to someone on your way to your motorcar? Are you sure you were home on December 31, 2003 and not out to celebrate the New Year?" Be very precise with your questioning. Also, let your imagination run wild with possibilities. Brainstorm. Sometimes this is when you are most likely to get the answer. Creativity is the essence of all science.

Hints

Dr. Wheeler's university office was never broken into. Poor Miss Mortimer and the kind lady who found the notebook had nothing to do with the disappearance of the notebook. Dr. Wheeler's dog Tut did not bury his notebook. So what did happen? There is, in fact, a correct answer that will explain the mystery. Try to find that answer! To do this, you will have to think like an archaeologist. It is a lot of fun, and it will reward you well!

Article

Prepared by: Mari Pritchard Parker, *Pasadena City College* and
Elvio Angeloni, *Pasadena City College*

Uncovering Secrets of the Sphinx

Who built it? Why? And how? After decades of research, American archaeologist Mark Lehner has answers.

EVAN HADINGHAM

Learning Outcomes

After reading this article, you will be able to:

- Discuss the construction of the Sphinx in terms of who built it and how.
- Describe the temple complex which includes the Sphinx as a "cosmic engine."

When Mark Lehner was a teenager in the late 1960s, his parents introduced him to the writings of the famed clairvoyant Edgar Cayce. During one of his trances, Cayce, who died in 1945, saw that refugees from the lost city of Atlantis buried their secrets in a hall of records under the Sphinx and that the hall would be discovered before the end of the 20th century.

In 1971, Lehner, a bored sophomore at the University of North Dakota, wasn't planning to search for lost civilizations, but he was "looking for something, a meaningful involvement." He dropped out of school, began hitchhiking and ended up in Virginia Beach, where he sought out Cayce's son, Hugh Lynn, the head of a holistic medicine and paranormal research foundation his father had started. When the foundation sponsored a group tour of the Giza plateau—the site of the Sphinx and the pyramids on the western outskirts of Cairo—Lehner tagged along. "It was hot and dusty and not very majestic," he remembers.

Still, he returned, finishing his undergraduate education at the American University of Cairo with support from Cayce's foundation. Even as he grew skeptical about a lost hall of records, the site's strange history exerted its pull. "There were thousands of tombs of real people, statues of real people with real names, and none of them figured in the Cayce stories," he says.

Lehner married an Egyptian woman and spent the ensuing years plying his drafting skills to win work mapping archaeological sites all over Egypt. In 1977, he joined Stanford Research Institute scientists using state-of-the-art remote-sensing equipment to analyze the bedrock under the Sphinx. They found only the cracks and fissures expected of ordinary limestone formations. Working closely with a young Egyptian archaeologist named Zahi Hawass, Lehner also explored and mapped a passage in the Sphinx's rump, concluding that treasure hunters likely had dug it after the statue was built.

No human endeavor has been more associated with mystery than the huge, ancient lion that has a human head and is seemingly resting on the rocky plateau a stroll from the great pyramids. Fortunately for Lehner, it wasn't just a metaphor that the Sphinx is a riddle. Little was known for certain about who erected it or when, what it represented and precisely how it related to the pharaonic monuments nearby. So Lehner settled in, working for five years out of a makeshift office between the Sphinx's colossal paws, subsisting on Nescafé and cheese sandwiches while he examined every square inch of the structure. He remembers "climbing all over the Sphinx like the Lilliputians on Gulliver, and mapping it stone by stone." The result was a uniquely detailed picture of the statue's worn, patched surface, which had been subjected to at least five major restoration efforts since 1,400 B.C. The research earned him a doctorate in Egyptology at Yale.

Recognized today as one of the world's leading Egyptologists and Sphinx authorities, Lehner has conducted field research at Giza during most of the 37 years since his first visit. (Hawass, his friend and frequent collaborator, is the secretary general of the Egyptian Supreme Council of Antiquities and controls access to the Sphinx, the pyramids and other government-owned sites and artifacts.) Applying his archaeological sleuthing to the surrounding two-square-mile Giza plateau with its pyramids, temples, quarries and thousands of tombs, Lehner helped confirm what others had speculated—that some parts of the Giza complex, the Sphinx included, make up a vast sacred machine designed to harness the power of the sun to sustain the earthly and divine order. And while he long ago gave up on the fabled library of Atlantis, it's curious, in light of his early wanderings, that he finally did discover a Lost City.

The sphinx was not assembled piece by piece but was carved from a single mass of limestone exposed when workers dug a horseshoe-shaped quarry in the Giza plateau. Approximately 66 feet tall and 240 feet long, it is one of the largest and oldest monolithic statues in the world. None of the photos or sketches I'd seen prepared me for the scale. It was a humbling sensation to stand between the creature's paws, each twice my height and longer than a city bus. I gained sudden empathy for what a mouse must feel like when cornered by a cat.

Nobody knows its original name. Sphinx is the human-headed lion in ancient Greek mythology; the term likely came into use some 2,000 years after the statue was built. There are hundreds of tombs at Giza with hieroglyphic inscriptions dating back some 4,500 years, but not one mentions the statue. "The Egyptians didn't write history," says James Allen, an Egyptologist at Brown University, "so we have no solid evidence for what its builders thought the Sphinx was.... Certainly something divine, presumably the image of a king, but beyond that is anyone's guess." Likewise, the statue's symbolism is unclear, though inscriptions from the era refer to Ruti, a double lion god that sat at the entrance to the underworld and guarded the horizon where the sun rose and set.

The face, though better preserved than most of the statue, has been battered by centuries of weathering and vandalism. In 1402, an Arab historian reported that a Sufi zealot had disfigured it "to remedy some religious errors." Yet there are clues to what the face looked like in its prime. Archaeological excavations in the early 19th century found pieces of its carved stone beard and a royal cobra emblem from its headdress. Residues of red pigment are still visible on the face, leading researchers to conclude that at some point, the Sphinx's entire visage was painted red. Traces of blue and yellow paint elsewhere suggest to Lehner that the Sphinx was once decked out in gaudy comic book colors.

For thousands of years, sand buried the colossus up to its shoulders, creating a vast disembodied head atop the eastern edge of the Sahara. Then, in 1817, a Genoese adventurer, Capt. Giovanni Battista Caviglia, led 160 men in the first modern attempt to dig out the Sphinx. They could not hold back the sand, which poured into their excavation pits nearly as fast as they could dig it out. The Egyptian archaeologist Selim Hassan finally freed the statue from the sand in the late 1930s. "The Sphinx has thus emerged into the landscape out of shadows of what seemed to be an impenetrable oblivion," *The New York Times* declared.

The question of who built the Sphinx has long vexed Egyptologists and archaeologists. Lehner, Hawass and others agree it was Pharaoh Khafre, who ruled Egypt during the Old Kingdom, which began around 2,600 B.C. and lasted some 500 years before giving way to civil war and famine. It's known from hieroglyphic texts that Khafre's father, Khufu, built the 481-foot-tall Great Pyramid, a quarter mile from where the Sphinx would later be built. Khafre, following a tough act, constructed his own pyramid, ten feet shorter than his father's, also a quarter of a mile behind the Sphinx. Some of the evidence linking Khafre with the Sphinx comes from Lehner's research, but the idea dates back to 1853.

That's when a French archaeologist named Auguste Mariette unearthed a life-size statue of Khafre, carved with startling realism from black volcanic rock, amid the ruins of a building he discovered adjacent to the Sphinx that would later be called the Valley Temple. What's more, Mariette found the remnants of a stone causeway—a paved, processional road—connecting the Valley Temple to a mortuary temple next to Khafre's pyramid. Then, in 1925, French archaeologist and engineer Emile Baraize probed the sand directly in front of the Sphinx and discovered yet another Old Kingdom building—now called the Sphinx Temple—strikingly similar in its ground plan to the ruins Mariette had already found.

Despite these clues that a single master building plan tied the Sphinx to Khafre's pyramid and his temples, some experts continued to speculate that Khufu or other pharaohs had built the statue. Then, in 1980, Lehner recruited a young German geologist, Tom Aigner, who suggested a novel way of showing that the Sphinx was an integral part of Khafre's larger building complex. Limestone is the result of mud, coral and the shells of plankton-like creatures compressed together over tens of millions of years. Looking at samples from the Sphinx Temple and the Sphinx itself, Aigner and Lehner inventoried the different fossils making up the limestone. The fossil fingerprints showed that the blocks used to build the wall of the temple must have come from the ditch surrounding the Sphinx. Apparently, workmen, probably using ropes and wooden sledges, hauled away the quarried blocks to construct the temple as the Sphinx was being carved out of the stone.

That Khafre arranged for construction of his pyramid, the temples and the Sphinx seems increasingly likely. "Most scholars believe, as I do," Hawass wrote in his 2006 book, *Mountain of the Pharaohs,* "that the Sphinx represents Khafre and forms an integral part of his pyramid complex."

But who carried out the backbreaking work of creating the Sphinx? In 1990, an American tourist was riding in the desert half a mile south of the Sphinx when she was thrown from her horse after it stumbled on a low mud-brick wall. Hawass investigated and discovered an Old Kingdom cemetery. Some 600 people were buried there, with tombs belonging to overseers—identified by inscriptions recording their names and titles—surrounded by the humbler tombs of ordinary laborers.

Near the cemetery, nine years later, Lehner discovered his Lost City. He and Hawass had been aware since the mid-1980s that there were buildings at that site. But it wasn't until they excavated and mapped the area that they realized it was a settlement bigger than ten football fields and dating to Khafre's reign. At its heart were four clusters of eight long mud-brick barracks. Each structure had the elements of an ordinary house—a pillared porch, sleeping platforms and a kitchen—that was enlarged to accommodate around 50 people sleeping side by side. The barracks, Lehner says, could have accommodated between 1,600 to 2,000 workers—or more, if the sleeping quarters were on two levels. The workers' diet indicates they weren't slaves. Lehner's team found remains of mostly male cattle under 2 years old—in other words, prime beef. Lehner thinks ordinary Egyptians may have rotated in and out of the work crew under some sort of national service or feudal obligation to their superiors.

This past fall, at the behest of "Nova" documentary makers, Lehner and Rick Brown, a professor of sculpture at the Massachusetts College of Art, attempted to learn more about construction of the Sphinx by sculpting a scaled-down version of its missing nose from a limestone block, using replicas of ancient tools found on the Giza plateau and depicted in tomb paintings. Forty-five centuries ago, the Egyptians lacked iron or bronze tools. They mainly used stone hammers, along with copper chisels for detailed finished work.

> **The Way it Was?**
>
> Egyptologists believe the Sphinx, pyramids and other parts of the two-square-mile Giza complex align with the sun at key times, reinforcing the pharoah's role in sustaining the divine order.
> Lehner's vision of the restored Sphinx after the 15th century B.C. includes a statue of Thutmose IV's father, Amenhotep II, atop an engraved granite slab.

Bashing away in the yard of Brown's studio near Boston, Brown, assisted by art students, found that the copper chisels became blunt after only a few blows before they had to be resharpened in a forge that Brown constructed out of a charcoal furnace. Lehner and Brown estimate one laborer might carve a cubic foot of stone in a week. At that rate, they say, it would take 100 people three years to complete the Sphinx.

Exactly what Khafre wanted the Sphinx to do for him or his kingdom is a matter of debate, but Lehner has theories about that, too, based partly on his work at the Sphinx Temple. Remnants of the temple walls are visible today in front of the Sphinx. They surround a courtyard enclosed by 24 pillars. The temple plan is laid out on an east-west axis, clearly marked by a pair of small niches or sanctuaries, each about the size of a closet. The Swiss archaeologist Herbert Ricke, who studied the temple in the late 1960s, concluded the axis symbolized the movements of the sun; an east-west line points to where the sun rises and sets twice a year at the equinoxes, halfway between midsummer and midwinter. Ricke further argued that each pillar represented an hour in the sun's daily circuit.

Lehner spotted something perhaps even more remarkable. If you stand in the eastern niche during sunset at the March or September equinoxes, you see a dramatic astronomical event: the sun appears to sink into the shoulder of the Sphinx and, beyond that, into the south side of the Pyramid of Khafre on the horizon. "At the very same moment," Lehner says, "the shadow of the Sphinx and the shadow of the pyramid, both symbols of the king, become merged silhouettes. The Sphinx itself, it seems, symbolized the pharaoh presenting offerings to the sun god in the court of the temple." Hawass concurs, saying the Sphinx represents Khafre as Horus, the Egyptians' revered royal falcon god, "who is giving offerings with his two paws to his father, Khufu, incarnated as the sun god, Ra, who rises and sets in that temple."

Equally intriguing, Lehner discovered that when one stands near the Sphinx during the summer solstice, the sun appears to set midway between the silhouettes of the pyramids of Khafre and Khufu. The scene resembles the hieroglyph *akhet*, which can be translated as "horizon" but also symbolized the cycle of life and rebirth. "Even if coincidental, it is hard to imagine the Egyptians not seeing this ideogram," Lehner wrote in the *Archive of Oriental Research*. "If somehow intentional, it ranks as an example of architectural illusionism on a grand, maybe the grandest, scale."

If Lehner and Hawass are right, Khafre's architects arranged for solar events to link the pyramid, Sphinx and temple. Collectively Lehner describes the complex as a cosmic engine, intended to harness the power of the sun and other gods to resurrect the soul of the pharaoh. This transformation not only guaranteed eternal life for the dead ruler but also sustained the universal natural order, including the passing of the seasons, the annual flooding of the Nile and the daily lives of the people. In this sacred cycle of death and revival, the Sphinx may have stood for many things: as an image of Khafre the dead king, as the sun god incarnated in the living ruler and as guardian of the underworld and the Giza tombs.

But it seems Khafre's vision was never fully realized. There are signs the Sphinx was unfinished. In 1978, in a corner of the statue's quarry, Hawass and Lehner found three stone blocks, abandoned as laborers were dragging them to build the Sphinx Temple. The north edge of the ditch surrounding the Sphinx contains segments of bedrock that are only partially quarried. Here the archaeologists also found the remnants of a workman's lunch and tool kit—fragments of a beer or water jar and stone hammers. Apparently the workers walked off the job.

The enormous temple-and-Sphinx complex might have been the pharaoh's resurrection machine, but, Lehner is fond of saying, "nobody turned the key and switched it on." By the time the Old Kingdom finally broke apart around 2,130 B.C., the desert sands had begun to reclaim the Sphinx. It would sit ignored for the next seven centuries, when it spoke to a young royal.

According to the legend engraved on a pink granite slab between the Sphinx's paws, the Egyptian prince Thutmose went hunting in the desert, grew tired and lay down in the shade of the Sphinx. In a dream, the statue, calling itself Horemakhet—or Horus-in-the-Horizon, the earliest known Egyptian name for the statue—addressed him. It complained about its ruined body and the encroaching sand. Horemakhet then offered Thutmose the throne in exchange for help.

Whether or not the prince actually had this dream is unknown. But when he became Pharaoh Thutmose IV, he helped introduce a Sphinx-worshiping cult to the New Kingdom (1550–1070 B.C.). Across Egypt, sphinxes appeared everywhere in sculptures, reliefs and paintings, often depicted as a potent symbol of royalty and the sacred power of the sun.

Based on Lehner's analysis of the many layers of stone slabs placed like tilework over the Sphinx's crumbling surface, he believes the oldest slabs may date back as far as 3,400 years to Thutmose's time. In keeping with the legend of Horemakhet, Thutmose may well have led the first attempt to restore the Sphinx.

When Lehner is in the United States, typically about six months per year, he works out of an office in Boston, the headquarters of Ancient Egypt Research Associates, a nonprofit organization Lehner directs that excavates the Lost City and trains young Egyptologists. At a meeting with him at his office this past fall, he unrolled one of his countless maps of the Sphinx on a table. Pointing to a section where an old tunnel had cut into the statue, he said the elements had taken a toll on the Sphinx in the first few centuries after it was built. The porous rock soaks up moisture, degrading the limestone. For Lehner, this posed yet another riddle—what was the source of so much moisture in Giza's seemingly bone-dry desert?

The Sahara has not always been a wilderness of sand dunes. German climatologists Rudolph Kuper and Stefan Kröpelin, analyzing the radiocarbon dates of archaeological sites, recently concluded that the region's prevailing climate pattern changed around 8,500 B.C., with the monsoon rains that covered the tropics moving north. The desert sands sprouted rolling grasslands punctuated by verdant valleys, prompting people to begin settling the region in 7,000 B.C. Kuper and Kröpelin say this green Sahara came to an end between 3,500 B.C. and 1,500 B.C., when the monsoon belt returned to the tropics and the desert reemerged. That date range is 500 years later than prevailing theories had suggested.

Further studies led by Kröpelin revealed that the return to a desert climate was a gradual process spanning centuries. This transitional period was characterized by cycles of ever-decreasing rains and extended dry spells. Support for this theory can be found in recent research conducted by Judith Bunbury, a geologist at the University of Cambridge. After studying sediment samples in the Nile Valley, she concluded that climate change in the Giza region began early in the Old Kingdom, with desert sands arriving in force late in the era.

The work helps explain some of Lehner's findings. His investigations at the Lost City revealed that the site had eroded dramatically—with some structures reduced to ankle level over a period of three to four centuries after their construction. "So I had this realization," he says, "Oh my God, this buzz saw that cut our site down is probably what also eroded the Sphinx." In his view of the patterns of erosion on the Sphinx, intermittent wet periods dissolved salt deposits in the limestone, which recrystallized on the surface, causing softer stone to crumble while harder layers formed large flakes that would be blown away by desert winds. The Sphinx, Lehner says, was subjected to constant "scouring" during this transitional era of climate change.

"It's a theory in progress," says Lehner. "If I'm right, this episode could represent a kind of 'tipping point' between different climate states—from the wetter conditions of Khufu and Khafre's era to a much drier environment in the last centuries of the Old Kingdom."

The implication is that the Sphinx and the pyramids, epic feats of engineering and architecture, were built at the end of a special time of more dependable rainfall, when pharaohs could marshal labor forces on an epic scale. But then, over the centuries, the landscape dried out and harvests grew more precarious. The pharaoh's central authority gradually weakened, allowing provincial officials to assert themselves—culminating in an era of civil war.

Today, the Sphinx is still eroding. Three years ago, Egyptian authorities learned that sewage dumped in a nearby canal was causing a rise in the local water table. Moisture was drawn up into the body of the Sphinx and large flakes of limestone were peeling off the statue.

Hawass arranged for workers to drill test holes in the bedrock around the Sphinx. They found the water table was only 15 feet beneath the statue. Pumps have been installed nearby to divert the groundwater. So far, so good. "Never say to anyone that we saved the Sphinx," he says. "The Sphinx is the oldest patient in the world. All of us have to dedicate our lives to nursing the Sphinx all the time."

Critical Thinking

1. In what sense does the Sphinx represent one of the largest and oldest monolithic statues in the world?
2. Why is there no mention of the Sphinx in hieroglyphic inscriptions? What is the significance of Ruti, the double-headed lion?
3. What indications are there that the pharaoh Khafre built the complex including his pyramid, the Sphinx Temple, the Valley Temple, and the Sphinx itself?
4. What can be said about who did the backbreaking work of building the Sphinx? What kinds of tools did they use? What is the estimate regarding the amount of labor involved and for how long?
5. What does Lehner think the pharaoh Khafre had in mind in building the Sphinx and what is his evidence?
6. Why does it seem that Khafre's vision was never fully realized?
7. What is the significance of the fact that the climate in the Sahara was changing from the wetter conditions of Khufu and Khafre's era to a much drier environment in the last centuries of the Old Kingdom?

Create Central

www.mhhe.com/createcentral

Internet References

NOVA Online/Pyramids—The Inside Story
www.pbs.org/wgbh/nova/pyramid
The Ancient Egyptian Pharaohs
www.ancient-egypt-online.com/ancient-egyptian-pharaohs.html

EVAN HADINGHAM is senior science editor of the PBS series "Nova." Its *"Riddles of the Sphinx"* was to air January 19.

From *Smithsonian*, February 2010, pp. 32, 34–42. Copyright © 2010 by Evan Hadingham. Reprinted by permission of the author.

Article

Prepared by: Mari Pritchard Parker, *Pasadena City College* and
Elvio Angeloni, *Pasadena City College*

Home away from Rome

Excavations of villas where Roman emperors escaped the office are giving archaeologists new insights into the imperial way of life.

PAUL BENNETT

Learning Outcomes

After reading this article, you will be able to:

- Discuss the Roman villas in terms of the way they reflect contrast between the emperor's official and private lives.
- Discuss the importance of the imperial Roman villas as part of the economy of the empire.

In A.D 143 or 144, when he was in his early 20s, the future Roman emperor Marcus Aurelius set out for the country estate of his adoptive father, Emperor Antoninus Pius. The property, Villa Magna (Great Estate), boasted hundreds of acres of wheat, grapes and other crops, a grand mansion, baths and temples, as well as rooms for the emperor and his entourage to retreat from the world or curl up with a good book.

Which is just what young Marcus did, as he related in a letter written to his tutor, Fronto, during the excursion. He describes reading Cato's *De agri cultura,* which was to the gentlemanly farmer of the Roman Empire what Henry David Thoreau's *Walden* was to nature lovers in the 19th century. He hunted boar, without success ("We did hear that boars had been captured but saw nothing ourselves"), and climbed a hill. And since the emperor was also the head of the Roman religion, he helped his father with the daily sacrifices—a ritual that made offerings of bread, milk or a slaughtered animal. The father, son and the emperor's retinue dined in a chamber adjacent to the pressing room—where grapes were crushed for making wine—and there enjoyed some kind of show, perhaps a dance performed by the peasant farmworkers or slaves as they stomped the grapes.

We know what became of Marcus Aurelius—considered the last of the "Five Good Emperors." He ruled for nearly two decades from A.D 161 to his death in A.D 180, a tenure marked by wars in Asia and what is now Germany. As for the Villa Magna, it faded into neglect. Documents from the Middle Ages and later mention a church "at Villa Magna" lying southeast of Rome near the town of Anagni, in the region of Lazio. There, on privately owned land, remains of Roman walls are partially covered by a 19th-century farmhouse and a long-ruined medieval monastery. Sections of the complex were half-heartedly excavated in the 18th century by the Scottish painter and amateur treasure hunter Gavin Hamilton, who failed to find marble statues or frescoed rooms and decided that the site held little interest.

As a result, archaeologists mostly ignored the site for 200 years. Then, in 2006, archaeologist Elizabeth Fentress—working under the auspices of the University of Pennsylvania and the British School at Rome—got permission from the property owner and the Italian government to excavate the area and began to make some interesting discoveries. Most important, near the old farmhouse, her team—accompanied by Sandra Gatti from the Italian Archaeological Superintendency—found a marble-paved rectangular room. At one end was a raised platform, and there were circular indentations in the ground where large terra-cotta pots, or *dolia,* would have been set in an ancient Roman *cella vinaria*—a wine pressing room.

The following summer, Fentress and a team discovered a chamber shaped like a semicircular auditorium attached to the pressing room. She was thrilled. Here was the dining area described by Marcus Aurelius where the imperial retinue watched the local workers stomp grapes and, presumably, dance and sing. "If there was any doubt about the villa," says Fentress, "the discovery of the marble-paved *cella vinaria* and the banquet room looking into it sealed it."

In all, roman emperors constructed dozens of villas over the roughly 350-year span of imperial rule, from the rise of Augustus in 27 B.C. to the death of Constantine in A.D 337. Since treasure hunters first discovered the villas in the 18th century (followed by archaeologists in the 19th and 20th), nearly 30 such properties have been documented in the Italian region of Lazio alone. Some, such as Hadrian's, at Tivoli, have yielded marble statues, frescoes and ornate architecture, evidence of the luxuries enjoyed by wealthy, powerful men (and their wives and mistresses). As archaeological investigations continue at several sites throughout the Mediterranean, a more nuanced picture of these properties and the men who built them is emerging. "This idea that the villa is just about conspicuous consumption, that's only the beginning," says Columbia University archaeologist Marco Maiuro, who works with Fentress at Villa Magna.

The villas also point up the sharp contrast between the emperors' official and private lives. "In Rome," says Steven Tuck, a classical art historian at Miami University of Ohio, "you constantly see them through their service to the state—dedications of buildings, triumphal columns and arches and monuments." But battles and bureaucracy are left at the villa's door. Tuck points to his favorite villa—that of Tiberius, Augustus' stepson, son-in-law and successor. It lies at the end of a sandy beach near Sperlonga, a resort between Rome and Naples on the Mediterranean coast. Wedged between a twisting mountain road and crashing waves, the Villa Tiberio features a natural grotto fashioned into a banquet hall. When archaeologists discovered the grotto in the 1950s, the entrance was filled with thousands of marble fragments. Once the pieces were put together, they yielded some of the greatest sculptural groups ever created—enormous statues depicting the sea monster Scylla and the blinding of the Cyclops Polyphemus. Both are characters from Homer's *Odyssey* as retold in Virgil's *Aeneid*, itself a celebration of Rome's mythic founding written just before Tiberius' reign. Both also vividly illustrate man locked in epic battle with primal forces. "We don't see this kind of thing in Rome," says Tuck. It was evocative of a *nymphaeum*, a dark, primeval place supposedly inhabited by nymphs and beloved by the capricious sea god Neptune. Imagine dining here, with the sound of the sea and torchlight flickering off the fish tail of the monster Scylla as she tossed Odysseus' shipmates into the ocean.

If the imperial villa provided opportunities for Roman emperors to experiment with new images and ideas, then the one that Hadrian (A.D 76–138) built at Tivoli in the first decades of the second century may be the ultimate in freewheeling expression. Occupying about 250 acres at the base of the Apennine Hills, Villa Adriana was originally a farm. When Hadrian became emperor in A.D 117, he began renovating the existing structure into something extraordinary. The villa unfolded into a grand interlocking of halls, baths and gathering spaces designed to tantalize and amaze visitors. "This villa has been studied for five centuries, ever since its discovery during the Renaissance," says Marina De Franceschini, an archaeologist working with the University of Trento. "And yet there's still a lot to discover."

Franceschini is especially beguiled by the villa's outlandish architecture. Take the so-called Maritime Theater, where Hadrian designed a villa within a villa. On an island ringed by a water channel, it is reached by a drawbridge and equipped with two sleeping areas, two bathrooms, a dining room, living room and a thermal bath. The circular design and forced perspective make it appear larger than it is. "The emperor was interested in experimental architecture," says Franceschini. "It's an extremely complicated place. Everything is curved. It's unique."

What exact statement Hadrian wanted to make with his villa has been the subject of debate since the Renaissance, when the great artists of Italy—including Raphael and Michelangelo—studied it. Perhaps to a greater extent than any other emperor, Hadrian possessed an aesthetic sensibility, which found expression in the many beautiful statues discovered on the site, some of which now grace the halls of the Vatican museums and the National Museum of Rome, as well as the Metropolitan Museum of Art in New York City and the Louvre in Paris.

Hadrian traveled frequently, and whenever he returned to Italy, Tivoli became his preferred residence, away from the imperial palace on the Palatine Hill. Part business, part pleasure, the villa contains many rooms designed to accommodate large gatherings. One of the most spacious is the *canopus*—a long structure marked by a reflecting pool said to symbolize a canal Hadrian visited in Alexandria, Egypt, in A.D 130, where his lover Antinous drowned that same year. Ringing the pool was a colonnade connected by an elaborate architrave (carved marble connecting the top of each column). At the far end is a grotto, similar to that at Sperlonga but completely man-made, which scholars have named the Temple of Serapis, after a temple originally found at Alexandria.

Today, the canopus and grotto may look austere, but with the emperor seated there with up to 100 other diners around the pool, it must have been something to see. A network of underground tunnels some three miles long trace a labyrinth beneath the villa, which allowed servants to appear, almost magically, to refill a glass or serve a plate of food. The pool on a warm summer night, reflecting the curvilinear architrave, was surely enchanting.

Standing at the grotto today, one can barely see the line made by two small aqueducts running from a hillside behind the grotto to the top of this half-domed pavilion. Water would have entered a series of pipes at its height, run down into walls and eventually exploded from niches into a semi-circular pool and passed under the emperor. Franceschini believes the water was mostly decorative. "It reflected the buildings," he says. "It also ran through fountains and grand waterworks. It was conceived to amaze the visitor. If you came to a banquet in the canopus and saw the water coming, that would have been really spectacular."

Hadrian was not the only emperor to prefer country life to Rome's imperial palace. Several generations earlier, Tiberius had retired to villas constructed by his predecessor Augustus. Installing a regent in Rome, the gloomy and reclusive Tiberius walled himself off from the world at the Villa Jovis, which still stands on the island of Capri, near Neapolis (today's Naples hills). Tiberius' retreat from Rome bred rumor and suspicion. The historian Suetonius, in his epic work *The Lives of the Twelve Caesars,* would later accuse him of setting up a licentious colony where sadomasochism, pederasty and cruelty were practiced. (Most historians believe these accusations to be false.) "Tradition still associates the great villas of Capri with this negative image," says Eduardo Federico, a historian at the University of Naples who grew up on the island. Excavated largely in the 1930s and boasting some of the most spectacular vistas of the Mediterranean Sea of any Roman estate, the Villa Jovis remains a popular tourist destination. "The legend of Tiberius as a tyrant still prevails," says Federico. "Hostile history has made the Villa Jovis a place of cruelty and Tiberian lust."

Perhaps the best-known retirement villa belonged to the emperor Diocletian (A.D 245–316), who ruled at the end of the third century and into the fourth. Besides his tireless persecution of Christians, Diocletian is known for ending a half-century of instability and consolidating the empire—before dividing it into eastern and western halves (thereby setting the stage for the rise of the Byzantine Empire). Much of this work involved quelling rebellions on the perimeter and keeping the ever-agitating senatorial class under control. By A.D 305, at the age of 60, Diocletian had had enough. In a bold, unprecedented move—previous emperors had all died in office—he announced his retirement and sought refuge in a seaside villa on the coast of Dalmatia (today's Croatia).

Now called Diocletian's Palace, the ten-acre complex includes a mausoleum, temples, a residential suite and a magnificent peristyle courtyard complete with a dais and throne. Even out of power, Diocletian remained a force in the empire, and when it fell into chaos in 309, various factions pleaded for him to take up rule again. Diocletian demurred, famously writing that if they could see the incredible cabbages he'd grown with his own hands, they wouldn't ask him to trade the peace and happiness of his palace for the "storms of a never-satisfied greed," as one historian put it. He died there seven years later.

Located in the modern city of Split, Diocletian's Palace is one of the most stunning ancient sites in the world. Most of its walls still stand; and although the villa has been looted for treasure, a surprising number of statues—mostly Egyptian, pillaged during a successful military campaign—still stand. The villa owes its excellent condition to local inhabitants, who moved into the sprawling residence not long after the fall of Rome and whose descendants live there to this day. "Everything is interwoven in Split," says Josko Belamaric, an art historian with the Croatian Ministry of Culture who is responsible for conservation of the palace. "It's so dense. You open a cupboard in someone's apartment, and you're looking at a 1,700-year-old wall."

Belamaric has been measuring and studying Diocletian's Palace for more than a decade, aiming to strike a balance between its 2,000 residents and the needs of preservation. (Wiring high-speed Internet into an ancient villa, for instance, is not done with a staple gun.) Belamaric's studies of the structure have yielded some surprises. Working with local architect Goran Niksic, the art historian realized that the aqueduct to the villa was large enough to supply water to 173,000 people (too big for a residence, but about right for a factory). The local water contains natural sulfur, which can be used to fix dyes. Belamaric concluded that Diocletian's estate included some sort of manufacturing center—probably for textiles, as the surrounding hills were filled with sheep and the region was known for its fabrics.

It's long been thought that Diocletian built his villa here because of the accommodating harbor and beautiful seascape, not to mention his own humble roots in the region. But Belamaric speculates it was also an existing textile plant that drew the emperor here, "and it probably continued during his residence, generating valuable income."

In fact, most imperial Roman villas were likely working farms or factories beneficial to the economy of the empire. "The Roman world was an agriculturally based one," says Fentress. "During the late republic we begin to see small farms replaced by larger villas." Although fish and grains were important, the predominant crop was grapes, and the main product wine. By the first century B.C., wealthy landowners—the emperors among them—were bottling huge amounts of wine and shipping it throughout the Roman Empire. One of the first global export commodities was born.

At Tiberius' villa at Sperlonga, a series of rectangular pools, fed by the ocean nearby, lay in front of the grotto. At first they seem merely decorative. But upon closer inspection, one notices a series of terra-cotta-lined holes, each about six inches in diameter, set into the sides of the pools, just beneath the water's surface. Their likely use? To provide a safe space in which fish could lay their eggs. The villa operated as a fish farm, producing enough fish, Tuck estimates, not only to feed the villa and its guests but also to supply markets in Rome. "It's fantastic to see this dining space that also doubled as a fish farm," says Tuck. "It emphasizes the practical workings of these places."

Maiuro believes that the economic power of the larger villas, which tended to expand as Rome grew more politically unstable, may even have contributed to the empire's decline, by sucking economic—and eventually political—power away from Rome and concentrating it in the hands of wealthy landowners, precursors of the feudal lords who would dominate the medieval period. "Rome was never very well centralized," says Maiuro, "and as the villas grow, Rome fades."

Critical Thinking

1. In what sense do the emperors' villas point up the sharp contrast between their official and private lives?
2. In what respects did the imperial villas reflect the emperors' experimentation with "new images and ideas"?
3. How did Hadrian transform the villa at Tivoli? What evidence is there that he possessed an "aesthetic sensibility"?
4. How and why was Tiberius the object of rumor and suspicion?
5. What was Diocletian known for? In what respects did he remain a "force in the empire"?
6. What was the significance for the Roman Empire that "most imperial Roman villas were likely working farms or factories beneficial to the economy of the empire"? How did this lead to the fading of Rome and the shift to feudalism?

Create Central

www.mhhe.com/createcentral

Internet References

Society for Historical Archaeology
www.sha.org

WWW Classical Archaeology
www.archaeology.org/wwwarky/classical.html

From *Smithsonian*, June 2010. Copyright © 2010 by Paul Bennett. Reprinted by permission of the author.

Carthage: The Lost Mediterranean Civilisation

Little remains of the great North African empire that was Rome's most formidable enemy. Because, explains Richard Miles, only its complete annihilation could satisfy its younger rival.

RICHARD MILES

Learning Outcomes

After reading this article, you will be able to:

- Discuss the motivations behind the Roman Empire's complete destruction of Carthage.
- Explain how Carthage came into existence and describe its place as a major manufacturing and trade center as well as an agricultural powerhouse.

In the spring of 146 B.C. the North African city state of Carthage finally fell. After three years of embarrassing setbacks, the Roman army under their new and relatively inexperienced commander, Scipio Aemilianus, had managed to break through the Carthaginian defences and establish an all-important bridgehead at Carthage's circular war harbour, an engineering masterpiece with capacity for at least 170 ships and ramps to drag the craft from and to the water's edge.

The Roman forces were in a position to launch a final assault on the Byrsa, the citadel of Carthage and the religious and administrative heart of the city. The legionaries were, however, forced to fight every step of the way on the narrow streets that led up the hill as desperate defenders rained missiles down on them. Despite this stiff resistance, it was now a question of when rather than if Carthage would fall.

The Carthaginians who had sought refuge in the tall houses that flanked the city's streets were flushed out by fire and sword. The Greek historian Appian, who is the main surviving source for this episode, wrote of how Scipio employed squads of soldiers to drag burnt and mutilated corpses off the streets so that the progress of his legionaries was impeded no further.

It still took six days and nights to break Carthaginian resolve, with Scipio deploying his forces in rotation to preserve both their strength and sanity for the ghastly work in which they were engaged. On the seventh day a party of Carthaginian elders bearing a peace offering of olive branches from the sacred Temple of Eshmoun, the Carthaginian god of healing, which sat on the highest point of the Byrsa citadel, came to the Roman general begging that their lives and those of their fellow citizens be spared. Scipio acceded to their request and later that day 50,000 men, women and children left the citadel through a narrow gate in the wall.

Although the vast majority of its surviving citizenry had surrendered, a rump consisting of Carthage's commander-in-chief, Hasdrubal, his family and 900 Roman deserters—who could expect no mercy from Scipio—were still holed up in the precinct of the Temple of Eshmoun. Time, however, was on the side of the Romans and eventually this small group of diehards was forced up onto the roof of the building to make a final stand. It was then that Hasdrubal's nerve finally broke. Deserting his wife and children, he went in secret to Scipio and surrendered. It would be left to his wife to deliver a fittingly defiant epitaph for the dying city by throwing herself and her children into the flames of the burning temple after venting scorn at her husband's cowardice.

Although it is a myth that Scipio had the site of Carthage ploughed with salt to ensure that nothing would flourish there again, he was certainly keen to ensure that the city bore the full force of Roman opprobrium. As the fires burnt on the Byrsa Hill, Scipio ordered his troops to demolish the city's walls and ramparts. Following military custom, the Roman general also allowed the soldiers to loot the city and rewards were handed out to those legionaries who had displayed conspicuous bravery during the campaign. Scipio then personally distributed all gold, silver and religious offerings, while other spoils were either sent to Rome or sold to raise funds. The surviving arms, siege engines and warships were burnt as offerings to the gods Mars and Minerva and the city's wretched inhabitants sent to the slave markets, with the exception of a few grandees, including Hasdrubal, who, after being led through Rome as part of Scipio's triumph, was allowed to lead a life of comfortable confinement in various Italian cities.

The brutal destruction of Carthage by the Romans has retained its power to both shock and provoke. When in the 1950s the poet and playwright Bertolt Brecht cast around for a historical metaphor to remind his fellow Germans about the dangers of re-militarisation, he instinctively turned to an event that had taken place over 2,000 years before:

Great Carthage drove three wars. After the first one it was still powerful. After the second one it was still inhabitable. After the third one it was no longer possible to find her.

In recent years the ongoing crisis in Iraq has also afforded political commentators many opportunities to equate the situation in that unfortunate land with what befell Carthage.

The following words by the American sociologist and historian Franz Schurmann are typical of the kind of emotive comparisons that have been drawn:

Two thousand years ago the Roman statesman Cato the Elder kept crying out, 'Delenda est Carthago'—Carthage must be destroyed! To Cato it was clear either Rome or Carthage but not both could dominate the western Mediterranean. Rome won and Carthage was levelled to the ground. Iraq is now Washington's Carthage.

Brecht and Schurmann use the example of Carthage to make seemingly conflicting points: one sees the fall of the city as the result of a hubristic desire for military might; the other views it as the supreme example of destructive bullying by a more powerful and ruthless rival. In fact, whether you view Carthage as villain or victim, those judgments are based almost exclusively on the historical testimony of Carthage's greatest enemy, Rome.

It was not just the physical fabric of Carthage that Scipio sought to obliterate. The learned tomes that graced the shelves of the city's libraries, with the exception of the famous Carthaginian agricultural treatise by Mago which was spirited back to Rome, were dispersed among the local Numidian princes who had aided Rome in their war of extermination against Carthage. Nothing more starkly reflects the success of this Roman project than the fact that less than a couple of thousand words of Punic—the Carthaginian tongue—are known and many of these are proper names. The spoils of war not only included the ownership of Carthage's territory, resources and people but also its past. Destruction did not mean total oblivion. A far worse fate awaited Carthage as a mute, misrepresented ghoul in the historical annals of its enemies.

Both Greek and Latin literature would consistently portray the Carthaginians as mendacious, greedy, untrustworthy, cruel, arrogant and irreligious. Particularly shocking to modern sensibilities are the lurid accounts of hundreds of children being sacrificed by immolation in order to placate Baal Hammon and Tanit, the bloodthirsty chief deities of Carthage. Such was the emphasis placed by the Romans on Carthaginian treachery that the Latin phrase *Fides Punica*, literally 'Punic Faith', became a popular ironic expression denoting gross faithlessness.

Carthage was, of course, not the only city to suffer destruction at the hands of Rome. In the very same year that Scipio's troops were carrying out their grim work in North Africa, the venerable Greek city of Corinth was suffering a similarly traumatic fate at the hands of another Roman army. However, it is Carthage's fate that history remembers. It was not the demolishing of the walls, the burning of the houses or the enslaving and killing of the population that made this episode so infamous but its completeness and the cold-blooded determination with which it was carried out.

Many explanations have been put forward as to why Rome invested so much in the destruction of Carthage. Hatred and vengeance certainly played their part. After all, the two states had fought two of the greatest and bloodiest wars—the Punic Wars—that the ancient world had known. Many Romans considered Carthage to have been their greatest enemy, the 'whetstone' of their greatness. Victory over Carthage in the First Punic War (264–241 B.C.) had demanded that the Romans, who had no previous naval experience, develop their own fleet and defeat the pre-eminent sea power of the ancient world in a period of a little over three decades. In that short time the Mediterranean had been transformed in the Roman mind from a dangerous unknown to *Mare Nostrum*, 'our sea'. For many Romans the final defeat and destruction of Carthage was the great watershed moment of a glorious and eventful history because it marked the transformation of Rome from Italian to 'world' power.

Moreover, Carthage had taken Rome to the brink of total defeat. During the Second Punic War (218–201 B.C.), the great Carthaginian general Hannibal had blazed a trail of devastation across Italy, humiliating a series of Roman armies along the way. It had taken every ounce of Roman resilience and resources to eventually dislodge Hannibal from the Italian peninsula but not before he had come close to capturing Rome itself and, in all likelihood, final victory. Even a century later, the Roman poet Statius was still evoking the ghoulish spectre of 'Libyan hordes' marauding through the Italian countryside.

There was also the question of Rome's ruthless application of realpolitik. By the time of the third and final Punic War (149–146 B.C.), Carthage, despite having made an impressive economic recovery from the disastrous depredations of its defeat in the Second Punic War, was a mere shadow of the power that it had once been. It was really no threat to Rome, who by that time controlled much of the Mediterranean. Despite this, a powerful clique within the Roman senate, led by Cato the Elder of 'Delenda est Carthago' fame, had pushed hard for Carthage to be neutralised permanently. With the argument won, Carthage had been harassed into a foolhardy act of defiance that had at last given the Roman senate the justification to send their legions back to North Africa.

Yet, despite the contemporary emphasis on the destruction of Carthage being the result of the desire for a final settling of accounts, it is clear that more pragmatic considerations were at the fore of Roman thinking on this matter. The sacking of what was still one of the richest port cities in the ancient Mediterranean was unquestionably a hugely profitable business. The slave auctions and the seizure of a large swathe of previous Carthaginian territory which now became public land owned by the Roman state, unequivocally contributed to a massive infusion of wealth into both public and private Roman coffers. At the same time, the conspicuous destruction of such a famous city sent an unequivocal message: dissent from Rome would not be tolerated and past glories counted for nothing in this new world. The destruction of Carthage now stood as a bloody memorial to the cost of resistance to Rome and a suitably apocalyptic fanfare for Rome's coming of age as a new world power.

In the face of such a litany of destruction and misrepresentation both ancient and modern, one might legitimately ask whether it is really possible to write a history of Carthage that is anything more than just another extended essay on victimhood and vilification.

There are some intriguing but equally frustrating clues. Within the burnt-out structure of a temple (thought by its discoverer, the German archaeologist Friedrich Rakob, to have been the Temple of Apollo ransacked by Roman soldiers), were the remains of an archive thought to have contained wills and business contracts, stored there so that their integrity and safekeeping was guaranteed by the sacred authority of the god. The papyrus on which the document was written was rolled up and string wrapped around it before a piece of wet clay was placed on the string to stop the document from unravelling and a personal seal was imprinted upon it. However, in this particular case, the same set of circumstances that ensured the seals were wonderfully preserved because they were fired by the inferno which engulfed the city also meant that the precious documents that they enclosed were burnt to ashes.

When faced with such historical lacunae there is always a temptation to overcompensate when imagining what has actually been lost. However, we should be wary of assuming that the shelves of Carthage's famous libraries groaned under the weight of a vast corpus of Punic and earlier Near Eastern knowledge now destroyed. Although rumours circulated in the ancient world of mysterious sacred parchments which had been hidden away before Carthage fell and there are scattered references in much later Roman literature of Punic histories, it is difficult to gauge whether the city was really a great literary centre comparable with Athens or Alexandria.

At times, researching a history of Carthage is rather like reading a transcript of a conversation in which one interlocutor's contribution has been deleted. However, the responses of the existing protagonists, in this case Greek and Roman writers, allows one to follow the thread of the discussion. Indeed, it is the sheer range and scale of these 'conversations' that allows the historian of Carthage to recreate some of what has been expunged. Ideology and egotism dictate that even historians united in hostility towards their subject still manage vehemently to disagree with one another and it is within the contradictions and differences of opinion that existed between these writers that this heavily biased monologue can be partially overcome.

As regards other material evidence, the ruins of Carthage have always stirred the imagination of those who visited them. Rumours that the Carthaginians had managed to bury their riches in the hope of returning to retrieve them in better times had led the troops of one first-century B.C. Roman general to commence an impromptu treasure hunt. For the modern archaeologist Carthage can resemble a complicated jigsaw of which many pieces have been intentionally thrown away. Yet history tells us that such final solutions are rarely as comprehensive as their perpetrators would have us believe.

Although the religious centre on the Byrsa was completely demolished, many of the outlying districts and, as we have already seen, some parts of the hill itself escaped total destruction. In fact, the Romans inadvertently did much to preserve parts of Punic Carthage by dumping thousands of cubic metres of rubble and debris on top of it. Even the ominous two-foot thick black tide-mark found in the stratigraphy of the western slopes of the Byrsa, the archaeological record of the razing of the city in 146 B.C., is packed full of southern Italian tableware, telling us what pottery styles were in vogue in Carthage at that time.

Then there are the thousands of monuments recording votive offerings made to Baal Hammon and Tanit, which, although extremely formulaic, have furnished invaluable information on Punic religious rites. This is especially so in the case of child sacrifice which is revealed in a different light to the hysterical ritualised savagery found in the historical accounts. There are also a small number of surviving inscriptions relating to other aspects of city life, such as the construction of public monuments and the carrying out of an assortment of religious rituals. This epigraphic evidence has been helpful in aiding understanding not only of Carthage's religious life but also the social hierarchies that existed within the city. It is from the writing on these slabs of stone that we learn of the faceless potters, metal smiths, cloth weavers, fullers, furniture makers, carters, butchers, stonemasons, jewellers, doctors, scribes, interpreters, cloak attendants, surveyors, priests, heralds, furnace workers and merchants who made up the population of the city.

The picture of Carthage that emerges from these very fragmentary glimpses is a strikingly different one from the barbarous, cruel and aggressive city-state found in the Greek and Roman historical canon. Carthage might have been founded by settlers from the Phoenician city of Tyre in what is now southern Lebanon, but it was older (early eighth century B.C.) than any Greek city in the central or western Mediterranean region; so much for their ill-founded reputation as oriental gatecrashers into a pristine Hellenic world. Its Phoenician name, Qart-Hadasht, or 'New City', suggests that Carthage was set up as a colonial settlement and not just as a trading post.

Strategically the site could not have been better chosen, for it stood on the nexus of the two most important trans-Mediterranean trading routes, the east-west route that brought silver from the mines of southern Spain to Tyre and its north-south Tyrrhenian counterpart that linked Greece, Italy, Sicily and North Africa.

It is now thought that Carthage might have actually been established to act as a larger civic centre for other smaller Phoenician colonies in the region. It certainly grew quickly. Although archaeologists are yet to locate any of the important public buildings or harbours from that early period, current evidence indicates that the littoral plain began to fill up with a densely packed network of dwellings made of sun-dried bricks laid out on streets with wells, gardens and squares, all situated on a fairly regular plan that ran parallel to the shoreline. By the early seventh century B.C., the settlement was surrounded by an impressive three-metre wide casement wall. So swift was the development that in the first hundred years of the city's existence there is evidence of some demolition and redevelopment within it's neighbourhoods, including the careful relocation of an early cemetery to make way for metal workshops. Three further large cemeteries ringing the early city indicate that, within a century or so of its foundation, Carthage was home to around 30,000 people, a very considerable number for that period.

Although at first luxury goods were imported from the Levant, Egypt and other areas of the Near East, by the mid-seventh century B.C. Carthage had become a major manufacturer itself through the establishment of an industrial area just outside the city walls, with potter's kilns and workshops for purple-dye production and metalworking. Carthage now became a major manufacturer of terracotta figurines, masks, jewellery, delicately carved ivories and decorated ostrich eggs, which were then exported throughout the western Phoenician colonies.

The decline of Tyre as an economic and political force in the first decades of the sixth century B.C., led to Carthage assuming the leadership of the old Phoenician colonies in the central and western Mediterranean. This was hardly surprising because already Carthage was the most populous and economically powerful member of that grouping. The real source of Carthaginian might was and would remain its fleet, the greatest in the Mediterranean for hundreds of years. A huge mercantile fleet ensured that Carthage was the nexus of a vast trading network, transporting foodstuffs, wine, oil, metals and luxury goods as well as other cargoes across the Mediterranean. If a couple of much later Greek and Roman sources are to be believed then Carthaginian expeditions also made their way into the Atlantic, travelling as far afield as West Africa and Britanny.

With the most feared fleet in the Mediterranean, Carthage remained one of the pacesetters in naval technological innovation. In the fourth century B.C. they were the first to develop the quadrireme, which was both bigger and more powerful than the trireme, the ship that had dominated naval warfare for the previous 200 years. Marine archaeologists who have studied the remains of several Carthaginian ships lying on the sea bed just off Marsala on the west coast of Sicily, were amazed to discover that each piece of the boat was carefully marked with a letter which ensured that the complex design could be easily and swiftly assembled. The Carthaginians had developed what was, in essence, a flatpack warship.

With Carthaginian leadership of the western Phoenician colonies confirmed, we see the growing influence of recognisably Carthaginian cultural traits in other western Phoenician colonies. These included the adoption of Punic, the Levantine dialect spoken in Carthage, as well as a new taste for the luxury goods and religious practices favoured in the city.

Yet the headship of the Phoenician community in the west was not the only source of Carthage's burgeoning power. For the first centuries of its existence the Carthaginians had been hampered by the very limited extent of their hinterland which meant that they had been forced to import much of their food. This began to change in the sixth century B.C. as Carthage sometimes expanded aggressively into the territory of their Libyan neighbours. A whole raft of farmsteads and small towns were developed on this new land with the result that Carthage also became an agricultural powerhouse, producing food and wine not only for its own population but also for export. The Carthaginians were also celebrated for certain technological advances in agriculture, such as the *tribulum plostellum Punicum,* or Punic cart, a primitive but highly effective threshing machine.

Interestingly, this economic and political dominance did not translate into any imperial aspirations until the last decades before the First Punic War. However, the Carthaginian leadership of a Punic bloc that took in North Africa, Sardinia, western Sicily, southern Spain, the Balearics and Malta, did become increasingly involved overseas, politically and militarily. The most significant of these ventures was on Sicily where heavy economic investment and the presence of strategically important Phoenician colonies meant that Carthage quickly became a major player in the highly volatile political landscape that existed there. Over the following two centuries Carthage was obliged to send a number of armies to Sicily in order to defend its own and its allies' interests there, particularly from encroachments by the most powerful Greek city-state on the island, Syracuse. Military action between the two powers and their allies was punctuated by periods of 'cold war' in which each side eyed the other warily.

Despite some Sicilian-Greek historians' claims to the contrary, this was never a straight conflict between the Punic and Greek blocs. Carthage, in particular, often co-operated with Sicilian Greek city-states worried about the growth in Syracusan power. More generally, Greek, Punic and indigenous communities on the island intermarried and worshipped each others' gods and goddesses as well as trading and making war and political alliances with one another. Indeed, it was often the deep and long-standing relationships that existed between supposedly bitter rivals that were the driving force in the creation of a surprisingly cohesive and interconnected central and western Mediterranean.

Politically Carthage was certainly influenced by the Hellenic world, introducing constitutional structures that resembled but did not ape those found in the Greek city-states. Carthage had long been an oligarchy, dominated by a cartel of rich and powerful merchant families represented in a Council of Elders with one dominant clan usually holding the role of first amongst equals. However, over time this led to the introduction of more representative bodies and officials. A body called the Tribunal of One Hundred and Four, made up of members of the aristocratic elite, now oversaw the conduct of officials and military commanders as well as acting as a kind of higher constitutional court. At the head of the Carthaginian state were two annually elected senior executive officers, the Suffetes, as well as a whole range of more junior officials and special commissioners who oversaw different aspects of governmental business such as public works, tax-collecting and the administration of the state treasury. A popular assembly that included all members of the citizen body was also introduced.

However, much to the approval of the Athenian political scientist Aristotle, its powers were strictly limited. In fact, Aristotle thought that the Carthaginian constitution of the fourth century B.C. was the best balanced in the Mediterranean world. Later, however, in line with many Greek states, the powers of the popular assembly increased markedly, leading to charges that Carthage was going down the road of demagogy.

One finds the same mixture of emulation and innovation in Carthage's interactions with Greek culture. There is good evidence for members of the Carthaginian elite being educated in Greek, and Greek artistic and architectural traits were often adopted and adapted for Punic tastes. This familiarity with Greek art, rather than leading to mere mimicry, allowed the Punic population of the island to express themselves in new and powerfully original ways. Traditional Phoenician artforms such as anthropoid sarcophagi, stone coffins whose human heads, arms and feet protruded out from a piece of smooth stone like human pupae, acquired Greek dress and hair decoration. And it was not just one-way traffic. Sicilian Greek art, and architecture in particular, was clearly influenced by the Punic world.

Perhaps the most striking example of Greco-Punic cultural interaction was found by archaeologists excavating on the site of the Punic city of Motya in Sicily in 1979. It was an oversized marble statue of a young man, standing 1.8 metres tall without his missing feet. Although the arms had also gone, it was relatively simple to reconstruct the pose of the left arm, as the hand has been carved resting on the hip. The head was framed by a fringe of curly hair and had once worn a crown or wreath kept in place by rivets. All in all, it appeared to conform to the severe Greek sculptural style of the early fifth century B.C. and, indeed, a very similar statue of an *ephebe,* a young man of military training age, has been discovered on the site of the Sicilian Greek city of Acragas.

It has been argued that only a Greek sculptor could have created such a high quality piece and that the Motya ephebe was a looted Greek work. However, there was a problem. Unlike other statues of ephebes from this period, who are depicted nude, the Motya young man is clothed in a fine long tunic with flowing pleats bounded by a high girdle. Many ingenious solutions have been proposed to explain this anomaly. The strange girdle and hand positions have led to the suggestion that the young man was either a Greek charioteer or a sponsor of a chariot race. However, the Motya figure is very different from other surviving statues of Greek charioteers. In fact, the closest parallels are found within the Punic world. Firstly, despite the clearly Greek sculptural form, the statue follows the Punic convention of not displaying the nude body; second, the clothes and headgear worn by the young man bear a marked resemblance to the ritual garments worn by priests of the cult of the Punic god Melqart, with whom Heracles would enjoy an increasingly close association in Sicily. Neither Greek nor Punic but Sicilian, the Motya ephebe stood as a glittering testament to the cultural syncretism that was such a powerful force in this region.

In such a brief survey it is simply impossible to do justice to all of the different ways that Carthaginian political, economic and cultural dynamism helped to create a western Mediterranean world that existed long before Rome came on the scene. Carthage was, in reality, the bedrock on which much of Rome's success as an imperial power was founded. Rome was not just the destroyer of Carthage but also the inheritor of a politically, economically and culturally joined-up world which was Carthage's greatest achievement. The Romans were always ready, although sometimes grudgingly so, to recognise their debt to the Greeks. However, these had tended to be in cultural fields such as philosophy, art and history that the Romans did not wish, or did not have the confidence, to claim as their own. In fact the creation of what we know as the classical world was founded on the recognition of the complementary nature of Greek and Roman talents. Greek innovation met Roman dynamism. The existence of Carthage, a dynamic Mediterranean power which had also enjoyed a similar complementary relationship with the Greek world, was an inconvenient truth that Rome was simply not willing to acknowledge. Thus Carthage's brutal end might have had as much to do with Roman insecurity about creating its own unique legacy as any desire for vengeance or plunder.

Critical Thinking

1. To what extent was Carthage destroyed by Rome? What was even worse than total destruction, according to the author?
2. How would Carthage be consistently portrayed in Roman and Greek literature? What was meant by "Fides Punica?"
3. Why is the fate of Carthage remembered more than the similar fate of the Greek city of Corinth?
4. Why did Rome invest so much in the destruction of Carthage?
5. What is the nature of the literary and material evidence used by the author to research the history of Carthage? What is the picture of Carthage that emerges?
6. In what respects was Carthage strategically located?
7. Why was Carthage established, according to the author? What evidence is there that it grew rapidly?
8. In what ways did Carthage become a major manufacturing and trade center its own right? How did it also become an "agricultural powerhouse?"
9. How and when did Carthage's imperialistic aspirations develop?
10. Why does the author describe Carthage as part of a "surprisingly cohesive and interconnected central and western Mediterranean?"
11. How is it that Carthage possessed both an oligarchy and constitutional structures?
12. What evidence is there of "Greek-Punic cultural interaction?"
13. Why does the author claim "Carthage was, in reality, the bedrock on which much of Rome's success as an imperial power was founded.?" Why does he say that this was an "inconvenient truth" for Rome?

Create Central

www.mhhe.com/createcentral

Internet References

Society for Historical Archaeology
www.sha.org

WWW Classical Archaeology
www.archaeology.org/wwwarky/classical.html

RICHARD MILES is a Newton Trust Lecturer in the Faculty of Classics and Fellow and Director of Studies in Classics at Trinity Hall, Cambridge. He is the author of *Carthage Must be Destroyed: The Rise and Fall of an Ancient Mediterranean Civilisation* (Allen Lane, 2010).

From *History Today,* February 2010. Copyright © 2010 by History Today, Ltd. Reprinted by permission.

Article

Prepared by: Mari Pritchard Parker, *Pasadena City College* and
Elvio Angeloni, *Pasadena City College*

The Weapon That Changed History

Evidence of Rome's decisive victory over Carthage is discovered in the waters off Sicily.

ANDREW CURRY

Learning Outcomes

After reading this article, you will be able to:

- Discuss the reasons for the First Punic War between Rome and Carthage and the significance of its outcome.
- Discuss the Battle of the Egadi Islands in terms of how well prepared each side was.
- Discuss the "lost wax" method used in ancient times for crafting weapons made of metal.

In his work *The Histories,* the second-century B.C. Greek historian Polybius chronicles the rise of the Romans as they battled for control of the Mediterranean. The central struggle pits the Romans against their archenemies the Carthaginians, a trading super power based in North Africa. For 23 years, beginning in 264 B.C., the two rivals fought what became known as the First Punic War.

As Polybius tells it, the war came to a head in 242 B.C., with both powers exhausted and nearly broke after two decades of fighting. The Carthaginian general Hamilcar Barca—the father of a later adversary of Rome, Hannibal—was pinned down on a mountaintop above the city of Drepana, now the Sicilian town of Trapani. As the Carthaginians assembled a relief force, the Romans scraped together the money for a fleet to cut them off. According to Polybius, in March 241 B.C., the two sides met in between the Egadi Islands, a trio of rocky outcrops a few miles off the coast of Sicily. The clash brought hundreds of ships and thousands of men together in a battle that helped shape the course of history.

A string of discoveries just a few miles off the coast of western Sicily are now supplying new evidence of that war and the battle that brought it to a close. Working from a well-equipped research vessel, a team from the United States and Italy has located what can only be artifacts from what is now known as the Battle of the Egadi Islands.

It's the first time archaeologists have gone looking for and successfully uncovered evidence of a particular ancient naval battle. While ancient accounts often exaggerate the numbers of men or weapons involved in a battle, or are vague about their exact locations, Polybius turns out to have been fairly reliable. His basic report about the Battle of the Egadi Islands has been confirmed. "Ships met in a battle, and ships sank," says Jeff Royal, the director of the Florida-based nonprofit RPM Nautical Foundation, which is leading the work.

In Polybius' description, the two sides were wildly unmatched—not in numbers, but in terms of battle readiness. Traditionally a land power, the Romans had learned a great deal over the course of the war with Carthage. They arrived ready to fight, their new quinqueremes—fast warships powered by rowers during combat—stripped for battle. Any extra weight would have been left on shore. "The Roman ships were loaded with well-trained troops and no extra stores," Royal says. "They were ready for business."

The Carthaginian fleet, on the other hand, was burdened by supplies and troops intended to relieve the besieged Hamilcar. "For the first time, the shoe's on the other foot," Royal says. Polybius is unsparing in his criticism of the Carthaginians. "Their ships, being loaded, were not in a serviceable condition for battle, while the crews were quite untrained, and had been put on board for the emergency, and their marines were recent levies whose first experience of the least hardship and danger this was," the historian wrote decades after the battle.

As dawn broke on March 22, 241 B.C., the Roman commander Lutatius faced a difficult choice. The seas were stormy and the wind was against him—not ideal conditions for a naval assault in the age of sail. But Lutatius knew this was his best chance to intercept the Carthaginians and catch them at a disadvantage. "He therefore decided not to let the present opportunity slip," Polybius writes. An order sent dozens of Roman ships sitting at anchor along the shore of Levanzo, the northernmost of the Egadi Islands, surging toward the Carthaginian fleet.

In the 1970s, divers working for local tuna fisheries told Sicilian archaeologist Sebastiano Tusa that fragments of lead anchors were a common find along the rocky coast of Levanzo. That led Tusa to speculate that the island may have been where Roman ships waited to ambush the Carthaginians. Perhaps, he says, the Romans cut their anchors loose as they prepared to attack. "That would have made a ship much lighter—each anchor weighed 600 pounds," says Tusa, who is now superintendent of archaeology for Trapani. Freed of their last loads, ranks of Roman rowers, moving in carefully practiced concert, propelled the sleek wooden ships across the blue water.

On a warm day in August 2011, RPM's turquoise-and-white painted research vessel floated where the Romans and the Carthaginians clashed more than 2,000 years ago. The ship, dubbed *Hercules,* used a combination of GPS and computer-controlled thrusters to hover in place. Nearly 300 feet straight down was the evidence the ship was seeking.

As Tusa and local dignitaries watched from the deck and wetsuit-clad Italian coast guard divers slid from a nearby motorboat into the water to film the proceedings, the *Hercules'* crew used a crane to lower a cage the size of a small car, containing a remotely operated submersible vehicle (ROV), into the water. In an air-conditioned control room sandwiched between the ship's galley and the crew's lounge, racks of servers named after the Greek gods Artemis, Dionysius, and Zeus hummed softly.

Lit by a wall of blue-tinted video screens that display images from the ROV's camera, the control room is the heart of RPM's operation. *Hercules* is equipped with some of the most sophisticated sonar imaging equipment in the world, capable of creating computerized, three-dimensional relief maps of the ocean floor accurate to within a few feet. The ship spends months each year sailing back and forth across the Mediterranean, mapping out areas that might have shipwrecks. In the last seven years, the team has located dozens of ships off the coasts of Albania and Montenegro ("The Adriatic's Uncharted Past," March/April 2011).

RPM began searching for finds off the Egadi Islands in 2005, after Royal and Tusa made an educated guess on the general location of the battle based on Polybius' accounts. Because the flat parts of the seafloor have been so thoroughly disturbed by bottom-dragging nets, the team first mapped the seafloor to find underwater areas with lots of rocks. They hoped more artifacts would have been preserved intact in places the trawl nets couldn't tear up.

Once they created an accurate map of the undersea geography, they began "flying" over it with their submersible robot, looking for artifacts that had been left behind or lost during the Egadi Islands battle. In 2008, a ship's bronze ram was spotted sitting on the seafloor and recovered using an ROV. In 2010, they located another ram and brought it to the surface. A year later, they were back to retrieve yet another artifact, spotted months earlier.

With a crowd of local archaeologists looking on, a professional ROV pilot on loan from a Swedish oil pipeline project maneuvered the craft to within a few inches of one of the rams. The ROV's thrusters sent clouds of sand billowing up, occasionally obscuring the view of the partly buried chunk of bronze. After two tense hours, with RPM founder George Robb controlling the robot's gripper arms and Royal looking on nervously, the ram was finally hoisted to the surface.

As it lay dripping on the deck, the ram's features were easier to make out. A triple stack of two-foot-wide blades swooped back into a fitting that once snugly capped a ship's prow The ram rode just at the waterline, designed to splinter the planks of an enemy vessel on impact and cripple it. More like an arrowhead than a blunt battering ram, weighing in at 600 pounds, it was the pointed end of a larger weapon—the ship itself. "With these, the ship provides 99.9 percent of the mass, and thus the force, that's coming at you," Royal explains. "Without the ram, you could conceivably still hit another ship and sink it. But you could do that only a certain number of times."

Once the *Hercules* docked in Trapani, the small Sicilian city that serves as a launching point for ferries to the Egadi Islands, Royal began measuring and cleaning the ram, scooping handfuls of dark mud from the inside and sealing them in plastic bags for later analysis. Because this ram was the fourth such ram discovered here, Royal dubbed it Egadi 4. Egadi 2 was recovered in 2008, Egadi 3 in 2010. Both are now in a tuna plant-turned-local museum on the island of Favignana. Egadi 1—the ram that tipped Tusa off to the possibility that there might be something worth looking for on the ocean floor—turned up in a dentist's office in Trapani in 2001. Local fisher men pulled the ram up in their nets and traded it for dental care before Italian police seized it and turned it over to Tusa.

By the time *Hercules* finished its season and headed to its home port in Malta a few weeks later, Royal and the RPM team had recovered two more rams, for a total of six. Before this discovery only four warship rams from this period had ever been found. Add to that more than half a dozen helmets and about 200 amphorae, and RPM has strong evidence that an ancient naval battle took place here. "It sounds plausible—helmets and rams together say there's military equipment in the area," says ancient ship expert Ronald Bockius, a curator at the Roman-Germanic Central Museum in Mainz. "The number of rams is an indication for me that these artifacts are related to a battle. The more that are found, the more clear it seems."

Other scholars are less reserved. William Murray, an archaeologist at the University of South Florida and author of the new book *The Age of Titans: The Rise and Fall of the Great Hellenistic Navies,* calls the finds "a technological, methodological, and scientific tour de force. For the first time, people went to find things from a naval battle and actually found them. They've demonstrated without a doubt the location of the last battle of the First Punic War," says Murray.

The finds promise to do more than just pinpoint the location of a battle that took place two millennia ago. Until now, archaeologists studying ancient warships often had to rely on artifacts and structures found on land, such as the covered "ship sheds" that housed warships in port. "That's like trying to find out how big the car was by looking at the garage," Royal says.

There are major holes in archaeologists' knowledge of naval warfare in the classical world. Classicists and historians are often baffled by ancient accounts of naval battles, which are filled with everything from familiar triremes to the more exotic-sounding quadriremes, quinqueremes and pentecouters. "We know a lot about ancient warship names, but we know much less about the character of the actual ships," Murray says. "It's like not knowing what a cruise missile or a drone is. When the battle actually begins and a heptareme attacks a quinquereme and is sunk by a *lembos,* what does that mean?"

The Egadi rams may help sort things out. Ancient craftsmen shaped them using what's called the "lost-wax" method. After the ship was built, a complete ram was sculpted out of beeswax directly on the prow. The wax ram was then carefully removed and encased in clay, creating a mold. Molten bronze was poured into the mold, melting and replacing the wax. When the bronze cooled, the clay was cracked off and the bronze ram—a perfect copy of the wax original—could be mounted on the ship.

For archaeologists, each ram is a cast of the business end of an ancient warship—invaluable information for those who want to know how naval battles were fought in antiquity. "We can get a sense of where the ship's wooden timbers were by looking at the hollow cavity inside the ram," says Murray "That allows you to make certain suppositions about what the physical characteristics of the warships were."

Once retrieved from the Mediterranean, the rams are stored in deionized water to remove the salt from their surface, and are then dried and painstakingly cleaned with dental picks and drills. The patina (the green film that makes weathered bronze so distinctive) is left to protect the metal underneath. Finally, the rams are covered in a wax coating to seal and protect them.

The rams bear the scars of battle. Dents abound and even entire fins are sheared off, most likely from head-on collisions with other rams. As conservators in Trapani clean and restore the artifacts RPM has found over the last four seasons, new details about them are being revealed. Egadi 3, which likely belonged to a Carthaginian ship, bears an inscription in Punic, the Carthaginians' language, dedicated to the god Baal: "We pray to Baal that this ram will go into the enemy ship and make a big hole."

Just weeks after they were lifted from the sea floor, two of the rams found in summer 2011, Egadi 4 and 6, yielded identifying details as well. Both carry images of Victoria, Roman goddess of victory in battle, in relief on their upper surfaces. Below the goddesses there are names, perhaps belonging to Roman *quaestors,* officials who oversaw and organized the ships' construction. "Because the names on both rams are the same, it's likely this was part of a larger building program," Royal says. Evidence for this program may also be found in Polybius' account, where he writes that with the Carthaginian army pinned down on a Sicilian mountaintop in 242 B.C., the Senate pressed Rome's 200 richest families to sponsor warships. In less than a year, the new fleet was organized and sailors were trained and equipped. "This was their last-ditch effort," Royal says. "If it had failed, it might have meant another five to ten years of stalemate before Rome could get the resources together to try again."

Instead, the Roman fleet was victorious, forcing Carthage to sign a ruinous peace deal with Rome, effectively ending the longest sea war in Roman history in one day. The battle's impact rippled far beyond the waters of Sicily As part of the treaty that Carthage agreed to in the battle's aftermath, Rome gained its first overseas possessions. In one fell swoop, all the islands of the Mediterranean, from Sicily to Sardinia, were in Rome's hands. "They took the shot, rolled the dice, and won the damn thing," Royal says. "It was a huge watershed moment."

Critical Thinking

1. How did the Romans and the Carthaginians compare with respect to their readiness for the Battle of the Egadi Islands?
2. What kinds of technology were available to the archaeologists for locating and examining the battle site?
3. What was the evidence found for the First Punic War?
4. How can the Egadi rams help to fill in gaps in the archaeologists' knowledge of naval warfare in the classical world?
5. What is the "lost wax" method used to craft such weapons as the rams?
6. What was the significance of this battle for Rome and Carthage?

Create Central

www.mhhe.com/createcentral

Internet References

Society for Historical Archaeology
www.sha.org

WWW Classical Archaeology
www.archaeology.org/wwwarky/classical.html

ANDREW CURRY is a contributing editor at *Archaeology.*

Curry, Andrew. From *Archaeology*, January/February 2012, pp. 33–37. Copyright © 2012 by Archaeological Institute of America. Reprinted by permission of *Archaeology Magazine*. www.archaeology.org

Article

Prepared by: Mari Pritchard Parker, *Pasadena City College* and Elvio Angeloni, *Pasadena City College*

Lofty Ambitions of the Inca

Rising from obscurity to the heights of power, a succession of Andean rulers subdued kingdoms, sculpted mountains, and forged a mighty empire.

HEATHER PRINGLE

Learning Outcomes

After reading this article, you will be able to:

- Discuss the circumstances of the Inca rise to power along with the tactics used.
- Discuss the Inca as the "organizational geniuses of the Americas."

On the remote Peruvian island of Taquile, in the middle of the great Lake Titicaca, hundreds of people stand in silence on the plaza as a local Roman Catholic priest recites a prayer. Descended in part from Inca colonists sent here more than 500 years ago, the inhabitants of Taquile keep the old ways. They weave brilliantly colored cloth, speak the traditional language of the Inca, and tend their fields as they have for centuries. On festival days they gather in the plaza to dance to the sound of wooden pipes and drums.

Today, on a fine summer afternoon, I watch from the sidelines as they celebrate the fiesta of Santiago, or St. James. In Inca times this would have been the festival of Illapa, the Inca god of lightning. As the prayers draw to a close, four men dressed in black raise a rustic wooden litter holding a painted statue of Santiago. Walking behind the priest in a small procession, the bearers carry the saint for all in the plaza to see, just as the Inca once shouldered the mummies of their revered kings.

The names of those Inca rulers still resonate with power and ambition centuries after their demise: Viracocha Inca (meaning Creator God Ruler), Huascar Inca (Golden Chain Ruler), and Pachacutec Inca Yupanqui (He Who Remakes the World). And remake the world they did. Rising from obscurity in Peru's Cusco Valley during the 13th century, a royal Inca dynasty charmed, bribed, intimidated, or conquered its rivals to create the largest pre-Columbian empire in the New World.

Scholars long possessed few clues about the lives of Inca kings, apart from flattering histories that Inca nobles told soon after the arrival of Spanish conquistadores. The Inca had no system of hieroglyphic writing, as the Maya did, and any portraits that Inca artists may have made of their rulers were lost.

The royal palaces of Cusco, the Inca capital, fell swiftly to the European conquerors, and a new Spanish colonial city rose on their ruins, burying or obliterating the Inca past. In more recent times, civil unrest broke out in the Peruvian Andes in the early 1980s, and few archaeologists ventured into the Inca heartland for more than a decade.

Now archaeologists are making up for lost time. Combing rugged mountain slopes near Cusco, they are discovering thousands of previously unknown sites, shedding new light on the origins of the Inca dynasty. Gleaning clues from colonial documents, they are relocating the lost estates of Inca rulers and examining the complex upstairs-and-downstairs lives of imperial households. And on the frontiers of the lost empire, they are piecing together dramatic evidence of the wars Inca kings fought and the psychological battles they waged to forge dozens of fractious ethnic groups into a united realm. Their extraordinary ability to triumph on the battlefield and to build a civilization, brick by brick, sent a clear message, says Dennis Ogburn, an archaeologist at the University of North Carolina at Charlotte: "I think they were saying, We are the most powerful people in the world, so don't even think of messing with us."

On a sun-washed July afternoon, Brian Bauer, an archaeologist from the University of Illinois at Chicago, stands in the plaza of the sprawling Inca ceremonial site of Maukallacta, south of Cusco. He takes a swig of water, then points to a towering outcrop of gray rock just to the east. Carved into its craggy summit are massive steps, part of a major Inca shrine. Some 500 years ago, says Bauer, pilgrims journeyed here to worship at the steep outcrop, once regarded as one of the most sacred places in the empire: the birthplace of the Inca dynasty.

Bauer, a wiry 54-year-old in a battered ball cap and blue jeans, first came to Maukallacta in the early 1980s to uncover the origins of the Inca Empire. At the time most historians and archaeologists believed that a brilliant, young Andean Alexander the Great named Pachacutec became the first Inca king in the early 1400s, transforming a small collection of mud huts into a mighty empire in just one generation. Bauer didn't buy it. He believed the Inca dynasty had far deeper roots, and Maukallacta seemed the logical place to look for them. To his bewilderment, two field seasons of digging turned up no trace of primeval Inca lords. So Bauer shifted north, to the Cusco Valley. With colleague R. Alan Covey, now an archaeologist at Southern Methodist University (SMU) in Dallas, and a team of Peruvian assistants, he marched up and down the steep mountain slopes in straight transect lines for four field seasons, recording every scattering of pottery sherds or toppled stone wall he came across. Persistence paid off. Bauer and his colleagues eventually discovered thousands of previously unknown Inca sites, and the new evidence revealed for the first time how an Inca state had risen much earlier than previously believed—sometime between 1200 and 1300. The ancient rulers of the region, the mighty Wari (Huari) lords who reigned from a capital near modern Ayacucho, had fallen by 1100, in part due to a severe drought that afflicted the Andes for a century or more. In the ensuing turmoil, local chiefs across the Peruvian highlands battled over scarce water and led raiders into neighboring villages in search of food. Hordes of refugees fled to frigid, windswept hideouts above 13,000 feet.

But in the fertile, well-watered valley around Cusco, Inca farmers stood their ground. Instead of splintering apart and warring among themselves, Inca villages united into a small state capable of mounting an organized defense. And between 1150 and 1300, the Inca around Cusco began to capitalize on a major warming trend in the Andes.

As temperatures climbed, Inca farmers moved up the slopes by 800 to 1,000 feet, building tiers of agricultural terraces, irrigating their fields, and reaping record corn harvests. "These surpluses," says Alex Chepstow-Lusty, a paleoecologist at the French Institute for Andean Studies in Lima who has been studying the region's ancient climate, allowed the Inca to "free up many people for other roles, whether building roads or maintaining a large army." In time Inca rulers could call up more conscripts and supply a larger army than any neighboring chief.

With this big stick, Inca kings began eyeing the lands and resources of others. They struck marriage alliances with neighboring lords, taking their daughters as wives, and dispensed generous gifts to new allies. When a rival lord spurned their advances or stirred up trouble, they flexed their military might. In all the surrounding valleys, local lords succumbed one by one, until there was only one mighty state and one capital, the sacred city of Cusco.

Flush with success, Inca kings set their sights farther afield, on the wealthy lands surrounding Lake Titicaca. Sometime after 1400, one of the greatest Inca rulers, Pachacutec Inca Yupanqui, began planning his conquest of the south. It was the dawn of an empire.

Massed on a high, cold Peruvian plain north of the great lake in the mid-1400s, the army of the Colla bristled with battle gear, daring the Inca invaders to make war. Pachacutec scanned the enemy ranks in silence, preparing for the great battle ahead. The lords of the Titicaca region were haughty men, ruling as many as 400,000 people in kingdoms arrayed around the lake. Their lands were rich and desirable. Gold and silver veined the mountains, and herds of alpacas and llamas fattened in lush meadows. Military success in the Andes depended on such livestock. A llama, the only draft animal on the continent, could carry 70 pounds of gear on its back. Llamas, along with alpacas, also provided meat, leather, and fiber for clothing. They were jeeps, K rations, and fatigues all rolled into one—crucial military assets. If the Inca king could not conquer the Titicaca lords who owned these vast herds, he would live in fear of the day these lords would come to conquer him. Seated on a shimmering litter, Pachacutec issued the order to attack. Playing panpipes carved from the bones of enemies and war drums fashioned from the flayed skins of dead foes, his soldiers advanced toward the Colla forces, a moving wall of terror and intimidation. Then both sides charged. When the fog of battle lifted, Colla bodies littered the landscape. In the years that followed, Pachacutec and his descendants subdued all the southern lords.

"The conquest of the Titicaca Basin was the jewel in the crown of the Inca Empire," says Charles Stanish, an archaeologist at the University of California, Los Angeles. But military victory was only the first step in the Inca's grand strategy of empire building. Officials next set about establishing civil control.

If provinces mounted resistance, Inca sovereigns reshuffled their populations, deporting restive inhabitants to the Inca heartland and replacing them with loyal subjects. Residents of remote walled villages were moved to new Inca-controlled towns sited along Inca roads—roads that sped the movement of Inca troops. Inca governors ordered the construction of roadside storehouses for those troops and commanded local communities to fill them with provisions. "The Inca were the organizational geniuses of the Americas," says Stanish. Under Inca rule, Andean civilization flowered as never before. Inca engineers transformed fragmentary road networks into interconnected highways. Inca farmers mastered high-altitude agriculture, cultivating some 70 different native crops and often stockpiling three to seven years' worth of food in vast storage complexes. Imperial officials excelled at the art of inventory control, tracking storehouse contents across the realm with an ancient Andean form of computer code—colored and knotted cords known as quipus. And Inca masons raised timeless architectural masterpieces like Machu Picchu, which continues to awe visitors today.

By the time the Inca king Huayna Capac took power around 1493, little seemed beyond the reach of the Inca dynasty. To bring grandeur to his new capital in Ecuador, Huayna Capac put more than 4,500 rebellious subjects to work hauling immense stone blocks all the way from Cusco—a distance of nearly a thousand miles up and down vertiginous mountain roads. And in the Inca heartland, a small army of men and women toiled to construct a royal estate for Huayna Capac and his family. At the king's bidding, they moved the Urubamba River to the southern side of the valley. They leveled hills and drained marshes, then planted corn and other crops such as cotton, peanuts, and hot peppers from far corners of the empire. In the center of the estate, they laid stones and bricks for Huayna Capac's new country palace, Quispiguanca.

As the late afternoon sun slants down, I wander the ruins of Quispiguanca with Alan Covey, the archaeologist from SMU. Situated on the outskirts of the modern town of Urubamba, Quispiguanca basks in one of the warmest and sunniest microclimates in the region, which provided the Inca royal family a welcome escape from the cold of Cusco. The estate's gatehouses now look out on a field of pungent cilantro, and its surviving walls enclose a royal compound that once sprawled over an area equivalent to some seven soccer fields. Encircled by parkland, fields, and gardens, Quispiguanca was an Inca version of Camp David, a retreat from the world, a place for a warrior-king to unwind after military campaigning. Here Huayna Capac entertained guests in the great halls and gambled with courtiers and other favorites, while his queen gardened and tended doves. The grounds boasted a secluded lodge and a forest reserved for hunting deer and other game. In the fields hundreds of workers cleared irrigation channels, raised and mended terrace walls, and sowed corn and a host of exotic crops. These provided Huayna Capac with bountiful harvests and enough corn beer to entertain his subjects royally during Cusco's annual festivals.

Quispiguanca was not the only spectacular estate. Inca kings inherited little more than their titles, so each new sovereign built a city palace and country home for himself and his lineage shortly after assuming power. To date archaeologists and historians have located ruins of roughly a dozen royal estates built by at least six Inca kings.

Even after these kings died, they remained the powers behind the throne. "The ancestors were a key element of Andean life," says Sonia Guillén, director of Peru's Museo Leymebamba. When Huayna Capac perished of a mysterious disease in Ecuador around 1527, retainers mummified his body and carried it back to Cusco. Members of the royal family frequently visited the deceased monarch, asking his advice on vital matters and heeding the replies given by an oracle sitting at his side. Years after his death, Huayna Capac remained the owner of Quispiguanca and the surrounding estate. Indeed, royal tradition dictated that its harvest keep his mummy, servants, wives, and descendants in style for eternity.

It was during the rainy season in 1533, an auspicious time for a coronation, and thousands of people were packed into the main plaza of Cusco to celebrate the arrival of their new teenage king. Two years earlier, amid a civil war, foreign invaders had landed in the north. Metal-clad and bearing lethal new weapons, the Spaniards had journeyed to the northern Inca town of Cajamarca, where they took prisoner the Inca king, Atahuallpa. Eight months later, they executed their royal captive, and in 1533 their leader, Francisco Pizarro, picked a young prince, Manco Inca Yupanqui, to rule as a puppet king.

In the far distance, voices of the young king's bearers echoed through the streets, singing songs of praise. Falling silent, celebrants watched the royal teenager enter the square, accompanied by the mummies of his ancestors, each richly attired and seated on a splendid litter. The wizened kings and their consorts reminded all that Manco Inca descended from a long line of kings. Rulers of other realms might content themselves with displaying carved or painted images of their glorious ancestors. The Inca kings went one better, displaying the expertly preserved bodies of their forefathers.

In the months that followed, the Spanish invaders seized the palaces of Cusco and the spacious country estates and took royal women as mistresses and wives. Incensed, Manco Inca rebelled and in 1536 tried to drive them from the realm. When his army suffered defeat, he fled Cusco for the jungle city of Vilcabamba, from which he launched guerrilla attacks. The Spanish wouldn't subdue the stronghold until 1572.

In the turmoil of those decades, the Inca's sprawling network of roads, storehouses, temples, and estates began slowly falling into ruin. As the empire crumbled, the Inca and their descendants made a valiant attempt to preserve the symbols of imperial authority. Servants collected the precious bodies of the sacred kings and concealed them around Cusco, where they were worshipped in secret—and in defiance of Spanish priests. In 1559 Cusco's chief magistrate, Juan Polo de Ondegardo, resolved to stamp out this idolatry. He launched an official search for the bodies, questioning hundreds. With this information he tracked down and seized the remains of 11 Inca kings and several queens.

For a time colonial officials in Lima displayed the mummies of Pachacutec, Huayna Capac, and two other royals as curiosities in the Hospital of San Andrés in Lima, a facility that admitted only European patients. But the damp coastal climate wreaked havoc with the bodies. So Spanish officials buried the greatest of the Inca kings in secrecy in Lima, far from the Andes and the people who loved and worshipped them.

In 2001 Brian Bauer and two Peruvian colleagues, historian Teodoro Hampe Martínez and archaeologist Antonio Coello Rodríguez, went looking for the mummies of the Inca kings, hoping to right a historic wrong and restore to Peruvians an important part of their cultural heritage. "Can you imagine," Bauer asks, "how American citizens would feel if the British had taken the bodies of the first several presidents back to London during the War of 1812?" For months Bauer and his colleagues pored over old architectural plans of the Hospital of San Andrés, now a girls' school in central Lima. Eventually they identified several possibilities for the burial site of Pachacutec and Huayna Capac. Using ground-penetrating radar, they scanned the likeliest areas, turning up what appeared to be a vaulted underground crypt. Bauer and his Peruvian teammates were thrilled.

When the archaeologists finally dug down and opened the door of the dusty chamber, they were crestfallen. The crypt lay empty. Quite possibly, says Bauer, workmen removed the contents while renovating the hospital after a severe earthquake. Today no one can say where Peru's greatest kings lie. Concludes Bauer sadly, "The fate of the royal Inca mummies remains unknown."

Critical Thinking

1. Why are there so few clues about the lives of Inca kings? In what ways are archaeologists making up for lost time?
2. Until recently, what did most historians and archaeologists believe about the founding of the Inca Empire? What did Brian Bauer find to the contrary?
3. How did the Inca kings of Cuzco come to power?
4. Why did Pachacutec decide that he would have to conquer the Titicaca Basin?
5. In what ways did the Inca become the "organizational geniuses of the Americas"?

6. How did the royal estates function as a retreat for the Inca kings?
7. What did the Spanish do to take control of the Inca? In what ways did the Inca resist?

Create Central

www.mhhe.com/createcentral

Internet References

National Geographic Magazine
http://ngm.nationalgeographic.com

Society for American Archaeology
www.saa.org

Society for Historical Archaeology
www.sha.org

From *National Geographic*, April 2011. Copyright © 2011 by National Geographic Society. Reprinted by permission.

Article

Prepared by: Mari Pritchard Parker, *Pasadena City College* and
Elvio Angeloni, *Pasadena City College*

Return to the Trail of Tears

Excavations at the untouched site of a U.S. Army fort are providing a rare look at the path along which thousands of Cherokee were forcibly moved to Oklahoma.

MARION BLACKBURN

Learning Outcomes

After reading this article, you will be able to:

- Describe the Cherokee removal to Oklahoma in terms of the reasons for it and the Cherokee resistance.
- Describe Fort Armistad as an important archaeological site for understanding the conditions of the Cherokee removal.

Long time we travel on way to new land. People feel bad when they leave Old Nation. Women cry and made sad wails. Children cry and many men cry, and all look sad like when friends die, but they say nothing and just put heads down and keep on go towards West. Many days pass and people die very much.

—A Cherokee account from *The Oklahoman*, 1929, cited by John Ehle in *Trail of Tears: The Rise and Fall of the Cherokee Nation*, 1988

It's easy to miss this subtle groove, covered in pine straw and vines, worn in the ground of eastern Tennessee. In the summer of 1838, about 13,000 Cherokee walked this path from their homes in the Appalachian Mountains to a new, government-mandated homeland in Oklahoma. They traveled over land and water and were held in military camps along the way. Unlike other settlers heading West, who saw in America's open expanses the hope of a new life, the Cherokee traveled with a military escort. They left behind highly coveted land that was, even as they walked, being divided up among white land speculators.

The Trail of Tears was a journey of some 900 miles that took approximately nine months to complete. After they were rounded up from their villages and homes, the Cherokee were assembled in large internment camps, where some waited for weeks before heading out in waves of approximately 1,000, following different paths, depending on the season. As many as 4,000 died along the way from dehydration, tuberculosis, whooping cough, and other hardships—by some accounts, a dozen or more were buried at each stop. Some escaped along the way and were caught and returned to the march like criminals. Still others refused to leave, hiding out in the mountains, joining others on small farms where, stripped of tribal connections and burdened with unclear legal status, they faced an uncertain future.

Despite all our historical knowledge of the forced removal, there has been little study of the archaeology of the trail, the internment camps along the way, and the farms that sheltered those who stayed behind. The military forts that held the Cherokee in crowded, unsanitary conditions have been largely consumed by development or otherwise lost. The homesteads back East, where resistors lived under constant threat of arrest, went undocumented. Buildings, roads, farms, and floods have claimed almost all of these sites. In addition to a lack of material evidence, there has long been an uneasy, even contentious, relationship between Native Americans and archaeologists. Through neglect and distrust, this sad chapter has been at risk of fading from collective memory, taking with it any chance to understand the relationships between refugees and soldiers, and cultural information about the Cherokee themselves—what they carried, how they traveled, why they died.

That now stands to change. In eastern Tennessee, archaeologists are excavating the site of Fort Armistead, a U.S. Army encampment that served as a holding area and one of the first stops for North Carolina Cherokee on their forced journey West. Hidden deep in Cherokee National Forest, the site has managed to escape the damage or destruction that has visited nearly every other significant trace of the trail and camps.

Fort Armistead lodged as many as 3,000 Cherokee over several months in 1838. Today, the site sits on about four acres of a mountaintop clearing. It consists of foundation blocks, collapsed piles of chimney stones, trash pits, and window glass—plus an enigmatic stone pipe—all settled gently into the ground, covered by only a thin layer of dirt, leaves, straw, and moss. For four weeks in the summer of 2011, archaeologists from the University of North Carolina at Chapel Hill (UNC), the U.S. Forest Service (USFS), and Lee University in Cleveland, Tennessee, held the fourth field season at the site. The same archaeologists also have been conducting excavations about 35 miles east, across the North Carolina border, at the sites of long-forgotten homesteads where fugitive Cherokee found refuge and community.

"Any [Cherokee] who came from North Carolina came through here," says archaeologist Brett Riggs, an adjunct associate professor at UNC, of the Fort Armistead site. "We have an archaeological site and records that speak directly to it."

Spindly hardwoods and pines surround the clearing. The archaeologists began their efforts in 2006 at the invitation of USFS officials, who had just purchased the property from private owners. Artifacts have been found throughout the immediate area, but the main digs of the 2011 field season focused on a space at the northern end about the size of two city buses. Exposed cut stones set in powdery soil, chimney blocks, and the remains of fire pits compose what was once the barracks area. Another foundation there probably supported the quartermaster's residence, and a pit across the site likely served as a powder magazine. "You are right in the footsteps of the Cherokee," says Quentin Bass, an archaeologist with the USFS. "[Fort Armistead] is the only example of a removal-era fort that essentially hasn't been disturbed since the soldiers left. It's the dream for an archaeologist—to find an untouched site to explore and preserve."

These undisturbed remains of apparently substantial structures suggest that the federal government poured significant staff and resources into the fort during its military occupation. Beyond the barrack foundations, in a sunny opening in the tree cover, is a key public place, the fort's parade ground. Wide dirt roads lead right and left beyond that, and a gentle slope leads down to a creek.

Fort Armistead was formally established in 1832, ostensibly to protect local Cherokee from gold prospectors. It was the only U.S. outpost in the Cherokee Nation, whose land at that time extended from western North Carolina and eastern Tennessee south through Georgia and into Alabama. The fort was near a corridor that already served as a major source of cultural interaction, where different tribes traded, especially the Cherokee and the Creek (also known as the Muscogee). Cattle and pig rustlers, slave traders heading to South Carolina, gold miners, trappers, and hunters all came through along this route, known as the Unicoi Turnpike. Indeed, soldiers stationed at the fort often appropriated goods (including whiskey) for themselves, Riggs says. For the next several years, the fort was irregularly staffed and maintained.

Prior to the Civil War, trade and land speculation in the South often put businessmen and speculators at odds with Native Americans who occupied the land they coveted. The federal response to this problem was the Indian Removal Act, which passed by a narrow margin in 1830. The law marked a monumental shift for the young nation by officially claiming Native lands for its expanding population and farming needs. The act granted the Natives money and land in the West if they left their homes in the South. To sell the act to the public, the federal government asserted that Native Americans were primitive migrants—hunter-gatherers who would not be able to modernize. It was also cast as a measure to protect Natives from more violent efforts to claim the land on which they lived. However, it clearly overlooked that many tribes throughout the Southeast lived in villages and towns and were adept pastoralists, farmers, and entrepreneurs, with strong spiritual ties to their lands. President Andrew Jackson, a land speculator himself, championed the controversial act and stood to profit from it. In the ensuing decades, the legislation stoked moral outrage that also helped fuel the abolitionist movement.

The Cherokee fought eviction through official channels, eventually winning support for independent status from the U.S. Supreme Court—a decision that prompted Jackson to say, "[Chief Justice] John Marshall has made his decision; let him enforce it now if he can." Harassment, uncertainty, and eroding negotiating leverage ultimately fatigued the Cherokee. In 1835, a minority Cherokee group agreed to relocation, or removal, under the terms of the Treaty of New Echota. Deportation might then have seemed a kind of escape. The treaty included $5 million for the tribe, along with compensation for the land and possessions they abandoned.

The Cherokee, which white Americans called one of the Five Civilized Tribes, considered themselves American and wanted to join the growing country as participating members. In 1827, the Cherokee ratified a constitution modeled after the American one. They also assumed some aspects of American culture, in an effort to acculturate and escape the fate they had seen befall other Southeastern tribes, such as the Choctaw, the first tribe to move to the West in 1830, or the Seminoles, who violently resisted removal from Florida.

"The Cherokee were trying to play by American rules," says archaeologist Lance Greene, who worked with Riggs at UNC and now works at the Fort Armistead dig. "They were forming their own national government. A large part of the population had converted to Christianity. They sang Christian hymns as they were marching. There's still an image of savage Indians living in tepees, but maybe the Cherokee, more than anybody, made an attempt [to acculturate]. But ultimately it failed."

Despite the apparent Cherokee desire to join instead of fight, the federal government began a military buildup in preparation for what it assumed would become a long, bloody conflict. As part of this militarization, they reactivated Fort Armistead in 1836 and occupied it with soldiers who marched there from Florida. By the summer of 1838, more than 7,000 federal and state troops were stationed throughout the Cherokee Nation—a remarkably high concentration for America's nascent military.

"What drove their idea of a protracted conflict in North Carolina was the unanimous opposition to the Treaty of New Echota and strong activism to prevent its ratification, and then to have it annulled," Riggs says. "There were rumors afoot that there would be a guerilla war in North Carolina. The military was poised for an eventuality that never happened."

There was no insurgency and little resistance when the military began the roundup of the Cherokee in June and July 1838. Most of them gathered what belongings they could and came together in their town squares or waited for a soldier's knock on the door (though some did seek refuge in the mountains).

Coming together as they accepted their fate became a final act of preservation for their families, communities, and values, Riggs says. "They were trying to promote the cohesion of their group," he adds. "They were making a political statement, a moral statement. They believed very strongly in the ideals of this country and the moral imperative to treat everybody fairly"

For Cherokee living in North Carolina, Fort Armistead was the first stop outside their home state. It held as many as 800 to 1,000 for stays of two or three nights. These included not only the Cherokee, but also those traveling with them, including Creek and African Americans, some of them slaves. They continued on to a series of other outposts (there were up to 30 forts or stops along the trail) in Tennessee, including Fort Cass, the main holding site, near present-day Charleston, which was known for its especially unbearable conditions. In summer 1838, when drought made river levels so low that a planned river route became impossible—and heat made an overland course deadly—the march was delayed until fall, leaving thousands of Cherokee to languish there to face disease and death.

Once the Cherokee were moved and soldiers left in 1838, Fort Armistead was abandoned. From the Civil War period through the turn of the century, the site was privately owned, until it was purchased by the USFS in 2005, and archaeological exploration began the next year.

"We poked around and realized that, in fact, the site had never been plowed," Riggs says, a common fate for many archaeological sites in the Southeast. "Many of the anomalies that we were seeing on the surface, which I thought were small piles pushed up by a bulldozer, were melted chimneys and cellar pits that had been filled in [by settling debris]." Riggs says the site is in "as nearly pristine condition as you find in the East.

"When you start, you are immediately within an archaeological feature. You have to approach it with kid gloves from the outset," he adds.

The 2011 dig season, which also included Bass and students from Lee University, focused on several large architectural features, primarily the quartermaster's house and the enlistedmen's quarters. The foundation stones easily emerged from the surrounding dirt, lying so near the surface that in many cases soil could be removed by vacuum. The archaeologists discovered a surprising solidity and permanence to these structures, suggesting a highly organized and militarized approach to the removal of the Cherokee. In addition, the stone most likely was brought from up to five miles away, indicating extensive manpower was likely needed for the construction.

"The structure was even more substantial than we thought," Greene says. "It's almost a solid rock floor. If you have something that heavy, then you're almost building it as a foundation for a cannon. But they didn't have that firepower at the camp. They may have overbuilt some of the structures to keep the soldiers occupied. They must have had a stonemason who was skilled enough to do that work. The stone is cut to make very tight joints. They've done some fine stone work."

The seemingly grand military scale of the fort was not necessary to control the Cherokee, the demeanor of whom has been described as subdued and orderly. The fort grounds ordinarily used for drills may instead have served as a sleeping and cooking area for the internees. Direct evidence of Cherokee at the fort—or anywhere along the Trail of Tears for that matter—is vanishingly rare. Yet one find at Fort Armistead not only confirms the Cherokee presence in the area before their removal, but also suggests what sort of artifacts might be unearthed that could help reveal how the Cherokee and the soldiers stationed there interacted.

The broken remains of a carved stone Cherokee pipe were discovered at the site of the soldiers' barracks. The pipe, which was probably discarded before it was fully carved, was found in a deposit with military regalia that date it to a time before removal. So while it says little about the experience of the Cherokee as they were interned there, it implies that before removal, "you had Cherokees coming in and hanging around the fort," Riggs says.

"To find evidence of their presence is amazing," Greene adds. "[The soldiers and Cherokee] are dealing with each other on a face-to-face basis. It brings up those questions, makes you think about what happened on the ground. How could you explain this?"

Other finds in 2011 include ceramics, such as pearl ware, and glass dating the site to the removal period. A faceted blue glass bead, from the 1820s or 1830s, emerged from the foundation stones (and may, in fact, be of Cherokee origin). Also, more than 4,200 distinct metal objects have been documented.

The excavation and study of the site of Fort Armistead is beginning to flesh out the story of those who left. Now, the Cherokee, whose capital is Tahlequah in eastern Oklahoma, number some 300,000—comprising the United States' second largest tribal nation. But the small band of Cherokee who stayed behind left a smaller but still significant legacy in southern Appalachia.

It is estimated that about 400 Cherokee remained in North Carolina after the others were removed. They hid in the mountains where, unable to trade publicly, they found ways to survive by cooperating with one another. They often lived together in homesteads, and the Eastern Band of the Cherokee, which today numbers about 10,000, descends from residents of those homesteads.

In Andrews, North Carolina, just over the border from his work at Fort Armistead, Greene is excavating a farm once owned by John Welch, a Cherokee, and his white wife, Elizabeth. After removal, the state took over their land. John avoided relocation to Oklahoma because of his marriage, and Elizabeth repurchased the farm, where they further defied the Indian Removal Act, Greene says. There, they sheltered about a hundred Cherokee refugees. At the homestead site, Greene has found bones of rabbit, deer, and small game animals, such as songbirds. Among the food traces, there is a notable lack of long bones, which Cherokee often cooked and cracked open for the marrow. Greene says this is a significant cultural marker—the family continued many Cherokee practices. "One of the strongest signs of that is the food remains," he says.

The Welch settlement and others, perhaps hundreds yet undiscovered, will help explain the different experiences and separate paths of the two groups of Cherokee split by the trauma of removal. "In a broad sense, for all Cherokees, the removal is a watershed event," Greene says. "It's tied to the broader tribal history of tragedy and trauma." It divided the tribe, but also, he suggests, forged the resilience and character of the modern Cherokee.

In 1987, Congress designated the Trail of Tears National Historic Trail, about 2,200 miles across nine states. Fort Armistead is on the trail and is a remarkably fragile site. Hidden cameras, motion monitors, and a high-tech security system protect it from looters and unauthorized visitors. Among the visitors allowed at the site are Cherokee from Oklahoma, whose ancestors surely passed through the fort.

For archaeology student Beau Carroll, a Cherokee who grew up in western North Carolina, excavating at the site of Fort Armistead allowed him to experience a deeper connection with his past. He remembers his late great-grandmother telling him of being sent to boarding school, as many Cherokee children were, where she was instructed to follow white American traditions. She cried when she remembered it, he says. Working at the site gave him "an indescribable feeling, a really sad feeling."

"When I'm working, the archaeologist in me gets really excited," says Carroll. "I forget where I am. But then I take a break and look at that trail, and I can't believe what happened."

Critical Thinking

1. What were the circumstances and conditions of the Cherokee removal to Oklahoma in 1838?
2. Why is Fort Armistad an important archaeological site for understanding the Cherokee removal?
3. What was the purpose of the Indian Removal Act and why did the Cherokee resist it?
4. Why did the Cherokee consider themselves American and want to join the growing country as participating members?
5. What is the importance of Armistad as an archaeological site?

Create Central

www.mhhe.com/createcentral

Internet References

Society for American Archaeology
www.saa.org

Society for Historical Archaeology
www.sha.org

USD Anthropology
www.usd.edu/anth

MARION BLACKBURN is a freelance writer based in Greenville, NC.

Blackburn, Marion. From *Archaeology*, March/April 2012, pp. 53–54, 56–58, 64. Copyright © 2012 by Archaeological Institute of America. Reprinted by permission of *Archaeology Magazine*. www.archaeology.org

Article

Prepared by: Mari Pritchard Parker, *Pasadena City College* and
Elvio Angeloni, *Pasadena City College*

Living through the Donner Party

The nineteenth-century survivors of the infamous Donner Party told cautionary tales of starvation and cannibalism, greed and self-sacrifice. But not until now are we learning why the survivors survived.

JARED DIAMOND

Learning Outcomes

After reading this article, you will be able to:

- Discuss cannibalism in the Donner Party in terms of why it happened and how it was practiced.
- Discuss the lessons of the Donner Party in terms of the importance of gender, age, family ties, and membership in social groups.

> "Mrs. Fosdick and Mrs. Foster, after eating, returned to the body of [Mr.] Fosdick. There, in spite of the widow's entreaties, Mrs. Foster took out the liver and heart from the body and removed the arms and legs. . . . [Mrs. Fosdick] was forced to see her husband's heart broiled over the fire." "He eat her body and found her flesh the best he had ever tasted! He further stated that he obtained from her body at least four pounds of fat." "Eat baby raw, stewed some of Jake and roasted his head, not good meat, taste like sheep with the rot."
>
> —George Stewart,
> Ordeal by *Hunger: The Story of the Donner Party*

Nearly a century and a half after it happened, the story of the Donner Party remains one of the most riveting tragedies in U.S. history. Partly that's because of its lurid elements: almost half the party died, and many of their bodies were defiled in an orgy of cannibalism. Partly, too, it's because of the human drama of noble self-sacrifice and base murder juxtaposed. The Donner Party began as just another nameless pioneer trek to California, but it came to symbolize the Great American Dream gone awry.

By now the tale of that disastrous journey has been told so often that seemingly nothing else remains to be said—or so I thought, until my friend Donald Grayson at the University of Washington sent me an analysis that he had published in the *Journal of Anthropological Research*. By comparing the fates of all Donner Party members, Grayson identified striking differences between those who came through the ordeal alive and those who were not so lucky. In doing so he has made the lessons of the Donner Party universal. Under more mundane life-threatening situations, who among us too will be "lucky"?

Grayson's insights did not depend on new discoveries about the ill-fated pioneers nor on new analytical techniques, but on that most elusive ingredient of great science: a new idea about an old problem. Given the same information, any of you could extract the same conclusions. In fact, on page 163 you'll find the roster of the Donner Party members along with a few personal details about each of them and their fate. If you like, you can try to figure out for yourself some general rules about who is most likely to die when the going gets tough.

The Lewis and Clark Expedition of 1804 to 1806 was the first to cross the continent, but they didn't take along ox-drawn wagons, which were a requirement for pioneer settlement. Clearing a wagon route through the West's unmapped deserts and mountains proved far more difficult than finding a footpath. Not until 1841 was the first attempt made to haul wagons and settlers overland to California, and only in 1844 did the effort succeed. Until the Gold Rush of 1848 unleashed a flood of emigrants, wagon traffic to California remained a trickle.

As of 1846, when the Donner Party set out, the usual wagon route headed west from St. Louis to Fort Bridger in Wyoming, then northwest into Idaho before turning southwest through Nevada and on to California. However, at that time a popular guidebook author named Lansford Hastings was touting a shortcut that purported to cut many miles from the long trek. Hastings's route continued west from Fort Bridger through the Wasatch mountain range, then south of Utah's Great Salt Lake across the Salt Lake Desert, and finally rejoined the usual California Trail in Nevada.

In the summer of 1846 a number of wagon parties set out for California from Fort Bridger. One, which left shortly before the Donner Party, was guided by Hastings himself. Using his shortcut, the party would eventually make it to California, albeit with great difficulty.

The pioneers who would become the members of the Donner Party were in fact all headed for Fort Bridger to join the Hastings expedition, but they arrived too late. With Hastings thus unavailable to serve as a guide, some of these California-bound emigrants opted for the usual route instead. Others, however, decided to try the Hastings Cutoff anyway. In all, 87 people in 23 wagons chose the cutoff. They consisted of 10 unrelated families and 16 lone individuals, most of them well-to-do midwestern farmers and townspeople who had met by chance and joined forces for protection. None had had any real experience of the western mountains or Indians. They became known as the Donner Party because they elected an elderly Illinois farmer named George Donner as their captain. They left Fort Bridger on July 31, one of the last parties of that summer to begin the long haul to California.

Within a fortnight the Donner Party suffered their first crushing setback, when they reached Utah's steep, brush-covered Wasatch Mountains. The terrain was so wild that, in order to cross, the men had first to build a wagon road. It took 16 backbreaking days to cover just 36 miles, and afterward the people and draft animals were worn out. A second blow followed almost immediately thereafter, west of the Great Salt Lake, when the party ran into an 80-mile stretch of desert. To save themselves from death by thirst, some of the pioneers were forced to unhitch their wagons, rush ahead with their precious animals to the next spring, and return to retrieve the wagons. The rush became a disorganized panic, and many of the animals died, wandered off, or were killed by Indians. Four wagons and large quantities of supplies had to be abandoned. Not until September 30—two full months after leaving Fort Bridger—did the Donner Party emerge from their fatal shortcut to rejoin the California Trail.

By November 1 they had struggled up to Truckee Lake— later renamed Donner Lake—at an elevation of 6,000 feet on the eastern flank of the Sierra Nevada, west of the present-day California-Nevada border. Snow had already begun to fall during the last days of October, and now a fierce snowstorm defeated the exhausted party as they attempted to cross a 7,200-foot pass just west of the lake. With that storm, a trap snapped shut around them: they had set out just a little too late and proceeded just a little too slowly. They now faced a long winter at the lake, with very little food.

Death had come to the Donner Party even before it reached the lake. There were five casualties: on August 29 Luke Halloran died of "consumption" (presumably tuberculosis); on October 5 James Reed knifed John Snyder in self-defense, during a fight that broke out when two teams of oxen became entangled; three days later Lewis Keseberg abandoned an old man named Hardkoop who had been riding in Keseberg's wagon, and most of the party refused to stop and search for him; sometime after October 13 two German emigrants, Joseph Reinhardt and Augustus Spitzer, murdered a rich German named Wolfinger while ostensibly helping him to cache his property; and on October 20 William Pike was shot as he and his brother-in-law were cleaning a pistol.

They cut off and roasted flesh from the corpses, restrained only by the rule that no one partook of his or her relative's body.

In addition, four party members had decided earlier to walk out ahead to Sutter's Fort (now Sacramento) to bring back supplies and help. One of those four, Charles Stanton, rejoined the party on October 19, bringing food and two Indians sent by Sutter. Thus, of the 87 original members of the Donner Party, 79—plus the two Indians—were pinned down in the winter camp at Donner Lake.

The trapped pioneers lay freezing inside crude tents and cabins. They quickly exhausted their little remaining food, then killed and ate their pack animals. Then they ate their dogs. Finally they boiled hides and blankets to make a glue-like soup. Gross selfishness became rampant, as families with food refused to share it with destitute families or demanded exorbitant payment. On December 16 the first death came to the winter camp when 24-year-old Baylis Williams succumbed to starvation. On that same day 15 of the strongest people—5 women and 10 men, including Charles Stanton and the two Indians—set out across the pass on homemade snowshoes, virtually without food and in appallingly cold and stormy weather, in the hope of reaching outside help. Four of the men left behind their families; three of the women left behind their children.

On the sixth morning an exhausted Stanton let the others go on ahead of him; he remained behind to die. On the ninth day the remaining 14 for the first time openly broached the subject of cannibalism which had already been on their minds. They debated drawing lots as to who should be eaten, or letting two people shoot it out until one was killed and could be eaten. Both proposals were rejected in favor of waiting for someone to die naturally.

Such opportunities soon arose. On Christmas Eve, as a 23-year-old man named Antoine, a bachelor, slept in a heavy stupor, he stretched out his arm such that his hand fell into the fire. A companion pulled it out at once. When it fell in a second time, however, no one intervened—they simply let it burn. Antoine died, then Franklin Graves, then Patrick Dolan, then Lemuel Murphy. The others cut off and roasted flesh from the corpses, restrained only by the rule that no one would partake of his or her own relative's body. When the corpses were consumed, the survivors began eating old shoes.

On January 5, 23-year-old Jay Fosdick died, only to be cut up and boiled by Mrs. Foster over the protests of Mrs. Fosdick. Soon after, the frenzied Mr. Foster chased down, shot, and killed the two Indians to eat them. That left 7 of the original 15 snowshoers to stagger into the first white settlement in California, after a midwinter trek of 33 days through the snow.

On January 31 the first rescue team set out from the settlement for Donner Lake. It would take three more teams and two and a half months before the ordeal was all over. During that time many more people died, either in the winter camp or while fighting their way out with the rescue teams. There was never enough food, and by the end of February, cannibalism had established itself at the lake.

When William Eddy and William Foster, who had gotten out with the snowshoers, reached the lake with the third rescue team on March 13, they found that Keseberg had eaten their sons. The Foster child's grandmother accused the starving Keseberg of having taken the child to bed with him one night, strangling him, and hanging the corpse on the wall before eating it. Keseberg, in his defense, claimed the children had died naturally. When the rescuers left the lake the next day to return to California, they left Keseberg behind with just four others: the elderly Lavina Murphy, the badly injured George Donner, his 4-year-old nephew Samuel and his healthy wife Tamsen, who could have traveled but insisted on staying with her dying husband.

The fourth and last rescue team reached the lake on April 17 to find Keseberg alone, surrounded by indescribable filth and mutilated corpses. George Donner's body lay with his skull split open to permit the extraction of his brains. Three frozen ox legs lay in plain view almost uneaten beside a kettle of cut-up human flesh. Near Keseberg sat two kettles of blood and a large pan full of fresh human liver and lungs. He alleged that his four companions had died natural deaths, but he was frank about having eaten them. As to why he had not eaten ox leg instead, he explained that it was too dry: human liver and lungs tasted better, and human brains made a good soup. As for Tamsen Donner, Keseberg noted that she tasted the best, being well endowed with fat. In a bundle held by Keseberg the rescuers found silk, jewelry, pistols, and money that had belonged to George Donner.

After returning to Sutter's Fort, one of the rescuers accused Keseberg of having murdered his companions, prompting Keseberg to sue for defamation of character. In the absence of legal proof of murder the court verdict was equivocal, and the issue of Keseberg's guilt remains disputed to this day. However, Tamsen Donner's death is especially suspicious since she had been in strong physical condition when last seen by the third rescue team.

> **Experience has taught us that the youngest and oldest people are the most vulnerable even under normal conditions, and their vulnerability increases under stress.**

Thus, out of 87 Donner Party members, 40 died: 5 before reaching Donner Lake, 22 in their winter camp at the lake, and 13 (plus the two Indians) during or just after efforts to leave the lake. Why those particular 40? From the facts given in the roster, can you draw conclusions, as Grayson did, as to who was in fact the most likely to die?

As a simple first test, compare the fates of Donner Party males and females irrespective of age. Most of the males (30 out of 53) died; most of the females (24 out of 34) survived. The 57 percent death rate among males was nearly double the 29 percent death rate among females.

Next, consider the effect of age irrespective of sex. The worst toll was among the young and the old. Without exception, everyone over the age of 50 died, as did most of the children below the age of 5. Surprisingly, children and teenagers between the ages of 5 and 19 fared better than did adults in their prime (age 20 to 39): half the latter, but less than one-fifth of the former, died.

By looking at the effects of age and sex simultaneously, the advantage the women had over the men becomes even more striking. Most of the female deaths were among the youngest and oldest, who were already doomed by their age. Among those party members aged 5 to 39—the ones whose ages left them some reasonable chance of survival—half the men but only 5 percent of the women died.

The dates of death provide deeper insight. Of the 35 unfortunates who died after reaching the lake, 14 men but not a single woman had died by the end of January. Only in February did women begin to buckle under. From February onward the death toll was essentially equal by sex—11 men, 10 women. The differences in dates of death simply underscore the lesson of the death rates themselves: the Donner Party women were far hardier than the men.

Thus, sex and age considered together account for much of the luck of the survivors. Most of those who died (39 of the 40 victims) had the misfortune to be of the wrong sex, or the wrong age, or both.

Experience has taught us that the youngest and oldest people are the most vulnerable even under normal conditions, and their vulnerability increases under stress. In many natural disasters, those under 10 or over 50 suffered the highest mortality. For instance, children under 10 accounted for over half the 240,000 deaths in the 1970 Bangladesh cyclone, though they constituted only one-third of the exposed population.

Much of the vulnerability of the old and young under stress is simply a matter of insufficient physical strength: these people are less able to walk out through deep snow (in the case of the Donner Party) or to cling to trees above the height of flood waters (in the case of the Bangladesh cyclone). Babies have special problems. Per pound of body weight a baby has twice an adult's surface area, which means double the area across which body heat can escape. To maintain body temperature, babies have to increase their metabolic rate when air temperature drops only a few degrees below body temperature, whereas adults don't have to do so until a drop of 20 to 35 degrees. At cold temperatures the factor by which babies must increase their metabolism to stay warm is several times that for adults. These considerations place even well-fed babies at risk under cold conditions. And the Donner Party babies were at a crippling further disadvantage because they had so little food to fuel their metabolism. They literally froze to death.

But what gave the women such an edge over the men? Were the pioneers practicing the noble motto "women and children first" when it came to dividing food? Unfortunately, "women and children last" is a more accurate description of how most men behave under stress. As the *Titanic* sank, male crew

Manifest of a Tragic Journey

Donner Family

Jacob Donner	M	65	died in Nov. in winter camp
George Donner	M	62	died in Apr. in winter camp
Elizabeth Donner	F	45	died in Mar. in winter camp
Tamsen Donner	F	45	died in Apr. in winter camp
Elitha Donner	F	14	
Solomon Hook	M	14	
William Hook	M	12	died Feb. 28 with first rescue team
Leanna Donner	F	12	
George Donner	M	9	
Mary Donner	F	7	
Frances Donner	F	6	
Isaac Donner	M	5	died Mar. 7 with second rescue team
Georgia Donner	F	4	
Samuel Donner	M	4	died in Apr. in winter camp
Lewis Donner	M	3	died Mar. 7 or 8 in winter camp
Eliza Donner	F	3	

Murphy-Foster-Pike Family

Lavina Murphy	F	50	died around Mar. 19 in winter camp
William Foster	M	28	
William Pike	M	25	died Oct. 20 by gunshot
Sara Foster	F	23	
Harriet Pike	F	21	
John Landrum Murphy	M	15	died Jan. 31 in winter camp
Mary Murphy	F	13	
Lemuel Murphy	M	12	died Dec. 27 with snowshoers
William Murphy	M	11	
Simon Murphy	M	10	
George Foster	M	4	died in early Mar. in winter camp
Naomi Pike	F	3	
Catherine Pike	F	1	died Feb. 20 in winter camp

Graves-Fosdick Family

Franklin Graves	M	57	died Dec 24. with snowshoers
Elizabeth Graves	F	47	died Mar. 8 with second rescue team
Jay Fosdick	M	23	died Jan. 5 with snowshoers
Sarah Fosdick	F	22	
William Graves	M	18	
Eleanor Graves	F	15	
Lavina Graves	F	13	
Nancy Graves	F	9	
Jonathan Graves	M	7	
Franklin Graves Jr.	M	5	died Mar. 8 with second rescue team
Elizabeth Graves	F	1	died soon after rescue by second team

Breen Family

Patrick Breen	M	40	
Mary Breen	F	40	
John Breen	M	14	
Edward Breen	M	13	
Patrick Breen Jr.	M	11	
Simon Breen	M	9	
Peter Breen	M	7	
James Breen	M	4	
Isabella Breen	F	1	

Reed Family

James Reed	M	46	
Margaret Reed	F	32	
Virginia Reed	F	12	
Patty Reed	F	8	
James Reed Jr.	M	5	
Thomas Reed	M	3	

Eddy Family

William Eddy	M	28	
Eleanor Eddy	F	25	died Feb. 7 in winter camp
James Eddy	M	3	died in early Mar. in winter camp
Margaret Eddy	F	1	died Feb. 4 in winter camp

Keseberg Family

Lewis Keseberg	M	32	
Phillipine Keseberg	F	32	
Ada Keseberg	F	3	died Feb. 24 with first rescue team
Lewis Keseberg Jr.	M	1	died Jan. 24 in winter camp

McCutchen Family

William McCutchen	M	30	
Amanda McCutchen	F	24	
Harriet McCutchen	F	1	died Feb. 2 in winter camp

Williams Family

Eliza Williams	F	25	
Baylis Williams	M	24	died Dec. 16 in winter camp

Wolfinger Family

Mr. Wolfinger	M	?	killed around Oct. 13 by Reinhardt and Spitzer
Mrs. Wolfinger	F	?	

Unrelated Individuals

Mr. Hardkoop	M	60	died around Oct. 8, abandoned by Lewis Keseberg
Patrick Dolan	M	40	died Dec. 25 with snowshoers
Charles Stanton	M	35	died around Dec. 21 with snowshoers
Charles Burger	M	30	died Dec. 29 in winter camp
Joseph Reinhardt	M	30	died in Nov. or early Dec. in winter camp
Augustus Spitzer	M	30	died Feb. 7 in winter camp
John Denton	M	28	died Feb. 24 with first rescue team
Milton Elliot	M	28	died Feb. 9 in winter camp
Luke Halloran	M	25	died Aug. 29 of consumption
William Herron	M	25	
Samuel Shoemaker	M	25	died in Nov. or early Dec. in winter camp
James Smith	M	25	died in Nov. or early Dec. in winter camp
James Smith	M	25	died in Nov. or early Dec. in winter camp
John Snyder	M	25	killed Oct. 5 by James Reed
Jean Baptiste Trubode	M	23	
Antoine	M	23	died Dec. 24 with snowshoers
Noah James	M	20	

members took many places in lifeboats while leaving women and children of steerage class below decks to drown. Much grosser male behavior emerged when the steamship *Atlantic* sank in 1879: the death toll included 294 of the 295 women and children on board, but only 187 of the 636 men. In the Biafran famine of the late 1960s, when relief agencies tried to distribute food to youngsters under 10 and to pregnant and nursing women, Biafran men gave a brutally frank response: "Stop all this rubbish, it is we men who shall have the food, let the children die, we will make new children after the war." Similarly, accounts by Donner Party members yield no evidence of hungry men deferring to women, and babies fared especially poorly.

Instead, we must seek some cause other than male self-sacrifice to account for the survival of Donner Party women. One contributing factor is that the men were busy killing each other. Four of the five deaths before the pioneers reached the lake, plus the deaths of the two Indians, involved male victims of male violence, a pattern that fits widespread human experience.

However, invoking male violence still leaves 26 of 30 Donner Party male deaths unexplained. It also fails to explain why men began starving and freezing to death nearly two months before women did. Evidently the women had a big physiological advantage. This could be an extreme expression of the fact that, at every age and for all leading causes of death—from cancer and car accidents to heart disease and suicide—the death rate is far higher for men than for women. While the reasons for this ubiquitous male vulnerability remain debated, there are several compelling reasons why men are more likely than women to die under the extreme conditions the Donner Party faced.

The Donner Party records make it vividly clear that family members stuck together and helped one another at the expense of the others.

First, men are bigger than women. Typical body weights for the world as a whole are about 140 pounds for men and only 120 pounds for women. Hence, even while lying down and doing nothing, men need more food to support their basal metabolism. They also need more energy than women do for equivalent physical activity. Even for sedentary people, the typical metabolic rate for an average-size woman is 25 percent lower than an average-size man's. Under conditions of cold temperatures and heavy physical activity, such as were faced by the Donner Party men when doing the backbreaking work of cutting the wagon road or hunting for food, men's metabolic rates can be double those of women.

To top it all off, women have more fat reserves than men: fat makes up 22 percent of the body weight of an average non-obese, well-nourished woman, but only 16 percent of a similar man. More of the man's weight is instead made up of muscle, which gets burned up much more quickly than does fat. Thus, when there simply was no more food left, the Donner Party men burned up their body reserves much faster than did the women. Furthermore, much of women's fat is distributed under the skin and acts as heat insulation, so that they can withstand cold temperatures better than men can. Women don't have to raise their metabolic rate to stay warm as soon as men do.

These physiological factors easily surpass male murderousness in accounting for all those extra male deaths in the Donner Party. Indeed, a microcosm of the whole disaster was the escape attempt by 15 people on snowshoes, lasting 33 days in midwinter. Of the ten men who set out, two were murdered by another man, six starved or froze to death, and only two survived. Not a single one of the five women with them died.

Even with all these explanations, there is still one puzzling finding to consider: the unexpectedly high death toll of people in their prime, age 20 to 39. That toll proves to be almost entirely of the men: 67 percent of the men in that age range (14 out of 21) died, a much higher proportion than among the teenage boys (only 20 percent). Closer scrutiny shows why most of those men were so unlucky.

Most of the Donner Party consisted of large families, but there were also 16 individuals traveling without any relatives. All those 16 happened to be men, and all but two were between 20 and 39. Those 16 unfortunates bore the brunt of the prime-age mortality. Thirteen of them died, and most of them died long before any of the women. Of the survivors, one—William Herron—reached California in October, so in reality only 2 survived the winter at the lake.

Of the 7 men in their prime who survived, 4 were family men. Only 3 of the 14 dead were. The prime-age women fared similarly: the 8 survivors belonged to families with an average size of 12 people, while Eleanor Eddy, the only woman to die in this age group, had no adult support. Her husband had escaped with the snowshoers, leaving her alone with their two small children.

The Donner Party records make it vividly clear that family members stuck together and helped one another at the expense of the others. A notorious example was the Breen family of nine, every one of whom (even two small children) survived through the luck of retaining their wagons and some pack animals much longer than the others, and through their considerable selfishness toward others. Compare this with the old bachelor Hardkoop, who was ordered out of the Keseberg family wagon and abandoned to die, or the fate of the young bachelor Antoine, whom none of the hungry snowshoers bothered to awaken when his hand fell into the fire.

Family ties can be a matter of life and death even under normal conditions. Married people, it turns out, have lower death rates than single, widowed, or divorced people. And marriage's life-promoting benefits have been found to be shared by all sorts of social ties, such as friendships and membership in social groups. Regardless of age or sex or initial health status, socially isolated individuals have well over twice the death rate of socially connected people.

For reasons about which we can only speculate, the lethal effects of social isolation are more marked for men than for women. It's clear, though, why social contacts are important for both sexes. They provide concrete help in case of need. They're our source of advice and shared information. They provide a sense of belonging and self-worth, and the courage to face tomorrow. They make stress more bearable.

All those benefits of social contact applied as well to the Donner Party members, who differed only in that their risk of death was much greater and their likely circumstances of death more grotesque than yours and mine. In that sense too, the harrowing story of the Donner Party grips us because it was ordinary life writ large.

Critical Thinking

1. Why was the Donner Party so late in getting to the eastern flank of the Sierra Nevada?
2. Why had death come to the Donner Party even before reaching Truckee Lake?
3. What did the trapped pioneers do once they exhausted their little remaining food?
4. Once the subject of cannibalism had been broached, how did they decide to go about it? What was the one rule that would restrain them?
5. What conclusions can we draw from the roster of the Donner Party with respect to gender and age? How does Jared Diamond explain these differences in death rate?
6. How important to survival are family ties and membership in social groups? Explain.

Create Central

www.mhhe.com/createcentral

Internet References

Library of Congress
www.loc.gov

Smithsonian Institution Website
www.si.edu

Society for American Archaeology
www.saa.org

Society for Historical Archaeology
www.sha.org

JARED DIAMOND is a contributing editor of *Discover*, a professor of physiology at UCLA School of Medicine, a recipient of a MacArthur genius award, and the author of *The Third Chimpanzee*.

From *Discover*, March 1992. Copyright © 1992 by Jared Diamond, Inc. Reprinted by permission of the author.

Article

Prepared by: Mari Pritchard Parker, *Pasadena City College* and Elvio Angeloni, *Pasadena City College*

The Great New England Vampire Panic

Two hundred years after the Salem witch trials, farm communities became convinced that their dearly departed relatives were returning from the grave to feed on the living.

ABIGAIL TUCKER

Learning Outcomes

After reading this article, you will be able to:

- Describe the Great New England Vampire Panic of the 19th century.
- Explain the medical, communal, and social forces at work leading up to the Great New England Vampire Panic.

Children playing near a hillside gravel mine found the first graves. One ran home to tell his mother, who was skeptical at first—until the boy produced a skull.

Because this was Griswold, Connecticut, in 1990, police initially thought the burials might be the work of a local serial killer named Michael Ross, and they taped off the area as a crime scene. But the brown, decaying bones turned out to be more than a century old. The Connecticut state archaeologist, Nick Bellantoni, soon determined that the hillside contained a colonial-era farm cemetery. New England is full of such unmarked family plots, and the 29 burials were typical of the 1700s and early 1800s: The dead, many of them children, were laid to rest in thrifty Yankee style, in simple wood coffins, without jewelry or even much clothing, their arms resting by their sides or crossed over their chests.

Except, that is, for Burial Number 4. Bellantoni was interested in the grave even before the excavation began. It was one of only two stone crypts in the cemetery, and it was partially visible from the mine face.

Scraping away soil with flat-edged shovels, and then brushes and bamboo picks, the archaeologist and his team worked through several feet of earth before reaching the top of the crypt. When Bellantoni lifted the first of the large, flat rocks that formed the roof, he uncovered the remains of a red-painted coffin and a pair of skeletal feet. They lay, he remembers, "in perfect anatomical position." But when he raised the next stone, Bellantoni saw that the rest of the individual "had been completely . . . rearranged." The skeleton had been beheaded; skull and thighbones rested atop the ribs and vertebrae. "It looked like a skull-and-cross-bones motif, a Jolly Roger. I'd never seen anything like it," Bellantoni recalls.

Subsequent analysis showed that the beheading, along with other injuries, including rib fractures, occurred roughly five years after death. Somebody had also smashed the coffin.

The other skeletons in the gravel hillside were packaged for reburial, but not "J.B.," as the 50ish male skeleton from the 1830s came to be called, because of the initials spelled out in brass tacks on his coffin lid. He was shipped to the National Museum of Health and Medicine, in Washington, D.C., for further study. Meanwhile, Bellantoni started networking. He invited archaeologists and historians to tour the excavation, soliciting theories. Simple vandalism seemed unlikely, as did robbery, because of the lack of valuables at the site.

Finally, one colleague asked: "Ever heard of the Jewett City vampires?"

In 1854, in neighboring Jewett City, Connecticut, townspeople had exhumed several corpses suspected to be vampires that were rising from their graves to kill the living. A few newspaper accounts of these events survived. Had the Griswold grave been desecrated for the same reason?

In the course of his far-flung research, Bellantoni placed a serendipitous phone call to Michael Bell, a Rhode Island folklorist, who had devoted much of the previous decade to studying New England vampire exhumations. The Griswold case occurred at roughly the same time as the other incidents Bell had investigated. And the setting was right: Griswold was rural, agrarian and bordering southern Rhode Island, where multiple exhumations had occurred. Many of the other "vampires," like J.B., had been disinterred, grotesquely tampered with and reburied.

In light of the tales Bell told of violated corpses, even the posthumous rib fractures began to make sense. J.B.'s accusers had likely rummaged around in his chest cavity, hoping to remove, and perhaps to burn, his heart.

Headquartered in a charming old schoolhouse, the Middletown Historical Society typically promotes such fortifying topics as Rhode Island gristmill restoration and Stone Wall Appreciation Day. Two nights before Halloween, though, the atmosphere is full of dry ice vapors and high silliness. Fake cobwebs cover the exhibits, warty gourds crowd the shelves and a skeleton with keen red eyes cackles in the corner. "We'll turn him off when you start talking," the society's president assures Michael Bell, who is readying his slide show.

Bell smiles. Although he lectures across the country and has taught at colleges, including Brown University, he is used to people having fun with his scholarship. "Vampires have gone from a source of fear to a source of entertainment," he says, a bit rueful. "Maybe I shouldn't trivialize entertainment, but to me it's not anywhere as interesting as what really happened." Bell's daughter, 37-year-old Gillian, a member of the audience that night, has made futile attempts to tempt her father with the Twilight series, but "there's Buffy and Twilight, and then there's what my dad does," she says. "I try to get him interested in the pop culture stuff, but he wants to keep his mind pure." Indeed, Bell seems only mildly aware that the vampire—appearing everywhere from *True Blood* to *The Vampire Diaries*—has once again sunk its fangs into the cultural jugular. As far as he's concerned, the undead are always with us.

Bell wears his hair in a sleek silver bob and has a strong Roman nose, but his extremely lean physique is evidence of a long-distance running habit, not some otherworldly hunger. He favors black sweaters and leather jackets, an ensemble he can easily accentuate with dark sunglasses to fit in with the goth crowd, if research requires it. A consulting folklorist at the Rhode Island Historical Preservation & Heritage Commission for most of his career, Bell has been investigating local vampires for 30 years now—long enough to watch lettering on fragile slate gravestones fade before his eyes and prosperous subdivisions arise beside once-lonely graveyards.

He has documented about 80 exhumations, reaching as far back as the late 1700s and as far west as Minnesota. But most are concentrated in backwoods New England, in the 1800s— startlingly later than the obvious local analogue, the Salem, Massachusetts, witch hunts of the 1690s.

Hundreds more cases await discovery, he believes. "You read an article that describes an exhumation, and they'll describe a similar thing that happened at a nearby town," says Bell, whose book, *Food for the Dead: On the Trail of New England's Vampires,* is seen as the last word on the subject, though he has lately found so many new cases that there's a second book on the way. "The ones that get recorded, and I actually find them, are just the tip of the iceberg."

Almost two decades after J.B.'s grave was discovered, it remains the only intact archaeological clue to the fear that swept the region. Most of the graves are lost to time (and even in the cases where they aren't, unnecessary exhumations are frowned on by the locals). Bell mostly hunts for handwritten records in town hall basements, consults tombstones and old cemetery maps, traces obscure genealogies and interviews descendants. "As a folklorist, I'm interested in recurring patterns in communication and ritual, as well as the stories that accompany these rituals," he says. "I'm interested in how this stuff is learned and carried on and how its meaning changes from group to group, and over time." In part because the events were relatively recent, evidence of historic vampires isn't as scarce as one might imagine. Incredulous city newspaper reporters dished about the "Horrible Superstition" on front pages. A traveling minister describes an exhumation in his daily log on September 3, 1810. (The "mouldy Specticle," he writes, was a "Solemn Site.") Even Henry David Thoreau mentions an exhumation in his journal on September 29, 1859.

Though scholars today still struggle to explain the vampire panics, a key detail unites them: The public hysteria almost invariably occurred in the midst of savage tuberculosis outbreaks. Indeed, the medical museum's tests ultimately revealed that J.B. had suffered from tuberculosis, or a lung disease very like it. Typically, a rural family contracted the wasting illness, and—even though they often received the standard medical diagnosis—the survivors blamed early victims as "vampires," responsible for preying upon family members who subsequently fell sick. Often an exhumation was called for, to stop the vampire's predations.

The particulars of the vampire exhumations, though, vary widely. In many cases, only family and neighbors participated. But sometimes town fathers voted on the matter, or medical doctors and clergymen gave their blessings or even pitched in. Some communities in Maine and Plymouth, Massachusetts, opted to simply flip the exhumed vampire facedown in the grave and leave it at that. In Connecticut, Rhode Island and Vermont, though, they frequently burned the dead person's heart, sometimes inhaling the smoke as a cure. (In Europe, too, exhumation protocol varied with region: Some beheaded suspected vampire corpses, while others bound their feet with thorns.)

Often these rituals were clandestine, lantern-lit affairs. But, particularly in Vermont, they could be quite public, even festive. One vampire heart was reportedly torched on the Woodstock, Vermont, town green in 1830. In Manchester, hundreds of people flocked to a 1793 heart-burning ceremony at a blacksmith's forge: "Timothy Mead officiated at the altar in the sacrifice to the Demon Vampire who it was believed was still sucking the blood of the then living wife of Captain Burton," an early town history says. "It was the month of February and good sleighing."

Bell attributes the openness of the Vermont exhumations to colonial settlement patterns. Rhode Island has about 260 cemeteries per 100 square miles, versus Vermont's mere 20 per 100 square miles. Rhode Island's cemeteries were small and scattered among private farms, whereas Vermont's tended to be much larger, often located in the center of town. In Vermont, it was much harder to keep a vampire hunt hush-hush.

As satisfying as such mini-theories are, Bell is consumed by larger questions. He wants to understand who the vampires and their accusers were, in death and life. During his Middletown lecture, he displays a picture of a man with salt-and-pepper sideburns and weary eyes: an artist's reconstruction of J.B.'s face, based on his skull. "I start with the assumption that people of past generations were just as intelligent as we are," Bell says. "I look for the logic: Why would they do this? Once you label something 'just a superstition' you lock off all inquiry into something that could have been reasonable. Reasonable is not always rational." He wrote his doctoral dissertation on African American voodoo practitioners in the South who cast love spells and curses; it's hard to imagine a population more different from the flinty, consumptive New Englanders he studies now, but Bell sees strong parallels in how they tried to manipulate the supernatural. "People find themselves in dire situations, where there's no recourse through regular channels," he explains. "The folk system offers an alternative, a choice." Sometimes, superstitions represent the only hope, he says.

The enduring sadness of the vampire stories lies in the fact that the accusers were usually direct kin of the deceased: parents, spouses and their children. "Think about what it would have taken to actually exhume the body of a relative," Bell says.

The tale he always returns to is in many ways the quintessential American vampire story, one of the last cases in New England and the first he investigated as a new PhD coming to Rhode Island in 1981 to direct a folk-life survey of Washington County funded by the National Endowment for the Humanities. History knows the 19-year-old, late-19th-century vampire as Mercy Brown. Her family, though, called her Lena.

Mercy Lena Brown lived in Exeter, Rhode Island—"Deserted Exeter," it was dubbed, or simply "one of the border towns." It was largely a subsistence farming community with barely fertile soil: "rocks, rocks and more rocks," says Sheila Reynolds-Boothroyd, president of the Exeter Historical Association. Farmers heaped stones into tumbledown walls, and rows of corn swerved around the biggest boulders.

In the late 19th century, Exeter, like much of agrarian New England, was even more sparsely populated than usual. Civil War casualties had taken their toll on the community, and the new railroads and the promise of richer land to the west lured young men away. By 1892, the year Lena died, Exeter's population had dipped to just 961, from a high of more than 2,500 in 1820. Farms were abandoned, many of them later to be seized and burned by the government. "Some sections looked like a ghost town," Reynolds-Boothroyd says.

And tuberculosis was harrying the remaining families. "Consumption," as it was called, had started to plague New England in the 1730s, a few decades before the first known vampire scares. By the 1800s, when the scares were at their height, the disease was the leading cause of mortality throughout the Northeast, responsible for almost a quarter of all deaths. It was a terrible end, often drawn out over years: a skyrocketing fever, a hacking, bloody cough and a visible wasting away of the body. "The emaciated figure strikes one with terror," reads one 18th-century description, "the forehead covered with drops of sweat; the cheeks painted with a livid crimson, the eyes sunk . . . the breath offensive, quick and laborious, and the cough so incessant as to scarce allow the wretched sufferer time to tell his complaints." Indeed, Bell says, symptoms "progressed in such a way that it seemed like something was draining the life and blood out of somebody."

People dreaded the disease without understanding it. Though Robert Koch had identified the tuberculosis bacterium in 1882, news of the discovery did not penetrate rural areas for some time, and even if it had, drug treatments wouldn't become available until the 1940s. The year Lena died, one physician blamed tuberculosis on "drunkenness, and want among the poor." Nineteenth-century cures included drinking brown sugar dissolved in water and frequent horseback riding. "If they were being honest," Bell says, "the medical establishment would have said, 'There's nothing we can do, and it's in the hands of God.'"

The Brown family, living on the eastern edge of town, probably on a modest homestead of 30 or 40 stony acres, began to succumb to the disease in December 1882. Lena's mother, Mary Eliza, was the first. Lena's sister, Mary Olive, a 20-year-old dressmaker, died the next year. A tender obituary from a local newspaper hints at what she endured: "The last few hours she lived was of great suffering, yet her faith was firm and she was ready for the change." The whole town turned out for her funeral, and sang "One Sweetly Solemn Thought," a hymn that Mary Olive herself had selected.

Within a few years, Lena's brother Edwin—a store clerk whom one newspaper columnist described as "a big, husky young man"—sickened too, and left for Colorado Springs hoping that the climate would improve his health.

Lena, who was just a child when her mother and sister died, didn't fall ill until nearly a decade after they were buried. Her tuberculosis was the "galloping" kind, which meant that she might have been infected but remained asymptomatic for years, only to fade fast after showing the first signs of the disease. A doctor attended her in "her last illness," a newspaper said, and "informed her father that further medical aid was useless." Her January 1892 obituary was much terser than her sister's: "Miss Lena Brown, who has been suffering from consumption, died Sunday morning."

As Lena was on her deathbed, her brother was, after a brief remission, taking a turn for the worse. Edwin had returned to Exeter from the Colorado resorts "in a dying condition," according to one account. "If the good wishes and prayers of his many friends could be realized, friend Eddie would speedily be restored to perfect health," another newspaper wrote.

But some neighbors, likely fearful for their own health, weren't content with prayers. Several approached George Brown, the children's father, and offered an alternative take on the recent tragedies: Perhaps an unseen diabolical force was preying on his family. It could be that one of the three Brown women wasn't dead after all, instead secretly feasting "on the living tissue and blood of Edwin," as the *Providence Journal* later summarized. If the offending corpse—the *Journal* uses the term "vampire" in some stories but the locals seemed not to—was discovered and destroyed, then Edwin would recover. The neighbors asked to exhume the bodies, in order to check for fresh blood in their hearts.

George Brown gave permission. On the morning of March 17, 1892, a party of men dug up the bodies, as the family doctor and a *Journal* correspondent looked on. George was absent, for unstated but understandable reasons.

After nearly a decade, Lena's sister and mother were barely more than bones. Lena, though, had been dead only a few months, and it was wintertime. "The body was in a fairly well-preserved state," the correspondent later wrote. "The heart and liver were removed, and in cutting open the heart, clotted and decomposed blood was found." During this impromptu autopsy, the doctor again emphasized that Lena's lungs "showed diffuse tuberculous germs."

Undeterred, the villagers burned her heart and liver on a nearby rock, feeding Edwin the ashes. He died less than two months later.

So-called vampires do escape the grave in at least one real sense: through stories. Lena Brown's surviving relatives saved local newspaper clippings in family scrapbooks, alongside carefully copied recipes. They discussed the events on Decoration Day, when Exeter residents adorned the town's cemeteries.

But the tale traveled much farther than they knew.

Even at the time, New England's vampire panics struck onlookers as a baffling anachronism. The late 1800s were a period of social progress and scientific flowering. Indeed, many of the Rhode Island exhumations occurred within 20 miles of Newport, high society's summer nucleus, where the scions of the industrial revolution vacationed. At first, only people who'd lived in or had visited the vampire-ridden communities knew about the scandal: "We seem to have been transported back to the darkest age of unreasoning ignorance and blind superstition, instead of living in the 19th century, and in a State calling itself enlightened and Christian," one writer at a small-town Connecticut paper opined in the wake of an 1854 exhumation.

But Lena Brown's exhumation made news. First, a reporter from the *Providence Journal* witnessed her unearthing. Then a well-known anthropologist named George Stetson traveled to Rhode Island to probe "the barbaric superstition" in the surrounding area.

Published in the venerable *American Anthropologist* journal, Stetson's account of New England's vampires made waves throughout the world. Before long, even members of the foreign press were offering various explanations for the phenomenon: Perhaps the "neurotic" modern novel was driving the New England madness, or maybe shrewd local farmers had simply been pulling Stetson's leg. A writer for the *London Post* declared that whatever forces drove the "Yankee vampire," it was an American problem and most certainly not the product of a British folk tradition (even though many families in the area could trace their lineage directly back to England). In the *Boston Daily Globe,* a writer went so far as to suggest that "perhaps the frequent intermarriage of families in these back country districts may partially account for some of their characteristics."

One 1896 *New York World* clipping even found its way into the papers of a London stage manager and aspiring novelist named Bram Stoker, whose theater company was touring the United States that same year. His gothic masterpiece, *Dracula,* was published in 1897. Some scholars have said that there wasn't enough time for the news accounts to have influenced the Dracula manuscript. Yet others see Lena in the character of Lucy (her very name a tempting amalgam of "Lena" and "Mercy"), a consumptive-seeming teenage girl turned vampire, who is exhumed in one of the novel's most memorable scenes. Fascinatingly, a medical doctor presides over Lucy's disinterment, just as one oversaw Lena's.

Whether or not Lucy's roots are in Rhode Island, Lena's historic exhumation is referenced in H.P. Lovecraft's "The Shunned House," a short story about a man being haunted by dead relatives that includes a living character named Mercy.

And, through fiction and fact, Lena's narrative continues today.

Part of Bell's research involves going along on "legend trips," the modern graveside pilgrimages made by those who believe, or want to believe, that the undead stalk Rhode Island. On legend trips, Bell is largely an academic presence. He can even be a bit of a killjoy, declaring that the main reason that "no grass grows on a vampire's grave" is that vampire graves have so many visitors, who crush all the vegetation.

Two days before Halloween, Bell and I head through forests of swamp maple and swamp oak to Exeter. For almost a century after Lena died, the town, still sparsely settled, remained remarkably unchanged. Electric lights weren't installed in the western part of Exeter until the 1940s, and the town had two pound keepers, charged with safekeeping stray cattle and pigs, until 1957. In the 1970s, when I-95 was built, Exeter evolved into an affluent bedroom community of Providence. But visitors still occasionally turn a corner to discover the past: a dirt road cluttered with wild turkeys, or deer hopping over stone fences. Some elderly locals square-dance in barns on the weekends, and streets keep their old names: Sodom Trail, Nooseneck Hill. The white wooden Chestnut Hill Baptist Church in front of Lena's cemetery, built in 1838, has its original blown-glass windows.

An early nor'easter is brewing as we pull into the church parking lot. The heavy rain will soon turn to snow, and there's a bullying wind. Our umbrellas bloom inside out, like black flowers. Though it's a somber place, there's no immediate clue that an accused vampire was buried here. (Except, perhaps, for an unfortunately timed Red Cross blood drive sign in front of the farmer's grange next door.) Unlike Salem, Exeter doesn't promote its dark claim to fame, and remains in some respects an insular community. Old-timers don't like the hooded figures who turn up this time of year, or the cars idling with the lights off. They say the legend should be left alone, perhaps with good reason: Last summer a couple of teenagers were killed on a pilgrimage to Lena's grave when they lost control of their car on Purgatory Road.

Most vampire graves stand apart, in wooded spots outside modern cemetery fences, where snow melts slower and there's a thick understory of ferns. But the Chestnut Hill Cemetery is still in use. And here is Lena. She lies beside the brother who ate her heart, and the father who let it happen. Other markers are freckled with lichen, but not hers. The stone looks to have been recently cleaned. It has been stolen over the years, and now an iron strap anchors it to the earth. People have scratched their names into the granite. They leave offerings: plastic vampire teeth, cough drops. "Once there was a note that said, 'You go, girl,'" Bell says. Today, there's a bunch of trampled daisies, and dangling from the headstone's iron collar, a butterfly charm on a chain.

How did 19th-century Yankees, remembered as the most pious and practical of peoples, come to believe in vampires—especially when the last known vampire panics at the time hadn't occurred since 18th-century Europe? Some modern scholars have linked the legend to vampiric symptoms of diseases like rabies and porphyria (a rare genetic disorder that can cause extreme sensitivity to sunlight and turn teeth reddish-brown). Exeter residents at the time claimed that the exhumations were "a tradition of the Indians."

The legend originated in Slavic Europe, where the word "vampire" first appeared in the tenth century. Bell believes that Slavic and Germanic immigrants brought the vampire superstitions with them in the 1700s, perhaps when Palatine Germans colonized Pennsylvania, or Hessian mercenaries served in the Revolutionary War. "My sense is that it came more than one time through more than one source," he says.

The first known reference to an American vampire scare is a scolding letter to the editor of the *Connecticut Courant and Weekly Intelligencer,* published in June 1784. Councilman Moses Holmes, from the town of Willington, warned people to beware of "a certain Quack Doctor, a foreigner" who had urged families to dig up and burn dead relatives to stop consumption. Holmes had witnessed several children disinterred at the doctor's request and wanted no more of it: "And that the bodies of the dead may rest quiet in their-graves without such interruption, I think the public ought to be aware of being led away by such an imposture."

But some modern scholars have argued that the vampire superstition made a certain degree of practical sense. In *Vampires, Burials and Death,* folklorist Paul Barber dissects the logic behind vampire myths, which he believes originally arose from unschooled but astute observations of decay. (Bloated dead bodies appear as if they have recently eaten; a staked corpse "screams" due to the escape of natural gases, etc.) The seemingly bizarre vampire beliefs, Barber argues, get at the essence of contagion: the insight that illness begets illness, and death, death.

Vampire believers "say that death comes to us from invisible agents," Barber says. "We say that death comes to us from invisible agents. The difference is that we can get out a microscope and look at the agents."

While New England's farmers may have been guided by something like reason, the spiritual climate of the day was also hospitable to vampire rumors. Contrary to their Puritanical reputation, rural New Englanders in the 1800s were a fairly heathen lot. Only about 10 percent belonged to a church. Rhode Island, originally founded as a haven for religious dissenters, was particularly lax: Christian missionaries were at various points dispatched there from more godly communities. "The missionaries come back and lament that there's no Bible in the home, no church-going whatsoever," says Linford Fisher, a Brown University colonial historian. "You have people out there essentially in cultural isolation." Mary Olive, Lena's sister, joined a church just two weeks before she died, her obituary said.

In place of organized worship, superstitions reigned: magical springs with healing powers, dead bodies that bled in the presence of their murderers. People buried shoes by fireplaces, to catch the Devil if he tried to come down the chimney. They nailed horseshoes above doors to ward off evil and carved daisy wheels, a kind of colonial hex sign, into the door frames.

If superstition likely fanned the vampire panics, perhaps the most powerful forces at play were communal and social. By 1893, there were just 17 people per square mile in Exeter. A fifth of the farms were fully abandoned, the fields turning slowly back into forest. In her monograph *The New England Vampire Belief: Image of the Decline,* gothic literature scholar Faye Ringel Hazel hints at a vampire metaphor behind the westward hemorrhage: The migration "seemed to drain rural New England of its most enterprising young citizens, leaving the old and unfit behind."

As Exeter teetered near collapse, maintaining social ties must have taken on new importance. An exhumation represented, first and foremost, a duty to one's own kin, dead or dying: the ritual "would alleviate the guilt someone might feel for not doing everything they could do to save a family, to leave no stone unturned," Bell says.

Even more significant, in small communities where disease could spread quickly, an exhumation was "an outward display that you are doing everything you can to fix the problem." Residents of the already beleaguered town were likely terrified. "They knew that if consumption wiped out the Brown family, it could take out the next family," Bell says. "George Brown was being entreated by the community." He had to make a gesture.

The strongest testament to the power of the vampire myth is that George Brown did not, in fact, believe in it, according to the *Providence Journal.* It was he who asked a doctor to perform an autopsy at the graveyard, and he who elected to be elsewhere during the ritual. He authorized his loved ones' exhumation, the *Journal* says, simply to "satisfy the neighbors," who were, according to another newspaper account, "worrying the life out of him"—a description with its own vampiric overtones.

Perhaps it was wise to let them have their way, since George Brown, apparently not prone to tuberculosis, had to coexist with his neighbors well into the next century. He died in 1922.

Relatives of the Browns still live in Exeter and are laid to rest on Chestnut Hill. Some, planning ahead, have erected their grave markers. It can be disconcerting to drive past somebody's tombstone on the way to his or her home for a vampire-oriented interview.

On a sunny Halloween morning, when Bell has left for a vampire folklore conference at the University of London, I return to the cemetery to meet several Brown descendants at the farmer's grange. They bring, swaddled in old sheets, a family treasure: a quilt that Lena sewed.

We spread it out on a scarred wooden table. The cotton bedspread is pink, blue and cream. What look from a distance like large patches of plain brown fabric are really fields of tiny daisies.

It's the work of a farm girl, without any wasteful appliqué; Lena clearly ran out of material in places and had to scrimp for more. Textile scholars at the University of Rhode Island have traced her snippets of florals, plaid and paisley to the 1870s and 1880s, when Lena was still a child; they wondered if she used her sister's and mother's old dresses for the project. Perhaps her mother's death, too, explains Lena's quilting abilities, which are considerable for a teenager: She might have had to learn household skills before other girls. The quilt is in immaculate condition and was likely being saved for something—Lena's hope chest, thinks her distant descendant Dorothy O'Neil, one of the quilt's recent custodians, and a knowledgeable quilter herself.

"I think the quilt is exquisite, especially in light of what she went through in her life," O'Neil says. "She ended up leaving something beautiful. She didn't know she'd have to leave it, but she did."

Lena hasn't left entirely. She is said to frequent a certain bridge, manifested as the smell of roses. She appears in children's books and paranormal television specials. She murmurs in the cemetery, say those who leave tape recorders there to capture her voice. She is rumored to visit the terminally ill, and to tell them that dying isn't so bad.

The quilt pattern that Lena used, very rare in Rhode Island, is sometimes called the Wandering Foot, and it carried a superstition of its own: Anybody who slept under it, the legend said, would be lost to her family, doomed to wander.

Critical Thinking

1. How has folklorist Michael Bell been able to accumulate evidence for vampire exhumations in New England?
2. How is vampire exhumation related to the incidence of tuberculosis? Be aware the details of exhumation varied.
3. Why were Vermont's exhumations more public as opposed to those of Rhode Island?
4. Why does Bell dismiss the notions that the vampire exhumers were not as as intelligent as we are and that they were simply "superstitious" and not reasonable?
5. What is the "enduring sadness" of the vampire stories? How does the case of Mercy Lena Brown and her family illustrate the point?
6. How did 19th-century Yankees come to believe in vampires?
7. In what respects did vampire beliefs make "a certain degree of practical sense"?
8. How was the spiritual climate of the day hospitable to vampire rumors? What were the communal and social forces at work?

Create Central

www.mhhe.com/createcentral

Internet References

Yahoo: Society and Culture: Death
http://dir.yahoo.com/Society_and_Culture/Death_and_Dying

Tucker, Abigail. From *Smithsonian*, vol. 43, no. 6, October 2012, pp. 58–65. Copyright © 2012 by the Smithsonian Institution. Reprinted by permission.

Unit 6

UNIT

Prepared by: Mari Pritchard Parker, *Pasadena City College* and
Elvio Angeloni, *Pasadena City College*

Contemporary Archaeology

While archaeology of the twenty-first century can trace its origins to the nineteenth century, it is an ever-evolving science. As new methods become available, they are incorporated into the archaeologist's tool kit. Advances in the understanding of the human genome, new radiometric dating techniques, and experimental archaeology have all added significantly to the field. New hominid fossil discoveries generate excitement and debate and add to the refinement of the history of our species. Additionally, the modern environmental effects associated with global warming have raised concerns about the possible loss of coastal sites due to rising sea levels.

The nineteenth century was unique in the way that several currents of thought and beliefs coalesced. Some say it started with a Frenchman named Boucher de Perthes who found odd-shaped stones on his property, stones that could comfortably be held in the human hand. Undoubtedly, thousands of other people made such finds throughout history. But to Monsieur de Perthes, these stones suggested a novel meaning. He wondered if these odd rocks might be tools made by humans long lost in the mists of time.

Other exciting changes were occurring in the epistemology of the nineteenth century that would soon lend credibility to this hypothesis. In 1859, there was the publication of "*On the Origin of Species* by Charles Darwin. In this book (which, by the way, never mentioned humans or any implied relationship they might have to apes), Darwin suggested a general process that became known as "natural selection." The theory suggested that species could change gradually in response to the environment. This was an idea counterintuitive to scientific thought. Even biologists believed that species were immutable. But this theory was to change forever the way human beings regarded their place in nature. If species could evolve, then the implication was—so could humans. And that idea knocked humans down from our lofty position and into the archaeological record.

Then there was the concurrent emergence of uniformitarianism, which implied that the Earth was old, very old. (It has, in fact, been around for about 5 billion years.) But with this idea, the revolutionary possibility that human beings could have existed *before* history, became plausible. Moreover, such a serious challenge to the established wisdom that the Earth was only about 6,000 years old contributed to the new age speculation about what it means to be human.

The newly emerging science of paleontology involving the discovery and recognition of extinct fossil species, seriously challenged the traditional, elevated status of our own species. Nineteenth-century philosophers were forced to reexamine the nature of humanity. Among the intellectuals of the Western world, the essential anthropocentrism of the Christian view gradually shifted to a more secular view of humankind as simply another part of nature. In this way, humans became subject to the rules of nature and natural events, without any necessary reference to theology.

So, it was within this new nineteenth-century enlightenment that Boucher de Perthes suggested his hypothesis regarding the antiquity of his stone tools, as others came declaring that they too had found these same, odd-shaped stones and had thought similar thoughts. Thus, the science called archaeology began. As any science evolves, it naturally diversifies. And because mainstream archaeology has been pulled in so many different directions during its development, there have been concerns that archaeologists will specialize themselves right out of the mainstream of anthropology. On the other hand, we archaeologists share with other anthropologists two important concepts in our attempt to understand ourselves as a species: the concept of culture and the holistic approach.

Our current economic climate presents yet other challenges: financing future archaeological endeavors and finding additional sources of labor. And then there are the ethical questions that archaeologists must consider. Because an archaeological site is a nonrenewable resource, excavation involves the systematic destruction of a site and its ecological context. Anything overlooked, mislaid, not measured, or in some way not observed is a lost piece of the past, and if the information that is retrieved is never shared with an audience, it is as if it had not existed in the first place.

Moreover, as the world population continues to expand, we are destined to impact this scarce and valuable resource. The applied field of archaeology, commonly referred to as Cultural Resource Management (CRM), deals with the complex needs of developers and state and federal agencies. Its practitioners derive their livelihood from this work, even if it means physically destroying archaeological sites. They do so while striving to mitigate adverse impact and collect data in a way that will enable the archaeological community of the future to answer questions that have yet to be asked.

One saving grace in the field may be found in the current trend toward a more "public archaeology"—the awareness that archaeologists should present their findings in a more palatable, story format. Now is the time for the archaeological community to start a give-and-take dialogue with the public; by portraying their projects within the larger framework that expresses more than just a set of tedious details in specialized archaeological lingo. It is for these reasons that the articles presented in this section deal with the archaeological community's current interest in the preservation, conservation, and reconstruction of archaeological sites, as well as their educational and aesthetic value.

Article

Prepared by: Mari Pritchard Parker, *Pasadena City College* and
Elvio Angeloni, *Pasadena City College*

Maya Archaeologists Turn to the Living to Help Save the Dead

To preserve ancient sites, pioneering archaeologists are trying to improve the lives of the Maya people now living near the ruins.

MICHAEL BAWAYA

Learning Outcomes

After reading this article, you will be able to:

- Discuss community archaeology as a means to improve the lives of local people as well as preserve the archaeological sites and the relics of their ancestors.
- Discuss the problems of funding community archaeology projects and various methods being used to do so.

Archaeologist Jonathan Kaplan tries to spend as much time as possible exploring Chocolá, a huge Maya site in southern Guatemala dating from 1200 B.C.E. So far his team has mapped more than 60 mounds, identified dozens of monuments, and found signs of the emergence of Maya civilization, including large, sophisticated waterworks that likely required social organization to build.

But today, instead of digging, Kaplan is lunching with the mayor of a municipality that includes the impoverished town of Chocolá. Kaplan, a research associate with the Museum of New Mexico's Office of Archaeological Studies in Santa Fe, is trying to enlist the mayor's support for a land swap that would give farmers land of no archaeological value in exchange for land that holds Maya ruins. The local people he's trying to help, many of them descended from the ancient Maya, are "clinging by their fingers to survival," says Kaplan. So, working with a Guatemalan archaeologist, he has established a trash-removal service, hired an environmental scientist to help improve the drinking water, and developed plans for two museums to attract tourists.

Kaplan and others are in the vanguard of a movement called community archaeology. From Africa to Uzbekistan, researchers are trying to boost local people's quality of life in order to preserve the relics of their ancestors. In the Maya region, the situation is urgent; the vestiges of the ancient Maya may be destroyed in 5 to 10 years unless something is done to curb looting, logging, poaching, and oil exploration, says Richard Hansen, president of the Foundation for Anthropological Research & Environmental Studies and an archaeologist at Idaho State University in Pocatello. Hansen, Kaplan, and others are using archaeology as an engine for development, driving associated tourism and education projects. The resultant intertwining of research and development is such that "I cannot accomplish the one without the other," says Kaplan, "because poverty is preventing the people from attending to the ancient remains in a responsible fashion."

It wasn't always that way. Until fairly recently, Maya researchers were solely focused on the hunt for "stones and bones," says Hansen. Archaeologist Arthur Demarest of Vanderbilt University in Nashville, Tennessee, says researchers often excavated a site with the help of local workers, only to abandon them when the project ended. Those who lost their income often resorted to looting and slash-and-burn agriculture to survive. "In the wake of every archaeological project is an economic and social disaster," says Demarest.

He offers one of his own projects as an example of what not to do. After employing about 300 people in the early 1990s at several sites in the Petén, the vast tropical forest in northern Guatemala, Demarest left the government with a continuing development plan for the region, much of it federal land. But the federal government brought in outsiders to implement it. Desperate at having lost their jobs, the local people plundered the sites.

"From that, I learned a lot of lessons," Demarest says. "Archaeology transforms a region." In his view, archaeologists themselves must take responsibility for helping the locals succeed. "The days of Indiana Jones, when archaeologists could go to a place, excavate, and then leave without concern about the impact that their actions are having on the people in the area, are gone," he has said.

Today, Demarest embraces this responsibility as he excavates part of the great trade route that ran through much of the Maya region, including along the Pasión River and through Cancuen, an ancient city in central Guatemala. He says his project is successful because it operates "bottom up—we're working through the village." Using ethnographic studies of the Maya people and working with leaders from several villages, Demarest designed a research and community development plan that enables the local people, rather than outsiders, to serve as custodians of their own heritage. The communities choose projects—archaeology, restoration, ecotourism, etc.—and run them with the guidance of experts, earning more than they would by farming.

One successful enterprise is a boat service, run by the Maya, that ferries tourists down the Pasión River from the village of La Union to Cancuen, now a national park. In addition to generating revenue, the service attracted a variety of agencies that provided potable water, electricity, and school improvements to La Union. The World Bank cited the boat service as one of the 10 most innovative rural development projects in the world in 2003.

Demarest also helped establish a visitor center, an inn, a guide service, and a campground at the park's entrance. Three nearby villages collaboratively manage these operations, and the profits pay for water systems, school expansions, and medical supplies. "The only way these things are going to succeed is if it's theirs," says Demarest, who has raised nearly $5 million for community development at Cancuen. Last year, he became the first U.S. citizen to be awarded the National Order of Cultural Patrimony by the Guatemalan government.

Other archaeologists are trying to achieve similar results in their own field areas. Hansen is exploring the origins, the cultural and ecological dynamics, and the collapse of the Preclassic Maya (circa 2000 B.C.E. to 250 C.E.) in the Mirador Basin. His project has a budget of $1.2 million, with about $400,000 going to development and $800,000 to archaeology. He raised roughly half of the funds from the Global Heritage Fund, a nonprofit organization that helps preserve cultural heritage sites in developing countries. The project employs more than 200 people who earn above-average wages while getting training; Hansen's team has also installed a new water system and bought 40 computers to boost locals' computer skills.

Looting in the basin has been devastating in the past, so Hansen has hired 27 guards—most of them former looters. They make good guards, he says, "because they know the tricks of the trade." The project has instilled "a sense of identity" in some residents, although Hansen acknowledges that others continue to loot. "It is a long battle to win the hearts and minds of these people," he says.

Although both Demarest and Hansen have won generous grants for their work, they agree that finding funding for community archaeology is "horrific," as Hansen puts it. Kaplan makes do with about $130,000 each year for his "terribly underfunded" project, although his ideal would be about $800,000. Traditional funders, such as the U.S. National Science Foundation (NSF), pay for research but not community development, says Demarest. NSF, with its modest budget of $5 million to $6 million, is most interested in the "intellectual merit" of a project, agrees archaeology program director John Yellen, although he adds that the foundation does consider "broader impacts," including community development.

Demarest, who is financed by some 20 organizations including the United States Agency for International Development and the Solar Foundation, says a big budget is a must for community projects: "You've got to have about $400,000 a season to do ethical archaeology."

But other researchers say it's possible to run such projects without big budgets. Archaeologist Anabel Ford of the University of California, Santa Barbara, who has been practicing small-scale community archaeology while studying land-use patterns at a large site called El Pilar on the Belize-Guatemala border since 1983, says that she can achieve her community development goals for as little as $12,000 a year. "I actually think it's not about tons of money," she says. "It's about consistency."

Ford operates on an annual budget of $30,000 to $75,000, with funding sources ranging from the Ford and MacArthur Foundations to her own pocket. Within El Pilar's lush tropical forest are numerous temples and other buildings that stand as high as 22 meters. Over the years, Ford has built a cultural center and a caretaker house, and El Pilar now attracts hundreds of ecotourists annually. Ford started an annual festival to celebrate cultural traditions and foster community involvement, and she's organizing a women's collective to sell local crafts. "We've built the first infrastructure at El Pilar since 1000 [C.E.]," she says.

Whether they operate with big money or on the cheap, community archaeologists face a delicate juggling act between development and research. Ford believes her academic career has suffered because of the time and effort she's invested in development projects. "I would have written much more substantive work on my research at El Pilar," she says, lamenting that she has yet to finish a book about her work. Kaplan and Demarest say that they spend about half their time on community development, leaving only half for archaeology.

As impressive and well-intentioned as these and other community archaeology projects seem, at least a few researchers are concerned about unintended consequences. "If you don't understand the local politics, you can really do damage," says Arlen Chase of the University of Central Florida in Orlando, who has investigated Caracol, a major Maya site in Belize, since 1984. It's difficult to determine just what archaeologists owe the community they work in, he adds. "This is a new endeavor, and we're learning how best to do it," agrees archaeologist Anne Pyburn, outgoing chair of the Ethics Committee of the American Anthropological Association.

Despite these concerns, Hansen and his colleagues seem convinced that they're making progress. Guatemalans who were "dedicated to looting and destroying these sites," Hansen says, are "now dedicated to preserving them."

Critical Thinking

1. What is "community archaeology"?
2. What must be done to save the vestiges of the Ancient Maya from being destroyed and why?
3. What was Maya research focused on until recently? What were the consequences when the project was over?

4. How has Arthur Demarest exercised his responsibility to the community where he excavates? Describe his research and community development plan. In what ways has the community benefited?
5. What have been the benefits of Richard Hansen's community development efforts in the Mirador Basin and how has he achieved them?
6. Why is it that finding funding for community archaeology is "horrific," according to Demarest and Hansen?
7. Why does Anabel Ford believe that her academic career has suffered because of the development projects?
8. What concerns do some archaeologists have about community archaeology?

Create Central

www.mhhe.com/createcentral

Internet References

Maya Archaeology Initiative
http://mayaarchaeology.org

Society for American Archaeology
www.saa.org

Society for Historical Archaeology
www.sha.org

MICHAEL BAWAYA is the editor of *American Archaeology*.

From *Science Magazine*, August 26, 2005, pp. 1317–1318. Copyright © 2005 by American Association for the Advancement of Science. Reprinted by permission via Rightslink. www.sciencemag.org

Article

Prepared by: Mari Pritchard Parker, *Pasadena City College* and Elvio Angeloni, *Pasadena City College*

Archaeologists Race Against Sea Change in Orkney

Coastal erosion, accelerated by climate change, is threatening the Orkney Islands' wealth of archaeology, but researchers are adapting to the changes.

SARA REARDON

Learning Outcomes

After reading this article, you will be able to:

- Discuss the importance of Skara Brae to archaeologists and to the local community.
- Discuss global warming and how it affects archaeological sites such as those in Orkney.
- Discuss the ways in which archaeologists are coping with the effects of weather on archaeological sites.

Holding her jacket shut against the powerful wind, archaeologist Julie Gibson picks her way along the foot of a rock-studded cliff face on the western shore of the main island in north Scotland's Orkney archipelago. "I never know what I'm going to find when I come down here," she says, brushing her fingers through the dirt at eye level to look for fragments of bone or pottery. "It's so different every time, all these new faces exposed on the cliff." At her touch, bits of the soil crumble and fall away, loosened by storms that lash rain and waves up against the sandstone cliff and rapidly erode it.

As Orkney's county archaeologist, Gibson is one of the leaders in a charge to understand how erosion affects the islands' abundance of coastal archaeological sites. The cliff she's examining is only about 50 meters away from the incredibly well-preserved 5000-year-old Neolithic village of Skara Brae, a World Heritage site that draws 70,000 tourists per year and is a major source of income for the islands. The tight cluster of little round stone houses, complete with intact stone dressers, beds, and garbage heaps, has been an unparalleled resource for archaeologists like Gibson to learn how northern Britain's earliest agrarians lived.

Skara Brae looks safe at the moment, perched near the cliff edge overlooking the Bay of Skaill and protected by a 3-meter-high seawall. Yet powerful waves from just one violent storm could overwhelm the site's defenses and suck the village out to sea. "Even without anthropogenic global warming, Skara Brae's in trouble," says archaeologist Caroline Wickham-Jones of the University of Aberdeen in the United Kingdom. "At some point, we're going to have to say, so be it."

Hundreds of coastal sites from Orkney's 10,000-year human history are similarly endangered by climate change. Archaeologists can't fight the ocean so, like the people whose climate adaptation they study, modern researchers continue to adapt themselves. They take advantage of the fact that destructive storms can reveal and even excavate sites, though they're not the most delicate of diggers. And, by adopting new techniques such as 3D laser scanning, they can record, if not save, sites before they are taken by the sea. For Orkney, whose dense archaeology is covered with shell sand that preserves both stone and bone unusually well, the danger from storms and sea level rise are especially acute because of its northern latitude.

The history of Skara Brae is marked out by storms. In about 2200 B.C.E., a catastrophic storm drove the villagers away and blew masses of shell sand, called machair, over their houses, preserving them intact. Another massive storm, during a warm period in 1850, blew the sand off again and revealed the village to a local landowner, who excavated it himself. The village was originally well inland but during the centuries it lay buried, the sea rose more than 40 meters and turned a freshwater lake into the Bay of Skaill.

Now storms threaten it again. As waves ricochet about in the bay, Gibson explains, "you've got the full weight of the Atlantic piling into soft stuff, with hardly any resistance to sea taking back the sand." That story is repeated all along northern coasts. Archaeologist Thomas Dawson of the University of St. Andrews in the United Kingdom estimates 50 meters of the coast on a beach in western Scotland was lost in a single night in 2005. "We were walking along the beach finding bits of human skulls and Iron Age pottery for weeks afterward," he says. The Intergovernmental Panel on Climate Change predicts that in the future the North Atlantic will become stormier and storm surges may raise sea levels by 2 meters.

Local archaeologists say smaller storms are already accelerating erosion. "There's been more change [to the area near Skara Brae] in the last 10 to 15 years than in 100 years," says archaeologist Jane Downes of Orkney College, part of the University of the Highlands and Islands here, as shown by historical maps and photos of the site. In the mid-1990s, a team from Orkney College excavated a butchery and garbage heap, or midden, close to the village, finding bones, beads, and other detritus that created a picture of the people's lifestyle. Today, that site is entirely gone, swept away by crashing waves that have scoured about 5 meters of coastline. "It's ferocious," Downes says.

Letting nature take its course, or "managed retreat," is now the approved method of dealing with coastal erosion, Dawson says. "Also called the do-nothing approach," he adds. Seawalls tend to exacerbate erosion by redirecting the energy from the waves in unnatural ways.

There's only so long that researchers can mourn the loss of sites. "The fact is that they are [disappearing]," Downes says, "so rather than just bleating about it, it's much better to turn it into a positive." Coastal erosion helps by exposing sites, taking what Gibson calls "sea bites" out of cliffs and providing peepholes into a layer cake of archaeology, the remnants of waves of settlers and invaders who built upon the same attractive spots. This can save a lot of digging but leaves very little time to decipher what's there.

On the small Orcadian island of Rousay, waves have been unearthing buried treasures along all of its beaches. Between rain showers, Rousay is haloed with multiple rainbows so vivid that it feels like you could drive beneath one. Archaeologist Ingrid Mainland of Orkney College squelches past several dozen sheep down a steep, grassy hill to the beach where she will inspect the remains of a 1000-year-old Iron Age building called a broch. Brochs, which were originally round stone towers several stories high, abound in northern Scotland, especially on Orkney. Built by late Iron Age people, it's still unknown whether they were defensive castles or summer homes for the wealthy.

"There's my broch." Mainland points out a large grassy mound in what was her backyard while she was growing up on Rousay. Although the mounds make brochs clearly visible, researchers hesitate to excavate new ones both for lack of funds and fear of exposing them to the elements.

But in this case, coastal erosion did the work for them. Mainland points out a site on a beach called Swandro where, in July, researchers from the University of Bradford spotted the remains of what appeared to be a broch half-claimed by the sea. Waves had unearthed it at an angle, revealing that the lowest accessible part dated from 400 to 200 B.C.E. while the top part was remodeled as a Viking longhouse in the 1200s, says lead investigator Steven Dockrill. Because so much of the building had gone, the members of the team, which had only 3 weeks to work on the site, realized they may be able to get down to its base without much digging when they return next summer, Dockrill says. This will allow them, using modern technology for the first time, to sample the soil from the floor of a broch for bones and plant remains, perhaps settling the question of what brochs were used for.

A nearby graveyard contains both Viking boat burials and graves of Picts, a Scottish Iron Age people, suggesting possible conflict or mixing. If Vikings spent time in the Pictish broch, Dockrill hopes they left clues for his team to discover next year. That is, if the site is still there. Covered with a tarp weighted by stones, it lies only a few meters from the sea at high tide.

But even if the broch disappears before the team can finish its excavation, it has already given the researchers an opportunity to test out a new tool: a high-resolution 3D laser scanner that took a digital record of the site. The device needs only 30 minutes to scan across 270° out to a distance of up to 300 meters, allowing the archaeologists to slip onto a threatened site at low tide, quickly scan it, and slip out again.

"It's a godsend," Gibson says. The speed of the scanner saves the team from the need to mark out a grid over the site with bits of string and meticulously record everything that is there, often while battling high winds and rain. Gibson hopes to use it extensively to monitor erosion season by season. Back in the lab, technicians overlay the 3D reconstruction onto high-resolution color photos also taken by the scanner. The detail is sufficient for researchers to see bits of the archaeology that have been eaten away "like a mad quarrier has been at it," Gibson says, and watch for new pieces to pop out. The group plans to put this and future data online so that colleagues can read and analyze it.

"These sites are very emotive," says architect Chris McGregor, who heads a team called the Scottish Ten—funded by the government agency Historic Scotland—that is systematically laser-scanning world heritage sites, preserving them as educational tools both online and for museums. One of their targets is the Heart of Neolithic Orkney site, which includes Skara Brae, a ring of standing stones called the Ring of Brodgar, and a Neolithic cairn called Maeshowe in which 12th century Vikings sheltered and left runic graffiti. Laser scanning, McGregor says, is useful for monitoring erosion as well as recreations for the public. "We could take you into Skara Brae's houses virtually," he says.

Given the threat to sites around Scotland's coast, Historic Scotland has been running a "coastal zone assessment survey" since 1996, sending out surveyors to tramp more than 16,000 kilometers of coastline, record what's there, and send the data back for archaeologists to prioritize and make tough decisions about what to excavate, what to preserve, and what to abandon.

Dawson directs a group called Scottish Coastal Archaeology and the Problem of Erosion (SCAPE), which has been carrying out the survey for Historic Scotland since 2000. So far, the survey has inspected only 30% of Scotland's coastline and identified 11,500 archaeological sites. Its archaeologists recommended some kind of action on 3750 of these sites, be it excavation, laser recording, or other preservation—if the money is available. "This [huge number] is one reason you're not going to get people jumping up and down saying let's build coastal defenses," Dawson says. To help prioritize, SCAPE has begun crowdsourcing: asking local communities to measure and photograph the state of erosion in an area. In return, communities have a say in which of their favorite beach sites get excavated.

When people get worried about climate change, Wickham-Jones says she wants to remind them that Orcadians have dealt with it for ages. Situated at the edge of an ice sheet that covered mainland Scotland, Orkney was particularly susceptible to sea level rise when the sheet melted at the end of the Ice Age. How ancient peoples dealt with a changing climate is one of the primary questions that archaeologists hope to answer by studying farming and migration patterns. "What do you do when you know your land is getting smaller around you?" Wickham-Jones asks.

The people of Orkney are grappling with similar problems today, although the current rate of sea level rise, about 2 millimeters per year, is a far cry from what people have often experienced in the past. But by studying ancient climate change and Orcadians' history of adaptation, "archaeology will start to pay dividends," Gibson says. "Now we're trying to foretell what happens to ourselves."

Critical Thinking

1. How important is Skara Brae as an archaeological site and as a source of income for Orkney?
2. How have weather patterns preserved, revealed, and threatened archaeological sites in Orkney?
3. How have archaeologists adapted to the weather conditions?
4. How important have 3D laser scanners become for archaeologists?
5. What is the purpose of the "coastal zone assessment survey?"
6. Is climate change new to Orkney? Explain.

Create Central

www.mhhe.com/createcentral

Internet References

Society for Archaeological Sciences
www.socarchsci.org

Society for Historical Archaeology
www.sha.org

Reardon, Sara. From *Science Magazine*, November 25, 2011. Copyright © 2011 by American Association for the Advancement of Science. Reprinted by permission via Rightslink. www.sciencemag.org

Article

Prepared by: Mari Pritchard Parker, *Pasadena City College* and Elvio Angeloni, *Pasadena City College*

Ruined

MICHAEL MARSHALL

Learning Outcomes

After reading this article, you will be able to:

- Discuss the relationship between climate change and the decline of civilizations in the past.
- Discuss the prospects of societal collapse as a result of climate change in the modern world.

The most beautiful woman in the world, Helen, is abducted by Paris of Troy. A Greek fleet of more than a thousand ships sets off in pursuit. After a long war, heroes like Achilles lead the Greeks to victory over Troy.

At least, this is the story told by the poet Homer around four centuries later. Yet Homer was not only writing about events long before his time, he was also describing a long-lost civilization. Achilles and his compatriots were part of the first great Greek civilization, a warlike culture centered on the city of Mycenae that thrived from around 1600 BC.

By 1100 BC, not long after the Trojan War, many of its cities and settlements had been destroyed or abandoned. The survivors reverted to a simpler rural lifestyle. Trade ground to a halt, and skills such as writing were lost. The script the Mycenaeans had used, Linear B, was not read again until 1952.

The region slowly recovered after around 800 BC. The Greeks adopted the Phoenician script, and the great city states of Athens and Sparta rose to power. "The collapse was one of the most important events in history, because it gave birth to two major cultures," says anthropologist Brandon Drake. "It's like the phoenix from the ashes." Classical Greece, as this second period of civilization is known, far outshone its predecessor. Its glory days lasted only a couple of centuries, but the ideas of its citizens were immensely influential. Their legacy is still all around us, from the math we learn in school to the idea of democracy.

But what caused the collapse of Mycenaean Greece, and thus had a huge impact on the course of world history? A change in the climate, according to the latest evidence. What's more, Mycenaean Greece is just one of a growing list of civilizations whose fate is being linked to the vagaries of climate. It seems big swings in the climate, handled badly, brought down whole societies, while smaller changes led to unrest and wars.

The notion that climate change toppled entire civilizations has been around for more than a century, but it was only in the 1990s that it gained a firm footing as researchers began to work out exactly how the climate had changed, using clues buried in lake beds or petrified in stalactites. Harvey Weiss of Yale University set the ball rolling with his studies of the collapse of one of the earliest empires: that of the Akkadians.

It began in the Fertile Crescent of the Middle East, a belt of rich farmland where an advanced regional culture had developed over many centuries. In 2334 BC, Sargon was born in the city state of Akkad. He started out as a gardener, was put in charge of clearing irrigation canals, and went on to seize power. Not content with that, he conquered many neighboring city states, too. The empire Sargon founded thrived for nearly a century after his death before it collapsed.

Excavating in what is now Syria, Weiss found dust deposits suggesting that the region's climate suddenly became drier around 2200 BC. The drought would have led to famine, he argued, explaining why major cities were abandoned at this time (*Science*, vol 261, p. 995). A piece of contemporary writing, called *The Curse of Akkad*, does describe a great famine (see end of article).

Weiss's work was influential, but there wasn't much evidence. In 2000, climatologist Peter deMenocal of Columbia University in New York found more. His team showed, based on modern records going back to 1700, that the flow of the region's two great rivers, the Tigris and the Euphrates, is linked to conditions in the north Atlantic: cooler waters reduce rainfall by altering the paths of weather systems. Next, they discovered that the north Atlantic cooled just before the Akkadian empire fell apart (*Science*, vol 288, p. 2198). "To our surprise we got this big whopping signal at the time of the Akkadian collapse."

It soon became clear that major changes in the climate coincided with the untimely ends of several other civilizations. Of these, the Maya became the poster child for climate-induced decline. Mayan society arose in Mexico and Central America around 2000 BC. Its farmers grew maize, squashes and beans, and it was the only American civilization to produce a written language. The Maya endured for millennia, reaching a peak between AD 250 and 800, when they built cities and huge stepped pyramids.

Then the Maya civilization collapsed. Many of its incredible structures were swallowed up by the jungle after being abandoned. Not all was lost, though—Mayan people and elements of their culture survive to the present day.

Numerous studies have shown that there were several prolonged droughts around the time of the civilisation's decline. In 2003, Gerald Haug of the Swiss Federal Institute of Technology in Zurich found it was worse than that. His year-by-year reconstruction based on lake sediments shows that rainfall was abundant from 550 to 750, perhaps leading to a rise in population and thus to the peak of monument-building around 721. But over the next century there were not only periods of particularly severe drought, each lasting years, but also less rain than normal in the intervening years (*Science,* vol 299, p. 1731). Monument construction ended during this prolonged dry period, around 830, although a few cities continued on for many centuries.

Even as the evidence grew, there was something of a backlash against the idea that changing climates shaped the fate of civilizations. "Many in the archaeological community are really reticent to accept a role of climate in human history," says deMenocal.

Much of this reluctance is for historical reasons. In the 18th and 19th centuries, anthropologists argued that a society's environment shaped its character, an idea known as environmental determinism. They claimed that the warm, predictable climates of the tropics bred indolence, while cold European climates produced intelligence and a strong work ethic. These ideas were often used to justify racism and exploitation.

Understandably, modern anthropologists resist anything resembling environmental determinism. "It's a very delicate issue," says Ulf Büntgen, also at the Swiss Federal Institute of Technology, whose work suggests the decline of the Western Roman Empire was linked to a period of highly variable weather. "The field is evolving really slowly, because people are afraid to make bold statements."

Yet this resistance is not really warranted, deMenocal says. No one today is claiming that climate determines people's characters, only that it sets limits on what is feasible. When the climate becomes less favorable, less food can be grown. Such changes can also cause plagues of locusts or other pests, and epidemics among people weakened by starvation. When it is no longer feasible to maintain a certain population level and way of life, the result can be collapse. "Climate isn't a determinant, but it is an important factor," says Drake, who is at the University of New Mexico in Albuquerque. "It enables or disables."

Some view even this notion as too simplistic. Karl Butzer of the University of Texas at Austin, who has studied the collapse of civilizations, thinks the role of climate has been exaggerated. It is the way societies handle crises that decides their fate, he says. "Things break through institutional failure." When it comes to the Akkadians, for instance, Butzer says not all records support the idea of a megadrought.

In the case of the Maya, though, the evidence is strong. Earlier this year, Eelco Rohling of the University of Southampton, UK, used lake sediments and isotope ratios in stalactites to work out how rainfall had changed. He concluded that annual rainfall fell 40 per cent over the prolonged dry period, drying up open water sources (*Science,* vol 335, p. 956). This would have seriously affected the Maya, he says, because the water table lay far underground and was effectively out of reach.

So after a century of plentiful rain, the Maya were suddenly confronted with a century of low rainfall. It is not clear how they could have avoided famine and population decline in these circumstances. Even today, our ability to defy hostile climes is limited. Saudi Arabia managed to become self-sufficient in wheat by tapping water reservoirs deep beneath its deserts and subsidising farmers, but is now discouraging farming to preserve what is left of the water. In dry regions where plenty of water is available for irrigation, the build-up of salts in the soil is a serious problem, just as it was for some ancient civilisations. And if modern farmers are still at the mercy of the climate despite all our knowledge and technology, what chance did ancient farmers have?

Greek Dark Ages

While many archaeologists remain unconvinced, the list of possible examples continues to grow. The Mycenaeans are the latest addition. The reason for their downfall has been the subject of much debate, with one of the most popular explanations being a series of invasions and attacks by the mysterious "Sea Peoples." In 2010, though, a study of river deposits in Syria suggested there was a prolonged dry period between 1200 and 850 BC—right at the time of the so-called Greek Dark Ages. Earlier this year, Drake analysed several climate records and concluded that there was a cooling of the Mediterranean at this time, reducing evaporation and rainfall over a huge area.

What's more, several other cultures around the Mediterranean, including the Hittite Empire and the "New Kingdom" of Egypt, collapsed around the same time as the Mycenaeans—a phenomenon known as the late Bronze Age collapse. Were all these civilisations unable to cope with the changing climate? Or were the invading Sea Peoples the real problem? The story could be complex: civilisations weakened by hunger may have become much more vulnerable to invaders, who may themselves have been driven to migrate by the changing climate. Or the collapse of one civilisation could have had knock-on effects on its trading partners.

Climate change on an even greater scale might be behind another striking coincidence. Around 900, as the Mayan civilisation was declining in South America, the Tang dynasty began losing its grip on China. At its height, the Tang ruled over 50 million subjects. Woodblock printing meant that written words, particularly poetry, were widely accessible. But the dynasty fell after local governors usurped its authority.

Since the two civilisations were not trading partners, there was clearly no knock-on effect. A study of lake sediments in China by Haug suggests that this region experienced a prolonged dry period at the same time as that in Central America. He thinks a shift in the tropical rain belt was to blame, causing civilisations to fall apart on either side of the Pacific (*Nature,* vol 445, p. 74).

Critics, however, point to examples of climate change that did not lead to collapse. "There was a documented drought and even famines during the period of the Aztec Empire," says archaeologist Gary Feinman of the Field Museum in Chicago. "These episodes caused hardships and possibly even famines, but no overall collapse."

Realizing that case studies of collapses were not enough to settle the debate, in 2005 David Zhang of Hong Kong University began to look for larger patterns. He began with the history of the Chinese dynasties. From 2500 BC until the 20th century, a series of powerful empires like the Tang controlled China. All were eventually toppled by civil unrest or invasions.

When Zhang compared climate records for the last 1200 years to the timeline of China's dynastic wars, the match was striking. Most of the dynastic transitions and periods of social unrest took place when temperatures were a few tenths of a degree colder. Warmer periods were more stable and peaceful (*Chinese Science Bulletin*, vol 50, p. 137).

The Thirty Years War

Zhang gradually built up a more detailed picture showing that harvests fell when the climate was cold, as did population levels, while wars were more common. Of 15 bouts of warfare he studied, 12 took place in cooler times. He then looked at records of war across Europe, Asia and North Africa between 1400 and 1900. Once again, there were more wars when the temperatures were lower. Cooler periods also saw more deaths and declines in the population.

These studies suggest that the effects of climate on societies can be profound. The problem is proving it. So what if wars and collapses often coincide with shifts in the climate? It doesn't prove one caused the other. "That's always been the beef," says deMenocal. "It's a completely valid point."

Trying to move beyond mere correlations, Zhang began studying the history of Europe from 1500 to 1800 AD. In the mid-1600s, Europe was plunged into the General Crisis, which coincided with a cooler period called the Little Ice Age. The Thirty Years War was fought then, and many other wars. Zhang analysed detailed records covering everything from population and migration to agricultural yields, wars, famines and epidemics in a bid to identify causal relationships. So, for instance, did climate change affect agricultural production and thus food prices? That in turn might lead to famine—revealed by a reduction in the average height of people—epidemics and a decline in population. High food prices might also lead to migration and social unrest, and even wars.

He then did a statistical analysis known as a Granger causality test, which showed that the proposed causes consistently occurred before the proposed effects, and that each cause was followed by the same effect. The Granger test isn't conclusive proof of causality, but short of rerunning history under different climes, it is about the best evidence there can be (*Proceedings of the National Academy of Sciences*, vol 108, p. 17296).

The paper hasn't bowled over the critics. Butzer, for instance, claims it is based on unreliable demographic data. Yet others are impressed. "It's a really remarkable study," deMenocal says. "It does seem like they did their homework." He adds that such a detailed breakdown is only possible for recent history, because older civilizations left fewer records.

So while further studies should reveal much more about how the climate changed in the past, the debate about how great an effect these changes had on societies is going to rumble on for many more decades. Let's assume, though, that changing climates did play a major role. What does that mean for us? On the face of it, things don't look so bad. It was often cooling that hurt past civilizations. What's more, studies of the past century have found little or no link between conflict and climate change. "Industrialized societies have been more robust against changing climatic conditions," says Jürgen Scheffran of the University of Hamburg, who studies the effects of climate change.

On the other hand, we are triggering the most extreme change for millions of years, and what seems to matter is food production rather than temperature. Production is expected to increase at first as the planet warms, but then begin to decline as warming exceeds 3°C. This point may not be that far away—it is possible that global average temperature will rise by 4°C as early as 2060. We've already seen regional food production hit by extreme heat waves like the one in Russia in 2010. Such extreme heat was not expected until much later this century.

And our society's interconnectedness is not always a strength. It can transmit shocks—the 2010 heat wave sent food prices soaring worldwide, and the drought in the US this year is having a similar effect. The growing complexity of modern society may make us more vulnerable to collapse rather than less.

We do have one enormous advantage, though—unlike the Mycenaeans and the Mayas, we know what's coming. We can prepare for what is to come and also slow the rate of change if we act soon. So far, though, we are doing neither.

The Curse of Akkad

'Look on my works, ye mighty, and despair!' All empires fall, but why?

A great drought did occur at the time this tablet was inscribed

For the first time since cities were built and founded,

The great agricultural tracts produced no grain,

The inundated tracts produced no fish,

The irrigated orchards produced neither syrup nor wine,

The gathered clouds did not rain, the masgurum did not grow.

At that time, one shekel's worth of oil was only one-half quart, One shekel's worth of grain was only one-half quart. . . .

These sold at such prices in the markets of all the cities!

He who slept on the roof, died on the roof,

He who slept in the house, had no burial,

People were flailing at themselves from hunger.

Critical Thinking

1. Discuss the causes of the decline of civilizations such as those of the Akkadian Empire and the Maya.
2. Why was there initially a backlash against the idea that changing climates shaped the fate of civilizations? Why is such resistance not warranted?
3. What are some of the specific consequences when the climate becomes less favorable?
4. Why does Karl Butzer view the notion of climate change's impact on civilizations as exaggerated?
5. What is the specific evidence for the impact of climate change on the Maya?
6. What evidence is there that our ability to defy hostile climes is limited even today?
7. Discuss the possible factors for the Bronze Age collapse, i.e., the decline of the civilizations of the Mycenaeans (the Greek Dark Ages), the Hittite Empire, and the "New Kingdom" of Egypt.
8. What is the significance of the "striking coincidence" of the simultaneous collapse of the Tang dynasty in China and the Mayan civilization?
9. In what respect are the Aztecs an exception?
10. What do the climate records say about China's dynastic wars and transitions? About wars in Europe, Asia, and North Africa?
11. How was David Zhang able to "move beyond mere correlations" by using the "Granger causality test" with respect to the effects of climate change in Europe?
12. Why does there seem to have been little or no link between conflict and climate change over the past century?
13. Why might we become more vulnerable to collapse rather than less?
14. What is the one "enormous advantage" that we have today?

Create Central

www.mhhe.com/createcentral

Internet References

Murray Research Center
www.radcliffe.edu/murray_redirect/index.php

Small Planet Institute
www.smallplanet.org/food

Society for Historical Archaeology
www.sha.org

MICHAEL MARSHALL is an environment reporter for *New Scientist*.

Marshall, Michael. From *New Scientist Magazine*, vol. 215, no. 2876, August 4, 2012, pp. 32–36. Copyright © 2012 by Reed Business Information, Ltd, UK. Reprinted by permission via Tribune Media Services.

Article

Prepared by: Mari Pritchard Parker, *Pasadena City College* and
Elvio Angeloni, *Pasadena City College*

Archaeology of the Homeless

Can scholars help the 800,000 Americans living on the streets?

NICOLE ALBERTSON

Learning Outcomes

After reading this article, you will be able to:

- Discuss the ways in which archaeology can better help us understand the lives of the homeless.
- Describe how archaeology can help provide better assistance to the homeless.

Beneath overpasses, under graffiti-covered walls, and amid piles of trash, America's homeless get by as best they can. They build cardboard and plastic shelters, insulate abandoned cars, sleep on discarded mattresses, and store their belongings in garbage bags. They live in a shadow country made of castoffs.

Larry Zimmerman, a professor of anthropology at Indiana University-Purdue University Indiana (IUPUI), and Jessica Welch, one of his former students, are applying archaeological thinking to the study of this subculture in Indianapolis. Their work is revealing the rules, realities, and patterns of an ignored world, and may help improve programs that aid the homeless.

Zimmerman first became interested in the material culture of homelessness as head of archaeology at the Minnesota Historical Society. On an excavation at the mansion of 19th-century railroad magnate James J. Hill, Zimmerman carefully observed the trash that had accumulated above garden deposits he had come to study. "There was a fair amount of time depth to the homeless materials we were finding on site," he says. "We began to see evidence of different time periods, a range of things that indicated a long-term presence."

There were pieces of clothing, sleeping bags, and cooking materials on the surface, and excavation revealed four layers left by homeless people since the 1940s. Zimmerman did not pursue the idea further until he began teaching at IUPUI and mentioned his interest during a class discussion, striking a chord with Welch. She had personal insight on the subject.

In the early 1990s, Welch moved from Indiana to California, where she struggled with drugs and alcohol. She was kicked out of shelters and eventually found herself living in abandoned houses. After 10 months of wandering aimlessly around Long Beach, Welch reached rock bottom when a crackhead kicked her out of the house in which she had been squatting. Determined to turn her life around, she returned home, began working at a grocery, and started taking classes at IUPUI. She also volunteered at Horizon House, a program that helps some of the 3,000 homeless people in Indianapolis find permanent housing. The collaboration with Zimmerman—an archaeological survey of homeless sites for her senior project—forced her to confront the time she spent on the streets. "I understand that I'm a success story," she says. "So now I can try to educate people."

Zimmerman and Welch surveyed 61 sites frequented by the homeless, from highway overpasses and rest stops to fields and railroad right-of-ways. They identified three types of site—route, short term, and camp—each with its own patterns. Route sites, along which the homeless pass, tend to be in outlying areas and used by individuals or small groups. Short-term sites, akin to the encampments of nomadic peoples, have more inhabitants and temporary, freestanding structures. Camp sites are like villages, and are usually located in abandoned structures and have multiple residents forming small, enduring communities.

"The notion of semipermanent shelters, shanties, and other makeshift dwellings is a part of the contemporary picture of homelessness," says Kim Hopper, a medical anthropologist at Columbia University who has spent decades studying homelessness. "But some 'voluntary' villages work pretty well until taken down or disbanded by force of officialdom."

Sites of all types share a certain ingenuity—some shelters are makeshift lean-tos, while others are more permanent, with separate kitchens and latrines. At one site, the researchers found a tent made from a windbreaker sewn into a new shape with twigs. At another, the occupants insulated an abandoned truck with blankets to endure the cold Midwestern winter. "This shows how adaptable we are as a species," says Zimmerman. "Homeless people see possibilities in things most of us would just walk by."

Another common feature of most sites is the practice of caching. The homeless often store belongings in a single place, bundled in plastic bags or shopping carts, or attached to trees or fences. Leaving one's possessions unsecured might not seem like a good idea, but caching is often a respected practice. "There is an honor code in many places that they don't violate each other's caches," says Zimmerman, though Hopper's research and Welch's experience suggest this is not always the case in other places.

For the project, professor and student examined some caches. Abiding by the unspoken rules, they did not touch or disturb any belongings, and to maintain an archaeological approach, the researchers deliberately avoided direct interaction. They saw many expected items—soda cans, fast-food containers, and clothing—but also made observations that might help provide better assistance to the homeless. While social programs and aid agencies often have the best intentions, sometimes their efforts fall short, in ways that became clear with the survey. Canned food, for example, the staple of the food drive, is not of much use to the homeless. The researchers found many cans unopened or mangled for want of an opener. Hotel shampoo bottles, another item often provided to the homeless, were also left unused.

"People tend to impose their own lives on the homeless without really understanding the ramifications," says Zimmerman. "The homeless have a tough time opening cans unless they have openers. They can't wash their hair because they don't have running water."

Donations can simply go to waste if complementary items are not also offered, the researchers speculate. Shoes, food, blankets, and clothing can be put to better and more creative use and reuse if they are given with common-sense items such as shoelaces, scissors, rope, glue, and razors.

"[Zimmerman and Welch] show why some social programs directed to helping the homeless will not work," says George Nicholas, an archaeologist at Simon Fraser University in British Columbia, who invited Zimmerman to give a lecture on the archaeology of homelessness this past April. "[Some organizations] are naive about what people need."

After that lecture, Zimmerman also gave a talk at the Carnegie Centre, in Vancouver's Downtown Eastside neighborhood, a center of poverty, crime, and homelessness in the city. He expected a handful of homeless people to show up, but the room soon filled with nearly a hundred, many of whom approved of his findings with subtle nods or exclamations of "That's right!" Zimmerman was surprised by their enthusiasm, intelligence, and mental toughness.

"I think the greatest relevance of this work is humanizing the homeless," says Nicholas. "This is about a people whose stories are not known to others and may not be in the position to present their stories. People on the streets are often invisible or feared, and they are certainly not understood."

Zimmerman and Welch plan to continue their research by engaging a new set of students to help explore more sites and speak with the homeless to understand the meaning and significance of their cultural habits.

"My aim is to make the lives of homeless people more understandable," says Welch. "Some of these folks are true survivalists and show amazing ingenuity. These aren't just throwaway people."

Critical Thinking

1. How did Larry Zimmerman and Jessica Welch each become interested in the archaeology of the homeless?
2. What is the significance of the three types of homeless sites?
3. In what sense is there ingenuity involved at such sites?
4. What is the practice of "caching"?
5. What did the archaeologists learn studying the caches that might help provide better assistance to the homeless?
6. Why is it important to "humanize" the homeless with studies like this?

Create Central

www.mhhe.com/createcentral

Internet References

Society for American Archaeology
www.saa.org

The Garbage Project
http://traumwerk.stanford.edu/projects/GarbologyOnline/48

The New York Times
www.nytimes.com

NICOLE ALBERTSON is a former *Archaeology* intern and a freelance writer based in New York.

Albertson, Nicole. From *Archaeology*, November/December 2009, pp. 42–43. Copyright © 2009 by Archaeological Institute of America. Reprinted by permission of Archaeology Magazine. www.archaeology.org